MEYERHOLD
A Revolution in Theatre

MEYERHOLD
A Revolution in Theatre

EDWARD BRAUN

Methuen

First published in Great Britain in 1979
by Eyre Methuen Ltd
Second edition, revised and expanded,
published in 1995 by Methuen
an imprint of Reed Consumer Books Ltd
Michelin House, 81 Fulham Road, London SW3 6RB
and Auckland, Melbourne, Singapore and Toronto

A CIP catalogue record for this book
is available at the British Library

ISBN 0 413 68770 8

Typeset by Falcon Graphic Art Ltd
Wallington, Surrey
Printed in England by
The Bath Press

To Sarah

'De la musique avant toute chose'
(Verlaine, *Art Poétique*)

Contents

List of Illustrations

Jacket illustrations: front board: painting of Meyerhold with his double,
 Doctor Dapertutto, by Boris Grigoriev (1916); back board: painting of
 Meyerhold by Alexander Golovin (1917)

SOURCES OF ILLUSTRATIONS

All illustrations are taken from the author's collection held in the University of Bristol
Theatre Collection apart from the following:

5 — V.E.Meierkhold, *Perepiska 1896–1939* (Iskusstvo, 1976); 8, 10 —
K.L. Rudnitsky, *Russkoe rezhisserskoe iskusstvo 1898–1907* (Nauka, 1989); 17, 83, 86,
87, 130, 142, 144, 145 — *Meierkholdovskiy sbornik*, vypusk pervy (Tvorcheskiy tsentr
im. Vs. Meierkholda, 1992); 20 — N. Gosling, *Leningrad* (Studio Vista, 1965); 35, 40,
41 — I. Glikman, *Meierkhold i muzykalny teatr* (Sovetskiy kompozitor, 1989); 42 —
N. Petrov, *50 i 500* (VTO, 1960); 19, 110, 133, 142 — *Teatr*, Moscow, 1990, no. 1.

Introduction

The execution of Vsevolod Meyerhold on 2 February 1940 immediately following his sentencing on falsified charges of treason and espionage remained a secret for the next fifteen years and his name was mentioned in the Soviet Union only in order to vilify his unique achievements in the theatre. Even his closest relatives were given conflicting reports of his fate, and when his death was finally confirmed it was still falsely reported. In the West his reputation survived largely on the strength of the enthusiastic accounts of those critics and directors who had made their way to Moscow in the twenties and thirties, including Edward Gordon Craig who in 1935 described him as 'this exceptional theatric genius'.* Whereas the Moscow Art Theatre had visited Europe as early as 1906 and the United States in 1923, and Tairov's Kamerny Theatre had spent seven months touring Germany and France in 1923, the Meyerhold Theatre was denied permission to travel until 1930, by which time it had passed its zenith.

When the original edition of this book was published in 1979 under the title *The Theatre of Meyerhold*, twenty-four years had elapsed since the official rehabilitation of Meyerhold by the Military Collegium of the Soviet Supreme Court. However, the process of *de facto* rehabilitation proved extremely slow, hampered as it was by continuing apprehension, suspicion, and often by undisguised obstruction from those still anxious to suppress Meyerhold's radical legacy.† Even so, from 1960 onwards many of his former pupils, assistants, actors, designers and composers published reminiscences, factual accounts, recorded utterances and analyses of his work. This collective undertaking culminated in the publication of four major works that together restored Meyerhold to an eminence approached only by Stanislavsky amongst Russian directors: first the six-hundred page anthology of memoirs and criticism *Encounters with Meyerhold* (Vstrechi s

---

See p. 86 below.
† For a detailed account of Meyerhold's rehabilitation see A.A.Sherel (ed.) *Meierkholdovskiy sbornik* (Moscow, 1922), vol.I, pp. 19-222.

Meierkholdom) published in 1967 in an edition of 100,000; second, the two-volume, thousand-page edition of Meyerhold's writings, lectures, interviews, rehearsal notes, etc., containing much unpublished archive material (1968, principal editor Fevralsky); third, the first full-length critical study *Rezhisser Meierkhold* by Konstantin Rudnitsky (1969); finally, in 1976 a scrupulously edited collection of over five hundred letters between Meyerhold and his contemporaries (*V.E. Meierkhold – Perepiska*, ed. Korshunova and Sitkovetskaya).

The first retrospective account of Meyerhold's work to appear in the West was Yury Yelagin's *The Dark Genius* (published in Russian under the title *Temny geniy*, New York, 1955). Unfortunately, it was rendered worthless by a quality of scholarship that varied between carelessness, faulty memory and sheer distortion – as has been demonstrated by the recently published transcript of Meyerhold's final speech to the All-Union Conference of Theatre Directors in June 1939, which refutes utterly Yelagin's own purported verbatim text.* Angelo Maria Ripellino's work in Italy was of an entirely different order; his *Il Trucco e l'Anima* (Turin, 1965) comprised a series of long essays devoted to Stanislavsky, Tairov, Vakhtangov and Meyerhold, vividly recreating the sensation of their productions and the Russian cultural world of the period by drawing widely on eye-witness accounts.

Prior to Ripellino, the Czech scholar, Dr Karel Martínek, had published the first serious full-length study of Meyerhold (*Mejerchold*, Prague, 1963), and a year earlier the first collection of his writings and utterances had appeared in Italian under the title *La Rivoluzione teatrale* (trans. G. Crino, Rome). My own anthology *Meyerhold on Theatre* was published by Eyre Methuen in 1969 (revised edition, 1991). Since then, Meyerhold has been translated into numerous languages throughout the world and, to date, over thirty monographs devoted to him have been published outside Russia. Outstanding and most recent amongst these is Béatrice Picon-Vallin's *Meyerhold* (CNRS, Paris, 1990), which draws extensively on archive sources to offer what is as yet the fullest analysis of the major post-revolutionary productions. In addition, Picon-Vallin's four-volume *Vsevolod Meyerhold – Ecrits sur le Théâtre* (Lausanne, 1973–92) now offers the fullest collection in translation of the director's writings and utterances, representing a monumental achievement of devoted scholarship.

My own work on Meyerhold originated with my doctoral research in the late 1960s at the University of Cambridge and in Leningrad at the State Institute of Theatre, Music and Cinematography, which led in turn to the publication of my two earlier books. I was convinced of the need for the reappraisal that follows by the unceasing torrent of work that has flowed from Russian sources in the intervening period. An indication of its volume is given by the bibliography published in the anthology *Meierkholdovskiy sbornik*, pub-

* See Chapter 12 below.

lished in 1992 and covering the period 1974–1990, which excludes periodical and newspaper sources yet still runs to over forty pages. The anthology itself, comprising largely unpublished material, is over 650 pages in length.

The range of this scholarship and the wealth of newly revealed writings and other material by Meyerhold himself, including speeches, rehearsal transcripts, production notes and letters, has enabled me to undertake a complete revision of my earlier work and to repair numerous omissions. With the help principally of Maya Sitkovetskaya's scholarship, I have been able to give a far fuller account of Meyerhold's early work in the provinces. The work of Abram Gozenpud and Isaac Glikman has furnished the basis for a more extended treatment of his crucial operatic productions. The pre-revolutionary studio experiments have been further illuminated by the publication of fresh reminiscences by Meyerhold's former pupils, enabling me to see a clearer continuity between this period and the development of the system of biomechanics in the early twenties, which I discuss at greater length in Chapter Seven. The scholarship of Béatrice Picon-Vallin and Alma Law has encouraged me to re-examine the radical reinterpretations of the nineteenth-century classics, *The Forest* and *Woe from Wit*. Similarly, Alexander Matskin's recent study of Gogol on the modern stage has thrown further light on the 1926 production of *The Government Inspector*, whilst Leonid Varpakhovsky's extended analysis of *The Lady of the Camellias* from a first-hand viewpoint has encouraged a much fuller appraisal of that late masterpiece. Recently published documents on the life and work of Nikolai Erdman, together with John Freedman's pioneering critical biography, have provided the material for an account of the abortive production of Erdman's major work *The Suicide*. Similarly, the unrealised projects for Bely's *Moscow* and Tretyakov's *I Want a Child* can now be appreciated fully as the missed opportunities that they were. Vera Turovskaya's sensitive biography of Maria Babanova adds a new dimension to one's appreciation of a number of key productions from *The Magnanimous Cuckold* up to *The Government Inspector*, and provides the focus for a consideration of Meyerhold's frequently troubled relations with his leading actors and the role in his company of his wife, Zinaida Raikh. Finally, the release and publication since 1989 of KGB files and other state documents has made possible a detailed account of Meyerhold's final months from his last public appearance in June 1939 up to his execution on 2 February 1940. This is contained in Chapter Eleven, much of which was originally published as an article in *New Theatre Quarterly* in February 1993.

In addition to these major additions, the text has been completely revised and I have added a new conclusion. There are also some fifty new illustrations, including production photographs, costume and set designs, poster reproductions and caricatures. As with *The Theatre of Meyerhold*, my aim has not been to write a biography, although in this book there is considerably greater reference to Meyerhold's personal life where it bears directly on his professional activities, together with a fuller examination of the cultural and political circumstances of the period. My aim is to provide a comprehensive appraisal of a unique career that spanned forty years and remains seminal in the development of Western theatre up to the present day. In the process I have attempted to establish the continuity of his ideas and practice whilst not concealing the occasional failures, inconsistencies and instances of personal fallibility. There were undoubtedly profound contradictions that were part of the man and the director, and these have not been obscured.

With intervals, my work on Meyerhold has now stretched over thirty years, and in that time I have enjoyed the help and support of more people than I can possibly acknowledge. My indebtedness to the many practitioners and scholars whose thoughts and information I have shared is conveyed in my notes and bibliography. Those individuals who must be singled out for their personal assistance are Professor Elizabeth Hill, Masha Valentei, Alexander Fevralsky, Isaac Schneidermann, Irina Meyerhold, Marina Ivanova, Nikolai Abramov, Slava Nechaev – and Konstantin Rudnitsky, whose work I have found a constant source of inspiration.

Finally, I am grateful to my wife for her constant enthusiasm and understanding and to my colleagues in the Drama Department of the University of Bristol for making possible my visits to Russia, the last of which in 1992 was funded by an award from the British Academy. The production of the final typescript was facilitated by an award from the University of Bristol Arts Faculty Research Fund.

All translations are my own except where otherwise indicated.

Edward Braun
Bristol, May 1994

ONE 1874–1905

Apprentice Years

In the second half of the nineteenth century the small town of Penza, some 350 miles to the south-east of Moscow, was a rapidly expanding trading centre and a popular haven for dissident writers and intellectuals expelled from Moscow and St Petersburg. Prominent amongst its solidly affluent middle-class was the German family of Meyerhold, of which the father Emil Fyodorovich Meyerhold was a distiller and the owner of four substantial properties in the town. His family originated from Lower Silesia, though his mother was French. His wife, Alvina Danilovna, born van der Neese, was a Baltic German from Riga.

The eighth and last of his children was born on 28th January 1874* and christened Karl-Theodor Kasimir. He was considered of little account by his father, who was concerned more about the proper schooling of the two eldest sons, the likely successors to the family business. In consequence, Karl grew up under the influence of his mother and came to share her passion for music and the theatre. The family subscribed to a box at the civic theatre and from an early age he became familiar with the Russian and foreign classics performed by leading actors on tour. At the age of eighteen, less than a week before his father's death, he himself played the part of Repetilov in a local amateur production of Griboedov's *Woe from Wit*. Through his formative years Karl circulated freely in the varied society of the busy little town, being on easy terms with the workmen in the distillery and more than once falling in with 'socialists' who offended the Bismarckian rectitude of Emil Fyodorovich. Untouched by his father's mercantile values, Karl enjoyed the typical upbringing of a nineteenth-century middle-class Russian liberal, though possessing the added benefit of fluent German to extend his cultural horizon.[1]

In 1895, after graduating with some difficulty from the Penza Second Gymnasium, the youngest Meyerhold entered Moscow University to read

* All dates before October 1917 are according to the old-style Julian calendar.

law. That year he renounced his family's Lutheran religion in favour of the Orthodox faith, became a Russian national and took the name and patronymic of Vsevolod Emilievich. Thus, he affirmed his perception of himself as essentially Russian, as well as contriving to avoid conscription into the Prussian army. This step also facilitated his marriage the following year to a local Russian girl, Olga Munt.

In Moscow Meyerhold soon tired of his law studies and found his fellow students shallow and obsessed with back-stage intrigues at the operetta and similar trivia. His visits to the theatre were frequent, but seldom measured up to his expectations. After seeing *The Power of Darkness* at the Korsh Theatre he wrote '. . . the actors no more resembled the peasants of Tolstoy's play than I do the Emperor of China'.[2] However, one production stood out: in January 1896 he paid his first visit to the Moscow Society of Art and Literature to see Stanislavsky's production of *Othello*. The following day he recorded his impressions: '. . . Stanislavsky is highly gifted. I have never seen such an Othello, and I don't suppose I ever shall in Russia . . . The ensemble work is splendid; every member of the crowd truly lives on stage. The setting is splendid too. With the exception of Desdemona, the other actors are rather weak.'[3]

By this time Meyerhold had already taken the decision to leave university and the possibility of a career in the theatre was stirring in his mind. Back home in Penza, he joined the open-air Popular Theatre, a company organised for the specific purpose of establishing links between the intelligentsia and the working class. Over the summer he gained a considerable reputation for his performances in comic roles, and he returned to Moscow in the autumn resolved to become an actor.

His sister-in-law, Katya Munt, was already a student at the drama school of the Moscow Philharmonic Society, and spoke highly of her teacher on the acting course, Vladimir Nemirovich-Danchenko, who at thirty-eight was a successful dramatist. For his audition Meyerhold read Othello's speech to the Senate in an interpretation that was evidently based on Stanislavsky. Deterred neither by this plagiarism nor by the young candidate's angular appearance and nervous movements, Nemirovich was sufficiently impressed to offer him a place on the second-year course. Another of his fellow-students was Olga Knipper, the future wife of Chekhov. Years later she recalled:

A new 'pupil' joined our course who immediately seized my attention. He was Vsevolod Emilievich Meyerhold. I clearly remember his fascinating appearance: those nervous, mobile features, those pensive eyes, that unruly tuft of hair above the clever, expressive forehead. He was reserved to the point of dryness. On closer acquaintance he astonished me with his level of culture, the sharpness of his mind, the intelligence of his whole being.[4]

In the mid-nineties the Russian stage bore few signs of its imminent flowering. The main reason for this had been the existence until 1882 of a state monopoly that forbade the existence of any public theatres in Moscow and St Petersburg save those few under the direct control of the Imperial court. In effect, this meant that only the Maly Theatre in Moscow and the Alexandrinsky Theatre in St Petersburg were devoted to the regular performance of drama. These bureaucratically managed Imperial theatres remained dominated by illustrious actors who made their own laws and admitted no change. Production, insofar as it existed at all, was a matter of discussion amongst the leading actors; the 'director' was a mere functionary (usually the prompter) who supervised rehearsals; stage design was non-existent, settings being taken from stock, and costumes were selected by the performers themselves. Thus, when *The Seagull* was given its disastrous première at the Alexandrinsky Theatre in October 1896 there were eight rehearsals and the part of Nina was recast five days before the opening night.

In 1880 Anna Brenko, a little-known actress from the Maly Theatre, had circumvented the Imperial monopoly by opening her Pushkin Theatre in the centre of Moscow. For two years it operated successfully as an artistically serious venture which challenged the standards of the Maly before being swallowed up by a commercial backer.[5] After 1882 a number of commercial theatres were established, but they merely pandered to current fashions, and such hope as there was for the future lay in the two independent, partly amateur theatre clubs attached to the Societies of Art and Literature of Moscow and St Petersburg. With Stanislavsky as principal director and leading actor, the Moscow theatre opened in 1888, one year after Antoine's Théâtre Libre in Paris. The repertoire was unremarkable, relying heavily on the classics, but the level of production set new standards, especially after the second Russian tour of the Meiningen Theatre in 1890, whose scrupulous naturalism, stage effects and studied ensemble work left a deep impression on Stanislavsky. Inspired by their example, he became Russia's first stage-director in the true sense of the term.

Russia's introduction to the modern European repertoire came in 1895 when the millionaire newspaper proprietor, critic and dramatist, Alexei Suvorin, opened a similar theatre in St Petersburg. During its first year it staged plays by Ibsen, Hauptmann, Sudermann, Maeterlinck and Rostand, together with the Russian première of Tolstoy's *The Power of Darkness* after a ban of nine years. But the level of production was indifferent and the theatre's sense of adventure short-lived; it soon became a predominantly commercial enterprise and as such survived up to the October Revolution.

At this time of theatrical stagnation Meyerhold and his fellow-students at the Philharmonic were singularly fortunate to have in Nemirovich-Danchenko a teacher who was alive to the advance of naturalism in the Western theatre and its implications for the art of acting. According to Meyerhold, he 'gave the actor a literary grounding (a proper regard for text and metre), and also taught him the analysis of character. Above all, he was concerned with the internal justification of the role. He demanded a clearly

1 Meyerhold in
1898

outlined personality.'[6] But at the same time Meyerhold was all too aware of
the limitations of a drama school education, and his notebooks from this
period reveal a remarkably wide range of reading embracing political theory,
philosophy, aesthetics, art history and psychiatry. Before he left Penza the
exiled young Social Democrat and future symbolist poet, Remizov, had
introduced him to Marxism, and he now embarked on a more systematic
study of it, together with the theories of the 'Legal Marxists', Struve and
Kamensky.[7]

By the end of two years Meyerhold was firmly established as the Philharmonic's outstanding student, and on graduating in March 1898 he was one of
two to be awarded the Society's silver medal, the other being Olga Knipper.
His final report from Nemirovich-Danchenko makes impressive reading:

> Amongst the students of the Philharmonic Academy Meyerhold must be
> considered a unique phenomenon. Suffice it to say that he is the first student
> to have gained maximum marks in the history of drama, literature and the
> arts. It is seldom that one encounters such conscientiousness and seriousness
> amongst male students. Despite a lack of that '*charme*' which makes it easy
> for an actor to gain his audience's sympathy, Meyerhold has every prospect
> of winning a leading position in any company. His principal quality as an
> actor is his versatility. During his time here, he has played over fifteen major
> roles, ranging from old men to vaudeville simpletons, and it is hard to choose
> between them. He works hard, comports himself well, is skilled at make-up,
> and shows all the temperament and experience of an accomplished actor.[8]

That same winter the firm of Meyerhold and Sons in Penza finally went bankrupt, leaving Meyerhold *déclassé* and penniless. He needed to find work as an actor in order to support his wife and Maria, the first of the three daughters they were to have. The inducements to accept the lucrative and secure commercial offers that he received were strong, but the appeal made by Nemirovich-Danchenko was far stronger. Plans for the inaugural season of the Moscow Art Theatre were well advanced; Meyerhold, Knipper, Katya Munt, and eight more of the Philharmonic's young graduates were invited to join the company.

II

The founders of the 'Moscow Popular Art Theatre', as it was initially titled, were first and foremost men of the theatre, but they also shared that sense of responsibility towards the underprivileged which characterised the Populist movement in post-emancipation Russia.* More explicitly than their forerunners in the independent theatre movement in Paris, Berlin, or London, they announced their commitment to social problems. At the opening rehearsal on 14 June 1898 Stanislavsky said in his address to the company:

> What we are undertaking is not a simple private affair but a social task.
> Never forget that we are striving to brighten the dark existence of the poor
> classes, to afford them minutes of happiness and aesthetic uplift, to relieve
> the murk that envelops them. Our aim is to create the first intelligent, moral,
> popular theatre, and to this end we are dedicating our lives.[9]

As his letters to his wife indicate, Meyerhold, for all his great admiration of Stanislavsky, was not over-impressed by these lofty sentiments. With two summers behind him spent bringing the theatre to the people in Penza, he clearly demanded a more concrete definition of aims, and indeed a readiness to take sides. The following January when Stanislavsky was rehearsing *Hedda Gabler*, Meyerhold wrote:

> Are we as actors required merely to act? Surely we should be thinking as
> well. We need to know *why* we are acting, *what* we are acting, and *whom*
> we are instructing or attacking through our performance. And to do that we
> need to know the psychological and social significance of the play, to establish
> whether a given character is positive or negative, to understand which society
> or section of society the author is for or against.[10]

Not only did Meyerhold object to Stanislavsky's failure to take account of the play's social implications, he was also critical of the production's lack of form; some years later he recalled: 'In *Hedda Gabler* breakfast was served during the scene between Tesman and Aunt Julie. I well recall how skilfully

* The Emancipation of the Serfs became law in 1861.

the actor playing Tesman ate, but I couldn't help missing the exposition of the plot.'[11]

This indiscriminate naturalism, the obsession with external detail, was typical of the Moscow Art Theatre in its early days and clearly bespoke the powerful influence of the Meiningen Theatre on Stanislavsky. It was a continuing source of contention between the company and Chekhov. Meyerhold recalls in his diary Chekhov's reaction to an early rehearsal of *The Seagull* in September 1898:

> . . . one of the actors told him that offstage there would be frogs croaking, dragon flies humming and dogs barking.
> 'Why?' – asked Anton Pavlovich in a dissatisfied tone.
> 'Because it's realistic,' replied the actor.
> 'Realistic!' repeated Chekhov with a laugh. Then after a short pause he said: 'The stage is art. There's a genre painting by Kramskoy in which the faces are portrayed superbly. What would happen if you cut the nose out of one of the paintings and substituted a real one? The nose would be "realistic" but the picture would be ruined.'
> One of the actors proudly told Chekhov that the director intended to bring the entire household, including a woman with a child crying, onto the stage at the close of the third act of *The Seagull*. Chekhov said: 'He mustn't. It would be like playing pianissimo on the piano and having the lid suddenly crash down.' 'But in life it often happens that the pianissimo is interrupted by the forte,' retorted one of the actors. 'Yes, but the stage demands a degree of artifice,' said A.P. 'You have no fourth wall. Besides, the stage is art, the stage reflects the quintessence of life and there is no need to introduce anything superfluous onto it.'[12]

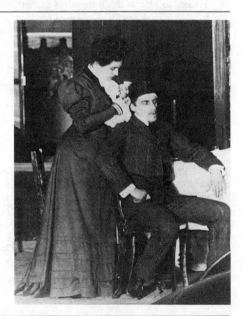

2 *The Seagull* at
the Moscow Art
Theatre.
Meyerhold as
Treplev with
Olga Knipper as
Arkadina

This was the first time that Meyerhold had met Chekhov in person, but *The Seagull* was a play that he and his fellow students at the Philharmonic had discovered through the enthusiasm of Nemirovich-Danchenko and had come to regard as their own. They saw the character of the young writer, Konstantin Treplev, as the very embodiment of the rising generation of artists and intellectuals of the 1890s, and they identified with his restless desire for change and with his exasperation at the smug routines of his elders. The casting of Meyerhold as Konstantin in the Art Theatre's historic production was a foregone conclusion, and predictably he played the part to the life. However, critical opinion of his interpretation was sharply divided. Years later, the perceptive and sympathetic Nikolai Efros recalled:

> The difficult and at times dangerous role of Treplev was played by Meyerhold, who in those days was a passionate advocate of Chekhov and his plays, and had a great instinct for them. But in Meyerhold's nature as an actor as I knew him in his years at the Art Theatre there was an extreme harshness, nothing soft, and vocally he had difficulty in conveying sincerity. . . . The Treplev exasperated by his literary failures, the Treplev yearning for recognition overshadowed the lyrically sorrowful Treplev, the Treplev of Chopin's waltzes . . . and that is why he was a distinctive Treplev, but he wasn't the character that Chekhov had written.[13]

However, whatever their opinion of his portrayal, few critics could have guessed that the very man playing Konstantin would in a few years be the one to respond to his demand: 'What we need is a new kind of theatre. We need new forms, and if we can't get them, we'd be better off with nothing at all.'[14]

Up to his death in 1904 Chekhov followed Meyerhold's progress with friendly concern, and Meyerhold regularly sought his advice on theatrical matters. From Chekhov, Meyerhold learned what the directors of the Art Theatre were slower to grasp: the need for economy and artifice. There is a clear link between Meyerhold's experiments as a director and the laconic style of Chekhov's latter years.

III

Stanislavsky shared Nemirovich-Danchenko's high opinion of Meyerhold, and in the first season Meyerhold was entrusted with eight roles, ranging from Treplev through Prince Ivan Shuisky in Alexei Tolstoy's *Tsar Fyodor Ioannovich*, and Tiresias in Sophocles' *Antigone* to the Prince of Aragon in *The Merchant of Venice* and the Marquis of Forlipopoli in Goldoni's *La Locandiera*. The following season he took over the part of Ivan from Stanislavsky after the first few performances of Alexei Tolstoy's *The Death of Ivan the Terrible* and played the leading role of Johannes Vockerat in Hauptmann's *Lonely People* when the theatre gave it its Russian première on 16 December 1899. At this time Hauptmann ranked with Chekhov in Meyerhold's estimation, and the following summer he translated Hauptmann's *Before Sunrise* into Russian. Something of what he admired in Hauptmann is conveyed by this extract from Meyerhold's notebook, dating from 1901:

> Hauptmann is criticised for rejecting the drama of the individual in favour of the everyday domestic drama. But how can one possibly dream of perfecting the spiritual life of separate units of the masses when the masses themselves are still unable to free themselves from the oppression that makes human existence impossible?[15]

It is easy to see how this conviction shaped Meyerhold's interpretation of the role of Baron Tusenbach in *Three Sisters* which he created in the Art Theatre's production in January 1901. There is in the character a contradiction, all too familiar in Chekhov, between on the one hand an urgent desire to be of use to the community, and on the other a resigned acceptance that whatever one does, nothing will change. Long as Meyerhold agonised over the part, the essential irony of the character seems to have eluded him, and more than one critic was reminded of his portrayal of Konstantin in *The Seagull*. However, Maria Andreeva, who played Irina, recalled later: 'It's impossible to imagine a better Tusenbach. Later I played opposite Kachalov, but I'm bound to say that despite his appalling hatchet face and rasping voice, Meyerhold was better than Kachalov.'[16]

Andreeva, soon to join the Bolshevik Party and become the mistress of Gorky, was part of the left-wing faction that was clearly emerging in the Art Theatre company, and this may well have biased her in favour of Meyerhold. Certainly as Russian society entered a new volatile phase, political factors could no longer remain divorced from artistic judgment. It was around this time that Meyerhold wrote in his diary:

> The bourgeois public takes pleasure in impressionism, moods, words so profound as to be incomprehensible, not words for the sake of their true meaning. . . It prefers works of art that leave it unscathed, that do not reprove or mock it. And as soon as there appears something straightforward that threatens the self-esteem of the bourgeoisie it either voices its outrage or affects an indifferent silence.[17]

Three Sisters received its première in St Petersburg on 31 January 1901, and it was during the company's visit that Meyerhold took part in a mass demonstration by students in front of the Kazan Cathedral and witnessed at close quarters its brutal suppression by the police and the Cossack cavalry. So angered was he by these events that he dispatched an account of them through a student intermediary to Lenin's newspaper *Iskra*.[18] Soon afterwards, in a letter that attracted the attention of the Okhrana secret police, he wrote to Chekhov:

> I feel frankly outraged at the police tyranny that I witnessed in St Petersburg

on 4 March, and I am incapable of devoting myself quietly to creative work while blood is flowing and everything is calling me to battle. I want to burn with the spirit of the times. I want all servants of the stage to recognise their lofty destiny. I am disturbed at my comrades' failure to rise above narrow caste interests which are alien to the interests of society at large. Yes, the theatre can play an enormous part in the transformation of the whole of existence.[19]

In the same letter Meyerhold described the audience's reaction to the Art Theatre's performance of *An Enemy of the People* on the day of the demonstration. The cast were nonplussed when line after line was interpreted as an overt political statement by the many academics and students in the audience. In *My Life in Art* Stanislavsky, who played Doctor Stockmann, recalled:

Up on the stage we had no thoughts of politics. On the contrary, the demonstration provoked by the play took us completely by surprise. For us, Stockmann was neither a politician nor a public orator; he was simply an honourable idealist, a just man, a friend to his country and his people such as any true and honest citizen should be.[20]

Stanislavsky conveys the essentially non-partisan attitude of his theatre at that time, an attitude that left Meyerhold and those like him in increasing isolation. To make matters worse, Tusenbach had been his only new role of any significance in the 1900–1901 season.

The following autumn it was decided to stage Gorky's first play, *Philistines*, a work which contrasted the pettiness of the Russian lower-middle classes with the vigour and optimism of the 'new man' of proletarian stock. Meyerhold was cast in the major part of the ex-student Peter. But mainly because of objections from the censor the première was repeatedly delayed. Meanwhile, in December 1901, the theatre put on Nemirovich-Danchenko's new play *In Dreams*. Bitterly frustrated, Meyerhold wrote to a friend:

The theatre is in a fog. It is a mistake to put on Nemirovich's play: it is uninspired, superficial and falsely heroic. It is all in the style of Boborykin:* the author's attitude to the social milieu, the petty dialogue, the style of writing. It's shameful that our theatre is stooping to such plays. And because of this Gorky's play is held up. That's what is so infuriating.[21]

Meyerhold's opinion of the play must have been well known, for he was accused of organising the barracking that occurred on the opening night. Rightly or wrongly, Stanislavsky seemed convinced of Meyerhold's involvement, and refused even to grant him an interview to discuss the matter.[22] It seemed now only a matter of time before Meyerhold parted company with his once admired mentors. The reasons were confused and various; the following summer Nemirovich wrote to Olga Knipper: 'The Meyerhold movement has subsided, thank God! It was a muddle, a crazy mixture of Nietzsche, Maeterlinck, and narrow liberalism verging on

* Pyotr Boborykin (1836–1921), minor Russian genre dramatist.

gloomy radicalism. The devil knows what! An omelette with onions. It was the muddle of someone who unearths several new truths every day, each one crowding out the next.'²³

This is probably a fair description of Meyerhold's confused state of mind at that time, but the times themselves were confused and Meyerhold was deeply concerned to define the changing position of himself and of the theatre in general. That is something that the Art Theatre itself was most reluctant to do. Meyerhold's early doubts were confirmed: both Stanislavsky and Nemirovich-Danchenko shied away from outright commitment, and in consequence Gorky was soon to be compelled to offer his more contentious plays such as *Summer Folk* and *Barbarians* to other companies.

The 1901–1902 season was an unhappy one both for the Art Theatre and for Meyerhold: the company enjoyed not a single success and the repeated postponements of *Philistines* left Meyerhold with only minor parts in *The Wild Duck* and *In Dreams*. What is more, the whole nature of the organisation was changing, due mainly to the power and influence of Savva Morozov, the millionaire industrialist who from the beginning had been its principal shareholder and benefactor. Before the start of the season the word 'Popular' (literally 'generally accessible') had been dropped from the Theatre's name, signalling its abandonment of the price concessions designed to attract a wider audience. In January 1902 the board of directors signed a twelve-year lease on a theatre in Kamergersky Lane that formerly had been used for operetta and cabaret. The company was already deeply in debt and the entire cost of 300,000 roubles was borne by Morozov, who leased it back for a modest 10,000 roubles a year whilst guaranteeing an annual subsidy of 30,000. He was now in a position to become the effective sole owner of the Art Theatre and to dictate its future financial structure. He proposed that by invitation some of its actors and others should become shareholders and own their own company. This was facilitated by Morozov buying out the existing shareholders and lending money to any actor who needed it. Thus, the Theatre was reorganised as a joint-stock company with sixteen shareholders, several of them already members of the company.²⁴ Apparently at the insistence of Morozov and Stanislavsky,²⁵ and despite strong objections from Chekhov, Meyerhold was not amongst those invited, and on 12 February he resigned. A few days later he and Alexander Kosheverov, a fellow-actor, stated in a letter to the press that their 'resignation from the company was totally unrelated to considerations of a material nature.'²⁶

The true reason was a combination of the personal and the political, greatly exacerbated by Meyerhold's growing frustration as an actor. In four seasons he had played a total of eighteen roles, but in the public eye at least, nothing had quite lived up to the early promise of his Konstantin, and it seems unlikely that he would have retained a leading place in the re-formed company. Meyerhold's biographer, Alexander Gladkov, offers an acute analysis of the problem posed by Meyerhold as a performer:

His indeterminate *emploi*, spanning the extremes of tragedy and clowning
. . . did not inspire confidence. He wasn't a tragedian; he wasn't a comedian;
he wasn't a hero; he wasn't a simpleton. So what was he? A neurasthenic?
That was no more than a convenient newspaper term. It's easier for us now
than it was for him: we know now that he was *Meyerhold*, and for us that's
quite enough. But for the contemporaries of his early years it was much more
difficult.[27]

Interestingly, soon after he had himself become a director, Meyerhold
made the following comment in his diary on the concept of the actor's
emploi:

At no point in his career should an actor specialise. With every day that
passes the division of actors according to their *emploi* recedes further into
the realm of legend. . . For the time being, we actors are obliged to rely on
a theatrical passport bearing our designated rank (*emploi*) because all values
have yet to be re-evaluated, but like any passport this defines nothing . . . I
need actors of a new kind, whose nature lies in impressionism, in undefined
outlines.[28]

3 Meyerhold as
Ivan in *The
Death of Ivan the
Terrible* at the
Moscow Art
Theatre

On the stage it was invariably Meyerhold's intelligence rather than his
natural talent that impressed the shrewdest observers. Chekhov remarked:
'You wouldn't call him an infectious actor, but you listen to him with
pleasure because he understands everything he says.'[29] Similarly, the leading
Petersburg critic, Alexander Kugel, had this to say some years later:

I recall Meyerhold at the very beginning of his stage career – purely as an actor. Even though he caught one's eye; it wasn't so much his acting talent, which is open to question, but rather something unrelated to acting, a most striking intellectual quality which stood out even in the company of the Art Theatre. . . He engraved the part, so to speak, on one's theatrical perception with the pressure of his intellect. His intellect far outstripped his powers of expression, and for this reason it was entirely natural that he should progress quickly from acting to directing.[30]

Soon after the announcement of Meyerhold and Kosheverov's resignation from the Art Theatre it was revealed that a month earlier they had arranged to hire the municipal theatre of Kherson in the Ukraine for the 1902–1903 season. Kosheverov's wife, Maria Vasilievna, had evidently arranged this through a contact on the Kherson city council and possessed the additional advantage of private means to help fund the venture, which she was to join as an actress, having also been with the Art Theatre.[31] Kosheverov seems to have had no previous professional experience as a director, whilst Meyerhold's had been limited to helping Nemirovich-Danchenko revive two Philharmonic student productions at the Society of Art and Literature in January 1899. However logical Meyerhold's progression to directing might seem in hindsight, it was not his real reason for moving to Kherson. Even after two highly successful seasons he was still to write to Chekhov: 'No matter how interesting directing might be, acting is far more interesting.'[32] Not only was his self-esteem severely damaged by his exclusion from the ranks of the Art Theatre's shareholders, but he needed to move elsewhere if he was to extend his range and experience as an actor. So long as the Art Theatre continued to mount only four or five new productions a year, there was little scope for junior members of the company, and that is why a number of them now decided to throw in their lot with Meyerhold and join him in the exodus to Kherson. It says much for his personal standing that they chose to go with him rather than accept a secure engagement with an established company in a major city.

Meyerhold remained with the Art Theatre until the expiry of his contract. His last engagement with the company was on tour in St Petersburg in March 1902, when he finally played Peter in the long delayed première of *Philistines*. The fear of demonstrations was so great that the occasion was attended by elaborate precautions, including burly policemen thinly disguised as theatre ushers. But such was the mutilation wrought on the text by the censor and so tentative was the production, that the play's significance was obscured and the event proved a mild anticlimax.

IV

Kherson is a port on the River Dnieper close to the Black Sea, which at the turn of the century numbered some 73,000 inhabitants. The 'troupe of Russian dramatic artists under the direction of A.S. Kosheverov and V.E. Meyerhold', as it was modestly titled, began rehearsals there in mid-August 1902. Yet there was nothing modest about the company's aspirations; from the start it was made known that they were a far cry from the provincial barnstormers who had inhabited the municipal theatre in previous years, seldom performing the same play twice in a season. Five weeks were set aside for uninterrupted rehearsals by the twenty-seven strong company, the repertoire was cut by half,[33] and the customary seasonal budget was more than doubled. It seemed a foolhardy undertaking in a remote town with no worthwhile theatrical tradition. Illarion Pevtsov, an actor with the company, has put the maximum number of local theatregoers at two thousand, of whom no more than three hundred could be regarded as regulars.[34] What is more, although the company was given the use of the theatre rent-free, it required extensive redecoration to meet Meyerhold's aspirations and Maria Kosheverova's capital fell far short of their initial needs. Facing a budget for the opening season of 27,000 roubles, they had at their disposal no more than 5000, of which 2000 had been borrowed by Meyerhold. Chekhov feared the worst, writing anxiously to Olga Knipper: 'I'd like to see Meyerhold and cheer him up. It isn't going to be easy for him in Kherson. There's no public for plays there; all they want is more travelling shows. After all Kherson isn't Russian or even Europe.'[35] His concern was understandable: although nominally Kherson was the seat of the provincial government, it remained a backwater, having been bypassed by the recently constructed railway linking Odessa with Moscow. It had no institute of higher education and no significant intellectual life. Importantly, though, it possessed a local newspaper, *The South (Yug)*, that was to provide unvaryingly constructive criticism and support for the brave new company.

On 22 September, Meyerhold and Kosheverov sent a telegram to Chekhov: 'Season opened today with your *Three Sisters*. Huge success. Beloved author of melancholy moods! You alone give true delight!'[36] Such was the interest aroused by the new venture that *Three Sisters* opened to a packed house, despite the fact that the previous season Meyerhold and Kosheverov's predecessor in the town, the experienced actress and entrepreneur, Zinaida Malinovskaya, had failed with it.[37] Within six weeks, *Ivanov*, *The Seagull*, and *Uncle Vanya* were added to the repertoire, with Meyerhold not only codirecting but playing Tusenbach, Ivanov, Treplev and Astrov. The style of the production was scrupulously naturalistic and openly indebted to the Moscow Art Theatre. In later years Meyerhold recalled: 'I began as a director by slavishly imitating Stanislavsky. In theory, I no longer accepted many points of his early production methods, but when I set about directing myself, I followed meekly in his footsteps. I don't regret it, because it was a short-lived phase; besides, it served as excellent practical schooling.'[38]

By now, the practice of copying the Moscow Art Theatre's productions of Chekhov and other dramatists was spreading rapidly to provincial theatres throughout Russia. At best, these were based on the firsthand observations of directors who had visited the capital. At worst, they were derived second hand from eyewitness reports, critical accounts, and even from postcard photographs of the originals. The practice was noted in such major centres as Nizhny Novgorod, Kiev, Kharkov, Voronezh, Kazan and Riga, even though in none of these theatres was it possible to allocate more than five or six rehearsals to a new production.[39] Meyerhold, of course, had the enormous advantage of having observed Stanislavsky and Nemirovich-Danchenko's work at length and as a performer. But as one shrewd local critic observed in some detail, Meyerhold's production of *Three Sisters* was by no means a slavish copy of the Moscow original, and in Act Three in particular was far more sparing in its use of naturalistic gesture and movement. Thus, from the start he seems to have heeded Chekhov's injunction concerning 'the quintessence of life'. Even so, his *mises-en-scènes* clearly owed much to Stanislavsky's fascination with minute detail, as a skit in *The South* from September 1902 confirms:

> *Leaving the Theatre after the performance of* Uncle Vanya.
>   Two ladies:
>   – Did you notice, darling, how the vase of flowers fell over?
>   – And how the clock ticked?
>   – And the curtains?
>   – And the crickets?
>   – And the thunder!
>   – And the rain!
>   – And how the pony and trap crossed the bridge?
>   – And how the harness bells tinkled?
>   – And the dress of the professor's wife?
>   – And the sleeves of her gown?
>   – With that lace!
>   – And the little ruches![40]

Similarly, the stage settings in Kherson were clearly indebted to the example of Victor Simov, the Art Theatre's head of design, in particular his device of locating the setting on the diagonal, often suggesting a suite of rooms rather than a single confined interior.[41]

On 17 February 1903 the season ended as it had begun with *Three Sisters*, receiving its fourth performance compared with five of *The Seagull*. *Uncle Vanya* sustained just two performances and *Ivanov* only one. Mindful of their financial position and of the need to husband precious rehearsal time for the more demanding works, the company was in no position to scorn the staple provincial repertoire of farce, melodrama and the ever-popular domestic comedies of Ostrovsky. But equally they had put on: the four Chekhov plays; Alexei Tolstoy's immensely demanding historical dramas, *Tsar Fyodor Ioannovich* and *The Death of Ivan the Terrible; Drayman Henschel, Lonely People, The Sunken Bell,* and *Michael Kramer* by Hauptmann; *The Wild Duck, Hedda Gabler,* and *An Enemy of the People* by Ibsen; *The Power of Darkness* by Tolstoy; *Thérèse Raquin* by Zola and Gorky's *Philistines.* Altogether, in five months the Kherson public had had the chance to see seventy-nine plays (a quarter of them one-act). Moreover, in contrast to the Art Theatre, they had successfully sustained a true policy of open access whereby reduced-price matinées were offered regularly for impoverished townspeople and free morning performances for schoolchildren. It is hard to believe how even a young and enthusiastic company of twenty-seven actors could sustain such a programme and still raise artistic standards to a level almost certainly without precedent on the Russian provincial stage. Understandably, Meyerhold surrendered some major roles to his fellow actors, notably Tsar Fyodor and Uncle Vanya, but he still played Astrov, Treplev, Tusenbach, Ivanov, Loevborg in *Hedda Gabler* and many others no less demanding. Altogether, he played in 83 of the 115 performances given in the course of the season.

One notable success was a little-known melodrama of circus life, *The Acrobats,* by the contemporary Austrian dramatist Franz von Schönthan, jointly translated by Meyerhold and Natalya Budkevich, an actress in the company. What most impressed the local critics was the authentic depiction of circus life backstage, on which Meyerhold lavished particular attention. But of equal importance for him was his own portrayal of the ageing and failing clown Landowski. His biographer, Konstantin Rudnitsky, gives a vivid evocation of his performance:

> For the first two acts the role remained within the predictable limits of
> the 'good father' stereotype. The clown loved his daughter Lily tenderly;
> pitiable and touching, he inspired the audience's sympathy. But in the third
> act everything changed: Landowski appeared with his white made-up face,
> ready to go into the ring. Now he was an old Pierrot, familiar with the
> bitterness of failure but still hoping to cheat fate, putting on airs and desperate
> to impress. Apprehensive at the prospect of failure, he struggled with his tight
> collar which 'stopped him from breathing', but he still struggled to believe in
> himself:
> 'The moment I enter the ring the laughter will start, and when I make
> my comic exit, just listen to them then!'
> It is easy to picture Meyerhold as Landowski: pitiful yet funny, the white
> face, the long, thin nose, the anxious eyes, the forced grimace of a smile.
> After his humiliating return from the ring, where he was greeted not with
> laughter but with cold silence, he stood for a long time on the forestage, not
> uttering a word, staring straight out into the auditorium, his ear still straining
> hopefully for some sound from the bleak silence of the circus. He so yearned

4 Meyerhold as
Landowski

for just one encouraging clap! But when the clapping finally broke out it was
clear that they weren't applauding Landowski but the acrobats who had come
on next.[42]

The modern transformation of the once rollicking clown Pierrot had begun
with Duburau père at the Théâtre des Funambules in the 1830s. Over the
years he became the new Everyman, the hapless butt of every cruel jest that
an inscrutable fate chose to play on him. Successively he has been taken up
by Leoncavallo, Picasso, Stravinsky, Chaplin, Carné, Fellini, Bergman. But,
as we shall see, the genealogy would be far from complete without the name
of Meyerhold, so this early acquaintance with von Schönthan's Landowski
has a particular significance.[43]

By Moscow standards both production methods and repertoire were
well-tried, but in Kherson they were a revelation and the season showed
a handsome profit of 6000 roubles which financed a tour of neighbouring
towns in the spring. In Sevastopol in May they presented *The Lower Depths*,
The Lady from the Sea, and 'an evening of new art' comprising *Last Masks*
by Schnitzler and *The Intruder* by Maeterlinck. It was Meyerhold's first
production of the Belgian symbolist.

V

In the summer of 1903 Meyerhold became the sole director of the Kherson company and renamed it 'The Fellowship of the New Drama'. It was a calculated indication of the new artistic policy that he intended to pursue, the term 'new drama' being synonymous with symbolist drama. By 1903 the impact of Western symbolism had been fully absorbed by Russian literature, and Alexander Blok was already engaged in the composition of his early masterpiece, the poetic cycle *Verses on the Beautiful Lady*. In the theatre, whilst no Russian symbolist drama of any consequence had appeared, isolated attempts at staging Maeterlinck had been made and both his plays and his theoretical writings had appeared in translation, notably *Le Trésor des humbles* in 1901, which contained the essay 'Everyday Tragedy'. The following year in Diaghilev's journal, *The World of Art*, Valery Bryusov had submitted the methods of the Moscow Art Theatre to symbolist scrutiny in a long essay entitled 'The Unnecessary Truth'.* But meanwhile, the practical problems posed by symbolist drama remained unsolved.

Meyerhold's plans for the new season included three works by Maeterlinck, four by Schnitzler, and four by the Polish Decadent dramatist, Stanislaw Przybyszewski. As the Fellowship's literary consultant he engaged Alexei Remizov, his Marxist friend from their days together in Penza who was now immersed in Symbolism and strongly influenced Meyerhold's thinking in this direction. Describing their aims, Remizov wrote:

> The theatre is not amusement and relaxation; the theatre is not an imitation of man's impoverishment. The theatre is an act of worship, a mass whose mysteries conceal perhaps redemption. . . It is of such a theatre that the 'New Drama' dreams. Its repertoire is composed of works whose words have cast a new light into the interminable nights of life, have smashed the gloomy, mouldering nests of mankind, have discovered new lands, sent forth strange calls, kindled new desires.[44]

The sentiments behind Remizov's portentous phrases were soon to become a familiar part of symbolist aspirations in Russia. Leading theorists and poets of the movement such as Vyacheslav Ivanov, Georgy Chulkov, and for a time Blok as well, sought a reunion of 'the poet' and 'the crowd' through a theatre delivered from the hands of its elitist audience and restored to its ancient origins in Dionysiac ritual.[45] For those like Meyerhold and Remizov with left-wing convictions the programme had the populist aims of repairing the separation of the intelligentsia from the people and of turning the theatre into a means of transforming society. This was to be achieved not by making the stage a platform for political oratory, but by creating a shared experience

* See pp. 30-31 below.

so compelling that it revealed the ineffable truths beneath the tawdry and illusory surface of everyday life.

Such was the theory, but for the present Meyerhold and Remizov had to come to terms with a public scarcely disposed towards transformation and unlikely to treat the theatre as 'an act of worship'. Still under the sign of Stanislavsky, the Fellowship opened its season on 15 September 1903 with Gorky's *Lower Depths*. This was followed by a sequence of works with similarly serious social content: Hauptmann's *Before Sunrise*, *The Reconciliation*, and *Colleague Krampton*, Ibsen's *A Doll's House*, *Ghosts*, and *Little Eyolf*, and Sudermann's *Homeland*, *St John's Fire*, and *Sodom's End*.

It was with Przybyszewski's *Snow*, performed on 19 December 1903 in the presence of the Polish author and his wife, that Meyerhold took his first tentative steps away from the verisimilitude of the Moscow Art Theatre. In the words of Remizov, the production 'reflected the considerable artistic flair of the director Meyerhold, who used tone, colours, and plasticity to blend the symbolism of the drama with its realistic plot'; it was '. . . a symphony of snow and winter, of consolation and irrepressible longing'.[46] Natalya Zvenigorodskaya has consulted Meyerhold's notes to establish what this amounted to in practical terms:

> Meyerhold employed here a technique that was completely new for the
> theatre of the time, based on a painstakingly worked-out lighting design
> that involved the most subtle shifts in nuance. The story of the love-triangle
> was accompanied by the play of light and shade. As the relationships between
> the principal characters developed and as their moods fluctuated, the fire in
> the hearth flared up or died down, dawn could be seen breaking through the
> window, or the room would be flooded with the crimson light of the setting
> sun.[47]

But either these carefully studied effects were lost on the Kherson public, or else it saw through them to the fundamental banality of Przybyszewski's text; either way, its baffled and scornful response to the single performance of *Snow* encouraged no further experiments that season.

The final production on 4 February 1904 was of Chekhov's last play, *The Cherry Orchard*, less than three weeks after its première at the Moscow Art Theatre. As well as directing, Meyerhold played the part of Trofimov. It is a measure of Chekhov's regard for Meyerhold that he released the play simultaneously to him and to the Art Theatre. In fact, the text performed in Kherson differed in places from the version that Chekhov finally agreed with Stanislavsky and Nemirovich-Danchenko. Soon after the close of the Kherson season Meyerhold saw the Moscow production and disliked it thoroughly. In his opinion, the play revealed an advance in Chekhov's style that the Art Theatre had failed to recognise. On 8 May he wrote to Chekhov:

> Your play is abstract, like a Tchaikovsky symphony. Above all else, the
> director must get the *sound* of it. In Act Three, against the background

of the mindless stamping of feet – it is this 'stamping' that must be heard
– enters Horror, completely unnoticed by the guests: 'The cherry orchard
is sold.' They dance on. 'Sold' – still they dance. And so on, to the end.
When one reads the play, the effect of the third act is the same as the ringing
in the ears of the sick man in your story *Typhus*. A sort of itching. Jollity with
overtones of death. In this act there is something Maeterlinckian, something
terrifying. I use the comparison only because I can't find words to express it
more precisely.[48]

There is a close resemblance between Meyerhold's analysis and the one
published shortly before in the Moscow symbolist journal *The Scales* by
Andrei Bely, who saw the guests in Act Three as 'incarnations of worldly
chaos' who 'dance and posture whilst the family drama is being enacted'.[49]

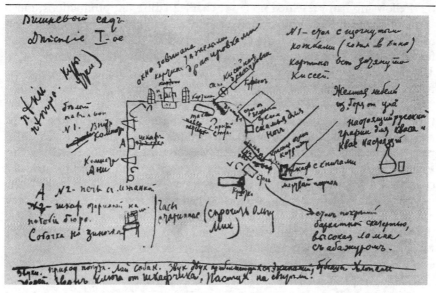

5 Meyerhold's ground-plan for Act One of *The Cherry Orchard* (1904). Amongst other
annotations he specifies 'real kvass in a real Russian carafe' and 'the yellow chairs from
Woe from Wit'

However, there seems to have been little trace of the symbolist influence
on Meyerhold's actual production of *The Cherry Orchard* in Kherson. His
prompt copy of the play survives, and the annotations appear to indicate
that the treatment was similar to his earlier productions of Chekhov.[50]
Furthermore, the local correspondent of the Petersburg journal *Theatre and
Art* saw nothing remarkable in the production and dismissed it as 'somewhat
commonplace'.[51] This is hardly surprising; in mid-season Meyerhold had
little time to rehearse what is an extremely complex play, and besides, he
would not have wanted to risk a further fiasco after *Snow*, least of all with
his beloved Chekhov.

Nevertheless, this does not alter the fact that in his letter to Chekhov, Meyerhold envisaged a production in which music and movement would be used not simply as components of a lifelike scene, but as the means of pointing theatrically what is truly significant in the action, the subtext, the unspoken dialogue of emotions, what Chekhov had called 'the quintessence of life'.* As we shall see, this concept of the expressive power of music and movement provided the foundation for the dramatic aesthetic that Meyerhold was to develop over the next few years.

Meyerhold's second season at Kherson ended on 8 February 1904 with the third performance of *The Cherry Orchard*. By now he was mentally and physically exhausted by the continual struggle to advance artistic standards whilst maintaining financial solvency. In the space of two five-month seasons the Fellowship had presented no fewer than 140 different productions, most of them staged by Meyerhold, and he himself had played forty-four major roles. So small was the potential audience and so resistant to change, that few plays could be staged more than twice in a season. The exception was *A Midsummer Night's Dream*, which with Mendelssohn's incidental music was presented seven times.

For a time Meyerhold was thought by his doctor to be suffering from tuberculosis and was ordered to rest in the country throughout the spring and summer. But in the autumn his fortunes took a new turn. For the past year he had been pressing Chekhov to use his influence to secure the Fellowship of New Drama an engagement for a season in a more theatrically conscious town, like Rostov or Chekhov's own birthplace Taganrog. Even before the start of the second season he had written to him: 'I need to get out of this hole Kherson. We've drawn a blank! We work hard, but what do we achieve . . .'52 When Chekhov died on 2 July 1904 in Badenweiler, Meyerhold lost a precious friend and protector, but by now his reputation as a practitioner of the new drama was beginning to speak for itself.

In May 1904 he was invited to join the new permanent company which had been formed in Petersburg by the actress Vera Komissarzhevskaya.† Interestingly enough, Meyerhold declined the offer because it made no mention of acting, for – as he explained to Chekhov – 'No matter how interesting directing might be, acting is far more interesting. For me, working as a director is interesting to the extent that it raises the artistic level of the whole ensemble, but no less because it contributes to the improvement of my own artistic personality.'53 In fact, Meyerhold did not give up working as an actor until after 1917.

Rather than accept Komissarzhevskaya's invitation, Meyerhold sought backing for a theatre of his own in Moscow, a 'theatre of fantasy, a theatre conceived as a reaction against naturalism'.54 However, money could not be secured so he took his company to the Georgian capital, Tiflis, where they

* See p. 10 above. † See pp. 50-51 below.

were offered a secure long-term engagement at the new and well-equipped theatre of the Artistic Society. Tiflis was well over twice the size of Kherson and, as *The Encyclopaedia Britannica* of 1911 reassured its readers: 'A large square, cathedrals, handsome streets, gardens, bridges, many fine buildings – among them the grand-ducal palace, the opera house and the museum – European shops, the club or "circle", hotels and public offices, are evidence of western civilisation.'

With a large number of tested productions, a strengthened company, and hopes of a much wider and more discerning public, Meyerhold could now afford to be more selective in his repertoire. But when the season opened on 26 September with a revival of *Three Sisters*, a local critic wrote:

> . . . the public was intrigued by various rumours that the Fellowship of the New Drama was going to give them something 'new', something Tiflis had never seen before. . . When the eagerly awaited something new was presented, it was found to consist mainly of a remarkably painstaking production of the play, with a host of minor details inspired by the desire to create an impression of the greatest possible illusion.[55]

The 'something new' was revealed a few days later when Meyerhold staged his previous year's production of *Snow*. Fragmentary reports give the impression that the entire action was played in semi-darkness, baffling public and critics alike. So confusing was the effect that some of the audience refused to leave at the end, arguing that the play couldn't possibly be over since it was still entirely incomprehensible. The local correspondent of *Theatre and Art* commented laconically '. . . if one is going to acquaint our public with the new trends in contemporary drama (an unquestionably laudable aspiration in itself) one must proceed with caution and certainly not begin with ultra-violet snow.'[56] The critic of the local newspaper *Kavkaz* was rather less restrained:

> If [Meyerhold] intends at all costs to infect us with the bacilli of the latest literary charlatanism and to transport us with the latest delights from the capital, he should know that it won't work here. . . The taste of Tiflis for drama is not yet that jaded; what we desire are clean, literary plays, free from unnatural contrivances.[57]

For a time this débâcle had an alarming effect on attendances at the Artistic Club and once again Meyerhold reluctantly abandoned his experiments. *The Acrobats* was revived and given an unprecedented ten performances during the season. Again, the critics were overwhelmed by its detailed realism:

> . . . the last act is staged with a skill that one could hardly expect even of a real circus. The artists of Mr Meyerhold's Fellowship are transformed into costumed clowns, jugglers, equestrians, equestriennes, acrobats, animal-trainers, and the like, and near the end there appears a strong man who must be the envy of Akim Nikitin himself, so skilfully does he exploit our public's passion for wrestling.[58]

But whilst remaining within the limits of orthodox theatre, Meyerhold contrived to introduce the works of a number of dramatists who at that time were little known in Russia, still less in Georgia; they included *The Father* by Strindberg and *The Concert-Singer* by Wedekind, which Meyerhold himself translated. On 15 February 1905 he staged Gorky's *Summer Folk*, barely five weeks after the Bloody Sunday massacre in St Petersburg and immediately following Gorky's release from prison for his involvement in that event. After this single performance the play, together with *An Enemy of the People* and Alexander Kosorotov's *Spring Torrent*, was summarily banned by the authorities.

The season ended on 27 February 1905 – once again with *Three Sisters*. The Tiflis public was finally well satisfied with its new company, but Meyerhold had good cause to regret his refusal of Vera Komissarzhevskaya's invitation. Even though the Fellowship could draw on the repertoire that they had built up in Kherson, they were still obliged to stage some eight new productions a month in order to sustain the box-office. Apart from *The Acrobats* and *An Enemy of the People*, which was given six times, no production received more than three performances. It was clear to Meyerhold that whether in the Ukraine or in Georgia, there was no future for experimental theatre outside Moscow and St Petersburg.

The Theatre-Studio

In February 1905 Stanislavsky determined finally to realise his long-cherished idea of a second company attached to the Moscow Art Theatre. It was to be the first of several such companies which would consist mainly of young actors graduated from the drama courses run by the Art Theatre. Each company would prepare a different repertoire of some ten plays in Moscow and then perform alternately in a number of major cities throughout the provinces. In this way many young actors would be guaranteed employment and the high artistic ideals of the Art Theatre would gradually be disseminated throughout Russia. But much more important initially than this missionary task was the opportunity that a second company would afford for experiments in new theatrical forms.

In fact, the practice of a company dividing its work between a main house and an experimental stage had been pioneered by Max Reinhardt and Richard Vallentin in February 1903, when they extended their activities in Berlin from the Kleines Theater to the larger Neues Theater. In the first season twenty-four productions were mounted in the two theatres. Although an account of Reinhardt's work appeared in Russian early in 1904 (*Vesy*, No.1), it wasn't until April 1907 that Meyerhold visited Berlin and saw his productions.* Equally, he seems to have had no knowledge of Paul Fort or Lugné-Poe's early attempts at symbolist staging in Paris in the 1890s. On the other hand, Stanislavsky saw the première of Maeterlinck's *Pelléas and Mélisande* in Lugné-Poe's production in 1893, though it seems to have made little impression on him.[1]

Notwithstanding the new problems posed by Chekhov's plays, the dominant influence on Stanislavsky's work as a director continued to be the Meiningen Theatre which he had studied at close quarters as long ago as 1890.

By the end of 1904 both Stanislavsky and Nemirovich-Danchenko were

* See p. 73 below.

forced to acknowledge that the Art Theatre had exhausted its potential. Following the première in 1901 of *Three Sisters* their work had relied consistently for its success on external realism, reaching its nadir in 1903 with a leaden, historicist version of *Julius Caesar*, in which Stanislavsky suffered acute personal embarrassment in the role of Brutus. Finally, in January 1904 there was no escaping the mournful truth that even the long-awaited *Cherry Orchard* had somehow eluded the company's grasp. Many years later Nemirovich-Danchenko wrote:

> There is no denying that our theatre was at fault in failing to grasp the full meaning of Chekhov, his sensitive style and his amazingly delicate outlines. . . *Chekhov refined his realism to the point where it became symbolic*, [N.D.'s italics] and it was a long time before we succeeded in conveying the subtle texture of his work; maybe the theatre simply handled him too roughly.[2]*

It was Chekhov who shortly before his death suggested that the theatre might extend its range by staging Maeterlinck's trilogy of one-act plays *The Blind, The Intruder,* and *Inside.* In *My Life in Art* Stanislavsky describes how he sought to embody the spirit of the latest music, poetry, painting, and sculpture in a style of acting that would somehow overcome the grossness of the human form and convey the ineffable mystical truths of symbolism.[3] But he could not free himself from his naturalistic perception of the external world, and the production that opened the new season in October 1904 turned out to be an uneasy hybrid, a mixture of over-literal symbols and obscure gestures with the performers either sticking resolutely to the familiar naturalistic style of the Art Theatre or seeking to develop an exalted tone of 'mysticism'. The critic Sergei Glagol wrote: 'I cannot recall another occasion when there was such total incomprehension in the theatre, such absolute disharmony between the audience and the stage.'[4] The critics were unanimous in their condemnation, some concluding that the Art Theatre was simply too heavy-handed to realise Maeterlinck's fragile creations, others taking the view that they were inherently unstageable. Echoing the view that Maeterlinck himself had expressed some fifteen years earlier, Nikolai Efros wrote: '. . . the symbolism of these little dramas . . . is conceived for the puppet theatre, or rather, not for the theatre at all. . . (The theatre) which by it very nature is material and real, with its ponderous mechanism of living people and stage settings, does not enhance but actually harms drama of this kind.'[5] Nemirovich-Danchenko was in no doubt that the fault lay entirely with Maeterlinck, whose work he regarded as 'drawn-out and ponderous'.[6]

But the challenge of symbolism had still to be met; as Meyerhold had shown in the Ukraine and Georgia, there was a rich repertoire of new drama, '*The* New Drama' as it now came to be called, waiting to be brought

---

* Compare the comments of Meyerhold and Bely on pp. 22-23 above.

to the Russian public. In March 1905 Stanislavsky and Meyerhold met in Moscow to discuss the projected 'Theatre-Studio' (the name was coined by Meyerhold), and it was agreed that Meyerhold should become its artistic director, with Stanislavsky and Savva Mamontov* as co-directors. This risky venture was financed exclusively by Stanislavsky at a time when the main company was by no means financially viable. In these circumstances, his confidence in Meyerhold was remarkable, even foolhardy, given that he had seen none of his work as a director. In *My Life in Art* he writes:

At this time of self-doubt and exploration I met Vsevolod Emilievich Meyerhold, a former pupil and artist of the Moscow Art Theatre. During the fourth year of our enterprise's existence he had left us for the provinces where he assembled a company and set out in search of a new, more modern form of art. Between us there was the difference that whereas I was merely striving towards something new and as yet did not know the ways and means of attaining it, Meyerhold seemed already to have discovered new methods and devices but was prevented from realising them fully, partly by material circumstances and partly by the weak composition of his company. Thus I found the man I needed at this time of exploration. I decided to help Meyerhold in his new work which, it seemed to me, accorded largely with my own dreams.[7]

Whereas Stanislavsky and Meyerhold had completely resolved their differences and henceforth were to remain on terms of mutual respect, Nemirovich-Danchenko bitterly resented Meyerhold's return to the Art Theatre. In the course of a long and bitter letter to Stanislavsky he likened Meyerhold to 'those poets of the new art who are in favour of the new simply because they have realised that they are entirely incapable of achieving anything worthwhile with the old.' He claimed that Meyerhold had usurped his own ideas on symbolist staging which Stanislavsky had persistently ignored, and complained that Meyerhold had deliberately set Stanislavsky against him.[8] Stanislavsky's dismissal of these accusations was curt and to the point: Meyerhold's personal motives were of no concern to him; he needed him as an artist to create the new company.[9] Understandably, Nemirovich remained antagonistic towards the whole enterprise, and the hostility between him and Meyerhold continued to smoulder for many years, fuelled at intervals from both sides. Nemirovich frequently condemned Meyerhold's innovations as mere modishness, whilst Meyerhold blamed Nemirovich for stifling Stanislavsky's innate theatricality by confining him within the bounds of psychological realism.[10]

---

* See p. 32 below.

II

The Theatre-Studio company and directors met for the first time on 5
May 1905. Stanislavsky, Meyerhold, and Mamontov all spoke, but it was
left to Stanislavsky to articulate the new theatre's policy, and he took the
opportunity to emphasise its social function:

> At the present time when social forces are stirring in our country the theatre
> cannot and must not devote itself to art and art alone. It must respond to the
> moods of society, elucidate them to the public, and act as its teacher. And not
> forgetting its lofty social calling, the 'young' theatre must strive at the same
> time to achieve its principal aim – the rejuvenation of dramatic art with new
> forms and techniques of staging.[11]

The reminder was timely, coming as it did less than four months after
the events of Bloody Sunday in St Petersburg; but it must be said that
as the summer progressed artistic experiment was more evident than social
conscience as the driving force for Meyerhold and his company. What is
more, hard as he tried to discern a relevance to contemporary events in
Maeterlinck's dramas, there was in the symbolists' rejection of the material
world and their striving for the ideal a disengagement from everyday reality
that amounted to escapism and elitism. Genuine as Meyerhold's populist
sentiments remained, the more he embraced symbolism, the less his work
remained in touch with the momentous events being enacted beyond the
doors of the theatre.*

Initially it was agreed to aim at a repertoire of ten productions, of
which the first four (all directed by Meyerhold) would be *The Death of
Tintagiles* by Maeterlinck, Hauptmann's *Schluck and Jau*, Ibsen's *Love's
Comedy*, and Przybyszewski's *Snow*. Other dramatists in view included
Verhaeren, Hamsun, von Hofmannsthal, Strindberg, Vyacheslav Ivanov,
and Valery Bryusov. Repertoire planning was placed in the hands of
a 'literary bureau' headed by Bryusov. His appointment was in itself
significant: not only was he the author of one of the first symbolist plays
in Russian (*Earth*, 1904), but as we have seen, in 1902 he had published a
crucial article 'The Unnecessary Truth' which was generally recognised as
the first formulation of the 'New Theatre's' case against stage naturalism.[12]
It is worth summarising at some length, since Meyerhold acknowledges it
as the theoretical basis for his experiments at the Theatre-Studio and later
with Vera Komissarzhevskaya in St Petersburg.[13] Bryusov writes:

> The subject of art is the soul of the artist, his feelings and his ideas; it is
> this which is the *content* of a work of art; the plot, the theme are the *form*; the
> images, colours, sounds are the *materials*. . . [Bryusov's italics] An actor on the

* See pp. 150-151 below.

stage is the same as a sculptor before his clay: he must embody in tangible form the same content as the sculptor – the impulse of his soul, his feelings . . . The theatre's sole task is to help the actor reveal his soul to the audience.

Citing the Russian poet Tyutchev's dictum 'A thought expressed becomes a lie', Bryusov defines the eternal paradox of the theatre:

The subject of art lies always in the conceptual world, but all the means of art lie in the material world. It is not possible to overcome this fatal contradiction; one can only make it as painless as possible by sharpening, refining, spiritualising art.

And this, he maintains, is what naturalistic theatre (and in particular the Moscow Art Theatre) fails to recognise; on the contrary, it strives to reproduce the material world in as concrete terms as possible. But in this too it fails because of its refusal to recognise the insurmountable conventionality of the theatre. It is not possible to reproduce life faithfully on the stage. The stage is essentially based on conventions. All one can hope to do is to replace one convention with another. It is as much a convention for the actors in Chekhov to remove their fur coats and boots on entering as it was for the characters from afar in Greek tragedy to enter stage-left. In both cases the spectator is aware that the actors have come on from the wings.

On being confronted with an exact representation of reality, our first reaction is to discover how it is achieved, our second is to discover the discrepancies with reality. Only then do we begin to respond to it as a work of art, and when we do it is because we have accepted the *convention*. The more exact the representation, the less scrutable will be the convention and the more delayed our response to it as a work of art.

Such conventions, says Bryusov, are dictated by necessity, and we must reject them in favour of the 'deliberate convention' which '. . . furnishes the spectator with as much as he requires to picture most easily in his imagination the setting demanded by the play's story'. As a model he cites the theatre of Ancient Greece where 'Everything was totally conventionalised and totally life-like; the spectators watched the action, not the setting, for tragedy – in the words of Aristotle – is the imitation not of people but of action. . .' And in conclusion he says: 'I call for the rejection of the unnecessary truth of the contemporary stage and a return to the deliberate convention of the antique theatre.'

Even though it was Stanislavsky who invited Bryusov to work at the Studio, it is doubtful whether he anticipated the complete rejection of accepted methods that was soon to take place there. Meyerhold recalls Stanislavsky saying at the inaugural meeting: 'Obviously the Art Theatre with its naturalistic style does not represent the last word and has no intention of remaining frozen to the spot; the young theatre, together with its parent, the Art Theatre, must continue the process and move forward.'[14]

But Meyerhold quickly showed that he was not content to 'continue the process and move forward'; in his account of the Studio he writes: 'the Theatre-Studio had no desire to uphold and further the interests of the Art Theatre, but straightaway devoted itself to the construction of a new edifice, building from the foundations upwards'.[15]

To do Stanislavsky justice it must be added that, far from opposing Meyerhold's experiments, he actively encouraged them and staunchly defended him against his detractors within the Art Theatre. Anxious to allow the young company artistic freedom, he soon left for the south to prepare his own production of Hamsun's *Drama of Life* which was due for rehearsal in the main theatre later in the summer.

III

The month following the inaugural meeting of the Studio was devoted exclusively to the preparation of designs for the new productions in the repertoire. For the first time Meyerhold had the chance to work with true artists rather than artisan scene-painters. Just as Lugné-Poe had recruited members of the Nabis group to work with him at the Théâtre de l'Oeuvre in the 1890s, so for the next eighteen years Meyerhold was to work almost exclusively with painters.

Since the 1880s theatre design had begun to emerge as a creative art in Russia. The man chiefly responsible was Savva Mamontov, railway tycoon, singer, sculptor, stage director, dramatist, and munificent patron of the arts. On his estate at Abramtsevo near Moscow he created his 'Private Opera' in which the performers were amateurs, but the designers the leading painters of the day. There, and later at the professional 'Moscow Private Russian Opera' (1885–1904), such artists as Apollinarius and Victor Vasnetsov, Konstantin Korovin, and Mikhail Vrubel created a dazzling series of settings and costumes which embodied the traditional motifs and colours of Russian folk art in a highly stylised and uncompromisingly theatrical manner. The result was a fully integrated spectacle whose every element – setting, costume, gesture, movement, music, and dialogue – played an equal part.

In time, Mamontov's example helped to effect a similar transformation in the Imperial operas and ballets of Moscow and St Petersburg, especially after 1900 when they began to employ artists of the 'World of Art' group, among them Alexander Benois, Leon Bakst, and Alexander Golovin. A few years later, their work was to astonish Western audiences at the first of Diaghilev's Russian Seasons in Paris.[16]

Meanwhile, the status and function of the designer in the Russian dramatic theatre remained unaltered. The Moscow Art Theatre was virtually alone in recognising and exploiting the visual aspects of the drama. But, although Stanislavsky was a great admirer of Mamontov's productions and himself performed at Abramtsevo, it was the painstaking verisimilitude of the Meiningen Theatre that he and Nemirovich-Danchenko took as their model. From 1898 to 1906 every major production at the Art Theatre (including all Chekhov's plays) was designed by Victor Simov, and in subsequent years too he was responsible for many more. His work was distinguished by its impeccable authenticity and its revolutionary use of the stage area. He aimed to present a complete view of life in progress, frequently in a whole series of rooms at varying levels seen, as if by chance, from an oblique angle. In terms of stage realism, the theatre today has made no significant advance on what Simov first accomplished eighty years ago – which is perhaps a measure both of the achievement and of the limitations of his method.

Amongst the young artists who joined Meyerhold and his fellow stage-directors* at the Art Theatre's model workshop in May 1905 were Nikolai Sapunov and Sergei Sudeikin, both in their early twenties. Previously, they had worked under Korovin: Sapunov as his assistant at the Bolshoi Theatre and Sudeikin as his pupil at the College of Painting, Sculpture and Architecture in Moscow. Jointly they were entrusted with the designs for Meyerhold's production of *The Death of Tintagiles*. In a short time they had refused flatly to conform to the accepted practice in the naturalistic theatre of constructing true-to-life models of the exteriors and interiors specified in the play. Following the already accepted practice in opera and ballet, and in any case inexperienced in three-dimensional work, they produced a series of impressionistically figurative pictures imbued with the foreboding atmosphere of *The Death of Tintagiles* and designed for translation into scenic terms in collaboration with the director and scene-painters.

Their fellow designers quickly followed suit, rejecting the model in favour of the impressionistic sketch:

> In Act One of [Hauptmann's] *Krampton* (the artist's studio), instead of a
> full-sized room with all its furnishings, Denisov simply depicted a few bright
> areas, characteristic of a studio. When the curtain rose, the studio atmosphere
> was conveyed by a single huge canvas occupying half the stage and drawing the
> spectator's attention away from all other details; but in order that such a large
> picture should not distract the spectator with its subject, only one corner was
> completed, the rest being lightly sketched in with charcoal. In addition, there
> was the edge of a big skylight with a patch of sky, a stepladder for painting
> the canvas, a large table, an ottoman (necessary to the play's action), and a
> number of sketches strewn over the table. This marked the introduction of
> the principle of stylisation.[17]

Meyerhold defines his conception of the term 'stylisation' (*uslovnost*) at that time:

> With the word 'stylisation' I do not imply the exact reproduction of the style
> of a certain period or of a certain phenomenon, such as a photographer might

* Alexander Kosheverov, Sergei Popov and Vladimir Repman.

6 Costume and
make-up design
by Nikolai
Ulyanov for
Schluck and Jau

7 Set design by Ulyanov for *Schluck and Jau*

achieve. In my opinion the concept of 'stylisation' is indivisibly tied up with the idea of convention, generalisation and symbol. To 'stylise' a given period or phenomenon means to employ every possible means of expression in order to reveal the inner synthesis of that period or phenomenon, to bring out those hidden features that are deeply rooted in the style of any work of art.[18]

The principle was pursued to its extreme in *Schluck and Jau*, directed jointly by Meyerhold and Vladimir Repman with designs by Nikolai Ulyanov. Hauptmann's 'ironical masque' about two vagrants ennobled for a day to amuse the gentry was transferred from its original setting in medieval Silesia to a stylised abstraction of the 'periwig age' of Louis XIV.* Here Meyerhold describes the treatment of the third scene:

The mood of idleness and whimsy is conveyed by a row of arbours resembling wicker baskets and stretching across the forestage. The back curtain depicts

* Apparently this was at Stanislavsky's suggestion after he had visited Diaghilev's brilliant exhibition of eighteenth-century portraits at the Tauride Palace in Petersburg. The exhibition's setting by Bakst was conceived as a dramatic unity of a garden with arbours, trellises and pavilions to set off the paintings.[20]

a blue sky with fluffy clouds. The horizon is bounded by crimson roses stretching the entire width of the stage. Crinolines, white periwigs, and the characters' costumes are blended with the colours of the setting into a single artistic design, a symphony in mother-of-pearl with all the charm of a painting by Konstantin Somov. The rise of the curtain is preceded by a duet in the style of the eighteenth century. It rises to disclose a figure seated in each arbour: in the centre is Sidselill, on either side – the ladies-in-waiting. They are embroidering a single broad ribbon with ivory needles – all in perfect time, whilst in the distance is heard a duet to the accompaniment of harp and harpsichord. Everything conveys the musical rhythm: movements, lines, gestures, dialogue, the colours of the setting and costumes. Everything that needs to be hidden from the audience is concealed behind stylised flats, with no attempt to make the spectator forget that he is in a theatre.[19]

Meyerhold's comparison with Konstantin Somov is apt, for he was a prominent member of the 'World of Art', and it is that movement's conception of a unity of the arts that is reflected in the interpretation of *Schluck and Jau* – to the exclusion of all traces of 'unnecessary truth'. In contrast to the chilling menace of *The Death of Tintagiles* Hauptmann's masque was conceived as a lighthearted divertissement, an unashamed exercise in theatrical style.

IV

Just as the original Moscow Art Theatre company had done seven years earlier, the Theatre-Studio started rehearsals on 3 June 1905 in a barn near Pushkino some miles outside Moscow. The company was composed largely of graduates of the Art Theatre School and ex-members of the Fellowship of the New Drama, plus three graduates from the Alexandrinsky Theatre School in St Petersburg.[20]

By this time Meyerhold was firmly committed to the principle of stylisation, and he was faced with the problem of creating a style of acting consistent with it. Before approaching *The Death of Tintagiles*, he acquainted himself with all the available literature on the play.[21] He found the key to its interpretation in Maeterlinck's *Everyday Tragedy*. Originally conceived in 1894 as a preview of Ibsen's *The Master Builder*, Maeterlinck's essay dealt far less with Ibsen than with his own conception of the theatre and exerted a considerable influence on Lugné-Poe's work at the Théâtre de l'Oeuvre. Even though he had worked with painters as talented as Vuillard, Denis and Sérusier, Lugné-Poe's productions were tentative and hampered by minimal resources. Obliged to hire actors from the regular theatre to strengthen his part-professional company, he was never in a situation to develop a uniform style equal to the demands of symbolist theatre.[22] In 1905 at the Theatre-Studio Meyerhold was much better placed to explore the practical implications of Maeterlinck's thinking.

In *Everyday Tragedy* Maeterlinck[23] begins by rejecting as superficial the truth revealed in 'le tragique des grandes aventures' and suggests that the truly tragic is to be found in the simple fact of man's existence:

> Is it absolutely necessary to cry out like the Atridae before an eternal God reveals himself in our life? Does he never come and join us in the stillness of our lamplight? Is it not tranquillity, when we reflect on it with the stars looking down, that is most terrible? When does the meaning of life manifest itself – in tumult or in silence? . . .
>
> I admire Othello, but to me he does not seem to lead the august daily life of a Hamlet, who has time to live because he does not act. . .
>
> I have come to believe that the old man seated in an armchair, simply waiting in the lamplight and listening unconsciously to all the eternal laws that preside about his house, interpreting without realising it all that is contained in the silence of the doors and windows, and in the small voice of the lamplight, enduring the presence of his soul and its destiny, bowing his head a little, never suspecting that all the powers of this world watch and wait in the room like attentive servants, unaware that the little table on which he leans is held in suspense over the abyss by the sun itself, unaware that there is not a star in the sky, not a part of the soul, that remains indifferent to the lowering of an eyelid or the waking of a thought – I have come to believe that in reality this motionless old man leads a life that is more profound, more human and more significant than the lover who strangles his mistress, the captain who is victorious in battle, or the husband who avenges his honour.

Such a static theatre, argues Maeterlinck, is wholly practicable: consider the absence of direct action from Greek tragedy. The beauty and grandeur of Aeschylus and Sophocles resides in their dialogue; that is, not in the 'external, necessary dialogue' that advances the plot, but in the implicit, unvoiced, 'internal dialogue'. This internal dialogue determines the tragic moments of human existence when the spoken word conceals the truth:

> What I say often counts for little; but my presence, the attitude of my soul, my future and my past, what is yet to be born of me, what lies dead within me, my secret thoughts, the planets that vouchsafe their approval of me, my destiny, the thousand upon thousand of mysteries that bound my existence and yours: at the moment of tragedy it is all this that speaks to you and is contained in your reply to me.

It is this mystical dialogue, says Maeterlinck, whose echo is sometimes captured by Aeschylus and Sophocles, and which, he implies, underlies the still surface of his own 'tragédies immobiles'.

Prompted by Maeterlinck's essay, Meyerhold saw *The Death of Tintagiles* as 'above all a manifestation and purification of souls, . . . a chorus of souls singing softly of suffering, love, beauty, and death'. Often in the years to come he was to take inspiration, even specific images, from painting. Now he discerned the key to the play's realisation in the art of Il Perugino where 'the contemplative lyrical character of his subjects, the quiet grandeur and archaic splendour of his pictures could be achieved only with compositions whose harmony is unmarred by the slightest abrupt movement or the merest harsh contrast.'[24]

To this end a style of diction was developed incorporating 'a cold coining of the words, free from all tremolo and the customary sobbing. A total absence of tension and lugubrious intonation.' Conventional histrionic gestures were replaced by 'The inner trembling of mystical vibration [which] is conveyed through the eyes, the lips, the sound and the manner of delivery: the exterior calm conceals volcanic emotions, with everything light and unforced.'[25]

But, above all, Meyerhold exploited the expressive power of the actor's body. In his music-drama Wagner conveys the protagonists' true emotions, the inner dialogue, through the medium of the orchestral score which is frequently in counterpoint – emotional as well as musical – to the sung libretto. In *The Death of Tintagiles* Meyerhold tried to employ movement, gestures, and poses in precisely the same manner in order to suggest the inexorable tragedy of the little Prince trapped and destroyed by the unseen Queen.*

> The *truth* of human relationships is established by gestures, poses, glances and silences. Words alone cannot say everything. Hence there must be a *pattern of movement* to transform the spectator into a vigilant observer. . . The difference between the old theatre and the new is that in the new theatre speech and plasticity are each subordinated to their own particular rhythms and the two do not necessarily coincide.[26]

In order to achieve these effects, Meyerhold left as little as possible to chance, prescribing every possible detail, visual and oral, in his prompt-copy. He sketched in desired gestures and poses, placing particular emphasis on

8 Costume design
for Aglovale in
*The Death of
Tintagiles*

* Compare Meyerhold's interpretation of *Tristan and Isolde* (pp. 86 ff. below).

the performers in profile so what the spectator saw would resemble a two-dimensional bas-relief, motionless and punctuating the action. This prescriptive method was strikingly similar to Stanislavsky's in his early productions of Chekhov, and reflects the same wish for absolute control over the actors.

Valentina Verigina, herself a member of the Theatre-Studio company, has recorded some vivid impressions of *The Death of Tintagiles*:

> In this production statuesque plasticity was employed for the first time: the hands with fingers together, certain turns and inclinations of the head, were typical of primitive painting. But Meyerhold never copied poses or groupings from actual pictures; he imbued them with his own powerful imagination, making a splendid composition in the original style and appropriate to the actor in question. When I first saw the picture 'Madonna at the Strawberry Bed' (by an unknown Middle-Rhenish master in the museum at Solothurn), I immediately recalled Tintagiles and his sister Ygraine, even though there were no such poses and no such *mise-en-scène* in *The Death of Tintagiles*. I was reminded of the Theatre-Studio production of Maeterlinck's play because at certain moments the head of the little Tintagiles bent towards his shoulder just like Christ's in the picture, and his hand was raised with the fingers together in the same way. Ygraine and Bellangère pensively bent their heads like the Virgin in the picture. When I recall the production I see everything in one place, even though the characters sometimes moved around and made exits and entrances. They did it inconspicuously, simply appearing then disappearing. Right from the first act, but especially later, one sensed the sisters' anxiety for their little brother in every phrase they uttered, every gesture of their submissive hands. But most of all one felt it in the moments of silence; one felt energy concentrated in their frozen poses. In this way an almost unbearable dynamism was created beneath an outward calm. The Queen's three maidservants entered one after the other, their index fingers hooked like claws, their faces hidden by grey hoods. One recalls them motionless: unlike the other characters, they never once altered their pose. The voices of these dreadful executors of the will of fate echoed sinister yet melodious. First they all spoke in unison on one note: 'They are sle-eeping. . . No need to wa-it now. . .' Then separately: 'She wants everything done in secret. . .' and so on.[27]

In 1902, the company of Otodziro Kawakami, the first Japanese actors ever to be seen in the West, performed in Russia. Their repertoire was based mainly on traditional works of the Kabuki theatre and their style was a modernised version of Kabuki called 'Soshi Shibai': stylised, yet revelatory in its naked emotive power. Above all, the critics praised the grace and virtuosity of Kawakami's actress-dancer wife, Sada Yacco. The English *Japoniste*, Charles Ricketts wrote in his diary:

> The convention of our European stage demands likely gesture and intonation throughout, and a sustained pitch in delivery. This the Japanese observe in the minor characters; with the principals it is not the case; elaborate expression, intonation, and posturing in a deliberate and 'transcendent' temper are the rule. During elaborate scenes of facial expression the body will remain almost immobile or be kept in cramped or curtseying positions.[28]

In 1909 Meyerhold wrote: ' . . . Sada Yacco demonstrated the meaning of true stylisation on the stage, the ability to economise with gestures, to reveal all the beauty of the composition.'[29] He makes no reference to the Japanese theatre in his published account of the Theatre-Studio and he never actually saw Sada Yacco perform, yet it seems likely that his first experiments in stylised movement and gesture were influenced by what others wrote about her.[30] Twenty years later when rehearsing Faiko's *Bubus the Teacher* he was still citing her as an example to his actors.[31]

V

When Meyerhold described to Chekhov his interpretation of *The Cherry Orchard* in 1904, he compared the third act to a symphony, in which the actual music of the Jewish band was merely one part.* Significantly, he wrote: 'In this act there is something Maeterlinckian, something terrifying.' Although more overtly stylised, his production of *The Death of Tintagiles* a year later was remarkably similar in conception and the score composed by the young, little-known composer, Ilya Sats, was a vital element. As Meyerhold recalled, 'Both the external effects of the scenario of Maeterlinck's play (such as the howling of the wind, the beating of the waves, and the buzzing of voices) and all the points of the 'inner dialogue' picked out by the director were conveyed with the help of actual music (orchestra and choir *a capella*).'[32]

Just as in *Schluck and Jau*, and indeed in virtually all Meyerhold's work in the future, the aim was a production whose every element was strictly bound by a musical scheme. But whilst it was easy enough to synchronise gestures and movements with the musical score, the actors found it impossible to rid their diction entirely of lifelike intonation and to think in purely rhythmical terms. As Meyerhold says, their task might have been easier had there existed some form of notation to record the required variations in tempo, pitch, volume, and expression, thereby ensuring their consistency from one performance to the next.[33] But the root of the trouble lay in the actors' previous training in the realist tradition: as the tension of the drama mounted they would begin once more to 'live' their roles and all thoughts of musical discipline would vanish.

The extent of the actors' failure to master the new style of declamation did not become apparent while they were at Pushkino, and rehearsals there proceeded in an atmosphere of general optimism. On 12 August Meyerhold revealed the company's progress to Stanislavsky, who by now had returned to Moscow. Immediately afterwards, Stanislavsky wrote to Sergei Popov, the Studio's administrative director:

> Yesterday brought me great joy. It went off splendidly. Unexpectedly, the entire Art Theatre company attended. Gorky and Mamontov turned up, so

* See pp. 22-23 above.

the parade was graced by the generals. *Schluck* made a splendid impression and I was delighted for Vladimir Emilievich [Repman]. *Tintagiles* caused a furore and I was happy for Vsevolod Emilievich. *Love's Comedy* was weak but I think I know the solution and can offer some good advice. But the main thing which became clear yesterday is that *there is a company*, or rather good material for one. This question has tortured me all summer and yesterday I was reassured. Yesterday the pessimists began to believe in the possibility of success and conceded the first victory of the Studio over prejudice.[34]

A week later the Studio moved to its permanent theatre in Moscow. Stanislavsky had taken a two-year lease on the former Nemchinov Theatre in Povarskaya Street, an improbably large auditorium seating seven hundred which had been renovated at considerable expense in a style befitting the lofty ambitions of the enterprise. As Konstantin Rudnitsky describes it, 'The Studio was furnished with taste and elegance, as though the very blue and white front-of-house décor was a polemic directed at the deliberate unpretentiousness of the dull green and grey of the Art Theatre's interior.'[35]

For the first time the new productions were rehearsed on a full-size stage with music and scenery, and this revealed a number of serious problems, beginning with the difficulty in *The Death of Tintagiles* of synchronising the actors' voices with Sats' score. Worse still, it now became clear that Sapunov and Sudeikin had been incapable of translating their brilliant atmospheric sketches into three-dimensional scenic terms. Not only did they introduce crude naturalistic details which marred the overall impression of stylisation, but they had failed to allow for the effects of stage lighting, and it altered their original designs beyond recognition, despite the use of a front gauze to soften the outlines and lend an air of mystery to the poses and movements of the performers.

Despite these problems Stanislavsky remained enthusiastic, though most of his attention was directed towards rehearsing productions for the new season in the main house, including a revival of *The Seagull* in which Meyerhold was again to play Treplev. However, it was decided to put back the opening of the Theatre-Studio from 1 October, first to the 10th and then to the 21st. Posters were printed and the season was announced. But by now Russia was in the grip of a general strike and on 14 October Moscow was hit by a violent upsurge of revolutionary disturbances. Practically all theatres closed and the Art Theatre was turned into a casualty station with actresses from both companies serving as auxiliary nurses. On 19 October an imperial manifesto proclaimed the end of the autocratic rule of the Romanovs and the institution of a constitutional monarchy. Normal theatrical activities now resumed, but many of the public stayed away, fearing right-wing extremist reprisals in public places, and the newspapers paid little or no attention to artistic matters.

Clearly, at such a time the future of a risky venture like the Theatre-Studio was in extreme jeopardy, and on 16 October the decision was taken to postpone the opening indefinitely. Even so, sometime within the next week, probably after the 19th, the first dress-rehearsal took place.[36]

Nikolai Ulyanov describes what happened:

On stage semi-darkness, only the silhouettes of the actors visible, two-dimensional scenery, no wings, the back-drop hung almost level with the setting line. It's novel, and so is the rhythmical delivery of the actors on stage. Slowly the action unfolds, it seems as if time has come to a standstill. Suddenly Stanislavsky demands 'light!' The audience starts; there is noise and commotion. Sudeikin and Sapunov jump up protesting. Stanislavsky: 'The audience won't stand for darkness very long on stage, it's wrong psychologically, you need to see the actors' faces!' Sudeikin and Sapunov: 'But the settings are designed to be seen in half-darkness; they lose all artistic point if you light them!' Again silence, broken by the measured delivery of the actors, but this time with the lights full up. But once the stage was lit, it became lifeless, and the harmony between the figures and their setting was destroyed. Stanislavsky rose, followed by the rest of the audience. The rehearsal was broken off, the production rejected.[37]

To Stanislavsky the problems went deeper than settings and lighting design. Recalling the dress rehearsal in *My Life in Art*, he writes:

Everything became clear. The young inexperienced actors, aided by a talented director, were fit to show their new experiments to the public only in short extracts; when it was a question of coping with plays of profound inner content, with a subtle structure and, what is more, a stylised form, the young people revealed their childlike helplessness. The director tried to use his own talent to obscure the faults of artists who were simply clay in his hands for the modelling of beautiful groups and ideas. But with actors deficient in artistic technique he succeeded only in demonstrating his ideas, principles and explorations; there was nothing and nobody with which to realise them in full, and so the interesting concepts of the Studio turned into abstract theories and scientific formulae. Once again I became convinced that a great distance separates the dreams of a stage director from their fulfilment, that above all else the theatre is for the actor and cannot exist without him, that the new drama needs new actors with a completely new technique. Once I realised that such actors were not to be found at the Studio, its sad fate became plain to me. Under such conditions it might have been possible to create a studio for the stage director and his *mises-en-scène*, but by that time the director interested me only insofar as he could assist the creative art of the actor, and not for his ability to camouflage the actor's inadequacy. For this reason the director's studio, no matter how splendid, could not satisfy my dreams at that time, particularly in view of the fact that by then I had become disenchanted with the designers' work – with their canvas, their colours, their cardboard, with all the external means of production and the tricks of the director. I invested all my hopes in the actor and the development of a firm basis for his technique and creativity.[38]

Finally, on 24 October Stanislavsky informed Meyerhold that he had decided to liquidate the enterprise altogether. At a personal cost of 80,000 roubles, which represented half his entire capital, he paid off every member of the company up to May 1906. It was partly to recover this loss that the Art Theatre embarked on its first European tour in February 1906.[39]

Nemirovich-Danchenko's reaction to the Studio's failure was predictable; the day after the disastrous dress-rehearsal he wrote to Stanislavsky: 'If you had only shown me what I saw yesterday before seeking my advice on what you should do, I would have said: the sooner you put an end to this, the worst mistake of your life, the better it will be for the Art Theatre, for you personally, and for your reputation as an artist.'[40] Even those most passionately committed to the ideals embodied in the Studio's experiments, including Meyerhold himself, soon became reconciled to its closure. For, as Valery Bryusov said, 'it demonstrated to everyone who made its acquaintance that it is impossible to reconstruct the theatre on old foundations: either we must continue to build the theatre of Antoine and Stanislavsky or begin again from the beginning.'[41]

In October 1905 the Theatre-Studio must have seemed a dismal fiasco to all concerned, but its failure stemmed not so much from the fallaciousness of its aims as from the deep-rooted habits and prejudices that frustrated their complete realisation: in effect, stylisation failed because it was not stylised enough. Nevertheless, the lessons learnt at the Studio equipped Meyerhold with the experience to achieve the successes that were soon to follow in St Petersburg and which led to the establishment of a new movement in the Russian theatre, a movement to which the Moscow Art Theatre itself remained committed and to which it was soon to contribute with a series of productions culminating in 1911 with the *Hamlet* of Edward Gordon Craig.

In January 1906, Meyerhold wrote to his wife Olga, summing up his reactions to all the momentous events of the past year:

> . . . Actors divide their calendars into seasons. Just as landowners calculate their resources by what they sow and what they reap, so actors reckon their successes by the season. This year I lost a season because I wasn't acting, or so it would seem. But that is only how it looks from the outside.
>
> As I was climbing into the train to start the new season, I found myself looking back and I realised how much I had gained from the last one. This year something new was born in my soul, something that will put out branches and bear fruit; the fruit will ripen, and my life is certain to flourish abundantly. Somebody said recently that the life of a creative artist follows a curve – twenty-five years up, thirty years down and then another thirty-five years up. Well this year has been part of an upward curve for me, or so it seems. In May there was the work in the model-workshop alongside artists who helped to realise what had never before been realised, and my spirit gave birth to a new world. Summer revealed the theatre of Maeterlinck, and for the first time the Primitives were given living form on the stage. The collapse of the Studio was my salvation – it wasn't what I wanted, not what I wanted at all. It is only now that I realise how fortunate its failure was.

Then the Moscow revolution.* I often find myself trembling, not from fear but from a sudden realisation of the truth. I found myself drawn out onto the streets when other people were sheltering in their homes. It wasn't the danger that drew me, as it draws neurotics to throw themselves from church-towers or under trains. I was drawn by the desire to see the transfigured world. I still remember the square lit by a single lamp at one corner and looking as though it was on a slant. The unlit side fell away and was swallowed up in the darkness where a lonely bell-tower gleamed white. I was drawn by the desire to run from street-corner to street-corner and watch the other dark figures scurrying along against the background of white snow, unlit by street-lamps but giving light enough of its own. I was drawn by the desire to listen to those hurrying figures as they told each other in whispers where it was safe to go. I was drawn by the desire to freeze when a bullet whistled past – dry, malevolent and cold, yet at the same time hot. From this *terrible* week there has remained within me something that will give me strength to feel something later, but not yet. How the soul of a creative artist trembled! It trembled so much, but nobody even noticed, and still nobody knows. . .[42]

* The armed uprising, 9-17 December 1905.

From Symbolism to the Grotesque

Meyerhold did not leave the Art Theatre immediately after the closure of the Studio. Before the cancellation of the project he had been persuaded by Stanislavsky to recreate his original role of Konstantin in the revival of *The Seagull*, which opened on 30 September 1905. 'This was meant' – says Meyerhold – 'as a kind of bridge that might lead to my return to the Moscow Art Theatre, or so Konstantin Sergeevich indicated. But there were also obstacles: Vladimir Ivanovich's [Nemirovich-Danchenko] reaction to the suggestion was cool, to say the least. And I didn't know what I wanted either: I was completely disorientated. But the decision was made for me by the total absence of any friendly contact backstage between myself and my former fellow-actors in the cast: they irritated me, and I seemed strange to them.'[1]

So at the end of 1905 Meyerhold left the Moscow Art Theatre for the last time and moved to St Petersburg. There he met the leading figures of the capital's artistic and intellectual circles at the regular Wednesday soirées held in the 'Tower' flat of Vyacheslav Ivanov, the leading theorist of Russian symbolism. It was at this time that Georgy Chulkov enlisted the aid of a number of symbolist poets (among them Bely, Blok, Bryusov, Remizov, Sologub, and Vyacheslav Ivanov) to realise the familiar utopian dream of a 'mystical theatre' that would revive the spirit of Dionysus in a communal ritualistic drama. Maxim Gorky, who had been actively involved in the December uprising in Moscow, was an improbable member of this company. But at a meeting in the 'Tower' on 3 January he articulated the ambitions of many at the time, Meyerhold included: 'In our impoverished Russia only art exists; it is we here who are her "government"; we underestimate our importance: we must rule powerfully and our theatre needs to be realised on a vast scale. It must be a theatre-club that will bring together all literary fractions.'[2] It was a valedictory exhortation on Gorky's part, for the following day he fled to Finland to escape arrest and remained abroad for the next eight years.

Meyerhold was seen as the natural choice for artistic director and it was proposed to build a company round a nucleus of the best actors from the Theatre-Studio. 'The Torches' (*Fakely*), as the company was called, never materialised because no financial backer could be found for such an esoteric and idealistic venture at a time when Russia was still in ferment after the traumatic disturbances of 1905. Likewise, a similar project involving Sergei Diaghilev came to nothing.[3] After almost four months of inactivity as a director, Meyerhold could not afford to remain idle, so at short notice he seized the opportunity to revive the Fellowship of the New Drama in Tiflis, where he was offered a five-year contract on very attractive terms. Leaving Olga and their three daughters, Maria, Tanya, and Irina, in Kuokkalla outside St Petersburg, he hurried south to prepare a repertoire for the remainder of the season. The opening presentation on 20 February 1906 was a double bill comprising Ibsen's *Love's Comedy* and an adaptation of Chekhov's short story, *Surgery*. After five weeks in Tiflis the company went on tour for a month to Novocherkassk and Rostov, closing there at the end of April.

Once more, Meyerhold found the provincial public resistant to innovation and he was obliged by financial considerations to include a large proportion of pot-boilers in his repertoire. Nevertheless, he did contrive to further his propagation of modern drama by introducing such works as Ibsen's *Love's Comedy*, *A Doll's House* and *Ghosts*, Hauptmann's *The Assumption of Hannele*, Strindberg's *Miss Julie*, and Eugène Brieux's controversial play about venereal disease, *Damaged Goods*, which had only recently been licensed for public performance in France. No less contentious were the productions of Gorky's *Children of the Sun*, with its scenes of rioting provoked by a cholera epidemic, and *The Jews* (1903) by Gorky's fellow Marxist Chirikov, with its vivid representation of a Black Hundred pogrom, which had been widely banned. Meyerhold took great pride in this production, and his description of it in a letter to his wife suggests his growing mastery of the fully orchestrated *mise-en-scène*:

Today's performance went very, very interestingly. I devised an extremely intriguing solution for the closing scene. The point is that for the pogrom I use not noise but silence. Throughout the act you are kept on tenterhooks by the distant roar of the mob offstage. It comes nearer, but at the very moment when the audience is thinking that it is really close I make it recede again until it becomes inaudible. A pause. Everyone on-stage has frozen, the audience has relaxed. Then there is hammering on the doors, the shutters are smashed – but no one shouts, they only whisper (remember the sound of voices when they were building the barricades outside our house – like that). The people on-stage put out their lamps and candles. There is complete darkness. Then the doors are broken open and the mob bursts in. They ransack the room in silence. A silent struggle. Leah shoots herself. Beryozin is strangled. Bursts of fire from the Cossacks are heard offstage. The mob disappears. Nakhman enters with a lamp and to our horror reveals a row of corpses. Only Leiser is still sitting and whispering that a storm came and carried everyone off. Nakhman falls to his knees and weeps over the body of Leah. The clock chimes. The effect is shattering. I'm afraid that the play will be banned tomorrow. The Chief of Police was in the theatre for the last act.[4]

Meyerhold was right: after three performances to packed houses, with himself in the role of Nakhman, the production was taken off.

On 19 March Meyerhold finally expunged the memory of the Theatre-Studio débâcle by presenting the Russian première of *The Death of Tintagiles* in a double bill with *Miss Julie*. The *mise-en-scène* was similar to the original and Sats' score was again used, this time played on a harmonium. However, the new settings by Konstantin Kostin bore an unmistakable resemblance to the highly fashionable paintings of the Swiss artist, Arnold Böcklin. In a strenuous attempt to instil some social relevance into Maeterlinck's fragile vision of a malign universe Meyerhold prefaced the performance with a short address to the audience in which he related the fate of Tintagiles to the suffering of the Russian people in the recent abortive revolution.[5] If Meyerhold is to be believed, the production was greeted with 'grandiose ovations' (letter of 20 March 1906) and was given a second performance. But, much as it had elsewhere, *Miss Julie* offended many of the audience and was not repeated.

Even though Meyerhold was now succeeding in testing and modifying in actual performance the ideas that he had explored at the Theatre-Studio, his frequent letters to his wife convey his growing exasperation over working under insupportable pressure as both director and actor with a largely inexperienced company and for a public that was more than likely to reject all but the most accessible works after a single performance. Even after the brilliant first night of *The Jews* on 24 February he rails in his letter to Olga against his actors' inattention, their lack of commitment, their temperaments, even their voices. And he goes on:

> I dream of a theatre school and of much else that can never be achieved in the provinces. Why, oh why am I destroying myself? And I shall be destroyed if I remain in the provinces. That much has become clear now that this sequence of productions has been put on. Up till now I have restrained myself when writing to you, but now I see clearly that the provinces are nothing but a rubbish dump. It's fine to arrive with ready-made productions, because the provincial public is naïve and capable of sincere enjoyment. But to try and create something on the spot . . . no, I am against the provinces.[6]

But Tiflis in 1906 was little more than a staging-post in Meyerhold's career. Before the start of the season there he had been invited once more by Vera Komissarzhevskaya to join her Petersburg theatre, and in May he signed a contract with her, this time as both actor and artistic director for the 1906–1907 season. Meanwhile, the Fellowship's engagement in Tiflis was renewed for a further year, with Meyerhold agreeing to continue as artistic director *in absentia* on the understanding that he would rejoin the company on its summer tour to prepare the principal new productions for the following season.

It was about this time that Meyerhold first read Georg Fuchs' *The Stage of the Future*,[7] a work that, as he himself admitted, made the deepest impression on him.[8] Like the symbolist poets of Vyacheslav Ivanov's circle, Fuchs called for the restoration of the theatre as a festive ritual, involving performers and spectators in a common experience that would reveal the universal significance of their personal existence. The drama, he writes, has no life except as a shared experience: 'By virtue of their origins the player and the spectator, the stage and the auditorium, are not opposed to each other, they are a unity.'[9] Modern theatres, with their tiers of boxes and their peep-show stages are 'crude imitations of the ballet-houses of baroque courts' in which the performer is confined beyond the barrier of the footlights at a respectful distance from the spectator.[10] Instead, Fuchs proposes a steeply raked amphitheatre capable of accommodating a large audience in the closest possible proximity to the stage. The stage itself is to be wide rather than deep and divided into three ascending strips joined by shallow steps of the same width. The low forestage is located in front of the proscenium opening, extending in a shallow arc into the auditorium. The middle stage is in effect a narrow bridge joining two walls, between which the aperture is normally closed with a backcloth. In the event of the middle stage being used (for crowd scenes or to facilitate rapid scene changes), a painted backdrop may be hung behind the rear stage, but in order to furnish a flat decorative background rather than to create an illusion of distance or perspective. The main action is concentrated on the shallow plane of the forestage where the performers are meant to stand out against the background like the figures in a bas-relief.[11]

In this way, says Fuchs, all attention is focused on the most profound means of dramatic expression: the rhythmical movement of the human body in space. He reminds the actor that his art 'has its origins in the *dance*. The means of expression employed in the dance are equally the natural means of expression for the actor, the difference being merely one of *range*.'[12] Not only in Ancient Greece but, as Kawakami and Sada Yacco had demonstrated on their European tour, in the Japanese theatre to this day every movement is dictated by the choreographic rhythm of the action.[13]

For the Japanese there is no part of a production that is not directed towards the enhancement of the overall rhythmical scheme, and this in its turn reflects the inner psychological development of the drama:

> The Japanese stage-director makes the colour composition of the costumes and
> scenery follow the psychical [sic] progress of the play most wonderfully. . .
> The setting accords with the play, the actors' poses, the figures, groupings
> and costumes; it is treated as 'beautiful' in line, form and colour, but by itself
> it is *expressionless*, a rhythmical monotone with no independent significance.
> However, as a line in the moving spectrum of the whole it has the
> greatest importance, supplying the final element in the scheme.[14]

The text of the drama Fuchs leaves until last: 'The text is nothing but the musical score, from which the re-creative, performing intellects must extract the true embodiment of the work.'[15]

Fuchs' advocacy of a theatre based on rhythmical movement is close in spirit to what Meyerhold had attempted in Moscow in 1905, and it is significant that they both took as a paradigm the style of Sada Yacco. But in *The Stage of the Future* Fuchs was more coherent and more radical in his theories than Meyerhold had been in his experiments at the Theatre-Studio. On the other hand, Fuchs' ideas had yet to be tempered by the inevitable compromises involved in bringing a production to actual performance: he conducted his first experiments with the relief stage in May 1906 at the Prinzregenten-Theater in Munich, and it was not until 1908 that it was incorporated in modified form in the new Munich Artists' Theatre.[16]

As well as lending weight to Meyerhold's own views, *The Stage of the Future* drew his attention to certain aspects of the theatre that he had previously overlooked. An early opportunity to examine them presented itself in June when he rejoined the Fellowship of the New Drama for a six-week season in the small Ukrainian town of Poltava. Altogether, they presented eighteen plays, opening with *Miss Julie* and closing with Gorky's *Barbarians*.[17]

On their arrival Meyerhold and his company found a theatre in which the stage was separated from the audience by a wide orchestra pit. The solution was to remove the footlights and construct a forestage that extended six metres from the front curtain up to the first row of the stalls. The curtain itself was dispensed with, permanent settings being constructed on the main stage for each production. Settings were reduced to a minimum, sometimes consisting of no more than drapes, and often much of the action was located on the forestage. In *Ghosts*, for example, Meyerhold as Osvald played much of the last act seated at a piano downstage close to the audience. In 1912 he wrote in the foreword to his book *On the Theatre*: 'Even though the theme of the forestage is not dealt with comprehensively in any of the articles below, it will be easy for the reader to see that all the various threads in this book lead towards the question of the forestage.'[18] It was in the summer of 1906 that he first grasped the significance of what was to prove a vital element in his mature style.

The summer season in Poltava before an increasingly responsive audience afforded the opportunity for other fruitful experiments. In some productions the open expanse of the stage area encouraged a treatment of the setting that was altogether more expressive than purely representational – 'impressionistic' rather than naturalistic. Thus, Meyerhold describes his interpretation of Schnitzler's *The Call of Life*:

> In this production we experimented with a stage setting of exaggerated
> dimensions. A huge sofa, parallel to the setting line and extending right
> across the stage (slightly reduced in size, of course) was meant to convey
> with its ponderousness, with the mass of its oppressive shape, an interior in

which anyone would feel confined and crushed by the overwhelming power of material things. This impression was intensified by the abundance of carpets, hangings and sofa-cushions. Chekhovian moods were sacrificed for the sake of the fatal and the tragic.[19]

In the same production Meyerhold introduced choreography consciously modelled on oriental practice, so that the actors' moves '. . . either prefaced or concluded their speeches, each movement being treated as a dance (a Japanese device), even when there was no emotional motivation for it.'[20]

As the critic Yury Krasovsky has observed, Meyerhold's use of the forestage in Poltava placed a new emphasis on the actor's technique:

> In extreme proximity to the spectators, the performer found himself having to communicate directly and immediately with them. Performing face to face, the actor was forced to summon up all his resources; he could no longer 'lie', take refuge in technical devices. But for this the actor needed to be prepared, to be schooled in new habits. The forestage required considerable preliminary pedagogic work, a particular kind of training.[21]

Thus, Meyerhold now saw clearly that the creation of a new theatre was indivisible from the creation of a theatre-studio in which new forms could be explored and new actors trained. Henceforth, this ambition remained uppermost in his mind and was in fact realised in St Petersburg two years later. However, it was 1922 before he finally achieved the fusion of studio and permanent company.

II

At the beginning of the twentieth century Vera Komissarzhevskaya was generally recognised as the greatest interpreter in Russia of modern dramatic roles, a reputation she had won by her performances in such parts as Nina in *The Seagull*, Sonya in *Uncle Vanya*, Hilda in *The Master Builder*, and Nora in *A Doll's House*. In 1902, at the height of her fame she left the Imperial Alexandrinsky Theatre, determined to perform in plays of her own choosing in her own theatre. Eventually, after two seasons touring in the provinces, her ambition was realised when she returned to St Petersburg and leased the Passage Theatre to house a new permanent company. The season opened on 15 September 1904 with Gutzkow's *Uriel Acosta*. The repertoire was similar to that of the Moscow Art Theatre, with a strong bias towards Ibsen, Chekhov and Gorky, and the style of production was very close to the naturalism of Stanislavsky and Nemirovich-Danchenko.

Shortly before the end of the first season Komissarzhevskaya appointed Akim Volynsky, a leading symbolist critic and art historian, as the theatre's literary manager. Clearly thinking along the lines that Meyerhold was soon to follow in Moscow, Volynsky said to the company before their first rehearsal of *The Master Builder* in March 1905:

I regard this undertaking as most important: sooner or later it will serve as the means for breaking down the theatrical prose in which you have had to work hitherto. Whereas before the actor was both ready and required to surrender to psycho-physiological reflexes, now he must look for gestures and mime capable of symbolising Ibsen's ideas.[22]

However, the transformation apparently heralded by these words failed to materialise. This is hardly surprising, since most of the productions in the following season were the work of Nikolai Arbatov, a former pupil of Stanislavsky and a passionate advocate of naturalism. It is difficult to understand how Arbatov came to join Komissarzhevskaya at the same time as Volynsky, with whom she was clearly in far closer accord. Shortly after her first meeting with Meyerhold in 1906 she wrote:

For the first time in the existence of our theatre the thought of it does not make me feel like a fish out of water. That feeling came to me first on the evening of the dress rehearsal of *Uriel Acosta*; I failed to admit it and it lived on in the recesses of my soul, preventing it not only from creating but even from breathing as it must in order to live.[23]

Thus Vera Komissarzhevskaya believed – like Stanislavsky a year earlier – that Meyerhold held the key to the 'New Drama'.

That summer it was decided to move from the Passage to the former Nemetti Theatre on Ofitserskaya Street. Before the start of the new season the auditorium was rebuilt in a style appropriate to the company's lofty ideals and similar to the other elegant 'art theatres' that had opened elsewhere in Europe:

Everything was unusual about the new theatre and it amazed the spectator, winning the approval of its friends and provoking furious attacks from its enemies. Gay drapery, cheap ornamentation, a frivolous front curtain: all these customary embellishments of the temple of operetta or farce disappeared, and the theatre acquired an austere appearance. It was all white with columns and completely devoid of decoration, with a curtain of dark material which parted slowly to the sides. The only colourful spot was the front curtain designed by Bakst: with its Greek temple and sphinx it reflected the directors' preoccupation with the religious origins of scenic art, with antiquity and the East.[24]

The first season with Komissarzhevskaya put Meyerhold under constant strain. After nearly six months separation from his wife and daughters in Tiflis and Poltava, he soon found himself on the road again. During the rebuilding of the theatre in September he was obliged to join Komissarzhevskaya's company on tour in Lithuania and western Russia in order to rehearse *Hedda Gabler* for the opening of the new season.[25] During his absence the Petersburg press made the most of Arbatov's threatened resignation from Komissarzhevskaya's company, attributing it to 'the decadent elements that she was introducing into the company.'[26] In fact, Arbatov left at Komissarzhevskaya's insistence just before the beginning of the season, by which time the publicity the incident had received was a clear indication of the treatment Meyerhold could expect from the great majority of the Petersburg critics. During his absence he had left rehearsals with the remainder of the company in the hands of Peter Yartsev, the theatre's newly appointed literary manager. But on his return he was so alarmed at the state of the work that he assumed sole responsibility for it. By mid-October he was rehearsing no fewer than four productions in parallel. Such was the level of public and critical anticipation at the new venture, that Meyerhold was now under even greater pressure than he had experienced in the provinces. But he saw it as an opportunity that had to be seized – at whatever cost to his family relations and personal health. His letters to Olga bear eloquent witness to his dependence on her, intellectual as well as emotional.

Hedda Gabler opened on 10 November 1906, with Komissarzhevskaya playing Hedda. The precise description given by Yartsev is worth quoting in full:

The theatre has chosen to use a single backdrop as a setting, either representational or simply decorative. The costumes, instead of being naturalistically authentic, are intended to harmonise as colour-masses with the background and present a synthesis of the style of the period and society in question, the subjective view of the designer, and the externally simplified representation of the character's inner nature. For instance, . . . the costume of Tesman corresponds to no definite fashion; although it is somewhat reminiscent of the 1820s, one is reminded equally of the present day. But in giving Tesman a loose jacket with sloping shoulders, an exaggeratedly wide tie and broad trousers tapering sharply towards the bottoms, the designer, Vassily Milioti,

9 Set design by Nikolai Sapunov for *Hedda Gabler*

has sought to express the essence of 'Tesmanism', and this has been stressed by the director in the way Tesman is made to move and in the position he occupies in the general composition. To harmonise with the colours of Sapunov's painted back-cloth, Milioti has dressed Tesman in dull grey. The walls, the portières and the sky (seen through a vast ivy-fringed window) are all light blue; the tapestry that covers an entire wall and the open-work screens on either side of the stage are painted in pale gold autumnal tints. The colours of the costumes harmonise amongst themselves and with the background: green (Hedda), brown (Loevborg), pale pink (Thea), dark grey (Brack). The table in the centre, the pouffes and the long narrow divan standing against the wall under the tapestry are all covered in light blue fabric flecked with gold to give it the appearance of brocade. A huge armchair stage-left is covered entirely in white fur, the same fur being used to cover part of the divan; a white grand piano projects from behind the screen stage-right and has the same blue and gold fabric hanging from it.

Behind the left-hand screen is glimpsed the silhouette of a huge green vase encircled with ivy and standing on a pedestal also covered with blue and gold fabric. Behind it is supposed to stand the stove for the scene between Hedda and Tesman when Hedda burns Loevborg's manuscript. The stove is suggested by a reddish glow which appears at the appropriate moments.

In front of the divan stands a low square table with a drawer in which Hedda hides the manuscript. On it Loevborg and Brack lay their hats, and on it stands the green box containing the pistols (when it is not on the big table).

In small white and green vases on the piano and the table and in the large vase on the pedestal there are flowers, mostly white chrysanthemums. More chrysanthemums rest in the folds of the fur on the back of the armchair. The floor is covered with dark grey cloth, with a fine tracery in blue and gold. The sky is painted on a separate drop behind the cut out window; there is a day sky, and a night sky with coldly glittering stars (for Act Four).

The stage comprises a broad, shallow strip, 10 metres wide and 4 metres deep, higher than the usual stage level and as close as possible to the footlights. The lighting is from footlights and overhead battens.

This strange room, if indeed it is a room, resembles least of all the old-fashioned villa of [Minister Falk's widow]. What is the significance of this setting which gives the impression of a vast, cold blue, receding expanse but which actually looks like nothing whatsoever? Why are both sides (where there should be doors – or nothing, if the room is supposed to continue offstage) hung with gold net curtains where the actors make their exits and their entrances? Is life really like this? Is this what Ibsen wrote?

Life is not like this, and it is not what Ibsen wrote. *Hedda Gabler* on the stage of the Dramatic Theatre is *stylised*. Its aim is to reveal Ibsen's play to the spectator by employing unfamiliar new means of scenic presentation, to create an impression (but only an *impression*) of a vast, cold blue, receding expanse. Hedda is visualised in cool blue tones against a golden autumnal background. Instead of autumn being depicted outside the window where the blue sky is seen, it is suggested by the pale golden tints in the tapestry, the upholstery and

10 Vera
Komissarzhev-
skaya as Hedda
Gabler.
Caricature by
A. Lyubimov,
1906

the curtains. The theatre is attempting to give primitive, purified expression to
what it senses behind Ibsen's play: a cold, regal, autumnal Hedda.

Precisely the same aims are adopted in the actual production of the play, in
the work of the director with the actors. Rejecting authenticity, the customary
'lifelikeness', the theatre seeks to submit the spectator to its own inspiration
by adopting a barely mobile, stylised method of production with a minimum
of mime and gesture, with the emotions concealed and manifested externally
only by a brief lighting of the eyes or a flickering smile.

The wide stage, its width emphasised by its shallowness, is particularly
suited to widely spaced groupings and the director takes full advantage of
this by making two characters converse from opposite sides of the stage
(the opening of the scene between Hedda and Loevborg in Act Three), by
seating Hedda and Loevborg wide apart on the divan in Act Two. Sometimes
(particularly in the latter instance) there may seem to be little justification in

this, but it arises from the director's attempt to create an overall impression of cold majesty. The huge armchair covered with white fur is meant as a kind of throne for Hedda; she plays the majority of her scenes either on it or near it. The spectator is intended to associate Hedda with her throne and carry away this combined impression in his memory.

Brack is associated with the pedestal bearing the large vase. He sits by it with one leg crossed over the other and clasps his hands round his knee, keeping his eyes fixed on Hedda throughout their keen sparkling battle of wits. He reminds one of a faun. Admittedly, Brack moves about the stage and occupies other positions (as do Hedda and the other characters) but it is the pose of a faun by the pedestal that one associates with him – just as one associates the throne with Hedda.

The table serves as a pedestal for the motionless figures that the theatre seeks to imprint on the spectator's memory. When Loevborg produces the manuscript in Act Two he is standing upstage by the portière near Hedda and Tesman. Brack is by the curtain stage-left; the centre of the stage (the table) is empty. In order to look through the bulky manuscript more comfortably, Loevborg comes forward to rest it on the table and after the words 'This is my real book', he lapses into a thoughtful silence, straightening up and placing his hand on the open manuscript. After a few seconds' pause he starts to turn over the pages, explaining his work to Tesman, who has now joined him. But in those motionless few seconds Loevborg and the manuscript have impressed themselves on the spectator and he has an uneasy presentiment of the words' significance, of what Loevborg is really like, what links him with the manuscript, and what bearing it has on the tragedy of Hedda.

The first scene between Loevborg and Hedda also takes place at the table. Throughout the entire scene they sit side by side, tense and motionless, looking straight ahead. Their soft, disquieting words fall rhythmically from lips which seem dry and cold. Before them stand two glasses and a flame burns beneath the punch bowl (Ibsen stipulates Norwegian 'cold punch'). Not once throughout the entire long scene do they alter the direction of their gaze or their pose. Only on the line 'Then you too have a thirst for life!' does Loevborg make a violent motion towards Hedda, and at this point the scene comes to an abrupt conclusion.

Realistically speaking, it is inconceivable that Hedda and Loevborg should play the scene in this manner, that any two real people should ever converse like this. The spectator hears the lines as though they were being addressed directly at him; before him the whole time he sees the faces of Hedda and Loevborg, observes the slightest change of expression; behind the monotonous dialogue he senses the concealed inner dialogue of presentiments and emotions that are incapable of expression in mere words. The spectator may forget the actual words exchanged by Hedda and Loevborg, but he cannot possibly forget the overall impression that the scene creates.[27]

As the critic Alexander Kugel was quick to observe, Meyerhold's *Hedda Gabler* owed a great deal to the ideas of Georg Fuchs.[28] Despite the retention of footlights the broad, shallow stage backed by a decorative panel seemed an obvious attempt to realise Fuchs' conception of the 'relief stage'. Furthermore, as we can see from Yartsev's account, Meyerhold again demonstrated the extent to which, like Fuchs, he had assimilated the conventions of the Japanese. The form and colour of every visual element in the production were determined by Meyerhold and Sapunov's* subjective vision of Hedda, with no purely lifelike detail permitted to mar the stage tableau. Within the limits of this scheme each costume was designed to synthesise the essence of the type, regardless of inconsistencies in style or period. Fundamentally speaking, this was the same approach to costume as that advocated by Fuchs in *The Stage of the Future*, where he cites the example of the Japanese and draws an analogy between them and the style of various contemporary painters, notably Anselm Feuerbach, in whose pictures '. . . the costumes are neither antique nor modern [but] an extension and a synthesis of our present-day fashions in clothing for the sake of heightened expressiveness.'[29]

Finally, the 'barely mobile, stylised method of production with a minimum of mime and gesture and with the emotions concealed, manifested externally only by a brief lighting of the eyes or the flicker of a smile' was clearly influenced by the decorum of Eastern stylisation allied to the ideals propagated by Maeterlinck and the French symbolists.

Hedda Gabler was received coldly by the public and even those few critics who admired the elegant beauty of the décor considered that it was hopelessly at odds with Ibsen's intentions. They complained that Sapunov's sumptuous autumnal vision obscured the point of all Hedda's despairing efforts to escape the trap of the narrow conventions and tawdry bad taste of provincial society. Their objections were directed less against stylisation as such than against what was stylised in this instance: the theme should have been not a vision of beauty conjured up by Hedda's fervid imagination but the everyday banality of George's slippers and Aunt Juju's new hat.[30]

The criticism seems incontestable: *Hedda Gabler* was a classic example of a production subordinated to the director's ruling obsession. In his probing analysis of him, the Soviet critic Alexander Matskin refers to 'the tragedy of Meyerhold's one-sidedness' whereby 'at any given moment he had a single ruling idea which forced his more durable preoccupations to retreat into the background'.[31] In this particular instance Matskin suggests that Meyerhold felt overwhelmed by the weight of genius and erudition that he had encountered amongst the Petersburg symbolists, trying to compensate by emphasising the formal aspects of his work, the one area in which he felt truly confident. There may well be some truth in this; certainly the symbolist philosophical debates at this time were of an awesome complexity and abstruseness. But equally Meyerhold's interpretation of *Hedda Gabler* (to say nothing of his subsequent productions with Komissarzhevskaya) was conceived in part at least as a polemic against stage naturalism *and* the whole materialist philosophy from which it sprang. In this aim, certainly,

---

* Sapunov, Sudeikin, and Denisov all worked with Meyerhold in St Petersburg after the closure of the Theatre-Studio.

Meyerhold was at one with the symbolists. Konstantin Rudnitsky is making this point when he quotes the philosopher Nikolai Berdyaev:

> The vital core of symbolism [is found] in the evocation of the delicate
> varied nuances of the human soul, in the protest against bourgeois vulgarity
> and against the total absence of beauty from life. Symbolism justifies itself
> with an aesthetic that totally rejects the possibility of art as the reflection
> of reality. An idealistic world-view must recognise the *independent meaning of
> beauty* and of artistic creativity in the life of mankind. *Beauty is the ideal goal
> of existence*; it elevates and ennobles man. . . In bourgeois society and its art
> there is too little beauty, and in opposing it we must introduce into human
> existence as much beauty as we can: beauty in human thought, in art, in our
> whole way of life. To earlier forms of protest is now joined aesthetic protest
> against bourgeois society.[32]

The doctrine was hardly new: it had been expounded at least twenty years earlier by Mallarmé and the French symbolists; but nobody, with the arguable exception of Craig, had succeeded in bringing it to fruition in the theatre before Meyerhold. It is interesting to note that within a few weeks of Meyerhold's *Hedda Gabler* there were two other major symbolist productions of Ibsen elsewhere in Europe: Reinhardt's *Ghosts* in Berlin (with designs by Edvard Munch), and Craig's *Romersholm* with Duse's company in Florence.[33]

III

In the seven weeks from the Theatre's opening with *Hedda Gabler* to the end of the year Meyerhold presented six new productions plus a revival of the Passage Theatre's *A Doll's House* with Komissarzhevskaya's celebrated portrayal of Nora. Through all these his exploration of scenic space and stylised gesture and movement were constant features, although such inferior works as Yushkevich's *In the City* and Przybyszewski's *The Eternal Fable* hardly justified the care and resources that were lavished on them. However, when Maeterlinck's *Sister Beatrice* joined *Hedda Gabler* and *In the City* in the repertoire on 22 November it demonstrated beyond question that symbolist drama could be rendered effectively in scenic terms.

Meyerhold's production was nothing less than a programmatic statement of symbolism, intended to soothe the audience with a vision of harmony and to induce participation in a corporate mystical experience akin to the medieval miracle play. It proved to be the one generally acknowledged success that Meyerhold enjoyed with Komissarzhevskaya, and for her in the role of Beatrice her sole personal triumph with him.

Maeterlinck's '*petit jeu de scène*' tells in simple terms the story of a nun, Beatrice, who elopes from a convent with a prince. A statue of the Virgin comes to life and takes the place of Beatrice in the convent so that

11 Act Two of *Sister Beatrice* with Komissarzhevskaya as Beatrice

12 Act Three of *Sister Beatrice*

her absence is never discovered. After many years during which she sinks to the depths of depravity Beatrice returns in search of retribution. But the Virgin returns to her pedestal and Beatrice dies hallowed by the sisters for her life of selfless devotion.

Maeterlinck sets the play in fourteenth-century Louvain, but again Meyerhold applied the principle of stylisation, seeking to imbue the legend with universality by creating a synthesis based on the style of Pre-Raphaelite and early Renaissance painters.[34] Some critics identified a clear resemblance between Meyerhold's *tableaux vivants* and the works of such painters as Memling, Giotto and Botticelli. The director, Alexander Tairov, at that time a member of the company, later criticised Meyerhold for modelling poses and complete groupings on reproductions of their pictures, and certainly in the final act the tableau of the sisters holding the dying Beatrice was a conscious evocation of the traditional deposition of Christ.[35] Yet Meyerhold was insistent that he 'borrowed only the means of expression employed by the old masters; the movements, groupings, properties and costumes were simply a synthesis of the lines and colours found in the Primitives'.[36] Either way, the visual impact was powerfully emotive. Voloshin, the critic of the newspaper *Russ*, wrote:

> A Gothic wall in which the green and lilac-tinted stone blends with the grey tones of the tapestries and glimmers faintly with pale silver and old gold . . . the Sisters in greyish-blue, close-fitting garments with simple bonnets framing their rounded cheeks. I was constantly reminded of Giotto's frescoes in the Duomo in Florence, the glorious *Assumption of St Francis* portrayed with unsparing realism and idealised beauty. I dreamt that I was in love with this Catholic madonna who reminded me so strongly of the one I had seen in Seville; I felt the horror of the sinful body of the mortal Beatrice, glimpsed beneath her crimson rags.[37]

Dialogue and movement were treated in the style first developed by Meyerhold to render Maeterlinck's 'static tragedy', *The Death of Tintagiles*, 'The melodious style of delivery and movements in slow motion were designed to preserve the implicitness of expression, and each phrase was barely more than a whisper, the manifestation of an inner tragic experience.'[38] Meyerhold defined the style as 'tragedy with a smile on the lips', saying that he found the key to it in these words of Savonarola:

> Do not assume that Mary cried out at the death of her Son and roamed the streets, tearing her hair and acting like a madwoman. She followed Him with great humility. Certainly, she shed tears, but her appearance would have revealed not so much sheer grief as a combination of *grief and joy*. Even at the foot of the Cross she stood in grief and joy, engrossed in the mystery of God's great mercy.[39]

Meyerhold succeeded in disciplining his actors' movements by the simple expedient of confining them to a strip of stage in front of the proscenium arch no more than two metres in depth. Yevgeny Znosko-Borovsky describes the chorus of nuns:

All dressed as one, with completely identical gestures, with slow restrained movements and following one another precisely, they moved the whole time in profile in order to maintain the repose of a bas-relief; they passed before you like a wonderful design on the grey stone of an ancient cathedral. . . Here was a crowd, a mass in which no individual led a separate life or constituted a separate character which might disrupt the essential idea and impression of the mass. Here was a unity that by its unity, by the rhythm of all its movements, poses and gestures, produced a far deeper impression than a naturalistic crowd split up into separate elements.[40]

As Rudnitsky observes, the compositional approach to *Sister Beatrice* was sculptural rather than painterly, in contrast to *Hedda Gabler* which was treated frontally as a bas relief.[41] Sergei Sudeikin's setting amounted to little more than a simple 'gothic' wall standing almost on top of the footlights, a neutral background designed to throw the actors' figures into plastic relief. 'It provides only an accompaniment,' wrote Nikolai Yevreinov; '[Sudeikin's] art desires at all costs to remain neutral and quiet – at most a gentle echo of the dialogue.'[42] Although footlights were used, it was contrary to Meyerhold's own wishes; financial considerations frustrated his original intention to link the forestage with the auditorium by a flight of polished wooden steps and thereby make the actors stand farther from the flat background.[43] Once again the resemblance to Georg Fuchs' relief stage was unmistakable.

Meyerhold's production drew grudging praise from the previously hostile critics, but the acting (with the exception of Komissarzhevskaya and Meyerhold himself in the small part of a beggar) was condemned as lifeless and uneven. Many blamed Meyerhold's system which, they maintained, reduced the artist to a mere puppet. But probably Peter Yartsev came as close as anybody to the truth when he wrote the following year:'[Komissarzhevskaya's] theatre is seeking to express technically forms that the theatre of the future will have to fill out with content. That is why the new theatre concentrates exclusively on the visual side (settings, costumes, grouping, movements). As yet in the new theatre there is not and cannot be a new actor.'[44] Acutely aware of this problem, Meyerhold pressed Komissarzhevskaya to find the resources to set up a summer 'colony' in order to school the company in preparation for the following season. Rational though the idea was on artistic grounds, it was rejected by Vera's younger brother, Fyodor, who was the company's production manager.* In his view, not only was such a scheme financially extravagant but it assumed a degree of commitment on the part of the actors that in most cases did not exist.[45]

---

* Fyodor Komissarzhevsky (1882–1954) became a director after Meyerhold's departure from his sister's theatre. In 1919 he emigrated to England and as Theodore Komisarjevsky established a considerable reputation as both director and designer, particularly with his productions of Chekhov.

IV

When Meyerhold was invited in December 1905 to become the artistic director of the proposed 'Torches Theatre', Georgy Chulkov commissioned Alexander Blok to write a play on the theme of his poem *The Fairground Booth* (1905)* which the new company would perform. Although the theatre failed to materialise, Blok completed *The Fairground Booth* within the space of a few days in January 1906 and Chulkov published it in the first number of his journal (also called *Torches*) in April 1906. When Komissarzhevskaya's theatre opened in the autumn it was decided to stage Blok's play and it had its first performance on 30 December 1906 in a double bill with Maeterlinck's *The Miracle of St Antony*.

Like the poem, the short one-act play incorporates themes, figures, and images that had disturbed his lyrics intermittently for some years. In the first of the play's 'lyric scenes', an assembly of 'Mystics' awaits the arrival of Death in the person of a beautiful lady. Pierrot, 'in a white smock, dreamy, distraught, pale, with no moustache or eyebrows, like all Pierrots', protests that she is his sweetheart Columbine. She appears, silent and all in white; Pierrot despairs and is on the point of conceding the allegory to the Mystics, when Columbine speaks to reassure him. But at once Harlequin, 'eternally youthful, agile and handsome', his costume decked with silver bells, comes to abduct her, leaving Pierrot and the Mystics confounded. The scene changes quickly to a ball with masked couples gliding back and forth. In the centre sits Pierrot, 'on the bench where Venus and Tannhäuser usually embrace'. He tells how Harlequin carried off Columbine in a sleigh, only for her to turn into a lifeless cardboard doll, leaving Pierrot and Harlequin to roam the snow-covered streets together, singing and dancing to console themselves. Then there appear in turn three pairs of masked lovers. The first pair, in pink and blue, imagine themselves beneath the lofty dome of some church: a vision of sacred love menaced by a dark figure, the man's double, beckoning from behind a column. Dancing figures disclose the second couple, the embodiment of violent passion in red and black; they leave, again pursued by a third, 'a flickering tongue of black flame'. Finally we see courtly love: the knight in cardboard visor and bearing a huge wooden sword, the lady echoing his portentous phrases. Their dignity is rudely shattered by a clown who runs up and pokes out his tongue at the Knight. He strikes him on the head with his sword; the clown collapses over the footlights crying 'Help, I'm bleeding cranberry juice!' and then jumps up and leaves. A leaping, jostling torchlight procession of masks makes its entrance. Harlequin steps from the crowd to greet the world in the springtime:

* In Russian '*Balaganchik*'. Sometimes translated as 'the puppet show' or 'farce'.

> Here nobody dares to admit
> That spring is abroad in the air!
> Here nobody knows how to love;
> They all live best by sad dreams.
> Greetings world! You're with me again!
> So long your soul has been close to me!
> And now once more I will breath your spring
> Through your window of gold!

Then he leaps through the window, but the view is only painted on paper and he falls headlong through the hole.

Death reappears, a scythe over her back, and all the masks freeze in terror. But Pierrot recognises her again as his Columbine: the scythe fades in the morning light and colour floods her cheeks. They are about to embrace when 'The Author', who throughout has kept appearing to protest at the misrepresentation of his text, pokes his head between them to acclaim the happy ending of his simple tale. As he is joining their hands the scenery is abruptly whisked aloft and Columbine and all the masks disappear. The Author withdraws in hurried confusion, leaving the baffled Pierrot to face the audience alone and play a mournful tune on his pipe 'about his pale face, his hard life, and his sweetheart Columbine'.[46]

At the start of his career as a poet Blok was strongly influenced by the mystical philosophy of Vladimir Solovyov and the like-minded literary group that included Bely, Bryusov, Balmont, Zinaida Gippius, and Merezhovsky. But his work became coloured with a scepticism entirely at odds with their mystical idealism. As early as 1902 in his first major work, the poetic cycle *On the Beautiful Lady*, Blok had invoked the traditional figures of Pierrot, Harlequin, and Columbine to convey his doubts in the constancy of human relations and even in the coherence of personality itself.[47] The bold sceptic Harlequin and the childlike, innocent Pierrot came to represent the two conflicting aspects of the poet's own character, whilst Columbine was both the 'beautiful lady', the ideal of perfect womanhood venerated by the Russian symbolists, and the very counterfeit of beauty, the deception inherent in all outward appearances. There is often present in Blok's poems an onlooker (in the poem *Balaganchik*: two children) who registers the transformation of the scene; the situation is virtually dramatic, with audience and players enacting the pretence of life itself. Now in *The Fairground Booth* he exploited the theatre's irony to give his dualistic vision even greater power. Much of the invention was his own, but in Meyerhold he found an interpreter with the power and insight to extend it still further. The production is described by Meyerhold:

> The entire stage is hung at the sides and rear with blue drapes; this expanse of blue serves as a background as well as reflecting the colour of the settings in the little booth erected on the stage. This booth has its own stage, curtain, prompter's box, and proscenium opening. Instead of being masked with the

conventional border, the flies, together with all the ropes and wires, are visible to the audience. When the entire set in the booth is hauled aloft, the audience in the actual theatre sees the whole process. In front of the booth, the stage area adjacent to the footlights is left free. It is here that the 'Author' appears to serve as an intermediary between the public and the events enacted within the booth. The action begins at a signal on the big drum; the music starts and the audience sees the prompter crawl into his box and light a candle. The curtain of the booth rises to reveal a box-set with doors stage-right

13 *The Fairground Booth.* Sapunov's setting for the opening scene with Pierrot and the Mystics

and centre, and a window stage-left. . . There is a long table covered with a black cloth reaching to the floor and parallel to the footlights. Behind the table sit the 'Mystics', the top halves of their bodies visible to the audience. Frightened by some rejoinder, they duck their heads, and suddenly all that remains at the table is a row of torsos minus heads and hands. It transpires that the figures are cut out of cardboard with frock-coats, shirt-fronts, collars and cuffs drawn on with soot and chalk. The actors' heads are thrust through openings in the cardboard torsos and the heads simply rest on the cardboard collars. . . Harlequin makes his first entrance from under the Mystics' table. When the author runs on to the forestage his tirade is terminated by someone hidden in the wings pulling him off by his coat-tails; it turns out that he is tethered with a rope to prevent him from interrupting the solemn course of events onstage. In Scene Two, 'the dejected Pierrot sits in the middle of the stage on a bench'; behind him is a statue of Eros on a pedestal.

When Pierrot finishes his long soliloquy, the bench, the statue and the entire set are whisked aloft, and a traditional colonnaded hall is lowered in

their place. When the masked figures appear with cries of 'torches!' the hands
of the stage-hands appear from both wings holding flaming Bengal lights on
iron rods. As Andrei Bely remarked, 'All the characters are restricted to their
own typical gestures; Pierrot, for instance, always sighs and flaps his arms in
the same way.'[48]

The part of Pierrot was played by Meyerhold himself; Sergei Auslender
describes his portrayal: '. . . he is nothing like those familiar, falsely
sugary, whining Pierrots. Everything about him is sharply angular; in a
hushed voice he whispers words of strange sadness; somehow he contrives
to be caustic, heart-rending, gentle: all these things, yet at the same time
impudent. . .'[49] His mimetic skill offered a daunting example of what he
expected of the rest of the company. Alexander Deutsch recalls the moment

14 Meyerhold as
Pierrot (Nikolai
Ulyanov, 1906)

when Columbine deserts Pierrot for Harlequin: 'It was astonishing how
Meyerhold as Pierrot fell face-down onto the floor, completely flat like a
board, an object, a lifeless body. In Meyerhold's skill as an actor there was
a plasticity, a suppleness verging on the acrobatic, that was quite unique at
the time.'[50]

Valentina Verigina, who played the second masked lady in the ball
scene, writes:

On the stage direction 'Pierrot awakes from his reverie and brightens up'
[in Scene One], Meyerhold made an absurd wave with both his sleeves, and in
this movement was expressed the suddenly dawning hope of the clown. Further
waves of his sleeves conveyed various emotions. These stylised gestures were
inspired by the musical conception of the characterisation; they were eloquent
because . . . they were prompted by the inner rhythm of the role. The gestures
always followed the words, complementing them as though bringing a song to
its conclusion, saying without words something understood only by Pierrot

himself. . . It was as though he was listening to a song being sung by his heart of its own free will. He wore a strange expression, gazing intently into his own soul.[51]*

The closing scene carried a clear echo of his performance as Landowski in *The Acrobats* in Kherson four years earlier:

> . . . the curtain fell behind Pierrot-Meyerhold and he was left face to face with the audience. He stood staring at them, and it was as though Pierrot was looking into the eyes of every single person. There was something irresistible in his gaze. . . Then Pierrot looked away, took his pipe from his pocket and began to play the tune of a rejected and unappreciated heart. That moment was the most powerful in his whole performance. Behind his lowered eyelids one sensed a gaze, stern and full of reproach.[53]

Rudnitsky senses a deep personal significance in the role: '. . . Meyerhold, who only twice in his life (the other time being as Treplev in *The Seagull*) expressed his true self on stage and found lyrical expression through a character, saw and affirmed in this vulnerability of Pierrot the ultimate justification for the artist's calling. The theme of Pierrot was interpreted as the theme of the bitter yet splendid isolation of poetry, of art that is doomed to misunderstanding.'[54]†

The opening night and many subsequent performances provoked memorable scenes in the theatre. Sixteen years later Sergei Auslender recalled:

> The auditorium was in an uproar as though it were a real battle. Solid, respectable citizens were ready to come to blows; whistles and roars of anger alternated with piercing howls conveying a mixture of fervour, defiance, anger and despair: 'Blok – Sapunov – Kuzmin – M-e-y-e-r-h-o-l-d, Br-a-v-o-o-o' . . . And there before all the commotion, radiant like some splendid monument, in his severe black frock-coat and holding a bunch of white lilies, stood Alexander Alexandrovich Blok, his deep blue eyes reflecting both sadness and wry amusement. And at his side the white Pierrot ducked and recoiled as though devoid of any bones, disembodied like a spectre, flapping the long sleeves of his loose smock.[55]

Blok clearly revelled in the scandal; three weeks after the opening he wrote to a friend: '. . . at this very moment *The Fairground Booth* is being given its fifth performance at Komissarzhevskaya's theatre, and – I would say – successfully since at the first and second performances I took many curtain-calls and they heartily whistled and catcalled at

---

* In February 1910, Meyerhold danced the role of Pierrot in the first production of Mikhail Fokine's ballet *Carnival* (to Schumann's music) at a ball organised by the Petersburg journal *Satyricon*. Columbine was danced by Karsavina and Florestan by Nijinsky. Fokine writes: 'At the first two rehearsals, Meyerhold was like a man from another world: his gestures were out of time with the music, and frequently he misjudged his entrances and exits. But by the third rehearsal our new mime had blossomed forth, and on the night he gave a marvellous portrayal of the sorrowful dreamer, Pierrot.'[52] It was Meyerhold's only performance as a dancer.

† Cf. pp. 84, 265 below.

me. . .'[56] For his part, Meyerhold regarded the violent demonstrations as conclusive proof of the production's 'true theatricality'.[57] Almost to a man, the critics were nonplussed by *The Fairground Booth* and dismissed it as a joke in very poor taste. Their response is fairly represented by 'Objective', writing in the Petersburg *Theatre Review*: 'Truly what took place at Vera Komissarzhevskaya's theatre on the 30 December must be regarded as an insult, not only to the theatre, but also to literature, poetry, and dramatic writing; it lies beyond the pale no less of art than of common sense.'[58]

Many of Blok's fellow symbolists shared this indignation. Justifiably enough, they saw themselves lampooned in the figures of the Mystics, though equally in a preliminary draft of the play Blok draws attention to their resemblance to the death-fixated characters in the works of Maeterlinck and Verhaeren.[59] One does not exclude the other: Blok is clearly ridiculing all idealists who seek to impose a reassuring design on empirical confusion. The production drove a rift between Blok and his bosom companion, Andrei Bely. Bely called it a betrayal of symbolism and 'a bitter mockery of Blok's own past'. He took particular exception to the blasphemy implicit in the depiction of the 'beautiful lady' Columbine.[60] As Blok himself later said, there was essentially nothing new in what he was saying in *The Fairground Booth*; the difference was that he was saying it in public rather than in the personal isolation of the lyric.[61] What had previously been the occasional voicing of self-doubt was now an outright rejection of the transcendental, a sardonic picture of a spiritually exhausted world devoid of constant values. To no small degree Blok's innate pessimism was greatly exacerbated by the sense of dislocation experienced generally by the Russian intelligentsia in the aftermath of 1905. *The Fairground Booth* in Meyerhold's production captured this mood with acute poetic accuracy, and therein lies the main reason for the violently opposed responses to it. For young and disenchanted radicals it became a rallying point, some going so far as to interpret Columbine as a symbol for the long-awaited, but never-to-appear, Russian constitution.[62] Konstantin Rudnitsky draws attention to the near coincidence of the first production of *The Fairground Booth* and the completion by Picasso of his first great Cubist painting *Les Demoiselles d'Avignon*.[63] The similarity lies in the complete subordination of each work's form to the artist's perception of reality, asserting his primacy as observer and interpreter of a world totally unamenable to the traditional solutions of faith or logic. Similarly, dramatic parallels readily suggest themselves: in the ten years preceding *The Fairground Booth* – but unknown to Blok – Jarry, Wedekind, Strindberg (notably in *A Dream Play*) had all sought to transform their personal experiences into a theatrical event – like Blok, inviting their audience to share their confusion and identify it with their own. Writing about Jarry, Henri Rousseau, Satie and Apollinaire in *The Banquet Years*, Roger Shattuck says: '. . . there are subjects about which one cannot be clear without fraud. Every emotion and conviction has its reverse side, and ambiguity can stand for a profound frankness, an acknowledgement of the essential ambivalence of truth and experience, of life itself.'[64] The essential importance of *The Fairground Booth* was that it proved the means by which Blok and Meyerhold were able to articulate this same fundamental truth and in so doing give their art a crucial new direction away from the resigned immobility of symbolism.

Meyerhold's production of *The Fairground Booth* followed Blok's stage directions almost to the letter: the disappearing Mystics, the Author's intrusions, the clown bleeding cranberry juice, Harlequin's leap through the paper flat, the disappearing settings, were all conceived by Blok before his collaboration with Meyerhold, and appear in the first published edition in April 1906. The production introduced one crucial refinement: whereas Blok prescribes 'a normal theatrical room with three walls, a window and a door', Meyerhold and his designer Nikolai Sapunov devised the little show-booth with the prompter and all the scenery exposed, thereby lending a further dimension to the play's irony. Such was Sapunov's contribution, that he may be regarded as co-author of the production. His treatment of the box-set located the action clearly within the confines of a tawdry everyday Russia, whilst the use of the forestage took the ideas first explored in Poltava a stage further. The crucial advance was that now this architectural device was exploited fully to promote direct and disturbing contact between performer and spectator.

As the descriptions of Meyerhold as Pierrot suggest, the style of acting was far removed from the *tableaux vivants* of his earlier productions. The abrupt changes of mood, the sudden switches of personality, the deliberate disruption of illusion, the asides to the audience, all demanded a mental and physical dexterity, an ability to improvise, a capacity for acting not only the part but also one's attitude to it. These devices were all waiting to be rediscovered in the tradition of the popular theatre stretching back to the *commedia dell'arte* and beyond. It was this theatre, the theatre of masks and improvisation, that the experience of *The Fairgound Booth* led Meyerhold to explore. In this he was soon to be followed by a number of younger Russian directors, notably Alexander Tairov, Nikolai Yevreinov and Yevgeny Vakhtangov (and later Sergei Eisenstein), with experiments into every aspect of traditional popular theatre from the mystery-play and the pageant through to the circus and the music-hall. Together, they achieved a revival of conscious theatricality that was to inspire many of the greatest achievements of the early Soviet period.

For Meyerhold, *The Fairground Booth* was to furnish the basis for his entire style, a style that in a word can be called 'grotesque'. In 1912, in his article '*Balagan*', Meyerhold defined his conception of the grotesque:

> It is the style that reveals the most wonderful horizons to the creative artist. 'I', my personal attitude to life, precedes all else. . . The grotesque

does not recognise the *purely* debased or the *purely* exalted. The grotesque
mixes opposites, consciously creating harsh incongruity, *playing entirely on
its own originality*. . . The grotesque deepens life's outward appearance to the
point where it ceases to appear merely natural. . . The basis of the grotesque
is the artist's constant desire to switch the spectator from the plane he has just
reached to another that is totally unforeseen.[65]

But for him the grotesque was no mere stylistic device; it sprang from a
recognition of the irrational and an acceptance of it on its own terms. His
conviction was that 'Beneath what we see of life there are vast unfathomed
depths. In its search for the supernatural, the grotesque synthesises opposites, creates a picture of the incredible, and encourages the spectator to try to
solve the riddle of the inscrutable.'[66] Alexander Matskin writes: 'Once he had
met Blok, it became clear that for Meyerhold the grotesque was not merely
a means of expression, a way of heightening colours, it was no less than the
content of that reality, that dislocated world in which he found himself and
which formed the subject of his art.'[67]

There were times in the Soviet period when Meyerhold was inclined
to play down his affinity with Blok,[68] and certainly their association
after 1906 was far from one of unbroken harmony. Nevertheless, *The
Fairground Booth* remained a crucial experience for Meyerhold and one
which, as we shall see, continued to reverberate through his work long
after 1917.

V

Meyerhold's final production of the season on 22 February 1907 was the
first performance of *The Life of a Man* by Leonid Andreev. In five episodic
acts the play traces the course of a man's life from the moment of birth
through poverty, love, success and disaster to death; the figures involved
are allegorical, with little or no characterisation and are called 'The Man',
'The Wife', 'The Neighbours', etc. A prologue is spoken by 'Someone in
grey, called He', who then remains on stage throughout, invisible to the
protagonists, commenting occasionally on the action, and holding a burning
candle to symbolise the gradual ebb of the Man's life and his ultimate return
to oblivion.

Although impressionistic rather than naturalistic, Andreev's stage directions are detailed and explicit. But as with *Hedda Gabler* Meyerhold chose
once more to exercise his creative autonomy. He devised the settings himself,
employing a designer merely as an executant; the scenic space was handled
with unprecedented freedom. The key to the entire production was light,
exploited for the first time by Meyerhold for its sculptural power. The
effects achieved are clear from his own account:

15 Scene One of *A Man's Life*

I produced this play *without sets* as they are generally understood. The entire stage was hung with drapes, but not as in *The Fairground Booth* where the drapes were hung in the places usually occupied by scenery. . . Here the drapes were hung on the walls of the theatre itself and against the back wall of the stage where 'distant views' are normally depicted. We removed all footlights, borders and battens in order to achieve a 'grey, smoky, monochrome expanse. Grey walls, grey ceilings, grey floor.' 'From an unseen source issues a weak, even light which is just as grey, monotonous, monochrome and ghostly, casting no hard shadows, no brilliant spots of light.' [The quotations are from Andreev's stage directions.] In this light the Prologue is read. Then the curtain parts to reveal a deep, gloomy expanse in which everything stands motionless. After about three seconds the spectator begins to make out the shapes of furniture in one corner of the stage. 'Dimly visible are the grey forms of old women huddled together like a group of grey mice.' They are sitting on a big, old-fashioned divan flanked by two armchairs. Behind the divan is a screen, in front of it a lamp. The old women's silhouettes are lit only by the light falling from this lamp. The effect is the same in every scene; a section of the stage is seen in a pool of light from a single source, which is sufficient to illuminate only the furniture and the characters immediately adjacent to it. By enveloping the stage in grey shadow, using a single light-source to illuminate one area of it (the lamp behind the divan and the lamp over the round table in Scene One, the chandelier in the ball scene, the lamps above the tables in the drunk scene),* we managed to create the impression of actual walls which were invisible because the light

* The actual source of light was a spotlight in the flies.

16 The ball scene in *A Man's Life*

did not reach them. On a stage free from conventional settings, furniture and other properties assume a fresh significance; the nature and atmosphere of a room is determined by them alone. It becomes necessary to use properties of clearly exaggerated dimensions. And always very little furniture; a single typical object takes the place of a host of less typical ones. The spectator is forced to take note of the unusual contour of a divan, an ornate column, a gilded armchair, a bookcase extending across the entire stage, a ponderous sideboard; given all these separate parts, the imagination fills in the rest. Naturally, the characters' features had to be modelled as precisely as sculpture, with make-up sharply accentuated; the actors were obliged to accentuate the figures of the characters they were playing in the same way as Leonardo da Vinci or Goya.[69]

It is not certain when Meyerhold first encountered Adolphe Appia's theories on stage lighting, only that when he came to stage *Tristan and Isolde* in 1909 he was familiar with Appia's book *Die Musik und die Inscenierung*. In this revolutionary work published in 1899 Appia, at that time a little-known Swiss artist, rejected traditional painted flats as incompatible with the three dimensions of scenic space and the actor's body; instead he advocated, in detailed and practicable terms, a setting conceived plastically throughout, composed on varying levels to overcome the unnatural flatness of the stage floor and unified by the sculptural power of chiaroscuro. As Lee Simonson writes:

> The light and shade of Rembrandt, Piranesi, Daumier, and Meryon was finally brought into the theatre as an interpretative medium, not splashed on a

back-drop, as romantic scene-painters had used it, but as an ambient medium actually filling space and possessing actual volume; it was an impalpable bond which fused the actor, whenever and however he moved, with everything around him. The plastic unity of the stage picture was made continuous.[70]

Appia's conception of stage lighting was entirely without precedent in the theatre and attracted little attention before 1912, when his work was first seen on the stage of Jaques-Dalcroze's School of Eurhythmics at Hellerau.[71] Reading Meyerhold's description of *The Life of a Man* it is difficult to believe that he had no knowledge of Appia's theories in 1907.*

Although rehearsed for only twelve days from read-through to first night, *The Life of a Man* was a great popular success and played to full houses for the last two weeks of the season; Fyodor Komissarzhevsky, the Head of Design at his sister's theatre, described the production as 'the most fully integrated during the first two seasons in Ofitserskaya Street'.[72] Andreev himself preferred Meyerhold's version to Stanislavsky's at the Moscow Art Theatre soon afterwards, which he said had a refinement akin to Beardsley rather than the Goya-like harshness that he had in mind.[73] Yet so shallow and pretentious does the text seem today, and so far did Meyerhold diverge from Andreev's stage directions,[74] that one feels the production's success must have been due to its visual impact rather than to the intrinsic worth of the play itself.

In his essay *On the History and Technique of the Theatre* (written in 1906–1907),[75] in which he describes the origins and development of the stylised theatre, Meyerhold stresses again and again the active role of the spectator:

> In the theatre the spectator's imagination is able to supply that which is left unsaid. It is this mystery and the desire to solve it that draw so many people to the theatre. . . Bryusov indicates the active role of the spectator in the theatre:
> '. . . *The stage must supply as much as is necessary to help the spectator picture as easily as possible in his imagination the setting demanded by the plot of the play.*'
> Ultimately, the stylistic method presupposes the existence of a fourth *creator* in addition to the author, the director and the actor – namely the spectator. The stylised theatre produces a play in such a way that the spectator is compelled to employ his imagination *creatively* in order to *fill in* the details intimated by the action on the stage.

This principle is the very foundation of stylisation; it was demonstrated by all Meyerhold's productions for Komissarzhevskaya, but by none so clearly as *The Life of a Man*. It was precisely because the spectator was shown so little that he saw so much, superimposing his own imagined or remembered experiences on the events enacted before him. In this way the dialogue and

* For further indication of Meyerhold's debt to Appia see the account of *Tristan and Isolde* (pp. 88-91, 94-95).

characters assumed a significance and a profundity that overcame their intrinsic banality. Time and again in the Soviet period Meyerhold exploited this associative power of the spectator's imagination to transform a mediocre dramatic text into a powerful theatrical experience.

VI

By the autumn of 1907 Meyerhold's position with Komissarzhevskaya had deteriorated to the point where his impending resignation was being openly discussed in the press. In particular, Meyerhold resented the fact that the company had gone on tour in the summer with a number of their old productions in an effort to shore up the precarious finances of the company. For her part, Komissarzhevskaya was bitterly disappointed at the rejection of their new work in Moscow by most of the critics, who had ridiculed even her performance in *Sister Beatrice*. To make matters worse, Fyodor Komissarzhevsky, whom Meyerhold regarded as a worthless dilettante, was losing no opportunity to discredit him in his sister's eyes.[76]

But Meyerhold was far too single-minded to allow dwindling confidence within the company to curb his experimental zeal. Encouraged by

17 'They didn't understand us!' Caricature of Meyerhold and Komissarzhev-skaya by Lyubimov, 1907

his successes with Blok and Andreev, he was keen to explore still further the flexibility of the stage area. He proposed staging Fyodor Sologub's new play *The Gift of the Wise Bees* 'in the round' by building a platform in the centre of the auditorium and seating part of the audience on the permanent stage. Komissarzhevskaya supported the idea but Fyodor opposed it, seeing no prospect of challenging local theatre regulations.[77] It was left to Nikolai

Okhlopkov a quarter of a century later at the Realistic Theatre in Moscow to present the first modern productions on a stage completely surrounded by the audience.*

Even so, Meyerhold's first production in the autumn was hardly less bold – not only in conception but in subject matter too. In April he had gone to Berlin with Komissarzhevsky and whilst there they had visited Max Reinhardt's experimental theatre, the Berliner Kammerspiele. Meyerhold was reserved in his opinion of Reinhardt. Whilst admiring his boldness, he was quick to spot the influence of Craig, criticised the indiscriminate use of Art Nouveau, and deplored the traditional manner of most of the acting.[78] One of the productions he saw was the first production of Wedekind's tragi-grotesque of adolescent sexuality, *Spring Awakening*, and he resolved immediately to present it in St Petersburg, even though it had taken fifteen years for the ban on its public performance to be lifted in Germany.

It was a fashionable choice, no doubt calculated to provoke controversy. As Rudnitsky notes, it followed hard on the publication of Mikhail Artsybashev's sensational novel *Sanin*, which dealt with the theory and practice of sexual freedom in naturalistic detail, gratifying the current vogue for the erotic, the psychosexual and the blatantly pornographic.[79]

Surprisingly enough, *Spring Awakening* was passed by the Russian censor, albeit extensively cut, and on 15 September 1907 it opened the second season in Ofitserskaya Street – to be followed a week later by a second production at the Korsh Theatre in Moscow. Meyerhold describes his interpretation in a production note: 'We have looked for a soft, unemphatic tone. The aim is to tone down the realism of certain scenes, to tone down the physiological aspect of puberty in the children. Sunlight and joyousness in the settings to counteract the chaos and gloom in the souls of the children.'[80] Critics and friends of the theatre alike could find little of merit in Wedekind's text, castigating both its style and theme. Alexander Blok actually doubted that Russian parents ever had such problems with their children,[81] whilst even the ultra-progressive Chulkov wrote that Wedekind 'will please nobody, with the possible exception of Moscow decadents and those German bourgeois who take pride in posing as sated aesthetes'.[82]

Shortly after the opening night the following letter to Vera Komissarzhevskaya appeared in the Petersburg *Theatre Review*:

> We 'advise' you to remove from your repertoire the masonic and yid play *Spring Awakening*. You may put on whatever you like in your flea-pit, but we are not going to let you corrupt children and adolescents. If you persist in staging this filthy piece of work, then fifty of us will come along to hiss it off the stage and pelt you with rotten apples, because it is not theatre but pornographic trash.
>
> (signed) Outraged parents and theatre-lovers.[83]

* See p. 309 below.

Despite the play's scandalous subject-matter, the production was received coolly and Blok was probably voicing a common reaction when he remarked that 'the pornography was obliterated by boredom' – not least because the opening performance ran one hour and forty minutes to the interval.[84] The one redeeming feature seen in the production was the method of area-lighting that Meyerhold devised to eliminate constant scene changes and to ensure an uninterrupted flow of the play's eighteen* short scenes on a stage that lacked a revolve. To quote Valentina Verigina:

> In accordance with Meyerhold's plan the stage was divided into several levels [by the designer Denisov]. At the bottom left and right were two apartments with part of a room visible in each. Light fell only on the place where the action was taking place, with everything else left in darkness. Above the apartments there was a sloping roof which represented the meadow where Wendla played with her friends. Still higher there was a platform on which Ilse and Moritz met, and finally at the top there was another small platform representing the grave of Moritz visited at the end by Ilse and Martha.[85]

For all its originality, area lighting was a technique accorded little significance by Meyerhold at the time. In fact, *Spring Awakening* seems to have been a production he was anxious to forget, for he makes no mention of it in the survey of his first ten years' work published in 1913.[85] Nevertheless, the play's episodic structure lent the action both fluency and moments of abrupt contrast of a kind long absent from the theatre. Now that Meyerhold had recognised the limitations of the static drama he was beginning to exploit fully the dimensions of theatrical time and space in a manner that had no precedent on the modern stage. In retrospect, productions such as *The Fairground Booth*, *The Life of a Man*, and *Spring Awakening* appear unmistakably cinematic – cinematic at a time when the cinema itself was little more than filmed theatre. When Meyerhold came to make *The Picture of Dorian Gray* in 1915 he immediately applied his dramatic theories to such telling effect that the result was what Jay Leyda has called '. . . undoubtedly the most important Russian film made previous to the February Revolution.'[87]†

On 10 October 1907 Meyerhold presented Maeterlinck's *Pelléas and Mélisande* in a specially commissioned translation by Valery Bryusov, and with Komissarzhevskaya as Mélisande and Meyerhold as the old King Arkel. Despite the production's imposing credentials, it was a total failure that proved decisive in Meyerhold's career. The principal fault lay in the setting (by Denisov) which consisted of a small raised platform in the centre of the stage; the stage floor was removed to furnish an orchestra pit surrounding the platform. Volkov suggests that this was Meyerhold's attempt to realise within legal limits his frustrated project for a theatre in the round.[88] If this is so, then the whole point was lost by enclosing the platform from behind

---

* Nineteen in Wedekind's original text.

† Meyerhold's work in the cinema is discussed on pp. 135-139 below.

with walls painted, according to Blok, in the vulgar style of old-fashioned '*cartes postales*'.[89] As Meyerhold admitted afterwards, the effect was precisely that of his early productions against decorative panels: the three-dimensional figures of the actors lost all plasticity in their close proximity to the painted background and were so constricted in their movements that they had no choice but to move as automata in obedience to the scheme prescribed by the director.

By this time Meyerhold had lost faith in many of his actors, whilst *Pelléas and Mélisande*, the most fragile and elusive of all Maeterlinck's dramas, represented a style of static theatre that he had left behind. Assailed by the virulent criticism of *Spring Awakening*, he found little comfort in the bare three weeks allotted to the rehearsals of *Pelléas*.

Unfortunately, it was a production on which Komissarzhevskaya had staked her own reputation and the very future of the company. At the age of forty-three and involved in an intense love affair with Bryusov, she had set her heart on playing the part of the child-like Mélisande, having only recently yielded the fourteen-year old Wendla in *Spring Awakening* with extreme reluctance to Katya Munt (herself thirty-two). Even the most friendly critics were unanimous in pronouncing her Mélisande a personal disaster. The critic of *Theatre and Art* wrote:

> In common with the rest of the cast, Miss Komissarzhevskaya, in an attempt to create a primitive, universal character, deliberately moved and gesticulated like a doll; her wonderful voice with its rare tonal range and musical timbre was replaced by something between a bird-like twittering and a childish squeak. . . It was neither moving nor dramatic.[90]

The only true success that Komissarzhevskaya had enjoyed with Meyerhold was in *Sister Beatrice* almost a year earlier, and her total failure as Mélisande was more than she could bear; immediately after the performance she summoned the two other administrative directors of the theatre, Kasimir Bravich and her brother Fyodor, and told them '. . . that the theatre must admit its entire course as a mistake, and the artistic director must either abandon his method of production or leave the theatre'.[91]

Two days later Meyerhold was given a chance to justify his policy at a meeting of the company's 'artistic council'. According to the notes of that meeting, Meyerhold explained that *Pelléas and Mélisande*, far from foreshadowing the future course of his work, represented the close of a cycle of experiments that had begun at the Theatre-Studio with *The Death of Tintagiles*; in future he would pursue the 'sculptural' style of production already initiated in *The Fairground Booth* and *The Life of a Man*.[92] With some justification, Komissarzhevskaya doubted that this signified any greater creative freedom for the actor, whereupon Meyerhold, in Volkov's words '. . . declared categorically that whatever the method of production in the future, he would continue to exert pressure on any actors who failed to grasp his conception in order to realise that conception. Everything he had heard horrified him and he wanted to leave the theatre and go abroad.'[93]

Eventually, an uneasy rapprochement was achieved and Meyerhold continued as artistic director. In an atmosphere of confusion previously announced productions were cancelled, but somehow Meyerhold contrived to rehearse Fyodor Sologub's new tragedy, *Death's Victory*, and it was presented on 6 November 1907. With this production Meyerhold confirmed his repudiation of what he called the 'decorative stylisation' of *Pelléas and Mélisande* and his earlier work.

> The settings (devised by Meyerhold) – wrote Chulkov – had a stylised simplicity that was most agreeable: a broad flight of steps extended the entire breadth of the stage, massive columns and the muted, severe tones of the overall background facilitated a blend of the visual impressions with those created by the severe and precise style of the tragedy itself. . . At the very end, the orgiastic frenzy of the crowd around the magnificent Algista was imbued with the magic of true theatre. Apparently, at this point the author wanted to cross the sacred line, 'to destroy the footlights'. And it would have been possible to do this . . . by extending the steps on the stage into the auditorium,* thereby enabling the action of the tragedy to culminate amongst the audience.[95]

Alexander Benois, normally one of Meyerhold's sharpest critics, called the production 'truly splendid', admiring particularly the effect of the steps in the crowd scenes, in which the face of every extra could be clearly seen. In his review he wrote:

> One wants to take a pencil and sketch those balanced clusters of people, those combinations of gesture and expression, those beautiful lines – only a most gifted man could have made a whole mass of people submit in this manner to his will and to his fine inspiration, could have made them memorise such a complex formula within such an incredibly short space of time. This evening has made me believe in Meyerhold.[96]

It was high praise from so accomplished an artist.

The critical reception of *Death's Victory* was almost unanimously enthusiastic; even Tamarin in the hostile *Theatre and Art* described the production as 'a clear turning-point in style'.[97] However, Komissarzhevskaya (yet again without a part in a successful production) was not reassured, sourly dismissing the production in a letter to Bryusov as a capitulation to the critics, and condemning Meyerhold's reversion to 'Meiningen crowd scenes'.[98] Three days after the première, and a year to the day since the opening of the theatre, Komissarzhevskaya called a company meeting with Meyerhold present and read out the text of a letter that had been handed to him that morning:

> In recent days, Vsevolod Emilievich, after much thought I have arrived at the firm conviction that you and I do not share the same views on the theatre,

---

* Meyerhold maintained that he was prevented from extending the steps down into the auditorium by the cautiousness of the theatre's management.[94]

and that what you are seeking is not what I am seeking. The path we have been following the whole time is the path that leads to the puppet theatre – if one excepts those productions in which we combined the principles of the 'old' theatre with those of the puppet theatre, for example *Love's Comedy* and *Death's Victory*. . . In answer to your question at the last meeting of our artistic council 'perhaps I should leave?' I must say: yes, there is no choice for you but to leave.[99]

Meyerhold protested that his summary dismissal in mid-season was a violation of professional ethics and demanded that the affair be submitted to a court of arbitration. However, Komissarzhevskaya's decision was upheld by the court and Meyerhold's place as artistic director was taken by Fyodor Komissarzhevsky and Nikolai Yevreinov. Only two further productions were staged, a revival of *The Master Builder* and Remizov's mystery, *The Devil's Play*, and the season ended prematurely on 7 January 1908. The company survived until February 1909 in Ofitserskaya Street, pursuing a similar artistic policy and retaining a number of Meyerhold's productions in the repertoire, though accomplishing nothing new that approached his best work. In February 1910, while she was on tour with her company in Tashkent, Vera Komissarzhevskaya contracted smallpox and died at the age of forty-five.

18 Melchior-
Meyerhold at
the grave of
Wendla-
Komissarzhev-
skaya: 'I am her
murderer! . . .
But I wasn't
bad' (then in his
native tongue):
'Ich war nicht
schlecht!'
Caricature by
Lyubimov
following *Spring
Awakening*,
1907

On 14 November after a performance of *Death's Victory* Meyerhold took his final curtain calls as Komissarzhevskaya's artistic director. He had endured a bruising year, constantly attacked and ridiculed by a largely malevolent press, undermined by intrigue and lack of commitment within the company, and attempting to perform whilst rehearsing intricate texts, sometimes in as little as ten days and never for longer than three weeks. Against this, it must be admitted that he was ruthless in his dismissal of actors, tactless in his dealings with Komissarzhevskaya, and quite lacking

in a sense of financial reality. Yet his achievements were awesome: in the space of twelve months he had staged no fewer than thirteen productions of formidable complexity, shaken the staid theatrical world of St Petersburg to its foundations, and set most of the ground rules for the rest of his creative life.

Eventually Meyerhold and his fellow director Rudolph Ungern (who had resigned with him) assembled a company mainly from those actors who had remained loyal to them and in February 1908 they embarked on a three-month tour of western and southern towns, beginning in Vitebsk and ending in Mariupol. In addition to revivals of most of Meyerhold's successful Petersburg productions, the repertoire included Wedekind's *Earth Spirit* in Meyerhold's translation, Ibsen's *The Master Builder*, Knut Hamsun's *At the Gates of the Kingdom*, and von Hofmannsthal's *Elektra*.

Although Meyerhold's innovations were frequently curbed by the limitations of provincial theatres, he continued to exploit the stage to its limits and even beyond: in *Death's Victory* the spectators were shocked to find the performers in the prologue making their entrances and speaking from the rear of the auditorium,[100] whilst *The Fairground Booth* was performed entirely in front of 'lightweight screens *à la Japonaise*' on the forestage with the house lights up throughout and 'The Author' voicing his protests from the front row of the stalls.[101]

On 7 March 1908 he wrote to his wife: '. . . Just as Poltava resurrected me after the collapse of the Studio, so Minsk has resurrected me now.'[102] All his life he was nothing if not resilient, as he was to prove soon enough to the scornful public back in St Petersburg, many of whom doubtless imagined that they had seen the last of him.

Dapertutto Reborn

In November 1907 at the Tenishev Academy in St Petersburg Meyerhold delivered a lecture entitled 'On the History and Technique of the Theatre', based on his contribution to an anthology that was published early the following year under the title *Theatre. A Book on the New Theatre*.[1] In this article, begun in the summer of 1906, he gives his personal account of the Moscow Art Theatre's development, traces the origins of the stylised 'New Theatre', and describes his own attempts to realise it, first at the Theatre-Studio and then with Komissarzhevskaya. In the final section, 'The Stylised Theatre', he outlines the conclusions reached after his rejection of the two-dimensional method of staging in favour of the more flexible style of *The Fairground Booth* and subsequent productions. In particular, he emphasises the removal of the footlights and the use of the forestage; the expressive power of rhythm in diction and movement; the director's right to interpret the text freely; the active participation of the spectator in the creative act; and, above all, the dispelling of illusion and the heightening of theatricality.

Recalling Meyerhold's recent dispute with Komissarzhevskaya, it is significant that he now placed particular stress on the actor's role:

> [The Director] serves purely as a bridge, linking the soul of the author with the soul of the actor. Having assimilated the author's creation, the actor is left *alone*, face to face with the spectator; and from the friction between these two unadulterated elements, the actor's creativity and the spectator's imagination, a clear flame is kindled.[2]

In conclusion, he considered the kind of auditorium demanded by the new theatre:

> Architecturally, the Greek classical theatre is the very theatre that modern drama needs: it has three-dimensional space, no scenery, and it demands sculptural plasticity. Obviously its design will need to be modified, but with its simplicity, its horseshoe-shaped auditorium, and its orchestra, it is the only theatre capable of accommodating such a varied repertoire as Blok's *The Fairground Booth*, Andreev's *The Life of a Man*, Maeterlinck's

tragedies, Kuzmin's plays, Remizov's mysteries, Sologub's *The Gift of the Wise Bees* and all the other fine new works that have yet to find their theatre.[3]

It is possible that had Meyerhold remained with Komissarzhevskaya he would have continued to stage the symbolist dramatists. But as it was, *A Book on the New Theatre* marked the close of a chapter in the history of the Russian theatre. Fyodor Komissarzhevsky's production of *The Devil Play* at Ofitserskaya Street was not a success, and after that there were few significant attempts to produce symbolist drama in Russia, so that most of the works of Ivanov, Bely, Kuzmin, Bryusov, and Remizov never reached the stage at all. The symbolists' vision of a revived communal ritual, embraced by Meyerhold in 'The Stylised Theatre', never materialised – or at least not until it assumed the form of the political mass spectacle after the October Revolution. However, every idea expounded by Meyerhold in his article can be traced right through his work over the next thirty years. Even the Greek amphitheatre was built finally after a lifetime spent struggling to burst the bounds of the box-stage and obliterate the picture-frame of the proscenium arch.'*

II

The critics' earlier glee at Meyerhold's dismissal by Komissarzhevskaya gave way to consternation when it was confirmed in April 1908 that Meyerhold was to be engaged as stage director and actor at the Petersburg Imperial Theatres. In his statement to the press the Director of the Imperial Theatres, Vladimir Telyakovsky said: 'I consider that Meyerhold with his propensity for rousing people will prove very useful in the State theatres. As regards his extremes, I am confident that he will abandon them with us. . . I am even afraid that his new surroundings might turn him into a conformist.'[4]† Apparently, Telyakovsky had seen none of Meyerhold's productions before he approached him, but acted on the advice of the stage designer, Alexander Golovin. Bizarre as it appeared, the appointment was consistent with his desire to break the stranglehold of the old guard at the Alexandrinsky Theatre and to transform it into a company that could bear comparison with its Moscow counterpart, the Maly, not to mention the Moscow Art Theatre.

The danger of Meyerhold's boldness and originality being stifled was

---

* See pp. 267-269 below.

† In fact, Meyerhold was approached by Telyakovsky a week after his dismissal, and his engagement was agreed in principle in November 1907. But Telyakovsky was careful to conceal it until the excitement over the Komissarzhevskaya scandal had subsided. The official organ of the Imperial Theatres (*The Theatre Review*) went so far as to refute the 'silly gossip', commenting: 'As is well known, the Directorate of the Imperial Theatres is not such an eccentric body as to wish to transform an exemplary theatre into a puppet show.'[5]

19 'Telyakovsky dances to the music of Meyerhold.' Caricature by 'Uncle Petya', 1908

real; at that time the Alexandrinsky was virtually ruled by a small group of august veteran artists, headed by Maria Savina, the redoubtable 'Empress of the Russian stage'. In their eyes all the stage-directors and designers under contract to the Imperial Theatres were no more than craftsmen, of no greater account than stage-managers, carpenters, electricians and the like, and as such denied any creative pretensions of their own.[6] The company was huge, numbering eighty-seven performers and four directors. It was under these daunting circumstances that Meyerhold was engaged at less than a quarter of Savina's salary and much less than he had been paid by Komissarzhevskaya, for an initial twelve months from 1 September 1908 as a stage-director and actor at the Alexandrinsky Theatre and as an occasional director at the Mariinsky Opera. In fact, he remained there for the next ten years and, not counting his private studio work, staged over two dozen productions, eight of them operas.

In anticipation of the hostile reception in store for him, Meyerhold published an article in the summer number of the periodical *The Golden*

Fleece, outlining his conception of the future development of the theatre.[7] In it, he divides theatre companies into two broad categories: first, those with an established company and a style and repertoire aimed at a wide audience (these he terms 'big theatres'); second, the theatre-studios whose function it should be to create the 'theatre of the future'.

A theatre-studio – argues Meyerhold – must have a director and a company unhampered by stylistic preconceptions and unharassed by the commercial considerations of a public theatre. Only from the experiments of such a studio can a completely new form of theatre emerge. This is the lesson to be derived from the failure of the Moscow Theatre-Studio, the lesson (he implies) ignored by Komissarzhevskaya's Theatre, which sought to embrace the functions both of a 'big theatre' and of a studio. The big theatres, on the other hand, are the custodians of tradition; the talents of their great veteran actors should be allowed to flourish in the plays of the dramatists who inspired them: Shakespeare, Schiller, Goethe, and, above all, Ostrovsky, Gogol and Griboedov. But, continues Meyerhold, the great works of the traditional repertoire invariably suffer from inadequate production; either they are staged as they always were 'in the good old days' or the director assembles a host of naturalistic properties in an attempt to create a perfect illusion of the period in question. What is the proper approach?

> The underlying idea of a play can be brought out not only through the
> dialogue between the characters created by the actors' skill, but equally
> through the rhythm of the whole picture created on the stage by the colours
> of the designer and by the deployment of practicable scenery, the pattern of
> movement and the interrelationship of groupings, which are all determined by
> the director.[8]

The aim should be a new, more profound realism which '. . . far from avoiding true life, transcends it by seeking only the *symbol* of the object, its *mystical essence*.'*

Thus Meyerhold tried to anticipate the protests of his future company whilst at the same time reaffirming the major principles of his own artistic credo. Indeed, he went so far as to recommend 'the old actors' to study Dmitry Merezhkovsky's recent symbolist reinterpretation of *The Government Inspector*,† thereby implying that their own traditional reading of that immortal work was by no means sacrosanct. We shall see how far Meyerhold succeeded in overcoming the deep-rooted prejudices and preconceptions of the Imperial stage when we come on to his productions of *Tristan and Isolde*, *Dom Juan*, *The Storm*, and *Masquerade*.

Despite Meyerhold's remarks on the ideal repertoire for the 'big theatres' his first production at the Alexandrinsky Theatre was of a modern work, *At the Gates of the Kingdom*, by the highly fashionable Norwegian writer, Knut

---

* Compare Nemirovich-Danchenko's comment on *The Cherry Orchard* (p. 28 above).

† *Gogol and the Devil* (1906).

20 The Alexandrinsky Theatre (now Pushkin Theatre)

Hamsun.* Written in Ibsen's symbolic-realist manner, the play is the first part of a trilogy dealing with the life of a Nietzschean philosopher, Ivar Kareno. As Meyerhold said in an interview at the time, *At the Gates of the Kingdom* belonged to the same cycle of productions as his earlier work on Ibsen.[9] It was given its première at the Alexandrinsky Theatre on 30 September 1908.

In one respect, the visual treatment was strongly reminiscent of *Hedda Gabler*: the single setting depicting Kareno's room was executed in brilliant colours and framed with an ornate false proscenium opening, the intention being to reflect not Kareno's material poverty but rather his spiritual exaltation.[10] The result was like the ante-chamber of some fabulous palace which, as one critic remarked, could as well serve for *Ruslan and Ludmilla* or *La Traviata*.[11] The costumes were no less vivid in hue. A number of the cast took exception to Meyerhold's innovations and paid little attention to his directions; one of them, Roman Apollonsky, set out deliberately to sabotage the opening performance by treating his part as a burlesque. Inevitably, the outcome was a fiasco and Meyerhold, who himself played Kareno, had

* During the 1908–1909 season *At the Gates of the Kingdom* was also staged at Komissarzhevskaya's Theatre and at the Moscow Art Theatre. Meyerhold himself had already produced it once before whilst on tour in the Spring, also playing the part of Kareno.

difficulty in completing the performance.[12] Most of the company and all the critics, except the sympathetic Lyubov Gurevich in *The Word*, took malicious pleasure in Meyerhold's double failure. In part, he had himself to blame: against Telyakovsky's advice he had taken over the part of Kareno from another actor, clearly unable to resist the chance of playing yet another solitary dissident artist-thinker in the line of Hauptmann's Johannes Vockerath, Chekhov's Treplev, and of course Blok's Pierrot.[13] It was a mistake that he didn't repeat: only occasionally over the next ten years did he perform, and then only in roles from his previous repertoire, such as Konstantin in *The Seagull* and the Prince of Aragon in *The Merchant of Venice*.

Meyerhold's next scheduled production was Oscar Wilde's *Salome* at the Imperial Mikhailovsky Theatre, a benefit performance sponsored by the wealthy amateur actress Ida Rubinstein with designs by Bakst, music by Glazunov, choreography by Fokine, and with Rubinstein herself as Salome. This extravagant project foundered in October after lengthy preparation when the cuts demanded by the censor threatened to render it meaningless.[14] Within days *Salome* was also banned after its public dress rehearsal at Komissarzhevskaya's Theatre and it was October 1917 before it received its première in Russia at Tairov's Kamerny Theatre.

Meyerhold completed no major productions in his first season and for a time his future at the Imperial Theatres seemed seriously in doubt. However, *At the Gates of the Kingdom* was by no means a total disaster for him, since it initiated his partnership with Alexander Golovin. Eleven years his senior, Golovin had been a leading member of the 'World of Art' movement since its first exhibition in 1898. Having worked in the Imperial Theatres as a designer for opera and ballet with great success since 1902, he created the settings for Mussorgsky's *Boris Godunov* at Diaghilev's Russian season in the summer of 1908, and for the première of Stravinsky's *Firebird* in 1910. With the exception of *Tristan and Isolde* in 1909, Golovin's designs were a vital and integral part of all Meyerhold's major productions at the Imperial Theatres for the next ten years.

III

No sooner had Meyerhold joined the Alexandrinsky Theatre than he took steps to ensure the furtherance of his experiments into new dramatic forms. At the start of the 1908–1909 season he and the young composer, Mikhail Gnesin, organised a small theatre-studio in Meyerhold's flat in St Petersburg. Significantly, the curriculum included courses in 'choral and musical declamation in drama' and 'plastic gymnastics'.[15] It was Meyerhold's first attempt at formal theatrical teaching and reflected his declared ambition to create a new style of theatre with his own pupils. The course ran only one year but the following season, mainly to augment his meagre salary, Meyerhold taught acting technique to the second-year students of the well-established Pollak drama school. In the winter he spent there he paid particular attention to mime and movement, gaining experience that was to prove valuable when eventually he opened a permanent studio of his own in 1913.[16]

In Autumn 1908 he was invited to collaborate in the creation of an intimate theatre housed in the Petersburg Theatre Club. Called 'The Strand' (*'Lukomore'*), it was envisaged as the equivalent of the Berlin *'Überbrettl'*, the original German literary cabaret founded by Ernst von Wolzogen in 1901, and of Nikita Baliev's late-night theatre club 'The Bat' which had opened recently in Moscow. However, 'The Strand' differed from its counterparts to the extent that as well as presenting a late-night programme of parody and satire (called *The Distorting Mirror*), it also planned to stage a programme of one-act plays at normal theatre times. The three main items of the opening programme, all directed by Meyerhold, were *Petrushka*, a 'folk farce' by Peter Potemkin, *Honour and Vengeance*, a buffonade by Count Vladimir Sollogub, and a dramatic adaptation of Edgar Allan Poe's *The Fall of the House of Usher*. Although the costumes and settings for these productions were designed by such accomplished artists as Bilibin and Dobuzhinsky, they were a failure mainly because the programme proved far too long and far too earnest for the informal club atmosphere. Whereas *The Distorting Mirror* survived and continued to flourish right up until 1931, 'The Strand' closed within three days of its opening on 6 December.[17] Immediately, Meyerhold announced the intention to create a new intimate theatre, '. . . a haven of rest for the cultured Petersburg theatregoer . . . in an atmosphere unpolluted by the belches of clubmen (pardon the vulgarity)'.[18]

In fact, two years passed before this ambition was realised at 'The Interlude House', but meanwhile Meyerhold continued to pursue a variety of activities outside the Imperial Theatres. In February 1909 Benjamin Kazansky presented a programme of 'Parisian Grand Guignol' at his theatre on Liteiny Prospect in which one of the items was *The Kings of the Air and the Lady from the Box*, a 'sensational melodrama' of circus life based on a short story called *The Four Devils* by the Danish writer Herman Bang. In three short acts without intervals, it was written by Meyerhold in response to a challenge from a friend while confined to his house with influenza. The work remained in Kazansky's repertoire for the remainder of the season and was published in Moscow shortly afterwards.[19] Although trivial in content, it reflected Meyerhold's widening interest in all theatrical genres and, in particular, the conventions of popular entertainment. Later in the year he made a translation from German of Takeda Izumo's Kabuki play *Terakoya*, and that too was staged by Kazansky.

At the same time Meyerhold continued to compose and translate articles on dramatic theory. Following the publication of his long essay 'On the History and Technique of the Theatre', he made translations from the German of two articles by Edward Gordon Craig, 'Über Bühnen-Ausstattung' and 'Etwas über den Regisseur und die Bühnen-Ausstattung', which were published in St Petersburg in 1909. The first was prefaced by a short biographical sketch of Craig.[20] Whilst warm in his praise of the Englishman, Meyerhold was careful to point out that his own crucial experiments at the Theatre-Studio were carried out in ignorance of the ideas expressed in Craig's book *The Art of the Theatre*;* it was not until Meyerhold visited Berlin in 1907 that he heard of Craig's stylised productions of Purcell's *Dido and Aeneas* (London, 1900) and Ibsen's *The Vikings* (London, 1903), and identified his influence in the work of Max Reinhardt at the Kammerspiele.

IV

In contrast to the punishing demands of his early years as a director, culminating in the twelve months with Komissarzhevskaya, in his ten years at the Imperial Theatres Meyerhold was seldom called upon to stage more than two major works in a season. Hence, he was left with time to undertake extensive preliminary research, mostly in collaboration with Alexander Golovin. *Tristan and Isolde*, his inaugural production at the Mariinsky Opera was the product of a year's exhaustive study of Wagner and his background.†

Grateful as he must have been for this unprecedented opportunity to indulge his intellectual curiosity, he must have been no less motivated by the magnitude of the task that faced him and the need to prove his credentials on a new and daunting stage. *Tristan and Isolde* had received its first Russian production ten years earlier at the Mariinsky in a production replete with all the familiar 'Wagnerian' baronial trappings and faithful to the composer's stage directions. The conductor was Felix Blumenfeld, but the identity of the producer is lost – hardly surprising, given the menial status of his function. So with all the notoriety that his directorial debut at the Alexandrinsky had attracted, Meyerhold now had to contend with an even more entrenched audience and a company of singers for whom acting amounted to little more than a narrow range of stock gestures. What is more,

---

* Published originally in German as *Die Kunst des Theaters* (Berlin and Leipzig, 1905). A Russian version appeared in 1906. After visiting Moscow in 1935 Craig wrote: 'It is to see Meyerhold's work in its entirety that I want to visit Russian again . . . I shall enjoy being figuratively tied to my seat for a few weeks attending rehearsals and performances in the Meyerhold Theatre; and only then, undisturbed by having to visit twenty other theatres, I shall be able to watch, learn and understand this exceptional theatric [sic] genius.'[21]

† Meyerhold returned to the Tristan theme in March the following year with a production at the Alexandrinsky Theatre of *Tantris the Fool* by the German neo-romantic dramatist Ernst Hardt.

he had somehow to establish a working relationship with the seventy-year-old principal conductor, Eduard Nápravník, who was renowned for his rigid pedantry and viewed the upstart producer as little more than a superfluous irritant. In the event, it was a situation that Meyerhold handled with quite unexpected tact and delicacy.[22]

Shortly after the première of *Tristan and Isolde* on 30 October 1909 he delivered a lecture on the subject which furnished the text for a long article published subsequently in *The Yearbook of the Imperial Theatres*.[23] In the first section of this article Meyerhold discusses the nature of Wagnerian music-drama and the style of acting appropriate to its realisation on the stage:

> If an opera were produced without words [he begins] it would amount to
> *a pantomime.* In pantomime every single episode, each movement in each
> episode (its plastic modulations) – as well as the gestures of every character
> and the groupings of the ensemble – are determined precisely by the music,
> by its changes in tempo, its modulations, its overall structure. . . So why don't
> operatic artists make their movements and gestures follow the musical tempi,
> the tonic design of the score, with mathematical precision? Does the addition
> of the human voice to the art of the pantomime alter the relationship between
> music and stage action that exists in pantomime? I believe it does alter it,
> because the opera singer bases his dramatic interpretation on the libretto
> rather than on the musical score.

Depending on the period of the opera, continues Meyerhold, the gestures and movements of the singers will be either conventionally 'operatic' or restrained and lifelike. The 'operatic' style is comparatively innocuous, because although it is mechanical and meaningless it does not distract the spectator by contradicting the musical tempi. But the lifelike style not only ignores the music, it exposes the *apparent* absurdity of the operatic convention of people singing in 'real life'. '*Music-drama must be performed in such a way that the spectator never thinks to question why the actors are singing and not speaking.*' [Meyerhold's italics]

In Wagner, as opposed to the school of Mozart and Bizet, 'the libretto and the music are composed free from mutual enslavement'. The score does not merely provide an accompaniment to the libretto but reveals the world of the soul, gives voice to the inner dialogue of the characters' emotions. Hence, it is not the libretto but the orchestral score that the singer through his acting must manifest in visible, plastic terms. However, it is not from everyday life that he must draw his inspiration: 'Where does the human body possessing the flexibility of expression demanded by the stage attain its highest development? *In the dance.* Because the dance is the movement of the human body in the sphere of rhythm. The dance is to the body what music is to thought: form artificially yet instinctively created.' But at the same time the actor should remember the expressive power of music: his gestures should not duplicate what the orchestra is saying, but rather supply what it fails to say or leaves half-said. Finally, he should understand that he is only one of several means of expression in the opera, neither more nor less important than any other, and he must remain conscious of them throughout his performance.

In the course of this section Meyerhold quotes only once from Adolphe Appia's *Die Musik und die Inscenierung*. But, in fact, the greater part of what he says here is clearly based on that work, as the following quotations from Appia show:

> To understand how music can control the elements of production, let us look briefly at pantomime – that prototype of drama in which, because language has no place, music and the visual elements of theatre are most prominent. In pantomime, music determines the time-durations and the sequence of the action. . . Obviously, if we now add words to this music, the relationship between the music and the production remains unaltered.
>
> . . . the poet-musician [a composer of the Wagnerian school], thanks to the music, presents us not only with external effects of emotions, the appearance of dramatic life, but with the emotions themselves, the dramatic life in all its reality, as we can know it only in the most profound depths of our being.
>
> The overwhelming power attained by music in our time makes impossible any artistic role for the human body as it functions in daily life. . . But there is yet another means of involving the living body in the [poet-musician's] expression: and that is by communicating to the actor the basic proportions of music, without necessarily having recourse to song – in other words, by means of the *dance*. By dance, I do not mean those light parlour entertainments or what passes for dance in the opera, but the *rhythmic* life of the human body in its whole scope.
>
> Dance is to the body what pure music is to our feelings: an imaginative, non-ration form.
>
> . . . for the author of word-tone [Wagnerian] drama, the actor is not the sole or even the most important interpreter of the poet's intention, he is rather but one medium, neither more nor less important than the others, at the poet's disposal.[24]

We have already seen how in 1907 in *The Life of a Man* Meyerhold's exploration of the sculptural power of light resembled the revolutionary lighting plots described by Appia in *Die Musik und die Inscenierung*. Now again his approach to *Tristan and Isolde* undoubtedly owed a debt to Appia that has been ignored not only by Rudnitsky in his otherwise authoritative study of Meyerhold, but even more surprisingly by Isaac Glikman in his *Meyerhold and the Music Theatre*.[25]

To what extent was Meyerhold influenced by Appia's ideas? Let us consider the opening of Chapter Two of Appia's book:

> We have seen that if the *mise-en-scène* is to be totally expressive of the playwright's intention, the means of controlling it must exist within the text. The *mise-en-scène*, as a design in space with variations in time, presents essentially a question of proportion and sequence. Its regulating principle must therefore govern its proportions in space and their sequence in time, each dependent on the other.

In drama, the playwright seems to have this power through the quantity and order of his text. However, this is not the case, because the text itself has no fixed duration; and the time not filled by the text is impossible to calculate. Even if one were to measure the relative duration of speech and silence with a stop-watch, this duration would be fixed only by the arbitrary will of the author or the director, without *necessarily* having its origins in the original conception.

The quality and order of the text alone, therefore, are insufficient to govern its staging. Music, on the other hand, determines not only time-duration and continuity in the drama, but, as we have seen, should actually be considered from the visual point of view of dramatic action as being time itself.

It is the word-tone poet, then, who possesses the guiding principle which, springing as it does from the original intention, inexorably and of necessity dictates the *mise-en-scène* without being filtered through the will of the dramatist – and this principle is an integral part of his drama and shares its organic life.

Thus the production attains the rank of an expressive medium in the drama of the poet-musician; but note that it cannot achieve such rank except in this kind of drama.[26]

It is not clear when Meyerhold first discovered Appia, but from an early stage his anti-naturalistic experiments reveal a conception of the director's role in the dramatic theatre strikingly similar to that of Appia's 'word-tone poet' in Wagnerian opera. One need only recall his criticism of the Moscow Art Theatre's production of *The Cherry Orchard* in 1904 when he wrote to Chekhov: 'Your play is abstract, like a Tchaikovsky symphony. Before all else, the director must get the *sound* of it.'* This became the guiding principle of all his work from the Theatre-Studio onwards: having isolated the text's 'inner dialogue', he would 'orchestrate' it in terms of speech rhythms, pauses, gestures, and movements; that is, he used *music* to determine precisely the 'time-duration and continuity in the drama' – often actual music (for example, by Sats for *The Death of Tintagiles*, by Lyadov for *Sister Beatrice* and by Kuzmin for *The Fairground Booth*), but sometimes pure rhythm, and always with the rhythmical discipline reinforced by the purposely contrived spatial restrictions of the stage area (the shallow strip of stage in *Sister Beatrice*, the stage within a stage in *The Fairground Booth*, the flight of steps in *Death's Victory*).†

Thus, as early as 1905 Meyerhold had discovered what Appia himself still denied: that 'the production could attain the rank of an expressive medium' not only in the opera but also in the dramatic theatre. This he

---

* See p. 22 above.

† Vyacheslav Ivanov's daughter, Lydia, recalls how 'Meyerhold talked over dinner about his production of *Tristan*. He complained about the familiar gesticulating of the singers and did hilarious impersonations of them. He was proud of his invention. He ordered the construction of settings that were so complicated, uncomfortable and dangerous at the slightest movement that the unfortunate singers were obliged to stand stock-still for fear of breaking their legs. The actors were furious but the director rubbed his hands in glee because he had achieved the production he wanted.'[27]

did by seeing what Appia had failed to see: that 'music' is by no means the exclusive property of opera, that rhythm is an expressive quality latent in all the performing arts. Considerable as Meyerhold's debt to Appia was, this crucial realisation was his own.

In the second and third sections of his article on *Tristan and Isolde*, Meyerhold considers the kind of stage and stage setting that best complement the plasticity of the actor in the music-drama. He argues that the Bayreuth Festspielhaus, despite its apparently revolutionary design (a concealed orchestra pit, broad proscenium opening, fan-like auditorium with no boxes), was really no more than a refinement of the traditional Renaissance box-stage and did little to satisfy Wagner's dream of a stage as a pedestal for human sculpture. The first man, he says, to revive the tradition of the proscenium stage of the Ancient Greek and Shakespearian theatres was Georg Fuchs at the Munich Artists' Theatre.* It is Fuchs' 'relief stage' with its foreground of non-decorative, practicable reliefs and remote painted back-drop that furnishes the ideal setting for Wagnerian music-drama.

As well as the architecture of Bayreuth, Meyerhold rejects its so-called 'historical' treatment of Wagner. The pseudo-period costumes and settings invite the spectator to relate the action to a specific time and place, and in consequence the atmosphere of remote legend conjured up by the orchestral score is lost to his imagination. However, the fault lies not so much with Bayreuth as with Wagner himself: his banal stage directions show that his visual imagination was no match for his musical inspiration and extended no further than the vulgar stereotyped conventions of nineteenth-century opera. Wagner's instructions are best ignored:

> Let the designer and director of *Tristan* take the cue for their stage
> picture from the orchestra. What extraordinary medieval colouring there is
> in Kurwenal's song, in the shouts of the sailors' chorus, in the mysterious
> death *Leitmotiv*, in the calls of the hunting horns, and in the fanfares when
> King Mark meets the ship in which Tristan has brought Isolde home to him.
> Yet Wagner places equal emphasis on the traditional operatic couch where
> Isolde is supposed to recline in Act One, and where Tristan lies dying in Act
> Three. In Act Two he stipulates a *'Blumenbank'* where Tristan is supposed
> to place Isolde during the intermezzo of the love duet; yet the garden with
> the rustling of leaves blending with the sound of the horns is miraculously
> evoked by the orchestra. The mere contemplation of real foliage on the stage
> would be as flagrantly tasteless as illustrating Edgar Allen Poe. In the second
> act our designer depicts a huge towering castle wall and in front of it, right
> in the centre of the stage, there burns the mystical torch that plays such an
> important part in the drama.[28]

Summarising Meyerhold's operatic work in 1932, Ivan Sollertinsky wrote: 'Of the whole Wagnerian legacy, *Tristan* . . . with its philosophical medita-tion verging on Schopenhauer . . . was regarded by the Russian symbolists

* See pp. 48-49 above.

21 and 22 Shervashidze's costume designs for Tristan and Isolde

as peculiarly their own.'[29] Certainly, Meyerhold was well acquainted with the thinking of Vyacheslav Ivanov and his circle and through them was familiar enough with Wagner's debt to Schopenhauer, but his interpretation of *Tristan and Isolde* owed little to this. Responding to Alexander Benois' criticism of the production, he wrote:

> . . . we see how Wagner's dramatic architectonics suffered as a result of his intentionally concentrating at the axis of the drama those elements of the myth that facilitated the development of his complex philosophical conception of Life and Death . . . the content of the [Act Two] duet is too complex for a music-drama in which the listener, after all, must devote himself so completely to the music that he has no time for philosophy.[30]

As Abram Gozenpud says, whereas 'Appia chose the path of abstraction, separating the action from reality . . . Meyerhold, by contrast, strove for artistic universality on an historical basis. Whilst resisting the symbolism of Appia, he also rejected the decrepit neo-romanticism of Bayreuth.'[31] Instead of 'All those helmets and shields gleaming like samovars, clinking chain-mail, and make-up reminiscent of Shakespearian histories', Meyerhold wanted his designer 'to create a fantastic background, to clothe the characters with loving care in garments that are the purest product of his imagination and whose colours recall the crumbling pages of ancient tomes . . . which persuade us that at some time in the past everything was like this.'[32] Prompted by the 'medieval colouring' that he perceived in the orchestral score, he and his designer, Prince Shervashidze, turned to the thirteenth century of Gottfried von Strassburg, whose poem *Tristan and Iseut* had been Wagner's main inspiration, and recreated the highly formalised style of his miniaturist contemporaries. In reply to Alexander Benois' criticism that, like the Bayreuth style, this obscured the opera's symbolism, Meyerhold wrote:

> Why, given that the play contains symbols, should the cut of the cloth necessarily be imaginary and why should the ship not resemble a ship of the thirteenth century? The object does not exclude the symbol; on the contrary, as reality becomes more profound, it transcends its own reality. In other words, reality, in becoming supra-natural, is transformed into a symbol.[33]

This argument presumes that the essence of the reality of Tristan and Isolde as perceived by Wagner corresponds to that of von Strassburg and the miniaturist painters, and not to Wagner's own nineteenth-century Romantic vision of the Age of Chivalry. Furthermore, the success in practice of such an approach would depend on the designer's ability to synthesise that reality, and not merely reproduce it, as Shervashidze's sketches suggest he did. The principle underlying Meyerhold's subsequent work with Golovin was similar, but he was an altogether more accomplished designer and, as we shall see, the results were strikingly different.

Faced with the insuperable problem of transforming the conventional stage of the Mariinsky Theatre into a relief stage every night that *Tristan and Isolde* was performed in the repertoire, Meyerhold compromised by constructing the practicable reliefs for the second and third acts immediately behind the setting line, whilst in Act One the ship was built at normal stage level. The distant painted backdrop showed no more than a bleak expanse of horizon. The forestage in front of the proscenium arch and the curtains to either side (as well as the ship's huge sail) were covered in a traditional medieval red and white lozenge pattern. The lifeless photographs that survive of the settings are perhaps misleading, for they give no indication of their appearance under stage-lighting in performance. However, they do seem to suggest a degree of lifelike detail (the rigging and decorative shields in Act One, the tower and drawbridge in Act Two) that is hardly consistent with Meyerhold's declared approach. On the other hand, tentative as the realisation of the relief-stage was, it greatly enhanced the production's visual impact. Vladimir Kastorsky, who played King Mark, recalled: 'When I came on stage in Act Two I felt taller, more imposing against the background of the huge, towering walls, and I got the same sensation in Act Three when I was performing against the background of the open sky.' With a second singer as Mark for the second performance, he was able to observe the effect from the auditorium: 'Without question, all the performers gained in stature, were seen in sharper relief against the background of the remote painted backdrop prescribed by the producer. The two principals, Yershov and Cherkasskaya

23 Shervashidze's setting for Act One of *Tristan and Isolde*

24 Shervashidze's setting for Act Three of *Tristan and Isolde*

as Tristan and Isolde, benefited especially from this. Thus, the producer's objective in dividing the stage into two planes was realised.'[34]
There is no evidence that the other principals shared this degree of enthusiasm for Meyerhold's innovations, and certainly Cherkasskaya re-

mained intractable throughout. However, what proved incontestable was the sheer musicality of his approach, his conviction that the entire *mise-en-scène* should be constructed on the basis of Wagner's score. As he remarked to his young assistant, Valery Bebutov, when discussing the Day and Night symbolism in the opera: 'Just think how fortunate the opera singer is in *Tristan*. The whole sphere of his feelings is resolved for him by the composer and is entirely contained within the score. All that remains is to organize the movement.'[35] As Meyerhold recalled in the 1930s, he did this by insisting on an 'almost mathematically precise synchronising of the performers' movements and gestures with the tempo of the music and the tonic design'.[36]

The production stimulated a level of critical debate that with isolated exceptions, such as the ultra right-wing *New Times*, was unmarred by the scornful abuse that Meyerhold had suffered in the past. The more conservative critics took exception to his disregard for the letter of Wagner's stage directions, but most were forced to concede the powerful emotional impact of the performance as a whole and of Yershov and Cherkasskaya in particular. Meyerhold's staging was widely praised and even Benois, whilst disagreeing fundamentally with the 'historical style' of the production, was forced to admit that 'In *Tristan* Meyerhold created a dozen groupings of such grace and beauty that as an artist I bemoaned the impossibility of stopping the action in order to sketch them.'[37] In *Apollon*, describing the Act Two love duet, Sergei Auslender wrote:

> The duet, imbued with a passionate, almost superhuman languor that
> already seems to anticipate death, by its very nature suggests immobility,
> and the poses of Tristan on the rock with Isolde reclining at his feet were at
> once splendid, sublime and tender. Yet when rapid movements were dictated
> Meyerhold provided them: all the ardour of meeting was contained in the one
> gesture when Tristan enveloped Isolde in his (deep violet) cloak, when the fatal
> purple of his garment blended with the more delicate (pink) monochrome of
> her dress.[38]

Theatre and Art grudgingly acknowledged that 'On the production side there is much that is original. On the operatic stage static poses are entirely appropriate.'[39] Despite dissenting voices, there was widespread agreement that Meyerhold had achieved a visual, musical, and dramatic coherence in advance of any previous operatic production in Russia. Even the conservative *Theatre Review* commented enthusiastically that 'scarcely a stage in Europe has witnessed such a production of *Tristan and Isolde* as yesterday's première at the Mariinsky Theatre'.[40]

The following January the work was conducted by Felix Mottl, the celebrated interpreter of Wagner and conductor of the first Bayreuth performance of *Tristan and Isolde*. According to Valery Bebutov, Mottl said that he had seen no more accurate interpretation of the score on any stage.[41] Remembering that Appia himself did not succeed in actually staging

Wagner until 1923,* Meyerhold's *Tristan and Isolde* must be acknowledged as probably the first attempt to free the composer's conception of the '*Gesamtkunstwerk*' from the banal conventions of the nineteenth century and give it credible theatrical form.

V

Of the various manifestations of the revolt against naturalism in the Russian theatre before the October Revolution the most fruitful and long-lasting proved to be the resurrection of the plays and stage conventions from the exemplary theatres of the past. This movement, later known as 'Traditionalism', originated with the opening in 1907 of 'The Ancient Theatre' ('*Starinny teatr*') in Petersburg. Created at the initiative of Nikolai Yevreinov in association with his wealthy patron Baron Driezen, it presented in its first season two programmes devoted to medieval miracles, moralities, farces, and the thirteenth-century pastorale, *Le Jeu de Robin et Marion* by Adam de la Halle. The whole enterprise typified the stand taken by the aesthetic élite against bourgeois bad taste and materialism in the Russia of Tsar Nicholas II.

In collaboration with such leading designers as Benois, Bilibin, Dobuzhinsky, Lanseray, and Roerich, Yevreinov and his fellow directors sought to re-create in precise detail the stages, costumes, settings, and theatrical conventions of past ages. Furthermore, an attempt was made to locate each play in its period by building 'a stage within a stage'. In this way the spectator witnessed not only the performance but also the surroundings in which it might once have been presented. Yevgeny Znosko-Borovsky describes Yevreinov's production of *Le Jeu de Robin et Marion*:

> The pastorale was staged as it might have been in some castle in the
> Age of Chivalry. . . The setting by Dobuzhinsky represented part of the
> great hall to either side of which were seated old, grey-haired minstrels
> with coronets on their heads and instruments in their hands. A master of
> ceremonies appeared and invited the audience to witness a pastorale, and
> immediately in full view preparations were begun for the performance. A
> little cardboard hut represented the peasants' house, imitation lambs served
> as the flock that was tended by Marion, a drooping cardboard tree was set
> up to indicate that the action was located in a field, and four attendants with
> candles placed themselves at each corner. In the same style as all this was the
> horse on which the knight entered: made also of wood and cardboard, it rolled
> backwards and forwards on four brightly decorated wheels.[42]

Originally it was Yevreinov's intention to cover the entire history of the theatre, beginning with Attic drama, but after the medieval programme three years elapsed before the second season in 1911–1912. Staged according

* *Tristan and Isolde* at La Scala, Milan.

to the same principles as the earlier programme, this season was devoted to the golden age of Spanish theatre, with works by Lope de Vega, Tirso de Molina, Cervantes and Calderón.

Despite considerable public interest and critical acclaim, the Ancient Theatre's existence was fraught with internal discord and financial problems. After a further interval, detailed preparations were made for a season of *commedia dell'arte*, but the project was frustrated by the outbreak of war in 1914, and the theatre ceased to exist.[43]

In a short review of the Ancient Theatre's opening season written in 1908 Meyerhold applauded its aims but criticised the means chosen to achieve them. In his opinion, the theatre should either have staged the original works in a precise 'archaeological' reconstruction of the scenic conventions of the period, or have taken plays written in the manner of works of the past and staged them as 'a free composition on the theme of the primitive theatre', like his own production of *Sister Beatrice*. Instead, he maintained, the Ancient Theatre fell between two stools, choosing original medieval texts but staging them as stylised free compositions. The result was a pastiche in which the naïve conventions seemed to be a deliberate parody of the original style.[44]

Meyerhold's own initial venture in the field of 'traditionalism' took place in April 1910, when he assembled an amateur cast of poets and writers and staged a single performance of Calderón's 'religious comedy' *The Adoration of the Cross* at Vyacheslav Ivanov's 'Tower'. Turning the limited space of Ivanov's (admittedly large) dining-room to his own advantage, Meyerhold ignored Calderón's prescribed location of thirteenth-century Siena and tried instead to re-create the spirit of a performance by Spanish strolling players of Calderón's day. Settings and costumes were improvised by Sergei Sudeikin from Ivanov's abundant collection of rich and exotic fabrics and carpets. The only properties used were wooden crosses and swords; the lighting was by candelabra; and the acting conventions were of the simplest: exits and entrances were made through the auditorium, a character supposed to be concealing himself beneath fallen leaves merely wrapped himself in a curtain. The stage was on a level with the audience, separated by gold brocade curtains which were operated by the two small sons of the hall porter, costumed and made-up to resemble the traditional blackamoors of the eighteenth-century court theatre. Ephemeral and lighthearted as this makeshift production may have been, it marked the beginning of Meyerhold's exhaustive study of the theatres of the past and his extensive application of their techniques to the modern stage.[45]

In the autumn of 1910 the intimate theatre whose formation Meyerhold had announced after the closure of 'The Strand' finally opened in St Petersburg. Called The Interlude House (*Dom intermedii*), it was run by Meyerhold and the impresario Boris Pronin with 'The Fellowship of Actors, Writers, Musicians and Artists' and housed in the former Skazka Theatre.

25 Poster for the *Interlude House* by Nikolai Remi (1910)

With the footlights removed, the tiny low stage was joined to the auditorium by a flight of steps and the rows of seats were replaced by restaurant tables and chairs. As well as a late-night cabaret, Meyerhold and his fellow organisers aimed to present a varied repertoire including ancient and modern farces, comedies, pantomimes, and operettas.

The opening programme on 9 October 1910 comprised a musical comedy called *The Reformed Eccentric*, a pastorale, *Liza, the Dutch Girl*, a burlesque, *Black and White – a Negro Tragedy*, and one production by Meyerhold, Arthur Schnitzler's pantomime, *The Veil of Pierrette*, with music by Dohnányi and settings and costumes by Sapunov. The first three items were greeted with reactions ranging from indifference to derision, but Meyerhold's contribution remained a haunting memory for those present. Freely adapted by himself and with the title altered to *Columbine's Scarf*, the work bore little resemblance to Schnitzler's original. The aim was to eliminate the cloying sweetness so often associated with pantomime and to create a chilling grotesque in the manner of E.T.A. Hoffmann. The three scenes were broken down into fourteen brief episodes, in order that the spectator should be shocked by the constant abrupt switches of mood and have no time to doubt the play's own ghastly logic. It was fitting that Meyerhold should dedicate the work to Blok, for in style, content, and atmosphere it bore a marked resemblance to the 1906 version of *The Fairground Booth*. But, as Vadim Shcherbakov comments, his aim now was a production 'without any echo of abstruse symbolism, without any pious deference towards the beloved poet who had in some ways restricted his freedom as a director.'[46] Here is an eyewitness description of the scenario of *Columbine's Scarf*:

The frivolous Columbine, betrothed to Harlequin, spends a last evening with her devoted Pierrot. As usual, she deceives him, swearing that she loves him. Pierrot proposes a suicide pact and himself drinks the poison. Columbine lacks the courage to follow him and flees in terror to the wedding ball where the guests await her impatiently. The ball begins; then while an old-fashioned quadrille is playing, Pierrot's flapping white sleeve is glimpsed first through the windows, then through the doors. The dances, now fast, now slow, turn into an awful nightmare, with strange Hoffmannesque characters whirling to the time of a huge-headed *Kapellmeister*, who sits on a high stool and conducts four weird musicians. Columbine's terror reaches such a pitch that she can hide it no longer and she rushes back to Pierrot. Harlequin follows her and when he sees Pierrot's corpse he is convinced of his bride's infidelity. He forces her to dine before the corpse of the love-stricken Pierrot. Then he leaves, bolting the door fast. In vain Columbine tries to escape from her prison, from the ghastly dead body. Gradually, she succumbs to madness; she whirls in a frenzied dance, then finally drains the deadly cup and falls lifeless beside Pierrot.[47]

The rhythm of the entire production was dictated by the hideous *Kapellmeister* and his sinister band. When the corpses of Pierrot and Columbine were discovered he fled in terror through the auditorium, as though acknowledging his manipulation of the tragedy. Just as in Meyerhold's interpretation of Lermontov's *Masquerade* six years later, when again he devised a sequence of episodes to emphasise the inexorable advance of the tragedy, the luckless victims seemed to have been marked down by some devilish power from which there was no escape. The key to *Columbine's*

26 Sapunov's design for the ball scene of *Columbine's Scarf* (1910)

27 and 28 Sapunov's costume designs for the Kapellmeister and Harlequin in *Columbine's Scarf*

Scarf was its combination of the supernatural and the banal, the terrifying and the ridiculous. Again to quote Shcherbakov:

> The tireless *Kapellmeister* . . . and the master of ceremonies, the ginger-headed hunchback, Gigolo, seemed to be the parodic dual embodiment of the power of Fate itself. The power of the music was fatal, inexorable, but the grim appearance of inevitability was rendered chimerical, crude and almost comical. What drove the dancers was Absurdity itself; its will was fatal yet farcical. Every single pause, every arrest in the movement, was employed by the director to stress the readiness of the guests at any given moment to tear themselves from their places and surrender to the Satanic power of the music. Breathless, they preened themselves, straightening their gaudy red, green, orange, pink and yellow costumes; the ladies rearranged their tall hats and their outlandish coiffures. During these pauses Columbine would materialise, her expression unperturbed and entirely innocent. Then the *Kapellmeister* would again launch himself at the piano and ferociously strike the keys. At Gigolo's imperious gesture, the whole crowd of wedding guests would resume the dance, including even the terrified portly figures of Columbine's

29 Portrait by Boris Grigoriev showing Meyerhold with his double, Doctor Dapertutto (1916)

parents. The wild dance resumed, and at its head, as amicably as if they had never exchanged a cross word, there cavorted the happy couple, Harlequin and Columbine, executing the most improbable *entrechats*.[48]

As we have seen, the obliteration of the conventional division between stage and audience was already established as a Leitmotiv in Meyerhold's work, and never was it more effectively applied than in this production of *Columbine's Scarf* at the Interlude House.

In making great play with objects as an aid to mime (a letter, a rose, a glove, the fatal cup, the flapping white sleeves of the ghost of Pierrot) Meyerhold was paying implicit homage to the *commedia dell'arte* from which the principal characters were drawn. Of similar origin were the devices used to involve the audience more closely in the action: the *Kapellmeister's* flight through the auditorium; the nightmarish polka of the wedding guests weaving amongst the tables; the asides to the audience from the little blackamoor 'proscenium servant' as he offered them drinks.

Much of the impact of the production derived from the inspired designs by Nikolai Sapunov. No artist was closer in spirit to Meyerhold's understanding of the grotesque than Sapunov. First in *The Fairground Booth* and now again in *Columbine's Scarf* they both, as Volkov says, 'knew how to turn a piercing gaze on the surrounding world, and where others remained blind, they saw clearly into the ugliness of everyday life in Russia'.[49] Sapunov's vision of life as treacherous, two-faced and insecure was firmly rooted in a world of tawdry furnishings, assertive bad taste, and small-town claustrophobia; it was unmistakably the world of Gogol.[50] Tragically, the association of Meyerhold and Sapunov came to an untimely end in 1912 when the artist was drowned at the age of thirty-two in a summer boating accident on the Gulf of Finland. Even so, his influence on Meyerhold's work was an enduring one, no less powerful than Mayakovsky's after the Revolution.

While Meyerhold was working on *Columbine's Scarf* he was asked by Telyakovsky to adopt a pseudonym for his private theatrical activities, as they constituted a breach of contract and might cause mutual embarrassment. At the suggestion of the poet and composer, Mikhail Kuzmin, he took the name of 'Doctor Dapertutto', a character from E.T.A. Hoffmann's *Adventure on New Year's Eve*.[51] Dapertutto was a real-life manifestation of the mask, an ubiquitous Doppelgänger who assumed responsibility for all Meyerhold's unofficial experiments for the rest of his time at the Imperial theatres. As Shcherbakov says, it was a particularly appropriate name to choose:

Hoffmann's writing was unusually close to Meyerhold's views at that time – and not only to his. The tragic collision between the spiritual being of the artist and vulgar reality, so repugnant in all its forms to the artist, with its aptitude for transforming elevated thoughts into the reasonable gratification of instincts; the Romantic disjunction between ideas and life, which only the magic of art could resolve, though not without a certain admixture of irony; the insanity of a world directed by ludicrous 'common sense' in which works of genius are transformed into trash at the paws of a libidinous Cat – all these Hoffmannesque ideas and images were reflected in Meyerhold's *Columbine's Scarf*.[52]

The second programme at the Interlude House on 3 December 1910 included a production by Meyerhold of Znosko-Borovsky's new comedy, *The Transfigured Prince* (designs by Sudeikin, music by Kuzmin). Based loosely on the traditional conventions of the Spanish theatre, it was treated by Meyerhold as 'a free composition on the theme of the primitive theatre'. He describes two of the devices used:

> Here are the kind of horses on which the prince and his entourage managed to complete their long journey. The designer gave the horses' necks deep curves and stuck prancing ostrich feathers into their (papier mâché) heads, which were enough to make the clumsy caparisoned frames look like horses lightly prancing and proudly rearing on their hind legs. . .
>
> The youthful prince returns from his journey to learn that his father, the king, has died. The courtiers proclaim the prince king, place a grey wig on his head, and attach a long grey beard to his chin. In full view of the audience the youthful prince is transformed into the venerable old man which a king in the realm of fairy-tales is supposed to be.[53]

Znosko-Borovsky himself describes the battle scene in the production:

> Sudeikin's setting in clashing fiery red and gold gave the spectator an impression of raging blood and fire, which was intensified by terrifying rumblings and explosions backstage. An actor dressed as a warrior crawled from underneath the set – thereby emphasising that the theatre was only simulating a battle and dispelling any illusion of a real battle that the audience might have – and began to give a graphic picture of a violent conflict between two vast armies. As he spoke, shots rang out and bullets and cannonballs flew; eventually he took flight, tumbled down the steps and hid under the first available table. Recovering his breath, he said: 'I should imagine I'll be safer here.' However the continuing gunfire drove him from that refuge as well and finally he fled from the theatre, crying: 'Every man for himself'.[54]

The second programme at the Interlude House proved to be its last, but for Meyerhold the insights gained through his two short-lived productions in that modest little theatre were priceless. He realised the full significance of those aspects of the traditional popular theatre that he had glimpsed already through his productions of *The Fairground Booth* and, to a lesser extent, *The Adoration of the Cross*. Behind the familiar masks and knockabout tricks of the *commedia dell'arte* he discovered a fund of theatrical wisdom and drew on it to create a style that in its essentials remained unaltered for the rest of his creative life. In 1938, while rehearsing the final revival of *Masquerade*, he said:

> People say: 'Meyerhold? He's a lost cause; he's obsessed with the *commedia dell'arte*. Yes, they're right. But if I need to play some part, I always have to look for Brighella or Pantalone in him. Because these theatrical masks are to

be found in every character. They represent a common theatrical tradition. You find them in Shakespeare and everywhere. It's simply a matter of finding them.[55]

VI

On 9 November 1910, a month after the opening of the Interlude House, Meyerhold presented Molière's *Dom Juan* at the Alexandrinsky Theatre in a production that exactly reflected the revivalist mood then prevailing in the Russian theatre. As he himself admitted, his treatment of Molière's comedy contradicted the rules governing the re-creation of the exemplary ages of drama that he had formulated in his criticism of the Ancient Theatre.[56] It was neither an exact reconstruction of the theatre in question nor a new work conceived in the spirit of a former age; instead, like Yevreinov's productions, it was an original text staged as a free composition designed to evoke the atmosphere of the theatre for which it was written. The crucial difference, claimed Meyerhold, was that in *Dom Juan* he avoided any impression of pastiche by preserving only those stylistic features that he considered vital to the spirit of Molière's comedy. In saying this he had one particular feature in mind:

> If we go to the heart of Molière's works – he writes – we find that he
> was trying to remove the footlights from the contemporary stage, since they
> were better suited to the heroic drama of Corneille than to plays with their
> origins in the popular theatre. The academic theatre of the Renaissance failed
> to take advantage of the projecting forestage, keeping actor and audience at a
> mutually respectful distance. Sometimes, the front rows of the orchestra stalls
> were moved right back to the middle of the parterre, sometimes even further.
> How could Molière accept this segregation of actor and public? How could
> his overflowing humour have its proper effect under such conditions? How
> could the whole range of his bold, undisguisedly lifelike characterisation be
> accommodated within such a space? How could the waves of accusatory
> monologue of an author outraged by the banning of *Tartuffe* reach the spectator
> from such a distance? Surely the actor's ability and freedom of gesture were
> hemmed in by the wings? Molière was the first amongst the stage-masters of
> the *Roi Soleil* to attempt to shift the action from the back and centre of the
> stage forward to the very edge of the forestage.[57]

Meyerhold, usually the most scholarly of apologists for his own productions, seems here to have read into accounts of Molière's theatre what he himself wished to find. Despite Molière's long apprenticeship on improvised platform-stages in the provinces and his love of the intimate cut-and-thrust of the popular theatre, there is no evidence that when he became established in Paris he attempted to halt the retreat of the French theatre behind the Italianate proscenium arch and out of the range of the unruly parterre. On the contrary, it seems likely that out of necessity he came to prefer a less intimate relationship with his audience, for at that time it had become the custom for young noblemen to demand seats on the stage itself whence they frequently caused obstruction, bodily as well as vocal, to the performers. Molière voices his distaste for this practice through the person of Eraste (one of his own parts) at the opening of *Les Fâcheux*.[58]

But historically justifiable or not, the forestage was used to telling effect by Meyerhold in his production at the Alexandrinsky. The footlights were removed and the normal stage area was augmented by a deep semicircular apron that extended over the orchestra pit up to the first row of the stalls. The sense of intimacy thus achieved was enhanced by Golovin's permanent setting, which was designed to obliterate the division between stage and auditorium and thus engulf the spectator in all the grandiose splendour of Louis XIV's Versailles. To this end, the front curtain was discarded and the theatre left fully illuminated throughout the performance except at such dramatic moments as the final encounter with the Commander. Valery Bebutov describes the initial impact of the spectacle on the opening night:

> I enter the auditorium long before the start of the performance and stop short, amazed at the spectacle revealed before me. The oval of red velvet loges is joined to the stage in a harmonious ensemble by the huge false proscenium

30 A scene from *Dom Juan* showing the 'proscenium servants', with the prompters' screens and stools for Varlamov's Sganarelle to either side

arch designed for the production. My enraptured gaze is lost in the splendour of the wings, screens, lambrequins and the tapestry curtain in the background which for the present conceals the secrets of Golovin's artistic wonders. The forestage covering the deep orchestra pit makes the spectacle seem like a ship entering the harbour which is the auditorium. Above the forestage hang three big chandeliers with wax candles. . . To either side of the forestage there are big candelabra on pedestals which also bear real candles.[59]

Very few properties were used and no scenery at all in the conventional sense. Behind the false proscenium arch a series of ornate borders decreasing progressively in aperture led back to the tapestry mentioned by Bebutov, placed just beyond the actual proscenium opening. The scene was set by a series of painted flats, revealed when the tapestry was drawn aside.

Some critics, notably Kugel and Benois, objected that Meyerhold and Golovin's *Dom Juan* was mere spectacle for spectacle's sake which blunted the satire of Molière's text.[60] But Meyerhold maintained that his intention was precisely the reverse:

When a director sets about staging *Dom Juan*, his first task is to fill the stage and the auditorium with such a compelling atmosphere that the audience is bound to view the action through the prism of that atmosphere. When one reads Griboedov's *Woe from Wit*, every page seems to reflect some aspect of modern life, and it is this that makes the play so meaningful to the public today. But if Molière's *Dom Juan* is read without any knowledge of the age that shaped the genius of its author, what a dull play it seems! How

31 Two of the 'proscenium servants' from *Dom Juan*

tedious is the exposition of its plot compared with even Byron's *Dom Juan*, to say nothing of Tirso de Molina's *El Burlador de Sevilla*. If one reads Elvira's great speeches in Act One, or Juan's long attack on hypocrisy in Act Five, one soon gets bored. If the spectator is not to get bored too, and if whole passages are not to strike him as simply obscure, it is essential somehow to remind him constantly of the thousands of Lyonnais weavers manufacturing silk for the monstrously teeming court of Louis XIV, the 'Hôtel des Gobelins', the whole town of painters, sculptors, jewellers and carpenters under the supervision of the celebrated Le Brun, all the craftsmen producing Venetian glass and lace, English hosiery, Dutch mercery, German tin and bronze. . .

The more grandiose and colourful the costumes and properties – only remember to keep the design of the stage itself as simple as possible! – the more clearly the *comédien* in Molière stands out in contrast to the stiff formality of Versailles.[61]

One of the most potent means employed by Meyerhold to evoke the required atmosphere was a whole crew of the now-familiar liveried proscenium servants, inspired, as he says, by the '*kurogo*', the black-clad stage-hands of the Japanese theatre. He describes their ubiquitous role in the production:

. . . little blackamoors floating about the stage sprinkling intoxicating perfumes from crystal bottles on to red-hot platinum; little blackamoors darting about the stage picking up a lace handkerchief dropped by Dom Juan, offering a stool to a tired actor; little blackamoors fastening Dom Juan's shoelaces as he argues with Sganarelle; little blackamoors appearing with lanterns for the actors when the stage is plunged into semi-darkness; little blackamoors removing cloaks and rapiers from the stage after Dom Juan's desperate fight with the brigands; little blackamoors crawling under the table at the appearance of the Commander's statue; little blackamoors summoning the public with tinkling silver bells and announcing the intervals (in the absence of a curtain): all these are not merely tricks designed for the delectation of snobs, but serve the central purpose of enveloping the action in a mist redolent of the perfumed, gilded monarchy of Versailles.[62]

It was with good reason that Benois' review of the production was entitled 'Ballet at the Alexandrinka', for *Dom Juan* was a deliberate attempt to re-create a '*comédie-ballet*' of the kind so popular at the court of Versailles. Seemingly oblivious to the intended satirical overtones of the production, Znosko-Borovsky writes:

What most amazed the public and what caused greatest disagreement was the dance rhythm to which all the characters were subordinated. The actors were not actually transformed into dancers, and Sganarelle in the rich interpretation of Varlamov moved as he always did; but the majority of them (particularly Dom Juan, played with superb grace and beauty by Yuriev, one of the most decorative artists in the Russian theatre) assumed an ease, an elegance, a lightness and a melodiousness of gait and movement. It was as though every character was played to the constant accompaniment of Lully's music,* for it

* The actual music for the production was taken from Rameau's *Hippolyte et Aricie* and *Les Indes galantes*.

32 and 33 Golovin's costume designs for Dom Juan and Sganarelle

echoed in the floating cadences of their speech and movements. The spectator
was reminded irresistibly of that happy age when the whole world danced,
when the Sun-King himself opened the festive ballet that concluded the
performance.[63]

The mountainous Sganarelle of Konstantin Varlamov was the one stationary
figure in the entire production; not only did his bulk and a severe heart
condition seriously limit his mobility, but with his incorrigibly bad memory
he was left helpless by the removal of the downstage prompter's box which
the construction of the forestage necessitated. Rather than sacrifice his unique
comic genius, Meyerhold and Golovin devised two ornate prompters' screens
which were placed to either side of the stage. Before the performance, two
bewigged prompters entered bearing large folios and lighted candles and
seated themselves behind apertures in the screens. Varlamov was permitted
to spend most of the play happily ensconced on a stool adjacent to one screen
or the other and the entire *mise-en-scène* was adapted to accommodate him.
Furthermore, he was allowed a freedom to improvise that delighted the
audience and was wholly in keeping with the mood of the production.[64]
Nikolai Khodotov describes his perambulation with Dom Juan around the
forestage:

> Lantern in hand, Varlamov's vast Sganarelle appears on the proscenium
> behind Yuriev's Dom Juan. Raising the lantern to eye-level, he looks for his
> friends in the auditorium; then his gaze halts: 'Ah! Nikolai Platonovich! (the
> well-known lawyer, Karabchevsky) How do you like our play? I don't know

about you, but it suits me fine! By the way, don't forget that you're having
a bite with me on Tuesday, will you, old chap?' He spots the Director in his
box: 'My dear Vladimir Arkadievich, I'll be along at twelve to talk over that
business of mine with you. . . Mind you don't let anyone in before me. . .'
He spots a friend sitting with a young lady: 'Ah! So that's your better half.
You take her out to the theatre, but hide her away from me. . . Tut, tut!
Ivan Ivanovich, you should be ashamed of treating an old man like that!'[65]

Varlamov's lovable Sganarelle drew a warm response from every critic,
but the real point of Dom Juan, played with glacial elegance by the
haughty Yuriev, seems to have been missed by even the most discerning
of them. In reply to Benois' criticism that the production amounted to no
more than 'an elegant fairground show' ('naryadny balagan') Meyerhold said
that this was the greatest compliment that he and Golovin could wish for:
their Dom Juan was indeed inspired by the popular travelling show, 'based
on the apotheosis of the mask, gesture, and movement'.[66] Earlier in the same
article* he explains the implications of the mask:

> If you examine the dog-eared pages of old scenarios such as Flaminio
> Scala's anthology of 1611, you will discover the magical power of the mask.
>   Arlecchino, a native of Bergamo and the servant of the miserly Doctor,
> is forced to wear a coat with multicoloured patches because of his master's
> meanness. Arlecchino is a foolish buffoon, a roguish servant who seems always
> to wear a cheerful grin. But look closer! What is hidden behind the mask?
> Arlecchino, the all-powerful wizard, the enchanter, the magician; Arlecchino,
> the emissary of the infernal powers.
>   The mask may conceal more than just two aspects of a character. The
> two aspects of Arlecchino represent two opposite poles. Between them lies
> an infinite range of shades and variations. How does one reveal this extreme
> diversity of character to the spectator? With the aid of the mask. The actor
> who has mastered the art of gesture and movement (herein lies his power!)
> manipulates his masks in such a way that the spectator is never in any doubt
> as to the character he is watching: whether he is the foolish buffoon from
> Bergamo or the Devil.
>   This chameleonic power, concealed beneath the expressionless visage of
> the comedian, invests the theatre with all the enchantment of chiaroscuro. Is
> it not the mask that helps the spectator fly away to the land of make-believe?
> The mask enables the spectator to see not only the actual Arlecchino before him
> but all the Arlecchinos who live in his memory. Through the mask the spectator
> sees every person who bears the merest resemblance to the character.[67]

What Meyerhold means here is not the traditional half-mask of the commedia
dell'arte (which he never used in his productions), but rather the style of acting
that the mask signifies: the emotional detachment and physical dexterity that
enable the actor to assume the various aspects of his part ('to manipulate his
masks') and at the same time to comment – both implicitly and explicity –
on the actions of himself and his fellow-characters, thereby affording the

* 'Balagan' (1912) – see pp. 124-125 below.

spectator a montage of images, a multi-faceted portrait of every role. It was in such a manner that Meyerhold conceived the figure of Dom Juan:

> For Molière, Dom Juan is no more than a wearer of masks. At one moment we see on his face a mask that embodies all the dissoluteness, unbelief, cynicism and pretensions of a gallant of the court of *Le Roi Soleil*; then we see the mask of the author-accuser; then the nightmarish mask that stifled the author himself, the agonising mask he was forced to wear at court performances and in front of his perfidious wife. Not until the very end does he hand his puppet the mask of *El Burlador de Sevilla*, which he borrowed from the touring Italians.[68]

As we have seen, it was *The Fairground Booth* that revealed to Meyerhold the powerful magic of the mask, but only now through his studies of the *commedia dell'arte* was he able to grasp its full psychological complexity. Yet, although this is made eloquently clear by Meyerhold in his writings, it seems likely that in *Dom Juan* his complex reinterpretation of the central character was obscured by the opulence of the production as a whole, even supposing that Yury Yuriev himself had fully grasped it.[69] Alexander Benois ended his review by asking: 'How is it possible to establish a new order of theatre whilst ignoring human thoughts, human emotions, and human beings in general?'[70] And Sergei Volkonsky lamented: 'Where is the word here, where is the thought, where is the soul, where is man?'[71]

But however justified these criticisms may have been, they do not invalidate what Meyerhold was *attempting* to do in *Dom Juan*: not only is that explained in convincing detail by himself but it is corroborated by all his major productions in later years. *Masquerade*, *The Magnanimous Cuckold*, *The Forest*, *The Warrant*, *The Government Inspector*, *The Queen of Spades*: in each one of these the treatment of character is based on the principle of the mask, as it was first explored in *Dom Juan*. As we shall see, once Meyerhold was in a position to school his own actors, the principle of the mask became a practical reality: a fact convincingly demonstrated by descriptions of the performances of Igor Ilinsky, Erast Garin, and others in the 1920s.

Even if the full complexity of Meyerhold's conception never fully emerged, *Dom Juan* enjoyed an immediate and vast popular success. The first of a series of 'festive spectacles' mounted by himself and Golovin, it was performed many times, and after the Revolution was revived first in 1922 and then again ten years later.

A Double Life

Following the success of *Tristan and Isolde* in 1909 Meyerhold was entrusted with a production at the Mariinsky Opera in each of the three succeeding seasons. The first, *Boris Godunov*, is noteworthy mainly because it was the one occasion on which Meyerhold worked with Fyodor Chaliapin, who appeared as Boris in the first two performances that season. The settings and costumes were those which Golovin had designed for Alexander Sanin's hugely successful production during Diaghilev's 1908 Russian season in Paris.*

With much of his time taken up until December by his work on *Dom Juan* and *The Transfigured Prince*, Meyerhold was able to devote barely a month to the rehearsals of *Boris Godunov*. The first night fixed for 6 January 1911 was immovable, since that was the date when Tsar Nicholas II and the royal household were expected to attend. Consequently, Meyerhold could undertake no more than a revision of Sanin's production, although his treatment of the crowd scenes was markedly different. In an interview with the St Petersburg *Stock Exchange Gazette* he said:

> In his production of *Boris Godunov* Sanin treated the crowd as individuals, employing an analytical method. I have divided the crowd not into individuals but into groups. Take, for example, the blind pilgrims with their guides –
> they are a single group and the audience should immediately perceive them as such. . . Take the crowd of Boyars: why should they be depicted as distinct from each other when in fact they were a unified sycophantic group? No sooner did someone elevate himself above that crowd than unfailingly he became Tsar. Vassily Shuisky and Godunov were individuals of rare character.[1]

As Glikman observes, whatever the historical justification for Meyerhold's argument, it also coincided with the artistic principle that he had pursued ever since his rejection of the Meiningen influence on the Moscow Art

---

* Two scenes were restored that had been omitted from the Paris production, together with a new design for the Fountain scene in Act Three, which previously had been executed by Benois.

Theatre, which of course he himself had followed in his early days in the provinces. In his handling of the ensemble scenes in *Boris Godunov*, he applied the principle that he had evolved in such productions as *Sister Beatrice*, *Death's Victory* and, most recently, *Tristan and Isolde*.[2] When the Danish writer Hermann Bang saw the production the following winter he said to an interviewer: 'A work of genius. I was particularly struck by your crowd. It's strange: it barely moves yet at the same time it is so alive.'[3] Local critics were much less impressed. In the forty years since its original composition Mussorgsky's opera had acquired the status of a national epic which a 'modernist' such as Meyerhold approached at his peril. True to his paper's rabid chauvinist line, Suvorin wrote in *New Times*: 'Whilst I consider Mr Meyerhold to be a man of talent, I consider that he should not have been entrusted with so complex a Russian work as *Boris Godunov*. In order to produce it one needs to possess a Russian soul to sense instinctively so much that is so very important.'[4]

Suvorin's colleague, the notorious Menshikov, was even more direct. Referring to the depiction of the tsarist gendarmerie controlling the mob with whips, he wrote: 'I think Mr Meyerhold found these gendarmes in his Jewish soul and not in Pushkin, whose (*Boris Godunov*) contains neither gendarmes nor knouts.'[5]

Given the time at his disposal and Chaliapin's position of absolute dominance in Russian opera, Meyerhold was in no position to do other than accommodate his unique portrayal of Boris. This he did, even to

34 Play-bill for *Boris Godunov*, directed by Meyerhold with Chaliapin in the title role

35 Golovin's set design for Act One of *Boris Godunov*, 1911

the extent of personally removing an offending railing from the set when Chaliapin appeared for the first time at the public dress rehearsal, thereby placating him and averting a major scandal which could have jeopardised the whole production. The overall effect, according to Bebutov, was 'a stately guest appearance by Chaliapin, who towered like a monument above its bas-relief pedestal.'⁶ Fourteen months earlier in his lecture on *Tristan and Isolde* Meyerhold had cited Chaliapin as the very model of 'theatrical truth' . . . 'the slightly embellished truth of an art that is always elevated above life itself'.⁷ No record survives of Chaliapin's thoughts on the production, but certainly the relationship between the two men remained distant. In the context of Meyerhold's artistic development *Boris Godunov* must be seen as an opportunity lost, all the more tantalising given the unique regard he had for Chaliapin's genius.

By contrast, Gluck's *Orpheus and Eurydice* staged at the Mariinsky the following December was the most completely realised as well as the most widely acclaimed of all Meyerhold's operatic work. First performed in 1762 in Vienna, *Orpheus* was the first of Gluck's so-called 'reform operas' aimed at exposing the absurdities of the *opera seria* or 'concerts in costume' of the Neapolitan school and at restoring opera to the dramatic heights first attained by Monteverdi. With this in mind, Meyerhold set out to stage *Orpheus* not as the conventional sequence of arias and ballet interludes but as total drama in the manner of his *Tristan* two years earlier.

It seems to have been Golovin who as early as 1908 first conceived the production, and he may well have been prompted by Isadora Duncan who visited St Petersburg in 1904 and performed her dance interpretation of Orpheus to Gluck's music.⁸ In the face of opposition from Eduard Nápravník, Meyerhold and Golovin insisted that the part of Orpheus should be sung in the 1774 Paris version for tenor, which Gluck had transposed from contralto castrato, rather than in the 1859 revision by Berlioz for contralto.

Working in close collaboration and faced with a highly complex *mise-en-scène*, Meyerhold and Golovin enlisted the aid of Mikhail Fokine as choreographer. Six years younger than Meyerhold, Fokine had already established himself as the foremost innovator in modern ballet with his choreography for *Carnival*,* *Les Sylphides*, *The Firebird*, *Petrushka*, and other works performed during Diaghilev's Russian seasons.

This time Golovin's settings incorporated a richly embroidered pink, orange, gold and silver front curtain and gauze act-drops to facilitate uninterrupted scene changes. Otherwise, the production bore a distinct external resemblance to *Dom Juan* at the Alexandrinsky: the forestage was covered with an ornamental carpet, the proscenium opening was reduced in size by using decorative borders, exquisite painted backdrops located the scenes, the blue and white auditorium was illuminated throughout by

---

* His first association with Meyerhold (see footnote on p. 65 above).

means of specially designed blue lanterns, and the costumes were conceived in the style of antiquity as an artist in Gluck's time might have seen it – that is, like *Dom Juan*, 'the work was viewed, so to speak, through the prism of the age in which the author lived and worked',[9] with no attempt made to create an illusion of classical antiquity or to reconstruct in precise detail a production by Gluck himself. In fact, the critics variously identified the inspiration of Poussin's pastoral landscapes (the opening scene at Eurydice's tomb), Gustave Doré's illustrations for Dante's *Divina Commedia* (Orpheus

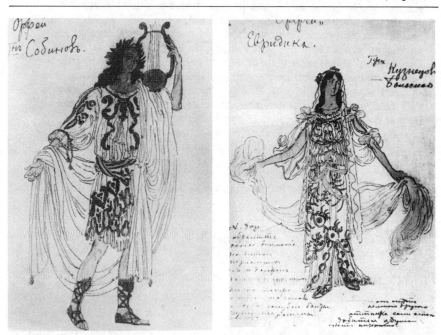

36 and 37 Golovin's costume designs for Orpheus and Eurydice

at the threshold of Hades), Botticelli's *La Primavera* (the Elysian Fields), and only Watteau from the eighteenth century. Golovin himself was happy to acknowledge such wide-ranging eclecticism, content that the success of his designs lay in the completeness of the synthesis and in their power to evoke complex associations in the mind of the spectator.[10]

The production made exceptional demands of the Mariinsky stage-crew. As Boris Almedingen, one of Golovin's design assistants recalls:

> It might seem improbable to modern theatre designers that the 'simple change' entailed by the transformation from 'Hades' to 'Elysium', which takes two minutes of music in *Orpheus*, proved such an extremely difficult task. In that time we had to strike four-metre high stepped rostra, close the traps and cover the entire stage area with a cloth, and set between ten

and fifteen cut-out bushes – all this while downstage a cloud-painted gauze roll-cloth was suspended, obscuring light from the stage. Nevertheless, after numerous rehearsals this 'simple change' was mastered and in performance was carried out perfectly smoothly.[11]

One outstanding feature that Meyerhold retained from the settings for *Tristan and Isolde* was the 'relief stage'. He describes its use in *Orpheus*:

Technically speaking, the stage was divided into two planes, the forestage, which remained devoid of painted scenery and was decorated exclusively with embroidered hangings; and the main stage, which was given over entirely to painted sets. Particular attention was paid to the so-called 'planes of action': practicable rostra deployed in such a way as to dictate the groupings and movements of the characters. For example, in Scene Two the descent of Orpheus into Hades takes place on a path descending steeply across the stage from a considerable height with two sheer cliffs falling away to either side and downstage of it. This arrangement of the places of action ensures that the figure of Orpheus dominates the chorus of Furies and does not become confused with them. With these cliffs on either side of the stage, the only possibility is to have the chorus and the corps de ballet in two groups straining upwards from the wings towards Orpheus. In this way, the scene at the threshold of Hades is not chopped up into a number of episodes but becomes a synthesis of two directly opposed movements: Orpheus descending, and the Furies first meeting him menacingly, then retreating before him.[12]

38 Sketch by Golovin for the opening scene of *Orpheus and Eurydice*

In scenes such as this, Golovin's settings became more than mere back-drops. There was absolute continuity between the painted setting, the lines of the three-dimensional practicable rostra and the precisely choreographed movements of the living figures. Thus, Golovin's sketches were not mere artist's impressions, but specific indications of the colour and rhythm of the eventual scene. This is nowhere more apparent than in his sketch of Scene One at the tomb of Eurydice where the very sky and trees seem to be sharing the grief of the mourners.[13] In the words of Yelena Katulskaya, who sang Amor:

> In the first scene of the opera the setting represented an overgrown clearing framed by dense trees. It was dominated by a huge tomb in which Eurydice was laid to rest. Surrounding the tomb were maidens in mournful poses, grouped picturesquely in the manner of Greek sculpture. The lighting, suggestive of dusk, created a mood of deep peace mingled with grief. Near the tomb stood the bowed figure of Orpheus. The opening chords from the orchestra and chorus stirred the depths of the soul with the austere beauty of the melody and the richness of the harmony. I can hardly recall a production that compares with the Mariinsky's *Orpheus* for the organic blending of all its elements: music, drama, painting, sculpture and the wonderful singing of Sobinov (as Orpheus).[14]

Leonid Sobinov's performance totally justified Meyerhold and Golovin's insistence on the tenor version of the score. In her memoirs the ballerina Vera Koralli writes:

> Sobinov's Orpheus was a truly remarkable incarnation of the mythical singer. He presented a wonderful appearance. His make-up was most restrained: the classical profile, the matt white of the face; on his light golden hair, seemingly fashioned by the chisel of some Ancient Greek sculptor, there glistened a laurel wreath of dark gold leaves. In Act One Orpheus appeared amongst the rocks near the tomb, clad in a dark tunic with a lyre in his hands, and in the seemingly chill silence gave voice to that aria of extraordinary emotional depth. In Sobinov's singing there was something unearthly: light and clear, yet imbued with inescapable mortal suffering and grief.[15]

The size of the chorus and corps de ballet, the complex rhythmical patterns dictated by the plot, and the use of practicable settings together created problems of choreography beyond the scope of any dramatic stage-director, even one with Meyerhold's appreciation of the role of movement in the theatre. For this reason Fokine's contribution was vital to the success of the production. Treating the chorus and corps de ballet (together some two hundred strong) as a single homogeneous mass, he created effects no less spectacular than those he had achieved with Golovin in Stravinsky's *Firebird* for Diaghilev a year earlier. Here is his description of the scene in Hades:

> . . . when the curtain rose the entire stage was covered with motionless bodies. Groups in the most unnatural poses, as though frozen in mid-convulsion, clung to the lofty cliffs and hung suspended over the abyss (open traps in the stage

floor) wracked by the ghastly torments of hell. As the chorus sang 'He who
strays here, knowing no fear. . .', the entire mass made a single slow movement,
one awful concerted gesture. It was as though some monster of unimaginable
size had been disturbed and was ominously raising itself up. A single gesture
that lasted for the duration of the chorus' long phrase. Then after freezing
for a few minutes in a new pose, the mass began slowly to curl up and then
to crawl about the stage. All those who represented the Shades – the whole
corps de ballet, the whole chorus of male and female voices, all the students
of the theatre school, plus hundreds of extras – were all crawling, changing
places. Some climbed from the traps up onto the cliffs, others slid into the
traps. The mass of performers was crawling all over the stage. They were all
exhausted from finding no place to rest.[16]

This scene and the descent into Hades described by Meyerhold illustrate
the extent to which all the elements of the production were synthesised and
subordinated to the rhythm of the musical score. In Fokine's demanding
scheme the chorus was spared as little as the corps de ballet. Fundamentally,
the conception was the same as that of *Tristan and Isolde*, the one difference
being that Fokine frequently moved the chorus in *Orpheus and Eurydice* in
counterpoint to the orchestra rather than in strict unison as Meyerhold
had done in *Tristan*. But in both cases it was the music rather than
any consideration of 'realism' or operatic convention that dictated every
movement and gesture. Fokine was anxious to extend the balletic principle to
the principals in the opera, choreographing Eurydice's movements in Scene

39 The closing scene of *Orpheus and Eurydice*

Three when she was reunited with Orpheus. However, Meyerhold opposed this, preferring the static sculptural method that he had employed in *Tristan*. Of the two sopranos who shared the role of Eurydice, one followed Fokine's instructions whilst the other remained true to Meyerhold. The critics were in no doubt as to their preference: 'Conceiving Eurydice in plastic terms, Bolska does not dance the part as other prima donnas do. She simply adopts a series of the most refined poses, but is that not enough in itself?'[17]

With the predictable exception of Alexander Benois, the critical response was wholly enthusiastic, and as Victor Kolomiitsev wrote in *The Studio* the following January, 'Such was the opening night of *Orpheus* that it was hailed as a great success even by the fashionably turned-out gala audience, and it has provoked more discussion than any other artistic event in the current season in St Petersburg.'[18] Telyakovsky, Director of the Imperial Theatres, noted with satisfaction in his diary: 'The Empress Maria Fyodorovna and almost the entire Royal family were present in the Royal box. They were all very pleased with the opera and with its production and performance. The Grand Duchess Maria Pavlovna lavished praise on every detail.' As Rudnitsky laconically observes, 'Meyerhold's stock was evidently rising.'[19]

However, the collaboration between Meyerhold and Fokine was far from harmonious: Fokine complained that Meyerhold belittled his contribution, and years later in his memoirs went so far as to claim that with the exception of a few scenes involving only the principal characters he staged the entire opera.[20] Fokine's claim seems extravagant: first, the original conception of the production and the plan to use the relief settings that dictated the whole pattern of the choreography belonged to Meyerhold and Golovin; secondly, the crucial factor in a work of such complexity is the co-ordinating of every element to produce a coherent whole – and this was indisputably Meyerhold's achievement. At the same time, though, it is significant that apart from their disagreement over the interpretation of Eurydice, Meyerhold and Fokine's differences in no way concerned the actual approach to the choreography in *Orpheus*: on this they were in complete accord, which indicates the affinity between what Meyerhold and the ballet-masters and stage-designers of Diaghilev's company were pursuing through their respective media at that time.

On 18 February 1913 Meyerhold staged Richard Strauss's *Elektra* at Mariinsky, the first opera by the German composer to be performed in Russia. As Gozenpud suggests, the choice of *Elektra* may well have been due to the growing reputation at the Mariinsky of Albert Coates, the young conductor of mixed English and Russian parentage who had returned to his native St Petersburg in 1910 after working for three years at the Dresden Opera where *Elektra* had received its première in 1909. Coates had collaborated with Meyerhold on *Boris Godunov* and was the obvious choice to conduct Strauss, a composer whom Nápravník and most of the Petersburg old guard dismissed as an incomprehensible modernist, with even the normally tolerant Glazunov complaining that *Elektra* reminded him of nothing so much as 'a poultry yard'.[21] But Meyerhold was not daunted, seeing Strauss as the natural successor to Wagner and being already familiar with von Hofmannsthal's reworking of the House of Atreus legend, which he had staged in its original dramatic version in Vitebsk in 1908.[22] Such are the demands of this one-act opera and such was the care that they devoted to it, that Meyerhold required no fewer than sixty full rehearsals whilst Coates brought the total up to an unprecedented one hundred and fifty.

The approach to the work adopted by Meyerhold and Golovin was in complete contrast to their previous productions: three years earlier during a study visit to Greece Meyerhold had visited the legendary palace and tombs of the House of Atreus at Mycenae; inspired by the memory of this and by the Minoan treasures recently excavated by Sir Arthur Evans in Crete, he resolved with Golovin 'not to modernise but to "archaise" the production'. Elaborating this concept in a newspaper interview a week before the opening, Meyerhold said: 'von Hofmannsthal has modernised the plot of *Elektra* by archaising it, but true to Strauss' music we are archaising it even more, "antiquitising" it, taking our inspiration from the colours and lines of the Minoan culture of the sixteenth to fourteenth centuries BC.'[23] Meyerhold and Golovin worked in close collaboration with Professor Bogaevsky, a Russian archaeologist who had worked with Evans. To quote Bogaevsky, they '. . . attempted as far as possible to convey the environment of the

40 and 41 Golovin's Costume designs for Clytemnestra and Elektra, executed by his assistant, Zandin, 1912

period in question whilst avoiding the appearance of a museum or indulging in excessive pedantry.'[24] Even the performers' movements were derived from poses depicted on Minoan relics, with particular attention paid to the expressive hand movements or '*chironomia*' of the ancient theatre.

In its spatial conception, the setting recalled Meyerhold's 1907 production of *Death's Victory*. On the elevated main stage, against a dark threatening sky shot through with yellow, stood Agamemnon's palace 'decorated with motifs typical of Aegean culture', with a broad flight of stone steps descending to the footlights. According to Golovin, 'The setting transported the spectator's imagination back to an historically accurate antiquity.'[25] At the same time, Meyerhold noted with satisfaction that the costumes, executed predominantly in tones of terra cotta and deep violet-blue, '. . . resembled in their cut the recent fashion for flared skirts, so that there is an astonishing correspondence between the stage picture and von Hofmannsthal's modernised text. By some miracle, the remote past and the present are drawn together . . .'[26] By no means all observers were so convinced; after the first dress rehearsal Telyakovsky noted in his diary: 'Golovin's designs are splendidly executed and very interesting, based on the recent excavations in Crete. Meyerhold's production is interesting too, but in places *style moderne* creeps in, which I pointed out to him afterwards. Some of the singers' movements are most comical.'[27] Many years later, Meyerhold himself admitted: 'Golovin and I made a mistake with *Elektra*. We got carried away by its design and paid insufficient attention to the music. We surrendered to archaeology, which became an end in itself. It was a mistake I never repeated.'[28]

His interpretation failed to take account of the demands of Strauss's savagely atonal score, which is far closer in spirit to the morbid visions of the German Expressionist painters than to the formalised tableaux on the frescoes and ceramics of Mycenae and Knossos. The critics were quick to seize on this contradiction; for instance, Vyacheslav Karatygin wrote:

> In itself most interesting and ingenious, the production . . . consistently evoked the spirit of the Mycenaean age and transported the spectator's imagination back to an historically authentic antiquity. But should this have been attempted? Whilst the stage spoke of archaeology, the orchestra emitted howls, cries and groans, giving voice to the writhing, tormented soul of the neurasthenic composer – an impressionist of the very latest mode! The contrast was most striking![29]

Ignoring Meyerhold's own admission of failure, Isaac Glikman has recently argued at length that the critics, both at the time and subsequently, have misread his intentions in *Elektra*. In particular, he makes the point that there was no inconsistency between the measured stylised movements of the performers and Strauss's frenetic score, citing the composer's own enthusiastic response to the production which he saw in rehearsal while on a concert tour to St Petersburg in January 1913. Rightly, Glikman draws a

comparison with Meyerhold's *Tristan and Isolde*, in which the music was left
to express the characters' deepest emotions while the singers' movements
and gestures were kept to a minimum.[30] Nevertheless, the view of even the
best disposed critics was that in *Elektra* the visual aspects of the production
distracted from the opera's deeper meaning. In the interpretation of Elektra
herself, Koptyaev missed the disturbing psychopathological aspect:

> The world concealed beneath the libretto may seem repellent. Elektra is
> without doubt an hysteric, which explains her fascination with the crime and
> her hymns in its praise. Her death following her terrible attack of insanity is
> fully comprehensible . . . but the channelling of all her feminine impulses into
> her desire for revenge (the very reason for regarding her as an hysteric) was not
> conveyed by Yermolenko-Yuzhina. Her ritual dance needed to be performed
> more vividly. Altogether, despite the singer's fine and powerful soprano voice,
> one never experienced the tense passion of Elektra.[31]

Elektra provoked at least as much discussion as *Orpheus and Eurydice*, but
after a stormy first night that split the audience down the middle, attendances
were poor and the opera was taken off after the third performance. Partly,
this may have been due to the failure of the public and most of the critics to
comprehend Strauss's music (even Blok dismissed it out of hand as 'worthless
ballyhoo').[32] But what finally sealed the production's fate was the reaction of
the conservative press, which pronounced that it was 'absolutely impermissible at the time of the three-hundredth anniversary of the Romanov
dynasty to put on an opera in which members of a royal house are be-
headed.'[33] In a letter to *New Times* signed by 'A Russian', 'the powers
that be' were urged to remind Telyakovsky 'to become a little more
Russian, to forget his Polish ancestry and to cease mocking the patriotic
sentiments of the poor artists and patrons of the Mariinsky Theatre.'[34]

As Rudnitsky rightly stresses, such productions as *Orpheus*, *Elektra*,
and D'Annunzio's *La Pisanelle** demonstrated Meyerhold's surrender to
the general mood of escapism that overtook St Petersburg in the last
pre-revolutionary decade. It was an escapism that took many forms: the
exotic, the archaic, the mystical, the supernatural, even the coyly pornographic. Its predominant decorative mode was art nouveau, or '*style moderne*'
as it was termed in Russia. In the theatre it embraced the Ancient Theatre,
the revival of *commedia dell'arte*, the early work of Tairov at the Kamerny
Theatre in Moscow, the numerous ornate productions of Molière – and
pre-eminently the dazzling Paris seasons of Diaghilev. So dominant was it,
that it completely overshadowed psychological realism, even at the Moscow
Art Theatre itself. Nor did it encounter much resistance, save the occasional
skirmish like *Columbine's Scarf* or the two isolated forays into the theatre by
the Futurists, Mayakovsky's tragedy *Vladimir Mayakovsky* and Matyushin
and Kruchenykh's opera *Victory over the Sun*, presented back-to-back in St

* In Paris, June 1913 (see p. 126 below).

Petersburg in December 1913.* Overwhelmingly, it was a period of rarefied taste, aesthetic extravagance and social disengagement. There is no denying that much of Meyerhold's work in St Petersburg served only to further such tendencies.

II

Despite his dual role as a director of drama and opera at the Imperial Theatres, Meyerhold continued to make time both for the activities of his alter ego, Doctor Dapertutto, and for further critical and theoretical writing. Immediately following an unsuccessful Moscow season in the summer of 1911 the Interlude House disbanded, but Meyerhold and the young director and theatre critic, Vladimir Solovyov, assembled a small group of actors, many of whom had worked with Meyerhold before, to pursue their interest in the *commedia dell'arte* and in pantomime in general. Over the next year they gave occasional performances in public halls, private houses, and in the summer at the seaside resort of Terijoki just over the Finnish border. The most frequently performed item was a one-act harlequinade devised by

42 Meyerhold at his company's dacha in Terijoki, 1912

* See p. 157 below.

Solovyov himself and called *Harlequin, the Marriage Broker*.* It is described here by Meyerhold:

> This Harlequinade, written with the specific aim of reviving the theatre of masks, was staged according to traditional principles and based on our studies of the scenarios of the *commedia dell'arte*. Rehearsals were conducted jointly by the author and the director; the author, in accordance with his aim of reviving the traditional theatre, would outline the *mise-en-scène*, moves, poses and gestures as he had found them described in the scenarios of improvised comedies; the director would add new tricks in the style of these traditional devices, blending the traditional with the new to produce a coherent whole. The Harlequinade was written in the form of a pantomime because, more than any dramatic form, the pantomime is conducive to the revival of the art of improvisation. In the pantomime the actor is given the general outline of the plot and in the intervals between the various key moments he is free to act *ex improviso*. However, the actor's freedom is only relative, because he is subject to the discipline of the musical score. The actor in a Harlequinade needs to possess an acute sense of rhythm, plus great agility and self-control. He must develop the equilibrist skills of an acrobat, because only an acrobat can master the problems posed by the grotesque style inherent in the fundamental conception of the Harlequinade.
>
> Instead of conventional sets there are two decorated screens, placed some distance apart to represent the houses of Pantalone and the Dottore (standing on stools, they appear above these screens and motion to one another in a mimed discussion of the Dottore's marriage to Aurelia). The stage groupings are invariably symmetrical and the actors' movements acrobatic. All the jokes (whether prescribed or improvised) conform to the style of a traditional buffonade: striking one's rival across the face with a glove; a character transformed into a magician with the aid of the traditional pointed cap and false beard; one character carrying off another pick-a-back; fights, blows with clubs, cutting off noses with wooden swords; actors jumping into the auditorium; dances, acrobatic numbers, Harlequin somersaulting; thumbing of noses from the wings; leaps and kisses; the final curtain with the actors forming up in a line and bowing comically to the audience; masks; shouts and whistles at the final exit; the introduction of short spoken phrases at moments of dramatic tension.[35]

June 1912 saw the creation of a new Fellowship of Actors, Writers, Musicians, and Artists at Terijoki. Meyerhold agreed to become artistic director, and with his family joined the young company who lived communally in a large seaside dacha with extensive grounds. Occasional performances were given at the Casino Theatre (in reality a wooden barn with a sand floor), the modest production budget being met largely by Blok's wife, Lyubov Dmitrievna, who also acted with the company. In addition to new productions of *The Adoration of the Cross* and *Harlequin, the Marriage Broker*, the repertoire included comic interludes by Cervantes, Shaw's *You Never Can Tell*, and at Blok's recommendation, Strindberg's *There are Crimes and*

---

* First performed at the Assembly Hall of the Nobility, Petersburg, 8 November 1911.

43 Valentina Verigina as Henriette in *There are Crimes and Crimes*, 1912

Crimes. This highly successful potboiler, which Strindberg had written in 1899, was presented on 14 July in memory of the dramatist who had died in Stockholm two months earlier. In fact, the production, staged within a black frame, served as a double memorial since it was a month to the day that Nikolai Sapunov had drowned in the Gulf of Finland.

In Strindberg's 'serious comedy' the part of the sculptress, Henriette, was played by Valentina Verigina, with Lyubov Blok as Jeanne. In her memoirs Verigina gives a detailed account of the summer in Terijoki, including a description of *There are Crimes and Crimes*. She tells how once again Meyerhold employed a deep forestage, though on this occasion much of the action was played upstage with the actors in silhouette against back-lit cut-out settings. They advanced onto the dimly lit forestage only when the action dictated their detachment from the other characters. But mostly, it was a question of drawing the spectator into the world of the play: a rare instance of Meyerhold focusing the audience's emotional attention in a manner akin to Stanislavsky. However, the use of measured pauses, stretches of calculated silence and telling poses was maintained. Consistent with Meyerhold's growing fascination with the *commedia dell'arte*, much play was made with significant objects – a yellow glove, a glass of champagne, a bunch of long-stemmed roses.[36]

The relaxed atmosphere of Terijoki enabled Meyerhold to complete his essay 'The Fairground Booth' (*Balagan*) which was published together with his other theatrical writings under the collective title *On the Theatre* in 1913. Apart from the article 'On the History and Technique of the Theatre' and those on the productions of *Tristan and Isolde* and *Dom Juan*, 'The Fairground Booth' forms the major part of *On the Theatre*. It is an erudite disquisition on the theatrical traditions that Meyerhold had been exploring since he left Komissarzhevskaya: the theatre of the grotesque, the theatre of the *cabotin*, the theatre of mime, the theatre of the juggler and the acrobat, the theatre of improvisation, the theatre of the *mask*.* He begins by quoting a recent article by Benois which hailed the Moscow Art Theatre's adaptation of *The Brothers Karamazov* (first staged in October 1910) as a revival of the tradition of the mystery-play and which saw in it the means of arresting the decline in the theatre that had been brought about by 'the deception and *cabotinage*' of such theatres and directors as the Comédie Française, Max Reinhardt, and Meyerhold.[37] But, argued Meyerhold, the reverse was the case:

> . . . it is the 'mystery' (in Benois' sense) that is ruining the theatre, and
> *cabotinage* that can bring about its revival. In order to rescue the Russian
> theatre from its own desire to become the servant of literature, we must spare
> nothing to restore to the stage the cult of *cabotinage* in its broadest sense. . .
>
> In the contemporary theatre the comedian has been replaced by the 'educated
> reader'. 'The play will be read in costume and make-up' might as well be the
> announcement on playbills today. The new actor manages without the mask
> and the technique of the juggler. The mask has been replaced by make-up that
> facilitates the exact representation of every feature of the face as it is observed in
> real life. The actor has no need of the juggler's art, because he no longer 'plays'
> but simply 'lives' on the stage. 'Play-acting', that magic word of the theatre,
> means nothing to him, because as an imitator he is incapable of rising to the
> level of improvisation, which depends on infinite combinations and variations
> of all the tricks at the actor's command.
>
> The cult of *cabotinage*, which I am sure will reappear with the restoration
> of the theatre of the past, will help the modern actor to rediscover the basic
> laws of theatricality. Those who are restoring the old theatre by delving into
> long-forgotten theories of dramatic art, old theatrical records and iconography,
> are already forcing actors to believe in the power and the importance of the art
> of acting.
>
> In the same way as the stylistic novelist resurrects the past by embellishing
> the works of ancient chroniclers with his own imagination, the actor is able to
> re-create the technique of forgotten comedians by consulting material collected
> by scholars. Overjoyed at the simplicity, the refined grace, the extreme artistry

---

* For earlier references to this article see pp. 67-68, 108 above.

of the old yet eternally new trick of the histrions, mimi, atellanae, scurrae, jaculatores and ministrelli, the actor of the future should or, if he wishes to remain an actor, *must* co-ordinate his emotional responses with his technique, subjecting both to the traditional precepts of the old theatre.

Meyerhold called upon the dramatist to assist the actor in the renaissance of the theatre of improvisation by composing scenarios after the manner of the *fiabe* that Carlo Gozzi wrote for Sacchi's troupe during the eighteenth-century revival of the *commedia dell'arte* in Venice. This is a point of profound significance: Meyerhold had always insisted on the right of the director and the actor to interpret the written text as they saw fit; now he demanded that the author merely provide the actor with material on which to base his improvisations. For, he argued, 'drama in reading is primarily dialogue, argument and taut dialectic. Drama on the stage is primarily action, a taut struggle. The words are, so to speak, the mere overtones of the action. They should burst spontaneously from the actor gripped in the elemental movement of the dramatic struggle.'[38]

But while the actor is gripped in the dramatic struggle, continued Meyerhold, he remains in full control of his actions by virtue of the physical dexterity and self-control that he has inherited from the *cabotin*; at the tensest moments of the drama he continues to 'manipulate his masks', thereby conveying without ambiguity the most subtle shades of irony and the most complex patterns of emotions.* From this point Meyerhold proceeded to a discussion of the grotesque, not only as a stylistic approach but as the expression of a comprehensive view of existence. We have already seen in the accounts of *The Fairground Booth* and *Columbine's Scarf* the significance that Meyerhold attached to the grotesque. Now he saw that the dexterity and flexibility available to the actor through improvisation and all the varied skills of popular theatre contained the power to break the deadly grip of institutionalised drama.

In writing 'The Fairground Booth' Meyerhold undoubtedly took pleasure in flaunting his recondite erudition under Alexander Benois' sophisticated nose. Similarly, in his practical research with Solovyov he was probably motivated by a kind of archaeological zeal which paid little heed to the relevance of *commedia* for a modern audience. Then again, with his inveterate capacity for self-dramatisation, he must have enjoyed casting himself in the role of a latter-day Gozzi charged with the mission of routing the Goldonis of the established stage. All this said, the fact remains that the theatre that Meyerhold presented to a truly wide audience from 1920 onwards had its stylistic origins in the seemingly recherché experiments initiated with Vladimir Solovyov and their group of young actors some ten years earlier.

---

* Compare the discussion of *Dom Juan* on pp. 108-109 above.

III

In March 1913, shortly after the première of *Elektra* at the Mariinsky, Meyerhold went to Paris to work abroad for the first and only time in his career. He had accepted the invitation of the wealthy Russian actress, Ida Rubinstein, to direct her in *La Pisanelle, ou la mort parfumée*, a verse drama of some absurdity by Gabriele d'Annunzio devised especially to show off her talents. Lavishly staged at the huge Théâtre du Châtelet with settings by Bakst, choreography by Fokine, music by Pizzetti (under the pseudonym 'Ildebrando di Parma'), and a cast of almost two hundred dancers and actors, the production opened on 29 May and drew attendances surpassed only - as Meyerhold proudly noted – by those at the Grand Opera.[39] Even André Antoine, the celebrated pioneer of stage naturalism, came twice. However, apart from affording Meyerhold valuable experience in the handling of large-scale crowd scenes, *La Pisanelle* marked no particular advance in his technique. Like *Elektra*, it was a lavish indulgence of the exotic and the spectacular. Meyerhold's letters to his wife suggest that he was pleased enough with the production,[40] but many critics were uneasy. Lunacharsky concluded his review in *Theatre and Art*: 'I left *La Pisanelle* not only exhausted by the frantic whirl of colour, but also with a disagreeable sense of extravagance of every kind which turned the head but left the mind undernourished, and which infected the heart with a sense of aesthetic protest against a spectacle that somehow put one in mind of certain kinds of fun-fair.'[41]

Meyerhold's alliance with his fellow collaborators was uneasy (particularly with Ida Rubinstein, whom he considered 'weak-willed, unprincipled, and prepared to betray true art'), and although he personally gained the respect of many prominent artists, men of the theatre and writers (notably Guillaume Apollinaire) it was seventeen years before his work was seen in Paris again.[42]

In September 1913 Meyerhold achieved a long-cherished ambition when he opened his own permanent theatre-studio at 18 Troitskaya Street in St Petersburg. It functioned throughout the theatre season on four days a week from 4 to 7 p.m. Students were charged a small fee which did no more than cover running costs, the staff being unpaid. Many had no previous acting experience and those who attended included university students, theatre scholars, architects, artists, musicians and critics. Entry was conditional only upon a simple mimed improvisation exercise presented after the first month, though some known previously to Meyerhold were admitted automatically. The complement of students soon grew to over a hundred, but this was limited by a process of self-elimination which depended largely on whether or not the individual succeeded in stirring Meyerhold's interest.

Those who didn't were likely to receive little attention and soon gave up attending. Meyerhold was by nature friendly towards young people, but so absorbed was he in his own theatrical explorations that he acknowledged little responsibility towards all those who paid to receive instruction. In fact, its formal curriculum notwithstanding, the Studio functioned not so much as a drama school but more as a laboratory for collective experiment in which Meyerhold was engaged in a learning process alongside his students.

Soon, a core group of about a dozen favoured students emerged, growing later to twenty.[43] Alongside them, there was a senior group of similar size, the 'acting class' which comprised some of the younger actors from the Alexandrinsky company and others who had worked previously with Meyerhold. In this group Blok's wife, Lyubov, seems in the first year to have had the status of a kind of 'head girl'. Eventually, there was a further division into a Grotesque group, a *Commedia* group and an Eighteenth-century group, each made up of both senior and junior students. A leading member of the Eighteenth-century group was the future director, Sergei Radlov, who was undoubtedly influenced by his experience at Meyerhold's Studio when he founded the Theatre of Popular Comedy in Petrograd in 1920.

In September 1914 the Studio moved to 6 Borodin Street where it functioned in a small concert hall belonging to the St Petersburg Municipal Transport Engineers. The hall was equipped with a small stage linked by steps to a blue-carpeted oval proscenium area. Following the outbreak of war and the launching of Russia's offensive against Austria-Hungary, more and more of Meyerhold's students enlisted and the number remaining fell to fewer than seven. By November, however, the total had returned to about thirty and the courses continued as before up to the Studio's closure three years later. Throughout the war period the lower floor in Borodin Street functioned as a temporary military hospital, and often convalescent soldiers provided an audience for the students' exercises. After one rehearsal for a public presentation by his students in November 1914 Meyerhold was moved to write: 'In the way they responded to the performance of the comedians, the wounded soldiers represented the very audience for which the new theatre, the truly popular theatre is intended'.[44]

The starting point for all research and practical exercises was the popular theatre in the broadest sense. The director, Alexei Gripich, himself a pupil at Meyerhold's Studio, writes:

In his striving for a modern popular theatre Meyerhold used as his source the popular theatres of the past: the Russian fairground shows, the Italian *commedia dell'arte*, the Japanese Kabuki, the theatre of Shakespeare, the theatre of the Spanish Renaissance, the Russian theatre of the 1830s (Pushkin, Gogol, Lermontov). Meyerhold pursued this large-scale programme in opposition to the stifling influence of the literary and everyday naturalistic theatre that had taken root in Russia at that time. Equally, it signified his own break with symbolism.[45]

The aim was in no way to revive the conventions of the past, and slavish reconstruction was avoided at all costs. Thus, whilst the *lazzi*, the gags of the *commedia*, were employed to refine physical dexterity, the mask as such seldom figured. Similarly, the familiar characters of Pulcinella, Brighella, Tartaglia and others were studied, but students were encouraged to develop their own stage personae. Meyerhold's long-standing enthusiasm for the circus inspired the training in clowning, juggling and acrobatics. Visits to the circus were compulsory, and the celebrated aerialist clown Donato was an occasional visiting instructor.

Initially, the curriculum was made up of three subjects: 'musical reading in the drama' (taught by the composer, Mikhail Gnesin); 'the history and technique of the *commedia dell'arte*' (Vladimir Solovyov); and 'stage movement' (Meyerhold). Gnesin's class was concerned with the principles of rhythm and their application to verse speaking, practising on choruses from Greek tragedy. It had little bearing on the other activities of the Studio and after a year was discontinued.

Solovyov delivered a course of lectures devoted to the origins, development, and influence of the *commedia*, and also instructed the students in the traditional tricks or *lazzi* of the genre. Initially, the scenarios of existing works by Gozzi, Marivaux, Cervantes, and Solovyov himself were used for practice, but later the students composed their own pieces as well. From 1914 onwards Solovyov's programme was expanded to include the French, Spanish, and Italian theatres of the seventeenth and eighteenth centuries. Wide ranging, erudite and inspirational, his courses provided the necessary introduction to Meyerhold's, which were the focus for the Studio's core activities.

In Meyerhold's classes the students were instructed in the basic skills that previously he had always been obliged to impart in the course of rehearsals – often to unwilling or incorrigible pupils. The student was taught:

1. spontaneous control of the body in space, with the whole body involved in every gesture;
2. to adapt his movements to the area available for the performance;
3. to distinguish between the various kinds of movement to music: in melodrama, circus and variety theatre; in the Chinese and Japanese theatres; the style of Isadora Duncan and Loie Fuller;
4. to imbue every action on the stage with joy – the tragic as well as the comic;
5. the power of the grotesque ('the grotesque helps the actor to portray the real as symbolic and to replace caricature with exaggerated parody');
6. the self-sufficiency of the *form* of the actor's performance (his movements and gestures) in the absence of a conventional plot from an improvised mime, and the significance of this lesson for acting as a whole.[46]

These were the principles on which Meyerhold's classes were based throughout the four years of the Studio's existence. At the start of the second year he and Solovyov introduced an additional joint course devoted to 'the practical study of the material elements of the performance: the construction, decoration and lighting of the stage area; the actor's costume and hand properties'.[47]

On 12 February 1915 the Studio gave its first public presentation of 'interludes, études and pantomimes'. The thirty-one '*comédiens*' who took part were dressed in two uniform costumes, one for the actors and one for the actresses. The varied programme included Cervantes' interlude, *The Cave at Salamanca*, *commedia* scenes, a fragment from a Chinese play, *The Lady, the Kitten, the Bird and the Snake*, performed in the manner of Gozzi's *Princess Turandot*, an interlude with circus clowns, and two mimed excerpts from *Hamlet*: the murder of Gonzago and Ophelia's mad scene.[48] One of the students, Alexandra Smirnova, recalls:

> Ophelia was picking flowers by a pond, making them into a garland; from time to time she seemed to remember something, stopped what she was doing and pressed the flowers to her breast. Then she began to pick more flowers, and it was as though for her they were real, living creatures. She moved around the blue oval of the carpet below the stage, giving the impression that the action was taking place around some small pond. . . The étude was performed to music. The repetitive movement – the circling around the pond – created a heart rending sense of foreboding. At the same time, a curious picture was presented: the heightened lyricism of Ophelia's emotional state was contrasted with the everyday behaviour of her nurse who observed her closely but uncomprehendingly, sometimes helping her by picking up a flower that she had thrown away. But then she began to realise that something was wrong and expressed her horror and despair. At a loss what to do, she followed on Ophelia's heels, weeping as she now realised the absurdity of her behaviour.[49]

Some simple improvisations were developed into more complex exercises which were used repeatedly to train successive groups of students. One of these was 'the Hunt', developed from 'Shooting the Bow', in which a group of 'Eastern' huntsmen stalked a bird, finally shooting her with their arrows. The mime concluded with the bird's dance of death and the triumphal exit of the hunters, holding her body aloft. Both the stage and the forestage were used, and the mime was executed to piano accompaniment, usually Liszt's *Mephisto Waltz*.

In February 1914 the Studio published the first number of its own periodical, *The Love of Three Oranges – The Journal of Doctor Dapertutto*. The publication took its name from the Carlo Gozzi's 'fiaba teatrale', *The Love of Three Oranges*, of which a free adaptation by Meyerhold, Solovyov and Konstantin Vogak appeared in the inaugural edition.* Gozzi was adopted as

---

* Prokofiev used this version for his opera which he wrote in 1919. Meyerhold recalls: 'I gave Prokofiev the first number of our journal . . . just before he left for America (it must have been at the very end of 1918). I urged him to write an opera based on our *Love of Three Oranges*, and he replied that he would read it on the ship.' Apparently, as early as 1913 Meyerhold had considered approaching Richard Strauss with the proposal, but decided against it because of Strauss's 'lack of taste'.[50] This was shortly after his production of *Elektra*.

44 Cover design by Golovin for *The Love of Three Oranges – The Journal of Doctor Dapertutto*, 1915

the Studio's exemplar, since it was he who had revived the declining *commedia dell'arte* in the eighteenth century with fairy-tale plays that combined the conventions of the literary and improvised theatres. In addition to chronicling the Studio's activities, the Journal included articles on the history and theory of the theatre, texts of plays (including *The Transfigured Prince, Harlequin the Marriage Broker,* and new translations of Gozzi, Plautus, and Tieck), reviews of contemporary productions and books on the theatre, and a poetry section that contained the works of modern Russian poets. The poetry section was edited by Alexander Blok, and as well as his own verses* it introduced a number of the works of Anna Akhmatova, Konstantin Balmont, Zinaida Gippius, Fyodor Sologub, and others. As well as being editor, Meyerhold himself contributed occasional critical and theoretical articles. Following the outbreak of war in August 1914 the journal was published in tiny

* *To Anna Akhmatova* (1914, No. 1): *Carmen* (1914, No. 4–5); *A Voice from the Chorus* (1916, No. 1).

editions at irregular intervals, the ninth and last number appearing late in 1916.

The editorial board of *The Love of Three Oranges* was responsible for the staging of Blok's two plays *The Unknown Woman* and *The Fairground Booth*, which were performed together seven times at the Tenishev Academy in St Petersburg between 7 and 11 April 1914. Although these were not billed as Studio productions, the cast was composed largely of the Studio's senior 'acting class' and staff,* whilst the scenery and costumes, designed by Yury Bondi, were executed by them. The Academy amphitheatre was specially converted to resemble a Greek classical theatre with a semicircular *orchestra* and shallow raised *skena*. Blok had completed *The Unknown Woman* in November 1906, a few weeks before the première of *The Fairground Booth*. Meyerhold planned to stage it the following season, but it was rejected by the censor on the suspicion that the character of the Unknown Woman was meant to represent the Virgin Mary – although, as he admitted, he didn't pretend to understand 'such decadent obscurity'.[51] It was given its first performance in 1913 by drama students in Moscow. Znosko-Borovsky describes the St Petersburg production:

> The opening scene takes place in a tavern. A number of actors with no parts in the play acted as 'proscenium servants' and performed the task of scene-shifting. Dressed in special unobtrusive costumes and moving rhythmically, they brought on tables, stools, a bar, and to the rear raised a green curtain on bamboo poles. Then in half-darkness the actors appeared, carrying bottles and glasses which they tried to place unobtrusively on the tables; they took their seats and after a momentary silence began to laugh softly, creating a buzz of conversation to draw the public into the atmosphere of a tavern. One of the servants sat down on the floor close at hand, ready to act as prompter if need be, but only if someone really forgot his lines. When the scene ended there was a roll of drums and the servants who had been holding up the curtain walked forward, stretching the curtain above the actors and then lowering it to hide them from the audience whilst they removed all the properties from the stage. Then the proscenium servants behind the curtain climbed on to stools and raised their end of it to expose the white, reverse side to the audience. Meanwhile, directly in front of the platform other servants rolled on from either side the two component parts of a wooden bridge, and on the platform a further group erected a new curtain of blue gauze with gold stars. So finally, when the white curtain was lowered, the audience saw a hump-backed bridge against a sky sprinkled with stars. As the actors mounted the bridge, the servants waved tarlatan veils in front of them to represent a snowy, starlit night. When a star was supposed to fall, all the chandeliers in the hall were extinguished and one of the servants lit a simple sparkler on a long pole which another raised right to the ceiling and then lowered it for the first to extinguish in water; then the chandeliers came on again.

* Meyerhold acted as one of the proscenium servants and Solovyov played the Author in *The Fairground Booth*. Yury Bondi was named as co-director.

The last scene, a 'grotesque' representation of a drawing room in varying shades of yellow, was enacted on the platform itself. In front of it knelt the proscenium servants, holding candles to parody footlights. On a table were exaggeratedly artificial fruits and flowers which the actor-guests themselves removed as they went off. There was also a door onstage leading nowhere (to an entrance hall?), through which the guests entered, throwing off their overcoats and joining in a conversation in which some were audible, others not.

When the time came for the Unknown Woman to disappear, she simply went off between the wing curtains whilst a proscenium servant lit a blue star on a pole and held it in the window. To a roll of drums, the curtain fell once more on the furniture and it was borne away like the sailing ships mentioned in the text. The play was over.[52]

In the tavern scene the characters were dressed naturalistically, but the men wore false red noses (some had gaudy wigs as well) and the women's cheeks were daubed bright red like wooden dolls. The Unknown Woman had huge lashes painted round her eyes. Even more clearly than in Meyerhold's *Dom Juan* the role of the proscenium servants recalled the '*kurogo*' of traditional Japanese theatre: apart from their tasks of scene-shifting, prompting and scenic effects, one of them constantly rearranged the voluminous cloak of the Man in Blue.

45 An artist's impression of the Mystics scene in *The Fairground Booth* at the Tenishev Academy, 1914

For *The Fairground Booth* the little theatre was represented by blue canvas screens behind the platform and paper-covered lanterns were suspended above the acting area. Meyerhold retained the device of the cardboard cut-out mystics on the platform from the 1906 production, but the rest of the action was performed on the semicircular *orchestra* in front. Apparently, this greatly detracted from the play's original impact: it proved impossible to sustain the necessary aura of mystery in a space hemmed in by a largely sceptical audience.[53] In order to heighten the impression of contrived theatricality Meyerhold persuaded a troupe of itinerant Chinese jugglers to perform during the interval, and the proscenium servants threw real oranges to the audience – designed to advertise the sale of the Studio's journal in the foyer. By all accounts, the point of both these attractions was lost on those present.

How far did Meyerhold succeed in conveying Blok's peculiar blend of visionary lyricism and sardonic burlesque? In his review of the production, Znosko-Borovsky, one of the most balanced and perceptive of Meyerhold's admirers, suggests that so enamoured was he with all the tricks of the grotesque he had discovered through his researches and studio experiments, that he neglected the tragic aspects of the plays which had been such a poignant feature of the original *Fairground Booth*.[54] But on that occasion much had depended on Meyerhold's own haunting portrayal of Pierrot, whereas in 1914 the performers were almost entirely students who could hardly be expected to possess Meyerhold's own intuitive understanding of the poet or his exceptional powers of expression as an actor. Blok himself did not share Meyerhold's enthusiasm for the popular theatre; indeed it was often the cause of violent disagreement between them. Initially he was exasperated by the productions at the Tenishev Academy; but by the end of the run he conceded the point of Meyerhold's interpretation of his work and regretted not seeing every performance.[55]

In 1926 Meyerhold wrote: 'The first attempt at a stage setting in the Constructivist manner was the erection of the bridge in the second part of Blok's *The Unknown Woman* on the empty platform of the Tenishev Auditorium. . . In that part of the production there were no theatrical elements whatsoever: the stage was cleared even of stylised objects.'[56] Even if Meyerhold does use the term 'Constructivism' loosely and chooses to ignore the depictive aspect of the scene in question, what he says lends further weight to the contention that his style in the twenties had its roots far back in his studio experiments in St Petersburg before 1917.

The coming of the war did not halt the activities of the Studio, but its impact was reflected in the increasingly irregular appearances of *The Love of Three Oranges*. The combined sixth and seventh issue for 1914 (published in February 1915) contained a patriotic play by Meyerhold, Solovyov, and Yury Bondi entitled *Fire*. Based on actual events on the Belgian front, the work is a scenario in eight scenes with an apotheosis, and is designed to leave full scope for improvisation. Although never performed, it bears a close resemblance to another agitatory work, *Earth Rampant*, staged by Meyerhold in 1923. In particular, the stage directions for *Fire* ('a series of iron girders and beams, with the centre occupied by an observation platform joined by a system of catwalks to the invisible foundations of the whole structure. On the platform a series of levers for controlling a complex system of dykes. . .') strikingly if coincidentally anticipate Lyubov Popova's gantry construction for the later production.*

The Studio's patriotic fervour was short-lived and Meyerhold and his colleagues continued their experiments uninterrupted by the effects of mobilisation. War forced the curtailment of the 1915–1916 season and there were no further public performances. Meyerhold's plan to stage a full-length production of *Hamlet* with his pupils never materialised,[57] and after one further season the Studio closed in 1917. Although it never led to the permanent popular theatre that Meyerhold dreamt of, the four seasons there gave him the chance to consolidate his ideas in practice and to lay the foundations for the style that he perfected in Moscow after the civil war. To the *commedia dell'arte* above all he was indebted for fundamental insights that were to inform everything that he did in the future. It was at the Borodin Street Studio that he was able finally to explore the full implications of the mask, which had been revealed to him in his first production of *The Fairground Booth* in 1906 and which now opened his eyes to the cardinal importance of play and improvisation. To quote Vadim Shcherbakov:

> Already in his Petersburg Studio . . . Meyerhold arrives at a vital conclusion: the main object of the spectator's attention, the main hero on the stage, must be *man at play* [*homo ludens*] . . . The joyous comedian, freely and effortlessly creating the plastic forms of his mask, and just as easily setting it aside to give his own mimed commentary on the role he is performing – this is the ideal towards which he was leading his pupils both before and after the third Russian Revolution.[58]

In 1915 Boris Pronin, the impresario of the old Interlude House, had opened a new intimate cellar theatre in Petrograd† called 'The Comedians' Rest' ('*Prival komediantov*'), with Meyerhold as artistic director. It was there in April 1916 that Meyerhold presented a new version of *Columbine's Scarf*. However, the designs by Sudeikin were poor by comparison with Sapunov's for the original production, and the work was not a success. The one feature worthy of note was a rudimentary flying ballet performed by Harlequin on a wire from the flies. A planned production of Tieck's *Puss in Boots* failed to materialise, and Meyerhold soon became disenchanted with the whole venture. On this muted note the public career of Doctor Dapertutto closed.

* See pp. 188-191 below.

† On the outbreak of war in August 1914 St Petersburg was Russified to become Petrograd.

IV

Before returning to the Imperial Theatres, mention should be made of Meyerhold's work in the cinema. In 1912 he wrote: 'There is no place for the cinematograph in the world of art, even in a purely auxiliary capacity. . . The cinematograph, that dream come true of those who strive for the photographic representation of life, is a shining example of the obsession with quasi-verisimilitude.'[59] The following year, when he was in Paris for the production of *La Pisanelle*, he made the acquaintance of D'Annunzio, Guillaume Apollinaire, and the actor Edouard de Max.* As Jay Leyda suggests, it may well have been they who persuaded Meyerhold to reconsider the artistic possibilities of the cinema.[60] In any case, when in May 1915 he was invited by Paul Thiemann to make a film for the Moscow company of Thiemann and Reinhardt, he accepted, albeit cautiously. In an interview he said:

> Firstly, I must say that the technical aspect of cinematography is far more advanced than the artistic. My task is perhaps to discover unexplored techniques. To begin with, I want to study, to analyse the element of movement in the cinematograph. The screen demands its own actors. So often we have seen artists who are splendid in the theatre or opera prove themselves totally unsuited to the cinematograph. Their movements are either too free or too cramped, their gestures far too weighty . . .
>
> In my view, it is a grave mistake to try to transfer dramatic or operatic works to the cinematograph . . .
>
> My opinion of cinematography to date is totally negative. . . It is still too early to say whether the cinematograph will become an art form in its own right or simply an adjunct to the theatre.[61]

At Meyerhold's suggestion, it was decided to make a film of Oscar Wilde's novel, *The Picture of Dorian Gray*, and Meyerhold himself composed the scenario. The shooting was completed in rather less than three months, and the film was released in Moscow in December 1915. In order to enhance the effect of Dorian's unsullied youthful beauty, the part was played by the young actress Varcara Yanova, whilst Meyerhold himself played Lord Henry Wotton. Critical reactions to the casting of Yanova were unfavourable, but Meyerhold's performance was widely admired. From the description of his cameraman Alexander Levitsky, one can see how the principle of economy, fundamental to his teaching at his Studio, was applied to the realisation of Lord Henry: 'Meyerhold . . . did not alter his outward appearance, but simply added a few details: a centre parting, a monocle on a long ribbon and the inevitable chrysanthemum in

---

* De Max, as well as the young Abel Gance, played in *La Pisanelle*.

the buttonhole of his morning coat. But with the aid of this he became unrecognisable.'[62]

As Levitsky, the foremost cameraman in Russia before the Revolution, and Meyerhold both later admitted, their collaboration was fraught with discord.[63] The main trouble seems to have been Meyerhold's initial reluctance to concede the creative role of the cameraman, and his own slight appreciation of the practical difficulties of photography. For his part, Levitsky was astonished to be confronted for the first time with a series of

46 Yanova as Dorian Gray and Meyerhold as Lord Henry

sketches (prepared by Meyerhold and his designer, Yegorov) specifying the pictorial composition of each sequence, in which particular attention was paid to the disposition of colour masses and chiaroscuro effects. At that time, the normal practice in Russia was first to design a complete setting and then to shoot the whole scene against it from varying angles. Levitsky claims that much of what Meyerhold specified was impracticable, and indicates that it was he himself who suggested the use of dissolves, close-ups, brief takes, even rudimentary montage, to make Meyerhold's inspiration viable cinematically.

Certainly Meyerhold was avid to utilise every means of expression the cinema had to offer, and in return he brought to it his own unique understanding of the dramatic power of rhythm and gesture. As Jay Leyda writes:

> Meyerhold's theories of actors' movement seem from today's perspective ready-made for an adolescent cinema, and were indeed later adapted by Kuleshov to film use. . .[64]
>
> [The Picture of Dorian Gray] was original and daring as few films before it or since have dared to be. Russian artists who saw it and then The Cabinet of Doctor Caligari a few years later in Europe tell me that if it had been shown abroad it would have surpassed Caligari's reputation as a heightening of film art. It was undoubtedly the most important Russian film made previous to the February revolution.[65]

In his authoritative account of the pre-revolutionary Russian cinema, Semyon Ginsburg goes so far as to say that 'Meyerhold was the very first in the history of the cinema to put forward the idea of the silent cinematograph as, above all, a pictorial art'.[66] One scene in particular serves to illustrate this point. In the story, Dorian takes Lord Henry to the theatre to see Sybil play Juliet; as Sergei Yutkevich describes the sequence:

> On the screen one saw neither the auditorium nor the stage, but only the box which Dorian Gray and his companion entered in darkness. At first, when they sat down you didn't realise what was happening. But on the rear wall of the box there was a tall mirror and in it you saw the reflection of the stage-curtain opening and then a part of the balcony with a rope ladder suspended for the famous scene between Romeo and Juliet. The entire scene from Shakespeare was seen in the mirror, whilst the reactions on the faces of the seated onlookers could be observed in close-up.[67]

Keen to pursue his experiments, Meyerhold agreed the following summer to make a second film for Thiemann and Reinhardt, this time of Przybyszewski's novel, The Strong Man, with himself in the secondary role of the poet, Gursky. He chose a new cameraman, complaining that previously he had been held back by Levitsky's 'conservative ways'.[68] Learning from his previous experience, Meyerhold now placed more emphasis on close-ups, the action being located largely within the single setting of the artist's studio. Although the collaboration with his cameraman seems to have been far

47 Dorian and Lord Henry at the performance of *Romeo and Juliet* with Meyerhold (right) as Lord Henry. (Still from the film)

more harmonious on this occasion, work on the film was interrupted by Meyerhold's conflicting theatrical commitments and it was not completed until August 1916. It was given its first public screening in Petrograd on 9 October 1917. Understandably enough at that time, it attracted little attention and no substantial critical accounts appeared. In April 1917 there was talk of a film version of Blok's play *The Rose and the Cross*, which came to nothing. That summer Meyerhold started shooting a version of Fyodor Sologub's novel *The Spectre's Charms*, but the Revolution forced the studio to suspend work and the film was never finished. The original designer for the production was Vladimir Tatlin, soon to become a leading figure in the Constructivist movement, but he found the script 'gloomy and thoroughly mystical' and the collaboration soon faltered.[69]

Meyerhold never directed another film, although various projects were mooted. At the end of 1925 it was announced that he had agreed to film John Reed's *Ten Days that Shook the World* for Proletkino,[70] but work was never started by him and three years later it appeared under the title *October*, directed by his former pupil, Eisenstein. Finally, in 1929 Meyerhold began work on a version of Turgenev's *Fathers and Sons*. Initially, it was suggested that the part of Bazarov might be played by Mayakovsky, but eventually it was offered to the actor and director Nikolai Okhlopkov, with Meyerhold's second wife, Zinaida Raikh, playing Mme Odintsova. However, the start of shooting was delayed by the Meyerhold Theatre's departure on its foreign tour in March 1930 and by the time Meyerhold and Raikh returned in September the project had been dropped.[71]

Unfortunately, no trace of either of Meyerhold's completed films sur-

48 Still from *The White Eagle* with Meyerhold as the Senator (centre) and Kachalov as the Governor (right)

vives. However, in 1928 he played the role of the Senator in Protazanov's *The White Eagle*. A copy is still preserved in the Soviet State Film Archive, and although as a film highly derivative, it remains an intriguing record of acting styles, with Meyerhold's precise angularity contrasting sharply with the highly emotional playing of the celebrated Kachalov from the Moscow Art Theatre in the role of the Governor. It was Meyerhold's only appearance on stage or screen after the Revolution.[72]

V

In the years following his production of *Elektra* Meyerhold's various un-official activities did not prevent him from extending his repertoire at the Alexandrinsky Theatre. Between 1914 and 1917 he was responsible for the staging of such widely differing works as Pinero's *Mid-Channel*, Lermontov's *Two Brothers*, Zinaida Gippius' *The Green Ring* and Shaw's *Pygmalion*. Also, in 1915 there was a production of Calderón's *The Constant Prince*, treated in a similar stylised manner to *Dom Juan* and using the same basic setting and the convention of the 'proscenium servants'. In order to stress the 'womanly' virtues of passive courage and endurance, the part of Prince Fernando was played by an actress. However, none of these productions was distinguished by the experimentation and the adroit manipulation of theatrical conventions that continued to enhance his reputation elsewhere. Meyerhold remained true to his word and kept his studio and 'big theatre' activities strictly segregated.[73]

One production that did question accepted practice and foreshadowed a vital line in Meyerhold's development after the Revolution was Ostrovsky's *The Storm* (9 January 1916). In his opinion, the true nature of Ostrovsky had been distorted by the naturalistic school which saw him as a mere genre dramatist of scant modern interest. Stressing Ostrovsky's affinity with Pushkin, Lermontov, and traditional Spanish tragedy, Meyerhold reinterpreted *The Storm* as a Russian romantic tragedy. He rejected the conventional emphasis on the vernacular in Ostrovsky's dialogue and sought to reveal its underlying poetry. In an attempt to bring out the predominant national character of the drama, Golovin based the settings and costumes on the strong colours and ornamentation of traditional weaving and carving. Although restrained by comparison with his later productions of nineteenth-century works such as *Tarelkin's Death*, *The Forest*, and *The Government Inspector*, *The Storm* was a bold challenge to tradition and the first of Meyerhold's many invigorating reinterpretations of the Russian classics.[74]

Nearly four years elapsed after the short-lived production of *Elektra* before Meyerhold returned to the operatic stage with a production of Alexander Dargomyzhsky's *The Stone Guest*, which had its première at the Mariinsky under the baton of Nikolai Malko on 27 January 1917. Unfinished on the composer's death in 1869, then completed by Cui and orchestrated by Rimsky-Korsakov, the opera follows closely the text of the 'little tragedy' that Pushkin wrote in 1830. Hence, its production

49 Design by Golovin for Act Two of *The Storm*

was a further example of Meyerhold's interest in the powerful theatricality of the Russian drama of the nineteenth century. He admired its fidelity to Pushkin and the abrupt changes of mood as the action speeds towards the final confrontation between Dom Juan, Donna Anna and the statue of the Commandant. Again his designer was Golovin, and in some respects the staging recalled their earlier treatment of the Dom Juan legend: ornate decorative borders were used to reduce the stage dimensions to those appropriate to a chamber opera of deep psychological intensity; the scene changes were swiftly executed by young 'proscenium servants' dressed as Capuchin friars; the settings eschewed any literal depiction of Spain. In an interview just before the opening Meyerhold said: 'In *The Stone Guest* it is as though we see before us the "masquerade" Spain that the poet pictured in his imagination, reflecting all the aspects of Russian taste in the 1830s. Consequently, the production avoids the merest hint of the ethnographic in its evocation of Pushkin's Spain.'[75] Seemingly, Meyerhold and Golovin had learnt from their mistakes with *Elektra*; on this occasion there was a clear homogeneity of libretto, musical score and scenic interpretation which was received enthusiastically by the public and the great majority of critics. For the first time on the Russian stage since the work's première in 1872, Meyerhold had demonstrated the theatrical viability of *The Stone Guest* and its right to a place in the operatic repertoire.[76]

In 1917 the monumental production of Lermontov's *Masquerade* was revealed to the public. Although put on finally at eighteen day's notice, it had been in preparation and intermittently rehearsed for seven years.[77] Planned originally for autumn 1912, it was put back to November 1914 to coincide with the centenary of Lermontov's birth, but then postponed owing to the outbreak of war. Now in 1917 Meyerhold was warned that any further delays would mean the abandonment of the whole costly enterprise. The cast of over two hundred comprised the permanent Alexandrinsky company augmented by drama school students including those from Meyerhold's own Studio. His 'comédiens' were particularly suited to the production by virtue of their familiarity with the grotesque, which was so vital to the realisation of the work as he conceived it.

Lermontov's verse drama tells of the cynical and dissolute Petersburg nobleman, Arbenin, who has become reformed by the love of his young wife, Nina. They attend a masked ball and through the intrigue of the society that he despises, Arbenin is persuaded that Nina has been unfaithful to him. Enraged with jealousy, he poisons her and on discovering her innocence, goes mad himself. Written in 1835–1836, the play was repeatedly rejected by the censor, largely on account of the embittered trenchancy of its satire. Despite the many modifications that Lermontov made to the text (including even the substitution of a happy ending), it had yet to be performed when he died in 1841. Finally, a number of scenes from the work were staged at the Alexandrinsky Theatre in 1852 with Karatygin as Arbenin. From this

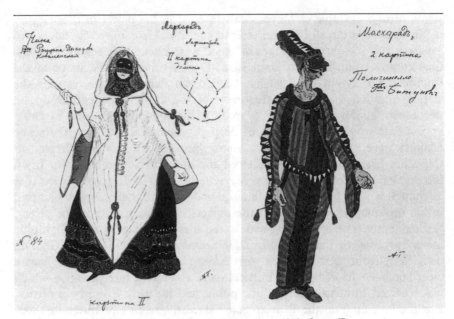

50 Costume design by Golovin for Nina in the masquerade in Scene Two

51 Costume design by Golovin for the mask of Pulcinella in the masquerade in Scene Two

and from the first complete stage version at the Maly Theatre ten years later there grew the tradition of interpreting *Masquerade* as a romantic melodrama in which Arbenin was driven to destroy his wife and himself by some demonic force within him.

Meyerhold, however, set out to restore the satirical emphasis of Lermontov's original version. One of his early notes reads '. . . whatever Arbenin might be, whatever horrors he might perpetrate, we shall castigate not him but the society that has made him what he is'.[78] He saw Arbenin's murder of Nina and his subsequent loss of reason not as the outcome of mistrust and jealousy but as the price exacted by a malign society from one who had sought to reject and discredit its corrupt way of life, having himself long pursued it. The figure of 'The Stranger' was made the principal agent of this vengeance, with Shprikh and Kazarin his henchmen to weave the deadly intrigue round Arbenin. In his preliminary notes on the characters Meyerhold writes:

> The Stranger is a hired assassin. Society has engaged the Stranger to take vengeance on Arbenin for 'his bitter disdain for everything in which once he took such pride'.
> The death of Pushkin and the death of Lermontov – one should remember the evil machinations of society in the 1830s – two deaths: the best sources for an explanation of the importance and the air of mystery surrounding the

Stranger. Martynov* stands behind Lermontov like a shadow, simply awaiting an order from 'his side'. . .[79]

Before he appears in the last act to reveal to Arbenin his ghastly mistake, the Stranger is glimpsed only fleetingly at the masked ball (Act One, Scene Two), when he warns Arbenin of the disaster that is shortly to befall him. In the text he is identified merely as 'A Mask', one amongst many at the ball, but Meyerhold left no doubt as to his menacing significance in the drama. Yury Yuriev, who on this occasion played Arbenin, describes his entrance.

Finally the mysterious figure of the Stranger appears, clad in a black domino cloak and a weirdly terrifying white Italian mask. He enters through the door in the proscenium arch to the left of the audience, and moves silently in an arc around the very edge of the forestage towards the opposite door. Behind him, as though in a magnetic field drawn by his hypnotic power, there floods on to the stage a long, broad ribbon of masked figures; suddenly he turns to face them, halts, and stares fixedly at them through his strange mask; they all freeze as one, riveted by his gaze.[80]

This vision of the supernatural is confirmed by Yakov Malyutin who played the Stranger in a later revival of the production:

He seemed to be the embodiment of an implacable tragic fate ruling and

52 Costume design by Golovin for Shprikh

* Nikolai Martynov killed Lermontov in a duel in 1841, four years after the death of Pushkin in the same manner.

pursuing the life and the future of man. In the interpretation of the director, the designer and the composer, the Stranger was a symbolic figure in every sense of the word: there was menace in his external appearance, menace in the musical theme that accompanied his appearance on stage, there was meant to be menace even in his voice, the stern, prophetic voice of a merciless, wrathful judge. The black cloak and the hideous mask in which he appeared at Engelhardt's masquerade, the tall hat and tightly buttoned frock-coat that he wore for his final appearance in the drama made the Stranger not so much a man as a devil in disguise, coldly inciting Arbenin to commit his crime and just as coldly punishing him for it.[81]

The Stranger's costume closely resembles a figure in the Venetian Pietro Longhi's painting 'Cavadenti'. This was no coincidence: in the summer of 1911 Meyerhold and Golovin read the recently published *Italian Images* by the art historian Pavel Muratov, in particular the chapter on eighteenth-century Venice.[82] Not long afterwards Meyerhold made the following note:

In my opinion the romanticism that colours *Masquerade* should be looked for in the surroundings that Lermontov discovered when he read Byron from cover to cover as a student in Moscow. Isn't it eighteenth-century Venice that appears between the lines of Byron's poetry and which revealed to Lermontov the world of fantasy and magic dreams that envelops *Masquerade*? 'The mask, the candle, and the mirror – that is the image of eighteenth-century Venice', writes Muratov. Isn't it masks, candles and mirrors, the passions of the gaming tables where the cards are scattered with gold . . . those intrigues born of tricks

53 Illarion Pevtsov
in the role of
'The Stranger'

54 The masquerade in Scene Two

played at masked-balls, those halls 'gloomy despite the glitter of candles in the many chandeliers' – isn't it all this that we find in Lermontov's *Masquerade*? Isn't it this very Venetian life 'imbued with the magic that always lies hidden in cards and in gold' that shows through the images of *Masquerade*, 'hovering on the borderline of delirium and hallucination'.[83]

Thus, in Meyerhold and Golovin's interpretation, Lermontov's St Petersburg setting took on these imagined attributes, and so became a true 'Venice of the North', sharing its atmosphere of outward show and inner corruption.

In the 1917 production the atmosphere of the supernatural, dominated by the Stranger as the emissary of infernal powers, tended to obscure the satirical aspect of the drama.* But this vision of man at the mercy of a malevolent capricious fate was familiar in Meyerhold's work: it appeared first in Blok's *Fairground Booth*, it inspired the phantasmagoria of *Columbine's Scarf*, it was embodied in his own portrayal of the satanic Lord Henry in *The Picture of Dorian Gray*, and above all it was germane to the sinister ambiguity of the mask as he interpreted it in his crucial essay, 'The Fairground Booth'. Even in the Soviet period Meyerhold did not suppress it

* Discussing the 1938 revival of *Masquerade*, Meyerhold said: 'The elements of mysticism have been removed from the figure of the Stranger. I am breaking free of Blok's influence, which I can now see in my production. Now I have emphasised that the actions of the Stranger are dictated by human feelings (revenge).'[84]

entirely: there was the spectral aspect of Khlestakov and his strange double in *The Government Inspector*, and the unexplained figure of 'The Stranger' who suddenly materialised to take up Hermann's fatal challenge in *The Queen of Spades*.*

From start to finish Meyerhold worked on *Masquerade* in closest collab-

55 Golovin's front-
   curtain design
   for *Masquerade*

oration with Golovin. In order to emphasise the remorseless advance of the tragedy, Lermontov's cumbersome five acts were treated as ten episodes; each had its own lavish setting, but the forestage and a series of five exquisitely figured act-drops were used to ensure no pause in the action, the concluding lines of one scene being spoken before the curtain as the scene behind was swiftly prepared for the next. Critical scenes were played at the edge of the semicircular forestage and a series of borders and screens was devised to reduce the stage area and frame the characters for the more intimate episodes. The full stage area was used only for the two ball scenes. The organisation of the stage space and the complex system of act-drops and borders helped Meyerhold to treat the text in the manner of a filmic montage, applying the experience gained from his work on *The Picture of Dorian Gray* and *The Strong Man*, on which he was still engaged. This greatly enhanced the sense of nightmarish unreality in a manner that was reminiscent of the episodic structure of such productions as *The Fairground Booth*, *The Life of a Man*, *Spring Awakening* and *Columbine's Scarf*, and anticipated his treatment of *The Government Inspector* nine years later. In his eye-witness account of the rehearsals for the 1938 revival of *Masquerade*, Isaac Schneidermann draws

* See pp. 228-230, 280-282.

56 The ball, Scene Eight

attention to a further cinematic element in the production, the use of the flashback to furnish a 'lyrical commentary on the events of the drama':

> The strains of Glinka's *Valse-fantaisie* were heard. To its elusive rhythm, disturbing yet enticing, and announced by the soft tinkling of the bells that fringed the apertures in the curtain, the two Harlequins made their silent entrance. Strangely identical, they noiselessly circled Nina, paying court to her, gently taking her by the hand. But their sport concealed a threat. One of them sat on the banquette and drew Nina down beside him. Tearing herself free, Nina left the fatal bracelet in his hands, and by design he let it fall onto the middle of the forestage. Then much later, during the ball scene when Arbenin brought Nina the poison and stood motionless by the proscenium arch, his arms crossed, the scene of the lost bracelet reappeared before the audience, lit by a yellow spot from the wings – this time quite lightly and silently, as though in an apparition. And again, like an echo from the past, Glinka's *Valse-fantaisie* was heard.[85]

As well as the many settings and costumes, Golovin designed all the furniture, china, glassware, candelabra, swords, walking-canes, fans – everything down to the last playing card, yielding a total of some four thousand design sketches. Not a single item was taken from stock and everything of significance was made slightly over life-size in order to ensure the required effect on the spectator through the expressive manipulation of props that was of fundamental importance in Meyerhold's Studio curriculum.[86] As with *Dom Juan* the auditorium was illuminated throughout, whilst tall mirrors flanking the proscenium opening helped to break down the barrier between stage and audience; not only did the reflected images emphasise the affinity between Golovin's settings and the 'Empire' style of Rossi's auditorium so redolent of Lermontov's own period (and between the St Petersburg society depicted onstage and that seated in the stalls), but they also served to heighten the all-prevailing atmosphere of illusion. Much of the action was accompanied by music specially composed by Glazunov and based on themes from Lermontov's contemporary, Glinka. On this occasion the entire choreography was arranged by Meyerhold, including the masked ball in which over a hundred and fifty guests took part.

The première on 25 February 1917, marking Yuriev's silver jubilee at the Alexandrinsky, was anticipated as the theatrical event of the decade. But on that day the tsarist régime was forced to a final confrontation with the Petrograd proletariat, and the first shots of the Revolution were exchanged. Even so, the theatre was packed with a brilliantly attired audience, but the response to the production was cool. Not entirely without justification, critics hostile to Meyerhold seized on the ironic coincidence of the occasion and condemned the profligacy of this, the richest spectacle the Russian theatre had ever seen, representing it as typical of Meyerhold's own decadence and megalomaniac extravagance. With his usual asperity Alexander Kugel commented in *Theatre and Art*:

> At the entrance to the theatre stood tight black lines of automobiles. All the rich, all the aristocratic, all the prosperous Petrograd pluto-, bureau-, and 'homefronto-crats' (*tylokratia*) were present in force . . . and when that Babylon of absurd extravagance was unveiled before us with all the artistic obscenity of a Semiramis, I was horrified. I knew – everybody knew – that two or three miles away crowds of people were crying 'bread' and Protopopov's policemen were getting seventy roubles a day for spraying those bread-starved people with bullets from their machine-guns. What is this – Rome after the Caesars? Should we go on afterwards to Lucullus and feast on swallows' tongues, leaving those starving wretches to go on shouting for bread and freedom?[87]

Rudnitsky refutes Kugel's condemnation; reading a deeper meaning into the drama's grim conclusion, he says, 'Meyerhold's production echoed like a grim requiem for the empire, like the stern, solemn, tragic, fatal funeral rites of the world that was perishing in those very days.'[88] Whether one regards the première as a masterpiece of instinctive timing or as a monumental gesture of social indifference, the fact remains that *Masquerade* survived all criticism to be performed over five hundred times after the October Revolution right up

57 Portrait of
Meyerhold by
Golovin, 1917

to 1941. The settings and costumes were destroyed by bombing during the Siege of Leningrad, but Meyerhold's legacy survived even that, for after the war *Masquerade* was revived for the last time as a production without décor at the Leningrad Philharmonic with Yuriev, then over 70, still in his original part of Arbenin.*

Although Meyerhold retained his posts at the Imperial Theatres for a further season after the October Revolution and completed several more productions, it is *Masquerade* that must be regarded as the culmination of his Petersburg period. Before the year was out he had declared his support for the Bolshevik cause and pledged himself to the democratisation of the new, Soviet theatre.[90]

---

* *Masquerade* was performed only thirteen times in 1917 but over five hundred times after the Revolution plus at least two hundred concert performances. The production was restored to the repertoire in 1919 and then revised twice by Meyerhold, first in 1933 and finally in December 1938. The second revival was Meyerhold's last completed work in the theatre.[89]

Revolution and Civil War

When Meyerhold left Moscow in 1902 to form his own company he was deeply concerned with the role of the theatre as a reforming influence in society. Indeed, the failure of the Moscow Art Theatre to discharge this function to his satisfaction was a major factor in his dispute with its directors. But although the repertoire of the Fellowship of the New Drama was based on the works of such 'progressive' dramatists as Chekhov, Gorky, Ibsen, and Hauptmann, it never made any attempt to exploit the theatre for overtly propagandist ends. Whatever Meyerhold's convictions, this was never a practical possibility, since any attempt at political involvement was instantly suppressed by the nervous local authorities.* After the events of 1905 they became more vigilant still, but in any case by that time Meyerhold was preoccupied with symbolist drama, which had no true bearing on the urgent problems of the day, whatever metaphorical significance might be attached to it.† In 1906 the Marxist critic, Anatoly Lunacharsky, stigmatised the 'New Theatre' as counter-revolutionary: in striving for a drama purged of all external action, in depicting the 'inner dialogue' of the spirit through the means of static poses and rhythmical movements, the New Theatre – he maintained – fostered a passive acceptance of life with all its imperfections. Its aesthetic could be compared to that of Schiller, of whom Karl Marx had said: 'Schiller's retreat from life to the ideal amounts to the rejection of everyday misery for the sake of grandiloquent misery.'[1]

The main objective of Lunacharsky's attack was the 'static theatre' of Meyerhold's early years as a director. But in any case his final rejection of that style after *Pelléas and Mélisande* in 1907 was largely for aesthetic

---

* In the winter of 1904-1905 during the period of unrest that followed the disastrous Russo-Japanese war, Ibsen's *An Enemy of the People*, Gorky's *Summer Folk*, and Kosorotov's *Spring Torrent* were all removed from the Fellowship's programme on the orders of the local police. In 1906 Chirikov's *The Jews* was banned by the Tiflis authorities after three highly successful performances (see pp. 46-47 above).

† See p. 47 above.

reasons, and his subsequent work continued to have little or no direct bearing on contemporary events. Besides, the terms of his employment once he joined the Imperial Theatres debarred him formally from any kind of political activity. In 1913, shortly after he had opened his Studio in St Petersburg, he said in an interview:

> A theatre that presents plays saturated in 'psychologism' with the motivation of every single event underlined, or which forces the spectator to rack his brains over the solution of all manner of social and philosophical problems – such a theatre destroys its own theatricality. . . The stage is a world of marvels and enchantment; it is breathless joy and strange magic.[2]

It took the outbreak of war to reopen Meyerhold's eyes to an alternative role for the theatre. As well as collaborating in the composition of *Fire*,* he was responsible in the autumn of 1914 for the staging of a number of propagandist pieces. One of them was a free adaption of Maupassant's story *Mademoiselle Fifi*, which was presented at the Suvorin Theatre on 15 August 1914. Meyerhold transformed it into 'a patriotic manifestation' in which 'All the performers spoke their parts clearly and precisely, like orators at a political meeting', and the play culminated with the entry of victorious French troops singing *La Marseillaise*.[3] Strictly speaking, this was Meyerhold's first encounter with agitatory theatre.

The demand for this kind of jingoism passed quickly enough once the true horror of war was grasped, and current events encroached no further on Meyerhold's theatrical activities. However, this is not to say that the social awareness of his youth had declined with the passage of time: in common with many other Russian intellectuals he shared a disdain for tsarist obscurantism, a disdain that in his case was greatly exacerbated by the languid indifference of the Alexandrinsky stalls patrons who resisted all his efforts to disturb them. Only on rare occasions, such as the visits of convalescent soldiers to his Studio, was he able to test his work against the responses of an audience that was unhampered by jaded preconceptions or over-refined aesthetic sensibility.† In April 1917, at a debate entitled *Revolution, Art, War*, Meyerhold castigated 'the silent, passionless parterre where people come for a rest', and asked 'Why don't the soldiers come to the theatre and liberate it from the parterre public?'[4] By this time, he had become recognised as a member of the 'left bloc' that had emerged in the newly-formed Arts Union and was agitating for a more democratic system of administration in the theatre.

The fall of the Romanov dynasty had been greeted with widespread relief throughout the Russian theatre. It signalled the end of repressive censorship, and was seen by the Imperial companies in Moscow and Petrograd as the opportunity to achieve the artistic autonomy for which they had long been agitating. The Provisional Government replaced the old Imperial

* See pp. 133-134 above. † See p. 127 above.

functionaries with its own nominees, and the well-meaning Telyakovsky was dismissed from the Alexandrinsky. With all tsarist insignia removed, May Day saw the renamed 'State Theatres' decked with red bunting, and the evening performances were preceded by celebratory speeches and the singing of the Marseillaise. That autumn, the season at the Mariinsky Opera opened not with the traditional performance of Glinka's *A Life for the Tsar* but with Borodin's *Prince Igor*.

In general, however, the major theatres saw little need to modify their repertoires and there was no rush to present the work of proscribed dramatists. Thus, Gorky's *Philistines* was given a single benefit performance by the Alexandrinsky Theatre in April 1917 but was not seen on the main stage for nearly a year, and then only three times. Similarly, at the Maly Theatre in Moscow the only new work of any significance in its first post-revolutionary programme was *The Decembrists*, a previously banned work by the popular contemporary dramatist, Gnedich. The Moscow Art Theatre's response to the momentous events of the day was one of artistic paralysis, from which it took some years to recover. Immediately following the October Revolution it suspended performances for over three weeks and formally dissociated itself from any political alignment. Elsewhere, reactions varied from watchful neutrality to overt hostility. Anticipating the early collapse of the new regime, the three State companies in Petrograd and several other theatres in Moscow went on strike against the violence of October. Of the eighty-strong Alexandrinsky company only four actors and Meyerhold alone amongst the directors declared their support for the Bolsheviks.[5]

As early as 9 November 1917 Lenin signed a decree transferring all theatres to the control of the newly created Commissariat for Enlightenment under Lunacharsky. Encouraged by his assurances, companies now entered into reluctant negotiations to salvage what they could of their artistic independence. For established theatres with proven repertoires this was surprisingly easy, since the Party's policy was to preserve and subsidise the traditional arts whilst rendering them more accessible to the new mass audience.

Within days of the October Revolution Lunacharsky had invited a hundred and twenty leading artists and intellectuals to a conference at the Smolny Institute to discuss the reorganisation of the arts in the new Soviet Russia. Only five accepted the invitation, and they included Blok, Mayakovsky, and Meyerhold.[6] In January 1918 the Petrograd paper *Our Gazette* reported sarcastically that 'The ranks of the Bolsheviks have been joined by the ultra-modernistic Mr Meyerhold, who for some unknown reason has acquired the title of "Red Guard"'.[7] It has been suggested that Meyerhold was merely exploiting the Revolution in order to propagate his own reforms.* However, the caution displayed by the majority

* Notably by the Russian artist Yury Annenkov in his autobiography *Dnevnik moikh vstrech* (New York, 1966). Vol. II, p. 46.

is significant: Bolshevik power was still far from secure and a declaration of solidarity amounted to a hazardous act of faith. This act Meyerhold committed, and soon affirmed it in August 1918 by joining the Bolshevik Party. Alexander Matskin speaks with justification of the 'saving clarity' that the Revolution brought to Meyerhold's relationship with the external world, and continues:

> No doubt Meyerhold linked his fate with the Revolution because he expected
> it to give him greater creative freedom, and there was no harm in that. After
> all, many Russian intellectuals, Pavlov and Stanislavsky among them, did just
> the same. But to Meyerhold . . . it brought an inner freedom as well; it broke
> the circle of alienation and at one stroke cut all the knots that he had struggled
> for so long to unravel. That was why he followed the Revolution to the very
> limit.[8]

II

Despite his involvement in external affairs and the increasingly alien atmosphere within the State theatres, Meyerhold's directorial activities did not slacken in the year following the Revolution. Only two days before that event he presented Alexander Sukhovo-Kobylin's *Tarelkin's Death* at the Alexandrinsky, having already that year staged the two earlier parts of his trilogy, *Krechinsky's Wedding* and *The Case*. Completed in 1869, this 'comedy-jest' is a savage satire on bureaucratic corruption and tsarist police methods. Sukhovo-Kobylin had to wait until 1900 when he was eighty-three to see it performed, and only then after he had been obliged to blunt its edge with numerous amendments. For the first time, Meyerhold restored the original text and interpreted it in the phantasmagorical, Hoffmanesque style of much of his own earlier work. With designs by Golovin's pupil, Boris Almedingen, that hovered on the margin between nightmare and reality in the manner of German expressionism, the production captured the public's imagination and was a great success.[9] No doubt, much of the appeal of *Tarelkin's Death*, both for Meyerhold and for the public, lay in its barely concealed denunciation of the old regime. There was no such justification for the next two productions that he was required to undertake, Rimsky-Korsakov's opera, *The Snow Maiden*, and Ibsen's *The Lady from the Sea*, both presented in December 1917. For him, they represented hack work and he did little more than supervise their staging by other directors.

Stravinsky's first opera *The Nightingale*, based on a fairy tale by Hans Christian Andersen and originally staged by Benois and Fokine in Paris in 1914, was another matter. Originally planned for the 1915–16 season and entrusted to Meyerhold with Stravinsky's full approval, it had the same qualities of oriental exoticism and naïve theatrical magic as the *fiabe teatrale* of Carlo Gozzi, who was the presiding genius at the Borodin Street Studio. However, Meyerhold's production, though undeniably innovative, was curiously formal in its conception. With a static chorus flanking the forestage, the parts of the Fisherman, Death and the Nightingale were sung by costumed performers standing at music stands while their actions were mimed by doubles on-stage. The remaining roles were performed conventionally by actor-singers. As Glikman points out, a similar convention had been employed more consistently and to controversial effect in 1914 when Benois and Fokine had staged Rimsky-Korsakov's *The Golden Cockerel* for Diaghilev in Paris, a production of which Meyerhold must have been aware. On the other hand, it has been suggested that his treatment of *The Nightingale* may have influenced the static conception of *Oedipus Rex* on which Stravinsky collaborated with Jean Cocteau in 1925. Stravinsky, who had readily entrusted the Russian première of his opera to Meyerhold and Golovin, was not present at the single performance conducted by Albert Coates on 30 May 1918 at the Mariinsky Opera. In common with most productions at that time, it received scant attention from the press and remains a tantalisingly under-documented anomaly in Meyerhold's career, oddly untheatrical and at odds with the prevailing mood.[10]

Whilst retaining his posts at the State Theatres, Meyerhold organised courses in production technique in Petrograd. These courses, the first of their kind in Russia, were held under the auspices of the newly established Theatre Department of the Commissariat of Enlightenment, of which Meyerhold was deputy head in Petrograd. The first, which ran from June to August 1918, was attended by nearly a hundred students with ages ranging from fourteen to fifty-three, and consisted of evening lectures designed to give a 'polytechnical education in the theatre arts'. There was a certain resemblance to Meyerhold's earlier Studio, with instruction in movement and mime; but equally, considerable stress was laid on the need for cooperation between the stage-director and the designer. Meyerhold continued with this work until ill health forced him to move south in May 1919. After a further term, the courses were discontinued.[11]

III

In addition to his teaching commitments in the summer of 1918 Meyerhold was engaged in setting up a company catering for the mainly working-class public of the Petrograd district of Kolomensky. At the poorly equipped Luna Park Theatre, hitherto associated with operetta, he supervised a number of productions, including *A Doll's House*, Shaw's *The Devil's Disciple*, Hauptmann's *The Weavers*, Cervantes' *The Theatre of Wonders* and Molière's *Georges Dandin*. It seems possible that he directed at least the latter two himself, but no details survive and the enterprise was short-lived.[12]

By now, his career at the former Imperial Theatres had nearly run its course. It only remained for him to discharge his obligation to stage Auber's romantic opera, *La Muette de Portici* (retitled *Fenella*) at the Mariinsky, or 'State Opera' as it was now called. Not surprisingly, given all his other commitments, he delegated most of the work on *Fenella* to his assistant, Sofya Maslovskaya, soon to become the first Russian woman to produce opera. *Fenella* had been staged at the Mariinsky as recently as January 1917, but was withdrawn on the orders of the Ministry of the Interior, presumably because of its provocative theme of a peasant revolt in seventeenth-century Naples. For the same reason, it was now decided to restage it on 7 November to mark the first anniversary of the October Revolution. Meyerhold and Maslovskaya were forced to use the indifferent designs by Lambin from the earlier production, and a second-rate conductor took the place of his regular collaborator, Albert Coates. Meyerhold's lack of commitment to the undertaking was undisguised and provoked angry complaints from the company. Eleven days after the single performance of *Fenella*, Meyerhold, supported by Lunacharsky, broke his contract with the State Opera and resigned.[13]

On the day of the opera's première Meyerhold was not even in the theatre, being wholly occupied nearby with an event of a very different kind. Six weeks earlier, plans had been made to celebrate the Revolution by staging Mayakovsky's newly-completed *Mystery-Bouffe*, the first play to be written by a Soviet dramatist. Lunacharsky and Meyerhold were present at Mayakovsky's first informal reading of the work and both were immediately enthusiastic.* Shortly afterwards, Meyerhold invited the author to read it again to the Alexandrinsky company with a view to staging it with them, but the absurdity of this idea was demonstrated by their scandalised reactions to the play's futuristic form, its overtly Bolshevik sympathies, and its outrageous blasphemy.[14]

With barely a month left for rehearsal Meyerhold was commissioned by the Narkompros (Commissariat for Enlightenment) to stage *Mystery-Bouffe* at the theatre of the Petrograd Conservatoire. Vladimir Solovyov and Mayakovsky himself were to be his assistants, and the Suprematist painter, Kazimir Malevich, was responsible for the settings and costumes. There remained the problem of casting: at that time all the Petrograd theatres were keeping their distance from the Bolshevik government, and the production was boycotted by the vast majority of professional actors. Consequently, on 12 October the organisers were forced to make an appeal through the press for actors and eventually all but a few main

* This was Meyerhold's first professional association with Mayakovsky. Their acquaintance originated in the winter of 1915–1916 when Mayakovsky came to Meyerhold's Studio and gave an impromptu reading of a number of his poems.

58 Poster for
Meyerhold's
production of
Mystery-Bouffe
(1918)

parts were played by students. Some had belated second thoughts, and
at the last minute Mayakovsky himself had to fill three roles, including
'Simply Man'.

The Bolshevik government was more than a little embarrassed by the
enthusiastic support it was receiving from the Futurists,* fearing that their
uncompromisingly brutalist vision of the new mechanised age might prove
insufficiently beguiling for the masses. Lunacharsky, himself a critic of
considerable liberality and perception, published an article in *Petrograd
Pravda*, championing *Mystery-Bouffe* and excusing in advance the worst
aberrations of the production:

> As a work of literature, it is most original, powerful and beautiful. But what
> it will turn out like in production I don't yet know. I fear very much that the
> futurist artists have made millions of mistakes . . . If *Mystery-Bouffe* is staged
> with all kinds of eccentricities, then whilst its content will be repugnant to
> the old world, its form will remain incomprehensible to the new. . . But
> even if the child turns out deformed, it will still be dear to us, because
> it is born of that same Revolution that we all look upon as our own great
> mother.[15]

As David Zolotnitsky remarks, the style of the play is what Lenin defined

* 'Futurism' was a term often applied to no specific group in Russia, but to the so-called
'left' avant-garde in general.

not unapprovingly some years later as 'hooligan communism'.[16] The play parodies the biblical story of the Ark, with the flood representing world revolution, the seven 'clean' couples who survive – the exploiters, and the seven 'unclean' couples – the international proletariat. Having overthrown the 'clean', the 'unclean' are led by 'Simply Man' through an innocuous hell and a tedious paradise to the promised land which is revealed as the utopian mechanised state of Socialism where the only servants are 'things' (tools, machines, etc). Meyerhold and his collaborators treated this allegory with all the rigid schematisation of the propaganda poster. In order to stress their solidarity, the 'unclean' spoke in the uniform elevated style of political oratory. The 'clean' were played in the broad, knockabout manner of the popular travelling show, a direct application of the skills explored in recent years by Meyerhold and Solovyov at their Studio, and an early demonstration of the style soon to be called 'eccentrism'.* Now added to the commedia *lazzi* and other tricks was the new element of circus acrobatics, which would be even more prominent when Meyerhold and Mayakovsky staged the second version of the play in 1921. In 1918, Mayakovsky as 'Simply Man' brought off one of the more spectacular effects:

> Hidden from the audience's view, he climbed four or five metres up an iron fire-escape behind the left-hand side of the proscenium arch. Then a broad leather strap was fixed to his waist, and at the appropriate moment he seemed to hurtle into view, soaring over the 'Unclean' crowded on the deck of the ark. . . In that position he hammered out the lines of his speech.[17]

Malevich's previous theatrical experience had been limited to the set and costume designs that he had prepared for the Futurist opera, *Victory over the Sun* in 1913.† Important as this project was in the artist's personal progression towards non-objective Suprematism, the isolated and hastily prepared event attracted little attention in avant-garde theatre circles and had no immediate impact on design or staging methods – even if affinities can be identified with Mayakovsky's later plays.[18]

No pictures of Malevich's designs for *Mystery-Bouffe* survive but some years later he talked about them to Alexander Fevralsky:

> My approach to the production was cubist. I saw the box-stage as the frame of a picture and the actors as contrasting elements (in cubism every object is a contrasting element in relation to another object). Planning the action on three or four levels, I tried to deploy the actors in space, predominantly in vertical compositions in the manner of the latest style of painting; the actors' movements were meant to accord rhythmically with the elements of the settings. I depicted a number of planes on a single canvas; I treated space not as illusionary but as cubist. I saw my task not as the creation of associations with the reality existing beyond the limits of the stage, but as the creation of a new reality.[19]

---

* See p.187 below. † See p. 120 above.

Fevralsky describes the effects produced:

> In Act One there was a three-dimensional ultramarine hemisphere (five
> metres in diameter) representing 'the Earth' in vertical cross-section against
> a skyline background and giving the spectator the impression of a globe. On
> the reverse, open side of the globe, and hidden from the public, there were
> steps which the actors playing the Eskimos could mount to appear on the
> 'Pole'. The hemisphere was made of light materials so that it was impossible
> to stand on it. Most of the action took place in front of 'the Earth'.
>
> The Ark in Act Two took the form of a three-dimensional ship-like
> construction with its prow pointing at the audience. The artist employed a
> variety of colour combinations that clashed rather than harmonised with each
> other.
>
> 'Hell' was represented by a red and green gothic hall, resembling a
> cave with stalactites. 'Paradise' was depicted in grey tones with clouds
> like aniline pink, blue, and raspberry-coloured cakes – to quote Malevich,
> the colour scheme was 'nauseating'.
>
> In the 'Promised Land' scene the audience saw a suprematist canvas
> and something like a big machine. The colours resembled iron and steel.
> The forestage lighting was slightly dimmed and the area upstage brightly
> illuminated. The 'Unclean' entered the 'City of the Future' through an arch.
>
> The costumes of the 'clean' bourgeoisie and the 'unclean' proletariat were
> realistic. The 'Devils' were clad half in red, half in black. The costumes of
> the 'Things' were particularly unusual, being made from sacks.[20]

Clearly, Malevich adopted a painter's approach to the production, which
led to his collaboration with Meyerhold and Mayakovsky being less than
harmonious. But in any case the play was put on in such a hurry that
confusion and misunderstandings were inevitable: the final cast, speaking
and non-speaking, seemed to vary in number between seventy and eighty;
the Conservatoire refused to sell copies of the play-text on its bookstall
and, according to Mayakovsky, even nailed up the doors into the theatre
to prevent rehearsals; the posters had to be finished off by Mayakovsky
himself on the day of the performance. There was no question of giving
more than the scheduled three performances since the Conservatoire was
due to follow them immediately with a programme of opera.

For Meyerhold and Mayakovsky, the production amounted to a declaration of war against the caution and routine of the established stage, and
in the prologue crude replicas of current theatre posters were ripped from
the front curtain. However, the reaction of the public to *Mystery-Bouffe* is
difficult to establish since few critics deemed the production worthy of
report. Andrei Levinson in the magazine *Life of Art* vilified the Futurists
for their calculated opportunism; yet wondered at the production's 'noisy
success'.[21] But some years later Vladimir Solovyov recalled: 'The production
had a rather cool reception; to be frank, it didn't get across to the audience.
The witty satirical passages . . . which had us doubled up with laughter
at rehearsals were greeted in performance with stony silence.'[22] However,
the unassailable fact remains that Mayakovsky had created a new dramatic

style that was soon to influence the course of the whole agitprop movement in Russia. The true vitality of *Mystery-Bouffe* was revealed in Meyerhold's production of the revised version in Moscow three years later, and thereafter the play was staged throughout the Soviet Union.[23]

In her recent study of Meyerhold Béatrice Picon-Vallin contrasts *Mystery-Bouffe* with *The Fairground Booth* twelve years earlier:

> Pierrot, the dreamer, mournful and solitary, the plaything of transformations in a deceptive reality, whose only means of self-affirmation is through his art, is succeeded by the poet, the worker of miracles who feels himself capable of transforming the world. . . With *Mystery-Bouffe* Meyerhold frees himself from the romantic approach to carnival, with its Venetian festivities or their provincial substitutes, with its black masks and ball-gowns. Instead of transplanting a democratic culture onto an aristocratic stage, thereby fashioning an image of a decadent world in decline whilst at the same time revitalising its theatre, resuscitating its theatricality, he now approaches the grotesque of the carnival directly through a heritage that is specifically Russian. It is a return to sources, brought about by the pressure of history: the irony of the 1910s gives way for the time being to a rough sense of the comic in which the individual and personal suffering are effaced.[24]

It remains to be seen whether the mood of Meyerhold's Petersburg period had been effaced for ever.

IV

In May 1919, weakened by illness and over-work, Meyerhold was forced to leave Petrograd for convalescence in the Crimea. He entered a sanatorium in Yalta, where he spent the summer receiving treatment for tuberculosis. The Civil War was at its height, and when the Whites captured the town he fled by sea to join his family in Novorossiisk, but there his Bolshevik sympathies were revealed by an informer and in September 1919 he was arrested. He spent several weeks in prison and narrowly escaped execution for alleged subversive activities. Still suffering from tuberculosis, Meyerhold was released on parole while the investigation of his case continued. He went into hiding and, fortunately for him, in March 1920 Novorossiisk was reoccupied by the Red Army. He immediately joined its political section and for the remainder of his stay in the South he participated in regular military training, spoke at both political and theatrical debates, and set up amateur drama groups in clubs and workplaces. He also managed to stage a hurried production of *A Doll's House* at the local Lenin Theatre. According to his nephew, Yury Goltsev, when the White general Baron Wrangel launched a counter offensive on the coast near Novorossiisk Meyerhold was amongst the irregulars who mobilised to aid the Red Army in repulsing the attack.[25]

As soon as Lunacharsky learnt of Meyerhold's vicissitudes, he summoned

59 Meyerhold in
1922–1923

him to Moscow to take charge of the Narkompros Theatre Department for
the entire Soviet Republic. The actor Igor Illinsky describes Meyerhold's
appearance on his arrival in Moscow in September 1920:

> He was wearing a soldier's greatcoat and on his cap there was a badge with
> Lenin's picture. . . In spite of its apparent simplicity, his appearance was
> somewhat theatrical, because although he was dressed modestly and without
> any superfluous 'Bolshevik' attributes, the style was still *à la Bolshevik*; the
> carelessly thrown-on greatcoat, the boots and puttees, the cap, the dark red
> woollen scarf – it was all quite unpretentious, but at the same time effective
> enough.[26]

Meyerhold's actions were no less dramatic than his appearance: he transformed the bureaucratic and ineffectual Theatre Department into a military
headquarters and proclaimed the advent of the October Revolution in the
theatre. Taking control of the Department's organ, *The Theatre Herald*
(*'Vestnik teatra'*), he initiated a violent polemic on behalf of the proletarian,
provincial, non-professional, and Red Army theatres, demanding a ruthless
redeployment of the manpower and material resources concentrated in the
small group of 'Academic Theatres' in Moscow. This group comprised the
Bolshoi, the Maly, the Moscow Art Theatre with its First and Second
Studios, Tairov's Kamerny Theatre, and the Moscow Children's Theatre.
These the State considered the most worthy custodians of Russian theatrical
traditions and rewarded them with its financial support. They were the true

objective of Meyerhold's offensive, and his tirades soon resolved into an undisguised assault on what he saw as their anachronistic styles and repertoires.

His hostility was not altogether objective: as Zolotnitsky records, certain well-known opera singers and members of the Art Theatre on tour in Novorossiisk in 1919 had made no effort to secure his release from prison.[27] Then again, there were his bitter memories of the haughty eminences of the Imperial stage and their languid public. But perhaps most influential was the desire to purge certain aspects of his own extravagant and over-refined artistic past by attacking similar tendencies in the work of others.[28] The targets were not hard to find; by 1920 the Revolution had left little impression on the Russian stage and not one Academic Theatre had attempted to present a Soviet play. Whilst the repertoire abounded in such works as Byron's *Cain* (Moscow Art Theatre), Wilde's *Salome* (Kamerny and Maly Theatres), Claudel's *The Tidings brought to Mary* (Kamerny Theatre), and Lecocq's operetta, *The Daughter of Madame Angot* (Moscow Art Theatre Musical Studio), not one serious attempt had been made to exploit the professional theatre for propaganda purposes since the three performances of *Mystery-Bouffe* in 1918. Tairov summed up the prevailing attitude in December 1920: 'A propagandist theatre after a revolution is like mustard after a meal.'[29] Immediately following the October Revolution Meyerhold had collaborated with Tairov on the production plan for Claudel's play *The Exchange* at the Kamerny Theatre (première 20 February, designs by Yakulov). At the same time, the two directors, together with Yevreinov, were contemplating the formation of a new 'left theatre' in Moscow to be directed by the three of them.[30] The project came to nothing and by 1920 Meyerhold and Tairov could find little in common; their mutual hostility then flared in the many public debates of the time.

Not content with mere exhortation, Meyerhold took control of the Free Theatre company, renamed it the 'R.S.F.S.R. Theatre No. 1', and augmented it with his own young and inexperienced nominees. In his opening speech to the company Meyerhold outlined his programme and policy:

> The Artistic Soviet of the R.S.F.S.R. Theatre has compiled a provisional
> repertoire that includes *The Dawn* (Verhaeren), *Mystery-Bouffe* (Mayakovsky),
> *Hamlet* (Shakespeare), *Great Catherine* (Bernard Shaw), *Golden Head* (Claudel)
> and *Women in Parliament* (Aristophanes). But since all this is merely literature,
> let it lie undisturbed in the libraries. We shall need scenarios and we shall often
> utilise even the classics as a basis for our theatrical creations. We shall tackle the
> task of adaptation without fear and fully confident of its necessity. It is possible
> that we shall adapt texts in cooperation with the actors of the company, and
> it is a great pity that they were not able to help Valery Bebutov and me with
> *The Dawn*. Joint work on texts by the company is envisaged as an integral
> part of the theatre's function. It is possible that such team-work will help us
> to realise the principle of improvisation, about which there is so much talk at
> the moment and which promises to prove most valuable.

> The psychological make-up of the actor will need to undergo a number
> of changes. There must be no pauses, no psychology, no 'authentic emotions'
> either on the stage or whilst building a role. Here is our theatrical programme:
> plenty of light, plenty of high spirits, plenty of grandeur, plenty of infectious
> enthusiasm, unlaboured creativity, the participation of the audience in the
> corporate creative act of the performance.[31]

The play chosen to inaugurate the new theatre was *The Dawn* ('*Les Aubes*') an epic verse drama written in 1898 by the Belgian symbolist poet Émile Verhaeren, depicting the transformation of a capitalist war into an

60 The Meyerhold
Theatre in the
1920s

international proletarian uprising by the opposing soldiers in the mythical town of Oppidomagne. It was translated by Georgy Chulkov and hurriedly adapted by Meyerhold and his assistant Valery Bebutov in an attempt to bring out its relevance to recent political events.

The first performance, timed to coincide with the third anniversary of the October Revolution, took place on 7 November 1920 at the former Sohn Theatre on what is now called Mayakovsky Square. The derelict, unheated auditorium with its flaking plaster and broken seats was more like a meeting-hall which was wholly appropriate, for it was in the spirit of a political meeting that Meyerhold conceived the production. Admission was free, the walls were hung with hortatory cartoons and placards, and the audience was showered at intervals during the play with leaflets. Also derived from the meeting was the declamatory style of the actors, who mostly remained motionless and addressed their speeches straight at the audience. Critics rightly compared the production with Greek tragedy, which furnished the precedent for the static manner of delivery and for

61 *The Dawn*, Scene Seven, showing the merging of the chorus in the orchestra pit with
the crowd onstage

the chorus commenting on the peripeteia of the drama. They extended from the
stage down into the orchestra pit, some in costume and some in everyday
clothes as though to merge performance and public. The chorus was assisted
in the task of guiding and stimulating audience reaction by a claque of actors
concealed throughout the auditorium.

A fortnight after the production had opened, the actor playing the
Herald interrupted his performance to deliver the news received the day
before that the Red Army had made the decisive breakthrough into the
Crimea at the Battle of Perekop. As the applause died down, a solo voice
began to sing the Revolutionary funeral march 'As Martyrs You Fell' and
the audience stood in silence. The action on stage then resumed its course.*
Meyerhold felt that his highest aspirations were gratified, and the practice

* Various myths have grown up around this event. The version given here seems to
be the most reliable.[32]

of inserting bulletins on the progress of the war continued. However, such unanimity of response did not occur every night, but usually only when military detachments attended *en bloc* – as they sometimes did, complete with banners flying and bands ready to strike up.

While the more sophisticated spectator was likely to find the conventions crude and the acting maladroit – not to mention the political message oversimplified or even repugnant – the new audience at whom ostensibly the production was aimed could not help but be puzzled by its appearance. Having failed to enlist the services of Tatlin as his designer, Meyerhold had turned to the twenty-year-old pupil of Petrov-Vodkin, Vladimir Dmitriev. He had attended the Borodin Street Studio from 1916 and continued his association with Meyerhold after the Revolution by studying design on his theatre arts course in Petrograd, where he had completed a project on *The Dawn* which was now hastily developed for the Moscow production.

62 *The Dawn*, Scene Four (the cemetery)

Dmitriev favoured the geometrical schematisation of the Cubo-Futurist school. His assembly of red, gold, and silver cubes, discs and cylinders, cut-out tin triangles, and intersecting ropes, which bore a clear resemblance to Tatlin's 'counter reliefs', blended uneasily with the occasional recognisable object such as a graveyard cross or the gates of a city, to say nothing of the soldiers' spears and shields, or the curious 'timeless' costumes of daubed canvas. Furthermore, the overall picture was made to look tawdry in the harsh glare of the floodlights, with which Meyerhold sought to dispel all illusion. Defending his choice of Dmitriev as a designer, Meyerhold said:

> We have only to talk to the latest followers of Picasso and Tatlin to know at once that we are dealing with kindred spirits . . . We are building just as they are building . . . For us, the handling of real materials ('*faktura*') is more important than any tediously pretty patterns and colours. What do we want with pleasing pictorial effects? What the *modern* spectator wants is the placard, the juxtaposing of the surfaces and shapes of *tangible materials*! . . . We are right to invite the Cubists to work with us, because we need settings like those that we shall be performing against tomorrow. The modern theatre wants to move out into the open air. We want our setting to be an iron pipe or the open sea or something constructed by the new man. I don't intend to engage in an appraisal of such settings; suffice it to say that for us they have the advantage of getting us out of the old theatre.[33]

His enthusiasm was not shared by Lunacharsky, who remarked drily: 'I was very much against that piano-lid flying through the sky of Oppidomagne.'[34]

As with *Mystery-Bouffe* in 1918, the Party was discomforted by this manifestation of the style of its Futurist supporters. Lenin's wife, Nadezhda Krupskaya, writing in *Pravda* had no complaint against the 'timelessness' of the production, but she objected violently to the ill-considered adaptation that related the action to a Soviet context and transformed the hero, Hérénien, into a traitor to his class who comes to terms with a capitalist power. Above all, she objected that it was a sheer insult 'to cast the Russian proletariat as a Shakespearian crowd which any self-opinionated fool can lead wherever the urge takes him.'[35] As a direct consequence of Krupskaya's criticism, the work was rewritten to render it dialectically more orthodox, but all the original theatrical devices were retained. With all its imperfections, *The Dawn* depended very much on the mood of the audience on the night for its success, but even so it ran for well over a hundred performances to full houses. It proclaimed an epoch in the Soviet theatre and is rightly considered a *locus classicus* in the history of the political theatre.

Whilst criticising the 'pretentiousness of the Futurist elements' in *The Dawn*, Lunacharsky considered it was a reasonable price to pay for the production's revolutionary fervour.[36] However, he refused point-blank to surrender the Academic Theatres to Meyerhold's demolition squad, saying: 'I am prepared to entrust Comrade Meyerhold with the destruction of the old and bad and the creation of the new and good. But I am not prepared to entrust him with the preservation of the old and good, the vital and strong, which must be allowed to develop in its own way in a revolutionary atmosphere.'[37]

All Academic Theatres in Moscow and Petrograd were brought under the direct aegis of Narkompras, thereby rendering Meyerhold's Theatre Department innocuous in the one sector it truly coveted. His ambitions were realised to the extent that the Academic Theatres began now to stage

Soviet works, but it was in their own good time and in their own well-tried manner.* The Nezlobin Theatre, the Korsh Theatre, and the Chaliapin Drama Studio rallied to Meyerhold and were renamed R.S.F.S.R. Theatres Nos. 2, 3 and 4 respectively, but they enjoyed only a brief existence in this guise and achieved no productions of note. On 26 February 1921 Meyerhold resigned as Head of the Theatre Department, and in May he severed his last effective connection with it.[38]

V

May Day 1921 saw the second production at the R.S.F.S.R. Theatre No. 1. It was *Mystery-Bouffe*, completely rewritten to make it relevant to the course of events since 1917. As a playwright, Mayakovsky was accorded unique status by Meyerhold. In 1933 he said:

> In his work with me, Mayakovsky showed himself to be not only a remarkable dramatist but a remarkable director as well. In all my years as a director I have never permitted myself the luxury of an author's cooperation when producing his work. I have always tried to keep the author as far from the theatre as possible during the period of actual production, because any truly creative director is bound to be hampered by the playwright's interference. In Mayakovsky's case I not only permitted him to attend, I simply couldn't begin to produce his plays without him.[39]

Mayakovsky was present from the first read-through of *Mystery-Bouffe* and added numerous topical couplets right up to the final rehearsal. The published text of this revised version is prefaced by the exhortation: 'Henceforth everyone who performs, stages, reads or prints *Mystery-Bouffe* should alter the contents in order to make it modern, up to date, up to the minute.'[40]

Among his amendments were the inclusion in the ranks of 'The Clean' of Lloyd George and Clemenceau, and the creation of a new central character 'The Conciliator', or Menshevik, who was brilliantly portrayed by the nineteen-year-old Igor Illinsky in red wig, steel gig-lamps, and flapping coat-tails, with an open umbrella to symbolise his readiness for flight. He was a figure derived from the traditional red-haired circus clown. His performance set the key for the whole production: an hilarious, dynamic, caricaturist rough-and-tumble, a carnival celebration of victory in the Civil War in total contrast to the still, hieratic solemnity of *The Dawn*. 'The Clean' wore costumes designed by Victor Kiselyov with much of the pith and vigour

---

* The Maly Theatre marked the fourth anniversary of the Revolution on 7 November 1921 with Lunacharsky's *Oliver Cromwell*, but the first Soviet play to be staged by the Moscow Art Theatre was *The Pugachov Rising* by Trenyov in September 1925. In the case of the Kamerny it was Levidov's *Conspiracy of Equals* in November 1927.

63 and 64 Ilinsky
as the
Menshevik and
one of the Devils
(sketches by
Victor Kiselyov)

that made the ROSTA satirical 'windows'* the most telling political posters of the early Soviet period. They were close in spirit to the sketches that Mayakovsky himself had made for the play in reaction against Malevich's original designs. As Fevralsky observes, these costumes were not unlike Picasso's cubist paintings in style, with pieces of newspaper and cardboard placards attached to them.[41] However, 'The Unclean', clad this time in blue overalls,† were of a uniform dullness which not even Mayakovsky's rousing rhetoric could hide. Meyerhold was soon to realise that the portrayal of virtue – even Socialist virtue – untarnished and triumphant, is inherently tedious and his avoidance of it at all costs was to cause him unending trouble in the years to come.

The proscenium which had been bridged by the placing of the chorus in the orchestra pit in *The Dawn* was demolished once and for all in *Mystery-Bouffe*.‡ The stage proper was taken up by a series of platforms of differing levels, interconnected by steps and vaguely suggestive of the various locations in the action. With several rows of seats removed, a broad ramp extended deep into the auditorium, bearing a huge hemisphere over which the cast clambered and which revolved to expose a 'hell-mouth'. In this scene, one of the devils was played by the celebrated circus clown, Vitaly Lazarenko, who entered by sliding down a wire and performed acrobatic

---

* A series of strip cartoons ('Okna ROSTA') on social and political themes issued by the Russian Telegraph Agency (ROSTA). Mayakovsky was a regular contributor.

† Soon to serve as the prototype for the uniforms of the 'Blue Blouse' agitprop theatre groups.

‡ The settings were by Anton Lavinsky and Vladimir Khrakovsky.

tricks in a red spotlight, greatly enlivening the performance but exposing the relative clumsiness of his fellow-performers. In the final act, set in the new *electrified* promised land, the action spilled into the boxes adjacent to the stage, and at the conclusion the audience was invited to mingle with the actors on stage.

In this production Meyerhold dispensed finally with a front curtain and flown scenery. The theatre was bursting at the seams, unable to accommodate the kind of popular spectacle that he was striving to achieve, and it was now that the questions arose whose answers he was shortly to seek in Constructivism. Reviewing the progress of the Meyerhold Theatre in 1931, the leading Constructivist theoretician, Nikolai Tarabukin, wrote:

> It can be seen as the source of two future lines of development in the theatre: constructivism and 'architecturalism'. Both features were present in *Mystery-Bouffe*, albeit in embryonic and undeveloped form. There was much that was purely decorative and superficial. Hence the treatment of the stage space, which both in conception and in execution was vague and undefined. But ten years ago it was daring in its impact and wholly in accord with developments in the other art-forms. Its echo resounded through a whole series of Moscow theatres, extended the length and breadth of the provinces, and probably survives to this day as an anachronism in some remote corners.[42]

Once again, Meyerhold and Mayakovsky were accused of 'Futurist' obscurity and the production was boycotted by all but three Moscow newspaper critics.

65 Model
reconstruction
of the setting for
Mystery-Bouffe

One of the few to subject it to constructive analysis was the Bolshevik writer Dmitry Furmanov, the future author of *Chapaev*. Reporting in a provincial paper, he found the play's form confused and its humour crude, but in conclusion he wrote:

> This new theatre is the theatre of the stormy age of the Revolution; it
> was born not of the tranquillity of *The Cherry Orchard*, but of the tempests
> and whirlwinds of the Civil War. . . This new theatre of storm and stress
> undoubtedly has a great future. It can't be dismissed as a mere aberration:
> it has its roots deep in our heroic, proletarian struggle.[43]

Despite all opposition, *Mystery-Bouffe* was performed daily until the close
of the season on 7 July. In the five months up to the end of May 1921, one
hundred and fifty-four performances of the two plays in the thousand-seat
Sohn Theatre were watched by roughly 120,000 spectators.[44]

In Spring 1921, when Soviet Russia was on the verge of bankruptcy as a
consequence of the privations and chaos wrought by the Civil War, Lenin
introduced his New Economic Policy in order to restore the economy. Under
its provisions, certain sectors of the economic system reverted to private
control and the ban on the investment of foreign capital was lifted. Its
effects were quickly felt in the theatre; all state subsidies were withdrawn,*
some companies reverted to private ownership and were required once more
to yield their investors a realistic profit, whilst those run by collectives or
state organisations such as the unions or the Red Army were subjected to
more stringent controls, and many were forced to close.

The R.S.F.S.R. Theatre No. 1 depended for its survival on *ad hoc* subsidy,
and in June 1921 the Moscow Soviet ordered its closure, implausibly accusing
it of overspending. Thanks largely to Lunacharsky's intervention, the theatre
continued to live a precarious existence throughout the summer, managing
to stage one more production, Ibsen's *The League of Youth*, in August. But
a 'revolutionised' version of Wagner's *Rienzi*, designed by Yakulov and
intended to celebrate the Third Congress of the Comintern in Moscow,
was abandoned after the second run-through, and on 6 September 1921 the
theatre closed. Thus Meyerhold, the first Bolshevik director, was left with
nowhere to work.[45]

---

* Subisidies were restored to the Academic Theatres in November 1921.

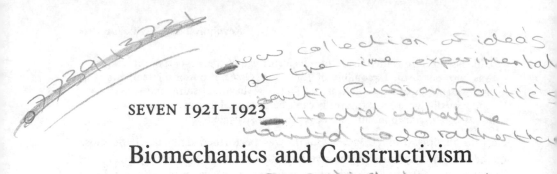

Biomechanics and Constructivism

Not for the first time, Meyerhold displayed remarkable resilience and powers of recovery after a disaster, fashioning virtue out of necessity. In the autumn of 1921 he was appointed director of the newly formed State Higher Theatre Workshops in Moscow.* He was joined on the staff by Valery Bebutov, his assistant director at the R.S.F.S.R. Theatre, and Ivan Aksyonov – ex-Civil War commissar, engineer by profession, leading member of the 'Centrifuge' group of poets, authority on Elizabethan and Jacobean drama, author of the first monograph in Russia on Picasso, and translator of English and French literature. Aksyonov was 'Rector', or dean, and gave courses in play-writing, the English theatre, and mathematics. His polymath skills typified the range of intellectual enquiry that invariably accompanied Meyerhold's work.

The Workshops opened at the start of October in sparse, poorly heated premises on Novinsky Boulevard, comprising a former gymnastics hall with a single lecture theatre below and a flat occupied by Meyerhold above. In the first year the courses in theatre history, theory and practice were attended by over eighty students; some had been with Meyerhold at the R.S.F.S.R. Theatre, but most were newcomers, no more than seventeen or eighteen years old. Henceforth, Meyerhold's company was composed exclusively of actors who had grown up during the Civil War period; many were of working-class origin or had seen military service, and were violently opposed to the traditions of pre-revolutionary art. Understandably, their devotion to the 'Master', as Meyerhold was now known to his students, bordered on the fanatical.

Applicants were required to present an improvisation, sometimes based on

* Called initially the State Higher Director's Workshops. In 1922 it was incorporated in the State Institute of Theatrical Art ('GITIS'), but shortly broke away to form the 'Meyerhold Workshop'. In 1924 this was given the new title of 'Meyerhold State Experimental Theatre Workshops' ('GEKTEMAS') and continued to function as such under various further names until 1938. It remained throughout an integral part of Meyerhold's theatre. (See also p. 184 below).

a simple *commedia* scenario. They also had to prepare a production proposal for a play of their choice and defend it in open discussion with the staff and other students. Amongst those accepted for the first course were the future film directors Sergei Eisenstein, Sergei Yutkevich, and Nikolai Ekk, together with many others who were to become leading actors and directors in the Soviet theatre and cinema, including Maria Babanova, Erast Garin, Igor Ilinsky, Vasily Zaichikov and Mikhail Zharov.

One student was Zinaida Raikh, the ex-wife of the poet Sergei Yesenin and soon to marry Meyerhold when he and Olga Munt were divorced. Twenty years younger than Meyerhold, Raikh had been abandoned by Yesenin a few weeks before the birth of their second child. In August 1920 she had found a job with Narkompros and joined the Bolshevik Party, having previously been a member of the Socialist Revolutionaries

66 Meyerhold and
Zinaida Raikh
in 1923

from the age of nineteen. Meyerhold's relationship with Olga Munt had been one of immense emotional dependency, but it was punctuated with long separations and breakdowns in communication. She was rooted in the old intelligentsia of his Petersburg period, whereas Raikh was working class in origin, the daughter of a railway worker from Odessa who had joined the Social Democrats in 1897. Worldly, elegant and politically well-connected, she was the obvious partner for Meyerhold in the new world of Moscow – and he loved her with an obsessive devotion that was often to distort his artistic judgement.[1] Beginning with Aksyusha in *The Forest*, Raikh played a series of leading roles in Meyerhold's productions right up to the day of his theatre's closure in 1938. His biographer Nikolai Volkov writes:

> Vsevolod Emilievich made an actress out of her. After the theatre's visit to Berlin* the Germans called Raikh 'die grosse Schauspielerin'; but she wasn't a great actress, or even a particularly outstanding one. The Moscow critics were harsh and emphatic in their rejection of her. But the fault for this unjustified rejection was largely Meyerhold's. His promotion of her as an actress was pursued aggressively. At times he neglected the interests of the other actors in his company by surrounding her with untalented actresses. . . He entrusted Raikh with the best parts, beginning with Anna Andreevna in *The Government Inspector* and ending with Marguerite in *The Lady of the Camellias*.[2]

Meyerhold's relationship with Raikh is inextricably bound up with his achievements and his errors as a director, and it is a theme that will recur repeatedly in the following chapters.

II

As early as January 1921 Meyerhold had made plans to open a 'theatrical technical school' attached to his theatre. It was designed to give actors methodical instruction in speech and movement 'based on the general physical laws of technology, as expressed most clearly in physics, mechanics, music and architecture'.[3] With Meyerhold's resignation from Narkompros, the school failed to materialise but now at the Higher Theatre Workshops the curriculum was very similar. As there had been at Meyerhold's earlier studios, there were courses in singing, voice, dance, fencing, boxing, acrobatics and gymnastics, as well as general cultural and technological topics. However, for the first time 'biomechanics' featured as a daily one-hour activity that was obligatory for all students. Meyerhold presented biomechanics as the theatrical equivalent of industrial time-and-motion study. He compared it on the one hand to the experiments in the scientific organisation of labour by the American Frederick Winslow Taylor and his Russian follower Gastev, and on the other to the theories of 'reflexology' developed by the 'objective psychologist' William James and the Russians, Bekhterev and Pavlov.[4] When the first public demonstration of his bio-mechanics exercises or '*études*' was given by Meyerhold and his students on 12 June 1922, he made the following points in his introductory lecture:

> In the past the actor has always conformed to the society for which his art was intended. In future the actor must go even further in relating his technique to

* In 1930 – see p. 260 below.

the industrial situation. For he will be working in a society where labour is no longer regarded as a curse but as a joyful, vital necessity. In these conditions of ideal labour art clearly requires a new foundation. . .

In art our constant concern is the organisation of raw material. Constructivism has forced the artist to become both artist and engineer. Art should be based on scientific principles; the entire creative act should be a conscious process. The art of the actor consists in organising his material: that is, in his capacity to utilise correctly his body's means of expression.

The actor embodies in himself both the organiser and that which is organised (i.e. the artist and his material). The formula for acting may be expressed as follows: $N = A_1 + A_2$ (where N = the actor; A_1 = the artist who conceives the idea and issues the instructions necessary for its execution; A_2 = the executant who executes the conception of A_1).

The actor must train his material (the body), so that it is capable of executing instantaneously those tasks that are dictated externally (by the actor, the director). . .

Since the art of the actor is the art of plastic forms in space, he must study the mechanics of his body. This is essential because any manifestations of a force (including the living organism) is subject to constant laws of mechanics (and obviously the creation by the actor of plastic forms in the space of the stage is a manifestation of the force of the human organism). . .

All psychological states are determined by specific physiological processes. By correctly resolving the nature of his state physically, the actor reaches the point where he experiences the *excitation* that communicates itself to the spectator and induces him to share in the actor's performance: what we used to call 'gripping' the spectator. It is this excitation that is the very essence of the actor's art. From a sequence of physical positions and situations there arise 'points of excitation' that are informed with some particular emotion. Throughout this process of 'rousing the emotions' the actor observes a rigid framework of physical prerequisites.[5]

The series of individual and group exercises, all performed to piano accompaniment, had such titles as 'Dagger thrust', 'Leap onto the chest', 'Lowering

67 Biomechanics exercises. Drawing by Vladimir Lyutse, 1922

a weight', and 'Shooting a bow'. One of the students, Erast Garin, describes 'Shooting a bow':

> An imaginary bow is held in the left hand. The student advances with the left shoulder forward. When he spots the target he stops, balanced equally on both feet. The right hand describes an arc in order to reach an arrow in an imaginary belt behind his back. The movement of the hand affects the whole body, causing the balance to shift to the back foot. The hand draws the arrow and loads the bow. The balance is transferred to the front foot. He aims. The bow is drawn with the balance shifting again to the back foot. The arrow is fired and the exercise completed with a leap and a cry.
>
> Through this, one of the earliest exercises, the pupil begins to comprehend himself in spatial terms, acquires physical self-control, develops elasticity and balance, realises that the merest gesture – say with the hand – resounds throughout the entire body, and gains practice in the so-called 'refusal' [or 'reaction' – EB]. In this exercise the 'pre-gesture', the 'refusal', is the hand reaching back for the arrow. The *étude* is an example of the 'acting sequence', which comprises intention, realisation and reaction.[6]

Meyerhold describes the 'acting sequence' or cycle* referred to by Garin:

> Each *acting cycle* comprises three invariable stages:
> 1. INTENTION   2. REALISATION   3. REACTION
> *The Intention* is the intellectual assimilation of a task prescribed externally by the dramatist, the director or the initiative of the performer.
> *The realisation* is the cycle of volitional, mimetic and vocal reflexes.
> *The reaction* is the attenuation of the volitional reflex after its realisation mimetically and vocally, preparatory to the reception of a new intention (the transition to a new acting cycle).[7]

In October 1922 Meyerhold and his students gave a further display of his system. Shortly afterwards, in an article entitled 'Biomechanics according to Meyerhold' the Imaginist poet Ippolit Sokolov, who was himself promoting an alternative system of 'Taylorised' actor-training,[8] dismissed Meyerhold's claim to the invention of biomechanics, referring to 'over 100 major works on the subject', most notably Jules Amar's *Le Moteur humain et les bases scientifiques du travail professionel* (Paris, 1914). Furthermore, he claimed that Meyerhold's exercises were either physiologically unsound and 'downright anti-Taylorist' or simply rehashed circus clowning.[9]

Meyerhold answered his critic in a lecture entitled 'Tartuffes of Communisim and Cuckolds of Morality'. Judging from the one brief résumé published, he made little attempt to refute Sokolov's charges, saying that his system had no scientific basis and that its underlying theory rested on 'one brochure by Coquelin'.[10] He doubtless meant either Constant Benoît Coquelin's *L'art et le comédien* (1880) or his *L'art du comédien* (1886), in which the remarks on the dual personality of the actor are strikingly similar to Meyerhold's formulation $N = A_1 + A_2$.[11] In his memoirs Meyerhold's

---

* The equivalent of Taylor's 'working cycles'.

68 'The Leap onto the Chest' in *The Magnanimous Cuckold* (1922)

pupil Erast Garin confirms that great emphasis was placed on Coquelin's theories in the early days of the Theatre Workshops.[12]

As we have seen, from 1905 when Meyerhold became director of the Theatre-Studio in Moscow his production methods were shaped by a preoccupation with mime and movement. With the opening of his Petersburg Studio in 1913 came the opportunity to explore the formal discipline of the *commedia dell'arte* and the conventions of the Oriental theatres. It was then that he laid the basis for what later became codified as biomechanics. One of the Studio's '*comédiens*', Alexei Gripich, recalls that '. . . from the exercise "Shooting a bow" there developed the *étude* "The Hunt", and then a whole pantomime which was used to train every "generation" in the Studio. A whole series of exercises and études became "classics" and were used later in the teaching of biomechanics.'[13] Similarly, Valery Bebutov says that Meyerhold got the idea for 'The Leap onto the Chest' from the Sicilian actor, Giovanni Grasso, who visited Petersburg before the First World War.[14]

Thus Meyerhold derived his exercises from various sources, refining them and adding new ones during the first year of the Theatre Workshops until they numbered more than twenty. As he said to Harold Clurman when he visited Moscow in 1935, 'each exercise is a melodrama. Each movement gives the actor a sense of performing on the stage.'[15] Biomechanics was designed to foster in the actor a sense of complete self-awareness and self-control in performance. In 1921 Meyerhold said to his students, 'On stage I can so enter a role that I suffer and cry real tears, but if at the same time my means of expression are not equal to my intention then my emotions will have no impact. I may sob, even die on stage, but the audience will feel nothing if I lack the means of conveying to them what I want.'[16] But it was not by means of *physical* training alone that biomechanics was intended to correct this lack of self-control; the function of the actor's *intelligence* was paramount. Again, to quote Meyerhold:

> The whole biomechanical system, the entire process of our movements is dictated by one basic principle – our capacity for thought, the human brain, the rational apparatus. . . That is why we verify every movement on stage against the thought that is provoked by the scene in question. . . Not only movements, not only words, but also the brain . . . the brain must occupy the primary position, because it is the brain that initiates the given task, that gives orientation, that determines the sequence of movements, the accent, and so on.[17]

In practice, however, the process was considerably more complex than this clear-cut statement seems to imply. Analysing the technique of some of Meyerhold's leading actors in 1926, two of his assistants wrote that ' . . . although the ability to control one's body is indeed one of the elements of the new acting system, the ability to control one's emotional apparatus is an equally fundamental requirement of the new system. We would say that the basis of Meyerhold's system is *the formal display of the emotional.*'[18] The productions from *Bubus the Teacher* (1925) onwards offer the best illustration of this formula.

There is no doubt that Meyerhold, spurred on by the polemical mood of the times, exaggerated the scientific aspect of biomechanics in order to show that his system was devised in response to the demands of the new machine age, in contrast to those of Stanislavsky, Tairov and others which he claimed were unscientific and anachronistic. But even though his initial claims may have been extravagant, biomechanics became accepted as a thoroughly viable system of theatrical training which he employed to school his actors up to the mid-thirties. Eventually, its practical success was largely responsible for the introduction of some form of systematised physical training into the curriculum of every Soviet drama school.[19] In 1934 Igor Ilinsky gave his view of the comprehensive scope of biomechanics:

> People think that essentially biomechanics is rather like acrobatics. At best, they know that it consists of a series of stage tricks like knowing how to box your partner's ears, how to leap onto his chest and so on, and so on. But not many realise that the biomechanical system of acting, starting from a series of devices

designed to develop the ability to control one's body within the stage space in the most advantageous manner, leads on to the most complex questions of acting technique, problems concerning the coordination of movement, words, the capacity to control one's emotions, one's excitability in performance. The emotional state of the actor, his temperament, his excitability, the emotional sympathy between the actor as artist and the imaginative processes of the character he is performing – all these are fundamental elements in the complex system of biomechanics.[20]

Over twenty years earlier Meyerhold had said: 'It is well known that the celebrated Coquelin began with externals when working on his roles, but does that mean he did not experience them? The difference here lies only in the method, in the way that one studies a role. What it boils down to is this: talent always experiences a role deeply, whereas mediocrity merely enacts it.'[21]

III

In February 1922 the former Sohn Theatre reopened under the new title of 'The Actor's Theatre'. Initially, the repertoire was composed entirely of revivals of productions by the former Nezlobin Theatre, but on 20 April Meyerhold presented Ibsen's A Doll's House as a joint production with the Nezlobin Company and his own students. It was his fifth production of the play since he had first staged it in Kherson nineteen years earlier. Rushed on after only five rehearsals and for five performances in order to establish Meyerhold's claim to the now empty theatre, it bore the subtitle 'The Tragedy of Nora Helmer, or how a woman of bourgeois upbringing came to prefer independence and labour'. On the day of the performance Meyerhold and his students moved into the Sohn Theatre and cleared the stage of all the curtains and ancient scenery that cluttered it. Then they constructed a setting for A Doll's House by taking flats from stock and propping them back to front against the stage walls in order to symbolise – or so Meyerhold claimed – 'the bourgeois milieu against which Nora rebels'.[22] Reviewing the production in Theatrical Moscow, Mikhail Zagorsky wrote: '. . . clearly it is a joke, a stroke of irony, a parody of itself, a long tongue poked out at NEP, but least of all a performance connected in any way with the name of Meyerhold. . .'[23] But he was not altogether right; insofar as it was a carefully calculated outrage against the tenets of illusionistic theatre, it had a most definite connection with the name of Meyerhold. And in one vital respect it was spectacularly successful: the scandal it caused was more than the 'Nezlobintsy' could stand; some fled at once and the remainder departed after the next production. Thus Meyerhold and his young company were left in sole occupation of the dilapidated theatre, which remained theirs until it closed for renovation in 1932.

The first production cast exclusively from the students of Meyerhold's Workshop was Fernand Crommelynck's *The Magnanimous Cuckold*, staged five days after *A Doll's House*. As Meyerhold himself said, circumstances forced him to seek a setting that was cheap and could be erected anywhere, without resort to conventional stage machinery.* It was a chance to realise the desire he had expressed a year earlier after his production of *The Dawn* 'to move out into the open air'. He came close to doing precisely that in April 1921 when he planned to stage a mass spectacle *Struggle and Victory*, devised by Aksyonov and involving some 2500 performers including artillery, aeroplanes, military bands, choirs, and gymnasts. Due to lack of funds the project had to be abandoned, but a design was completed by two young artists, Alexander Vesnin and Lyubov Popova, both of whom participated in the first exhibition of the Constructivists which opened under the title '5 x 5 = 25'† in Moscow later that year. In their constructions Meyerhold saw the possibility of a utilitarian, multi-purpose scaffolding that could be easily dismantled and erected in any surroundings. Furthermore, this industrial 'anti-art' which recognised practicability as its sole criterion and condemned all that was merely depictive, decorative, or atmospheric, seemed to Meyerhold a natural ally in his repudiation of naturalism and aestheticism.

Originally, Meyerhold had invited Medunetsky and the Stenberg brothers to design a setting for *The Magnanimous Cuckold* and the idea of a non-representational scaffold belonged to them. According to Vladimir Stenberg, the theatre failed to pay them an advance, which they had requested in the form of army rations in lieu of worthless inflated roubles, and in consequence they declined to submit a model. With time pressing, the work was handed over to Lyubov Popova who had joined the teaching staff of the Theatre Workshop subsequent to the '5 x 5 = 25' exhibition, and with minimal resources she developed the idea of a utilitarian construction.[25] It consisted of the frames of conventional theatre flats and platforms joined by steps, chutes, and catwalks; there were two wheels, a large disc bearing the letters 'CR-ML-NCK', and vestigial windmill sails, which all revolved at varying speeds as a kinetic accompaniment to the fluctuating passions of the characters.‡ Blank panels hinged to the framework served as doors and windows. As Rudnitsky says, the aim was simply 'to organise scenic space in the way most convenient for the actors, to create for them a "working area"'.[26] But despite the skeletal austerity, the grimy damp-stained brickwork of the exposed back wall, and the absence of wings to hide either stage-crew or cast, Popova's contraption evoked inevitable associations with

* Describing the setting for *The Magnanimous Cuckold*, Meyerhold wrote: 'After the closure of the R.S.F.S.R. Theatre No. 1 we were left without a theatre and began to work on the problem of productions without a stage.'[24]

† It consisted of five works by each of five artists, Vesnin, Popova, Rodchenko, Stepanova, Exter.

‡ The system was hand-operated, on the opening night by Meyerhold himself.

69 Design collage by Popova for *The Magnanimous Cuckold*

the windmill in which the play was supposed to be set, suggesting now a bedroom, now a balcony, now the grinding mechanism, now a chute for the discharging of the sacks of flour. Only in the episodes when it enhanced the synchronised movements of the complete ensemble did it work simply as a functional machine. In the theatre, whose whole allure depends on the associative power of the imagination, every venture by the Constructivists led to the unavoidable compromising of their utilitarian dogma and each time demonstrated the inherent contradiction in the term 'theatrical constructivism'. Popova herself conceded that, for all its innovative approach, her construction was a transitional work that bore the imprint of earlier painterly approaches to theatre design, and the leading art theorist, Nikolai Tarabukin, wrote in 1931:

> Lyubov Popova's work reflects the traditions of painting, albeit non-figurative painting. One is struck by the deliberate frontal emphasis of the *Cuckold* construction. The wheels of the windmill, the white letters on a black background, the combination of red with yellow and black – they are all decorative elements derived from painting. The 'installation' shows a predominance of flat surfaces and Suprematism. Its lightness and elegance are entirely in keeping with the style of Crommelynck's farce, but as a utilitarian construction it does not stand close scrutiny of all its components. One needs only to mention the door on the second level and the difficulty the actors have in making exits on to the landing behind it.[27]

But for all the solecisms of Popova's setting in the eyes of the Constructivists, it proved the ideal platform for a display of biomechanical agility, 'a spring-board for the actor which quite rightly was compared to the apparatus of a circus acrobat'.[28] Meyerhold himself fully acknowledged Popova's contribution. In a letter to *Izvestia* he wrote:

> I consider it my duty to point out that in the creation of the performance the work of Professor L S Popova was significant, . . . that the model of the construction was accepted by me before the beginning of the planning of the play, and that much in the tone of the performance was taken from the constructive set.[29]

Written in 1920, Crommelynck's tragi-farce tells of Bruno, a village scribe who is so infatuated with his beautiful and innocent young wife, Stella, that he convinces himself that no man could conceivably resist her. Deranged with jealousy, he forces her to share her bed with every man in the village in the hope of unmasking her true lover. Although still in love with Bruno, Stella eventually flees with the Cowherd on the condition that he will allow her to be faithful to him, leaving Bruno convinced that this is yet another trick to conceal 'the only one'. Some critics, notably Lunacharsky

70 Scene from *The Magnanimous Cuckold* (1922)

in *Izvestia*,[30] were scandalised by what they regarded as little more than a salacious bedroom farce, but the majority were agreed that the risqué plot was completely redeemed by the brio, the style, and the good humour of Meyerhold's production. Erast Garin describes the opening scene:

> . . . You heard an exultant voice ring out offstage, full of joyful strength, love and happiness; and then up the side ladder to the very top of the construction flew – and 'flew' is the word – Ilinsky as Bruno. His wife Stella (played by Babanova) ran to meet him and stood, indescribably youthful, lithe and athletic, with her straight legs planted wide apart like a pair of compasses. Without pausing, Bruno hoisted her onto his shoulder, then slid down the highly-polished chute and gently lowered his weightless load to the ground. Continuing this childishly innocent love-play, Stella ran from him and he caught her by the bench, where they remained face to face, excited and happy at the thought of being together again and full of the whole joy of living.[31]

The irresistible innocence of the production was exemplified by the performance of the twenty-one-year-old Maria Babanova, for whom it launched a long and scintillating career. On her own admission, Babanova in her naïveté barely comprehended the erotic implications of Stella's role, but

71 Maria Babanova
as Stella

she was wholly devoted to Meyerhold as a teacher and director and readily executed his most extreme demands. As Aksyonov wrote, 'She suffered in silence and worked like a mouse who has been set to turn a treadmill.'[32] In 1925 the actress, Vera Yureneva described the impact of Babanova's performance:

> A factory whistle is the signal for the spotlight to come on and the performance

begins. Up the side steps, with assured and agile strides, wearing tall, lace-up boots, a slender factory-girl bounds onstage.

A short, rough blue overall. A round, wicked little face. A simply-tied mop of flaxen hair. Eyes like two petrified violets . . .

Thus the new actress makes her appearance, the actress Babanova. Today no one knows her name, but tomorrow she will already be hailed as the first of a new galaxy of young actresses. Actresses magically born and reared amidst an arid expanse of wooden constructions, under the piercing gaze of a spotlight on a bare stage – stripped of curtains, wings, of all the mysteries of the old theatre. Actresses who owe that theatre nothing.

The impression is unusual: the age of innocence, an artless appearance, yet an unexpected assurance and a maturity of performance. Not a shadow of nerves or awkwardness at her first entrance . . .

Her performance is based on rhythms, precise and economical like a construction. Not the rhythms of speech, of words and pauses. No, the rhythms of steps, surfaces and space. Few words to speak of. The part is built on movement, and the words are thrown at the audience with unusual power, like a ball hitting a target. No modulation, no crescendo or piano. No psychology . . .

Her feet are trained not for the gentle rake of the ordinary stage, but for the dizzying cascades of steps, ramps, bridges and slopes.

The role develops, strengthens, matures without restraint – violently, yet according to plan. One moment she is talking innocently to a little bird, the next she is a grown-up woman, delighting in the return of her husband; in her passion and devotion she is tortured by his jealousy.

And now she is being attacked by a mob of blue-clad men, furiously fending them off with a hurricane of resounding blows.

But all to no avail, and finally she is carried off from under the marital roof on the shoulders of the man who loves her. Vengeful, seemingly entwined in him, she is a captivating little virago with a streaming white wave of hair and a stern, unwavering, blue gaze.[33]

Meyerhold transformed the play into a universal parable on the theme of jealousy, with the style of the performance furnishing a constant commentary on the dialogue and the situations. The characters all wore loose-fitting overalls with only the odd distinguishing mark such as a pair of clown's red pom-poms for Bruno, alluring button-boots for Stella, or a monocle and riding crop for the Count. The same principle of simplification was applied by Popova to the design of the hand-props. To quote Alma Law's description:

Many of the objects – for example, the inkstand and pen of Estrugo or the dustbin and shoe-brush of the Nurse – were intentionally exaggerated in size. Others, such as the key and keyhole that Bruno and Estrugo used to lock up Stella at the start of Act Two, were simply suggested through mimed action. The primula that Bruno sends Stella in Act One was not a flower at all but a little red wooden rattle, which was a very popular toy in the twenties. And the mask that Stella carries in Act Two was made from triangular and rectangular pieces of cardboard coloured red, white, black and grey. The exaggerated size of the props and their intentionally nonrealistic

72 *The Magnanimous Cuckold* (Act Three), with Ilinsky as Bruno (right) and Babanova as Stella (extreme right)

style served to emphasise the production's atmosphere of childlike innocence which constantly short-circuited the erotic content of Crommelynck's text.[34]

The actor's attitude to his part was conveyed through an eloquent succession of poses, gestures, and acrobatic tricks, many of them derived from the biomechanical études and all accomplished with the casual dexterity of a circus clown. Thus, 'as he is leaving, the Bourgmestre strikes the right-hand half of the revolving door with his behind, causing the left-hand half to hit Petrus who flies forward onto the bench. The Bourgmestre ("pardon me") accidentally leans on the right-hand half of the door, thereby causing the other half to hit his own nose. Finally he steps round the door and exits via the space between it and the left-hand corner of the set.'[35]

Boris Alpers describes Igor Ilinsky's performance:

Bruno . . . stood before the audience, his face pale and motionless, and with unvarying intonation, a monotonous declamatory style and identical sweeping gestures he uttered his grandiloquent monologues. But at the same time this Bruno was being ridiculed by the actor performing acrobatic stunts at the most impassioned moments of his speeches, belching, and comically rolling his eyes whilst enduring the most dramatic anguish.[36]

One needs only to compare this with Meyerhold's disquisition on the comedy of masks in his essay 'The Fairground Booth' or his analysis of the character of Dom Juan* to see that *The Magnanimous Cuckold*, for all its modernist exterior, was a revival of the spirit, and in good measure, the letter too of the *commedia dell'arte*. It was the culmination and the vindication of all the explorations into the traditions of the popular theatre that Meyerhold had been pursuing for the past fifteen years; at last he had realised his ambition of creating a new theatre with actors schooled by himself in a new style. Igor Ilinsky writes in his memoirs:

> Many of those who saw *The Magnanimous Cuckold* and many of the young actors (including myself) who worked with Meyerhold regard it as the most complete and the most significant of all his productions during the entire period of his theatre's existence – because of the way it revealed the fundamental purity of his style of acting, and the way it displayed most eloquently his system of biomechanics.[37]

IV

Despite the spectacular success of *The Magnanimous Cuckold*, Meyerhold was faced once more in June 1922 with the possible loss of the Sohn Theatre. This was averted only after violent protests from the theatrical Left and the Constructivists,[38] and an open letter from himself in which he threatened 'to cease work in the Republic altogether.'[39] Eventually, Meyerhold not only retained the use of the Actor's Theatre, but he became Artistic Director of the newly formed 'Theatre of the Revolution' as well. At the same time, he assumed overall control of the State Institute of Theatrical Art (GITIS), which was formed by an amalgamation of the former Theatre Workshops, the State Institute of Musical Drama and nine smaller autonomous theatre-studios. So disparate were the various factions that violent friction was bound to be generated, and this quickly led to the formation of an unofficial, quite separate Meyerhold Workshop within the Institute. Without official recognition and with only the box-office to support it, this Workshop ran the Actor's Theatre, with its young students discharging every function from door-keeper to scene-shifter. On 24 November 1922 *The Magnanimous Cuckold* was joined in the repertoire by Alexander Sukhovo-Kobylin's *Tarelkin's Death*, which he had first staged at the Alexandrinsky Theatre on the eve of the Revolution in October 1917.†

In a note on the play, Sukhovo-Kobylin writes: 'In keeping with the play's humorous nature, it must be played briskly, merrily, loudly – *avec*

* See pp. 108-109 above. † See p. 153 above.

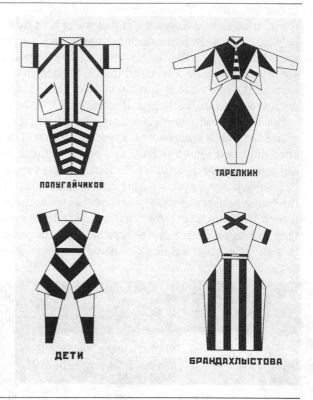

ПОПУГАЙЧИКОВ

ТАРЕЛКИН

ДЕТИ

БРАНДАХЛЫСТОВА

73 Costume
designs for
Tarelkin's Death
by Varvara
Stepanova
(1922)

entrain.'[40] Meyerhold's response was to employ once again the knockabout
tricks of circus clowns and strolling players. Varvara Stepanova designed a
series of drab, baggy costumes decorated with stripes, patches, and chevrons
which looked like nothing so much as convicts' uniforms. On the empty
stage there was an assortment of white-painted 'acting instruments' ready
to be shifted and used by the actors as required. Each one concealed a trap:
the table's legs gave way, the seat deposited its occupant onto the floor, the
stool detonated a blank cartridge. Most spectacular of all was the cage used
to simulate a prison cell into which the prisoner was propelled head-first
through something resembling a giant meat-mincer. As though all this was
not enough to tax the spectator's nerves and the actor's courage, an assistant
director (or 'laboratory assistant', as they were called) seated in the front
row announced the intervals by firing a pistol at the audience and shouting
'Entrrr-acte!'; there were helter-skelter chases with the pursuers brandishing
inflated bladders on sticks; at the end Tarelkin escaped by swinging across
the stage on a trapeze. Illusion was never given a chance to intrude: Ludmilla
Brandakhlystova, 'a colossal washerwoman of about forty', was played by the
slender, youthful Mikhail Zharov with no make-up and ridiculous padding

under his skirts;* Tarelkin, bound hand and foot in prison and frantic with thirst, tried in vain to reach a cup of water held by a warder – then suddenly he winked broadly at the audience and took a long draught from a bottle of wine he had concealed in his pocket. The overall intention, as Eisenstein and Vasily Fyodorov described it, was 'to circumvent the most "dangerous" parts of the play that in a naturalistic treatment would inevitably produce a distressing, almost pathological effect.'[41]

For all the production's vigour and invention, it failed to share the popular success of *The Magnanimous Cuckold* and was withdrawn from the repertoire after only two seasons. This was partly because Sukhovo-Kobylin's grim satire was hardly amenable to burlesque. But mainly it was due to practical deficiencies: Stepanova's 'acting instruments' functioned so capriciously that the young performers soon lost all confidence in them; the shapeless costumes tended to camouflage rather than enhance their movements; and frequently they had to perform in half-darkness when the erratic military searchlights that served as stage lighting fluctuated in power. Worst of all, throughout the

74 *Tarelkin's Death* (Act Three), showing the 'meat mincer' in use as a prison cell

* In fact the playing of Brandakhlystova by a man is authorised by Sukhovo-Kobylin himself in his prefatory note.

Moscow winter it was necessary to leave the draughty auditorium unheated due to the company's desperate financial position, and the sparse audiences were often augmented by the large brown rats that inhabited the theatre.[42] Nevertheless, *Tarelkin's Death* remains one of the most original products of the movement known as 'Eccentrism' which flourished in Russia in the early twenties.*

One of Meyerhold's two 'laboratory assistants' for the production was Sergei Eisenstein. Since joining the Theatre Workshop in 1921 Eisenstein had emerged as its most gifted student and had worked on a number of highly original projects, including the designs for Meyerhold's uncompleted production of Shaw's *Heartbreak House*, in which he proposed to augment his settings with cages of wild animals.[44] Shortly after *Tarelkin's Death* he left Meyerhold to return to the Moscow Proletkult Theatre where two years earlier he had worked as a designer. It was there that in April 1923 he staged Sergei Tretyakov's free adaptation of Ostrovsky's *Enough Simplicity in Every Wise Man* as a 'montage of attractions' on an arena stage and complete with a tightrope act by one of the characters.[45] Early in 1925 Eisenstein parted company with Proletkult and Meyerhold offered him a free hand to direct *Hamlet*, *The Government Inspector* or *Woe from Wit* at the Theatre of the Revolution. However, by that time Eisenstein had completed his first feature film *Strike* and had lost all faith in the theatre. In later years, though, he fully acknowledged the value of his early theatrical training, and in 1936 Meyerhold said: 'All Eisenstein's work had its origins in the laboratory where we once worked together as teacher and pupil. But our relationship was not so much of teacher and pupil as of two artists in revolt, up to our necks and afraid to swallow for fear of the disgusting slime in which we found the theatre wallowing in 1917.'[46]

---

* The term 'Eccentrism' was coined by Grigory Kozintsev, Georgy Kryzhitsky, and Leonid Trauberg to describe their experiments at the theatre-studio that they opened in Petrograd in 1921 and called the 'Factory of Eccentrism' of 'FEKS'.[43] The style may be said to have originated with Yury Annenkov's production of Tolstoy's comedy, *The First Distiller* in Petrograd (1919), when he staged a scene in hell with the aid of circus acrobats performing a flying ballet – that is, if one discounts the occasional use of circus devises by Meyerhold in *The Unknown Woman* and *The Fairground Booth* in 1914, and in the revival of *Columbine's Scarf* in 1916, to say nothing of the 1918 production of *Mystery-Bouffe*.

People's Artist

On 28 March 1923 it was announced in *Izvestia* that on his completion
of twenty years as a director and twenty-five in the theatre altogether,
Meyerhold had been awarded the title of 'People's Artist of the Republic'.
He was the first theatre director and only the sixth Soviet artist overall to
be so honoured. On 2 April his jubilee was celebrated with a programme
of extracts presented by his own theatre, the Theatre of the Revolution,
the Foregger Theatre Workshop, and the Proletkult Theatre together with
a display of biomechanics in the ornate and totally inappropriate setting of
the Bolshoi Theatre. Yet on the very same day the Sohn Theatre's electricity
was cut off because they could not pay the bills, and Meyerhold was obliged
to appeal yet again for a state subsidy.[1]

Fortunately, the theatre's position was soon eased by the great popular success of its latest production, Sergei Tretyakov's *Earth Rampant*,*
which had its première on 4 March and was performed forty-four times
in the remaining eleven weeks of the season. The text was freely adapted
by Tretyakov from a translation of Marcel Martinet's verse drama *La
Nuit* which had already been staged the previous October as the opening
production at the Theatre of the Revolution and a month later at the
Academic Dramatic Theatre in Petrograd, on both occasions with little
success. Originally published in 1921, the play concerns an abortive mutiny
of troops engaged in an imperialist war in an imaginary kingdom. As with
The Dawn, the aim of the radical adaptation of *La Nuit* was to transform the
play's vague universality into a direct commentary on recent Soviet history.
As a founder member of LEF (the Left Front of the Arts) Tretyakov had
little faith in theatre, being committed to 'the principle of production art,
whereby the former entertainer/joker/clown/conjurer/hanger-on of society's
entertainment world switched categorically to the ranks of the workers,
exchanging an aesthetic fantasy for the creation of things that were use-

---

* Also translated as *The Earth in Turmoil*.

ful and needed by the proletariat'.[2] However, he had been impressed by the utilitarianism of *The Magnanimous Cuckold* and accepted Meyerhold's invitation to join the teaching staff of his Workshop. He devised an anti-religious farce for the students to perform for Komsomols and workers' clubs, and also worked with Meyerhold to devise verbal elements to be combined with biomechanics.

Discarding over a third of the original text of *La Nuit* and simplifying the characters and their personal relationships, Tretyakov reduced the five acts to eight episodes, each self-contained and introduced by a title projected onto a screen above the stage. A second screen carried familiar Civil War slogans, stressing the action's relevance to recent historical events. The aim was to achieve the direct impact and tempo of the highly popular adventure film by constructing what Tretyakov called a 'speech montage' of 'word gestures', resembling the terse slogans of the agitatory poster. He schooled the actors in 'semaphore speech' in which, he explained, 'particular attention was paid to the precise delivery of the text and its phonetic expressiveness, requiring a shift in emphasis from the rhythmical aspect (the vowels) to the articulatory and the onomatopoeic (the consonants).'[3] As Huntly Carter observed following a visit to Moscow: 'The method of delivering the text is determined by the agitational effect which the actor must think of first of all. . . Gesture rests on a similar principle. It articulates the sound, just as sound articulates the meaning, and the arm-gesture has the same quality as the word-gesture, if such a term is permissible'.[4] Both in its objectives and in its form, Tretyakov's treatment anticipates the linguistic style and performance technique that Brecht began to develop a year later in Munich when he staged Marlowe's *Edward the Second*, adapted by himself and Leon Feuchtwanger.[5]* In *Earth Rampant*, Meyerhold and his designer, Popova, broke free from painterly influences and sought to eliminate all risk of aesthetic blandishment by resorting to purely utilitarian objects: cars, lorries, motor cycles, machine-guns, field telephones, a threshing machine, a field-kitchen, a model aeroplane – only what was required by the dramatic events. The one exception was a stark red wooden model of a gantry-crane, built only because a real crane proved too heavy for the stage floor to bear. The sole sources of light were huge front-of-house searchlights. The costumes of the soldiers were authentic and the actors wore no make-up.

As in *Mystery-Bouffe*, the negative characters were depicted as grotesque archetypes, performing what Meyerhold still referred to as '*lazzi*'.[6] Thus when the 'Emperor' received news of the mutiny he squatted down on a chamber-pot emblazoned with the Imperial eagle and relieved himself to the

---

* Some years later, Brecht and Tretyakov became closely acquainted and Tretyakov was largely responsible for introducing Brecht to the Soviet public. In 1934 under the title *Epic Dramas* he published a translation of *St Joan of the Stockyards*, *The Mother*, and *The Measures Taken*.

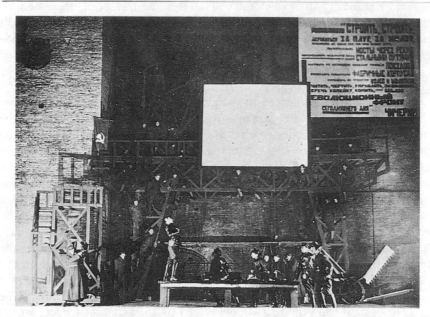

75 Scene from *Earth Rampant*, showing the two screens for projected titles and slogans

accompaniment of a band playing 'God save the Tsar', after which an orderly removed the pot, holding his nose. As David Zolotnitsky comments, 'The somewhat crude humour suited the nature of the production, as though it were being performed by soldiers for soldiers.'[7]

In contrast to earlier productions, the tedium of unalloyed virtue was completely overcome by the stirring evocation of Civil-War heroism which struck to the hearts of many of the spectators. For them, the receding throb of the lorry that had driven onto the stage with the coffin of a martyred Red soldier seemed like the finest and most fitting requiem for their own fallen comrades. Dedicated 'to the Red Army and the first Red Soldier of the R.S.F.S.R., Leon Trotsky',[8] *Earth Rampant* was first performed at a special preview on 23 February 1923 to mark the Army's fifth anniversary.* Ever since Meyerhold had returned from the Civil War, his theatre had shared a close relationship with the Red Army and had done much to foster the development of military drama groups. It was no empty gesture to dedicate *Earth Rampant* to the Army: at performances of the play regular collections were taken and in 1926 the money accumulated went to purchase a military aeroplane which entered service bearing the name 'Meyerhold'. On the occasion of his jubilee at the Bolshoi Theatre in 1923 Meyerhold was made an honorary soldier of the Moscow Garrison.[10]

* According to Yury Annenkov, Trotsky appeared on stage in the course of one of the early performances and delivered a speech to mark the fifth anniversary of the Red Army.[9]

76 *Earth Rampant*, Episode Seven

77 Meyerhold in
the uniform of
an honorary
soldier of the
Red Army
(1926)

Meyerhold conceived *Earth Rampant* in the spirit of a mass spectacle, and subsequently it was performed on a number of occasions in the open air, being freely adapted for various settings. The most memorable performance was that given in honour of the Fifth Congress of the Comintern in Moscow in June 1924 when a cast of 1500, including infantry and horse-cavalry took part and there was an audience of 25,000. For the occasion Tretyakov adapted the script to give it a victorious rather than tragic ending.[11]

As Fevralsky recalls, Meyerhold looked upon *Earth Rampant* as a production that it was necessary to stage. Apart from Mayakovsky, no Soviet dramatist had yet written a revolutionary play of any quality, and after the experimental ventures of *The Magnanimous Cuckold* and *Tarelkin's Death* the Meyerhold Theatre (as it was now officially known) urgently needed to confirm its reputation with the mass audience as the champion of revolutionary drama.[12] His judgement was confirmed in the summer when *Earth Rampant* was enthusiastically received in a variety of venues during the Theatre's tour of the Ukraine and Southern Russia.

78 and 79 The Curé and the Cook in *Earth Rampant* (caricatures by Ilya Shlepyanov, 1923)

Earth Rampant was conceived as a spectacle with wide popular appeal, and its impact was closely monitored by the Meyerhold Theatre. The integral relationship between the theatre and the Experimental Theatre Workshops placed at Meyerhold's disposal teachers and students who were in a position to pursue organised research into all aspects of theatre production. A number of 'laboratories' were set up, notably a 'dramaturgical laboratory' with the aim of collecting and evaluating objective data relating to plays in performance at the Meyerhold Theatre. Systematic attempts were made to monitor fluctuations in the performances of a given play; for example, audience response was recorded under a wide range of headings, namely: silence, noise, loud noise, collective reading (sic), singing, coughing, banging, shuffling, exclamations, weeping, laughter, sighing, movement, applause, whistling, hissing, the number of people leaving during the performance, the number getting to their feet, throwing objects onto the stage, people getting up onto the stage. As Fevralsky says, however unscientific these methods might appear today, they still represent the first serious attempt to subject performance to scientific analysis.[13]

Another important side to the activities of Meyerhold's company and students was the instruction and supervision of theatre groups in factories, military barracks, and student circles. During his work with Narkompros Meyerhold had become disillusioned with the theatrical activities of the Proletkult movement;* he felt it offered an easy refuge for out of work actors, who furnished the majority of Proletkult's drama instructors, and the general level of amateur theatre reflected their incompetence and outmoded ideas on acting.[14] Consequently, once his theatre and workshop became sufficiently established, he set about forging his own links between the professional and amateur stages without reference to the established Proletkult network.[15] Thus, far more than any other Soviet director of 1920s, Meyerhold took practical steps to open up the theatre to the new actor and the new audience.

II

During the period of the New Economic Policy (NEP) the incursions of private ownership into the legitimate theatre were relatively few; it was in the areas of cinema and light entertainment that the effects were most marked: there was a flood of foreign films, many of them light comedies or crime serials (notably *Judex*, *Fantômas*, *Nick Carter*, and *Pauline*); a fresh crop of operetta, cabaret, and variety theatres sprang up with such names as 'Trocadero', 'Merry Masks', 'Don't Cry' – even 'Empire'. Beginning in 1923, Meyerhold made the habits and fashions of the 'Nepman' the target for a series of satirical productions, linked either directly or by analogy to the portrayal of Western capitalist decadence.

The first of these was *Lake Lyul*, a 'romantic melodrama' by the young Soviet dramatist Alexei Faiko, which Meyerhold presented at the Theatre of the Revolution on 7 November 1923. Shortly before the play opened Faiko said in an interview:

In my opinion the modern revolutionary repertoire should not consist of schematised slogan-placard productions whose agitatory significance is ob-

* Proletkult was set up in 1917 as an association of proletarian cultural organisations sponsored and subsidised by the Narkompros as an independent body. In 1922 its theatre groups came under the control of the trade unions and attracted many directors from the professional stage. However, Meyerhold himself never worked with Proletkult. In 1932 the organisation was disbanded.

scured by raucous shouts and which lack any real relevance to the experience of the modern spectator; rather we should aim for entertaining plays, spectacular in conception and effective in performance, with complex subject matter, involved plots, and stirring emotions.[16]

In other words, Faiko proposed taking on the Nepman at his own beguiling game. Summarising *Lake Lyul*, he writes:

Location: somewhere in the Far West, or perhaps the Far East. Many characters. Crowd scenes. White, yellow and black races. Hotels, villas, shops. Advertisement hoardings and lifts. A revolutionary struggle on an island. An underground movement. Conspiracies. The basis of the plot – the rise and fall of the renegade, Anton Prim.[17]

The dialogue of the play was terse and the structure episodic, designed to convey the breakneck tempo of life in the 'big city', the dominant motif of the whole production. Faiko describes the setting and costumes:

The back wall of the theatre was bared. Girders stuck out and wires and cables dangled uncompromisingly. The centre of the stage was occupied by a three-storey construction with receding corridors, cages, ladders, platforms and lifts which moved both horizontally and vertically. There were illuminated titles and advertisements, silver screens lit from behind. Affording something of a contrast to this background were the brilliant colours of the somewhat more than life-like costumes: the elegant toilettes of the ladies, the gleaming white of starched shirt-fronts, aiguillettes, epaulettes, liveries trimmed with gold.[18]

80 Scene from *Lake Lyul* at the Theatre of the Revolution (1923)

The setting designed by Viktor Shestakov bore a distinct resemblance to Popova's construction for *The Magnanimous Cuckold*, though it was cheerfully representational and hardly 'constructivist' in the precise sense. Meyerhold exploited the construction to its limits, using area lighting to switch the action constantly from one level to another, sometimes playing two scenes simultaneously in different places. Its technical sophistication afforded him the flexibility that he had sought through the episodic adaptation of such works as *Columbine's Scarf* and *Masquerade*, and led him on to further experiments in montage at a time when that technique had scarcely been exploited in the cinema.* *Lake Lyul* epitomised the much criticised tendency of 'urbanism', the term used to describe a preoccupation with the dubious attractions of the big city. Shestakov's setting closely resembled Alexander Vesnin's construction for Chesterton's *The Man who was Thursday*, staged a month later by Tairov at the Kamerny Theatre, and a number of productions of German Expressionist drama which enjoyed a brief vogue at this time. At the beginning of 1923 Aksyonov had written: 'So-called "stage constructivism" started with a most impressive programme for the total abolition of aesthetic methods, but once it appeared on stage it began to show signs of being only too ready to adapt itself to its surroundings and now it has degenerated almost to a decorative device, albeit in a new style.'[19]

Aksyonov's diagnosis was to prove only too accurate: by the mid-twenties many theatres throughout the Soviet Union were exploiting Constructivism as the latest fashion in decorative style, often with little regard for the play's content, and often purporting to satirise 'Western decadence' whilst trading on its appeal as theatrical spectacle. At the same time, however, the theatre rendered a particular service to the Constructivists. As Christina Lodder writes:

> Constructivist theatrical sets played an enormous role in giving Constructivists, both designers and architects, experience in working with real materials in real space at a time when there was very little opportunity for realising such projects in the real world, thanks to material shortages and the slow rate of industrial recovery following the devastation of the seven years' hostilities in the First World War and Civil War.[20]

A far cry from Meyerhold's earlier work at his own theatre, *Lake Lyul* was a huge success with what Erast Garin has called the 'cleaner' public of the Theatre of the Revolution. It proved to be Meyerhold's second† and final production at that theatre; in effect, he ceased to be its artistic director after the 1923–1924 season, handing over the post to his former Petersburg pupil Alexei Gripich.

---

* Meyerhold's assistant director for *Lake Lyul* was Abram Room, soon to make his name as a director in the Soviet cinema.

† The first was Ostrovsky's *A Lucrative Post* (15 May 1923). It is referred to on pp. 204-205 below.

III

In January 1924 Meyerhold staged his brilliant reinterpretation of Ostrovsky's *The Forest*.* Then with his next production, *D.E.*, presented on 15 June 1924, he showed that his disregard for authors' rights was restricted by no means to the classics. This 'agit-sketch' was an amalgam by Mikhail Podgaetsky of two novels, *The D.E. Trust – The History of the Fall of Europe* by Ilya Ehrenburg and *The Tunnel* by Bernhard Kellermann, with additional material from Upton Sinclair and Pierre Hamp. Podgaetsky's scenario bore little resemblance to Ehrenburg's novel, from which the bulk of the material was taken, and after numerous further alterations in the course of rehearsals the connection was attenuated still further. Only two years before Ehrenburg had proclaimed: '*Away with the author!* Theatre shouldn't be written in the study, but built on the stage.'[21] Now he sprang to the defence of his novel, protesting 'I'm not some classic but a real, live person', and claimed to be working on a stage version of it himself.[22] In an open letter, playing on Ehrenburg's doubtful cosmopolitan status, and flaunting his own political credentials, Meyerhold retorted scornfully: '. . . even if you had undertaken an adaptation of your novel,† *The History of the Fall of Europe*, you would have produced the kind of play that could be put on in any city of the Entente, whereas in my theatre which serves and will continue to serve the cause of the Revolution, we need tendentious plays, plays with one aim only: to serve the cause of the Revolution.'[23]

D.E. was even more fragmented in structure than Meyerhold's previous episodic productions. It took the form of a political revue in seventeen episodes, of which only two or three featured the same characters twice. There were no fewer than ninety-five roles divided between forty-five performers, amongst whom the champion quick-change artist was Erast Garin, who appeared as seven different inventors in a scene lasting fifteen minutes. Later, so that the audience might fully savour Garin's skill, Meyerhold made a large peep-hole in the screen concealing the actor's on-stage wardrobe.[25]

Here is Fevralsky's synopsis of the bizarre plot:

> The international adventurer Jens Boot organises the 'D.E. Trust' (Trust for the Destruction of Europe), in which he is joined by three of America's most powerful capitalists. By various means the D.E. Trust succeeds in destroying the whole of Western Europe. A large proportion of the Western European proletariat manage to escape to the USSR, which joins with the Comintern to form a secret organisation under the cover-name of the 'USSR Radium Trust' in

* Discussed on pp. 205-213 below.

† In his memoirs, Ehrenburg claims that he had earlier refused Meyerhold's invitation to adapt the novel for the stage.[24]

order to build an undersea tunnel linking Leningrad to New York. The building of the tunnel provides employment for the European workers. The D.E. Trust is unable to follow up its triumph over Europe by overcoming the industrious zeal of the Soviet workers and is obliged to support the recognition of the Soviet Union *de facto* and *de jure*. But it is too late: the American proletariat rises in revolt and is supported by the International Red Army, arriving unexpectedly in New York through the tunnel which the capitalists have never discovered. The social revolution prevails.[26]

The production was remarkable for its settings, which were composed entirely of 'moving walls'. Devised by Meyerhold himself and executed by his former pupil Ilya Shlepyanov, these 'walls' were a series of eight to ten dark red wooden screens, about four metres long and three metres high, which were moved on wheels by members of the cast concealed behind each one. With the addition of the simplest properties, they were deployed to represent now a lecture hall, now a Moscow street, now the French National Assembly, now a Berlin café, now a sports stadium, and so on. The action never faltered and in some scenes the walls played an active part, their motion emphasised by weaving spotlights. For example, Jens Boot escaping from the Soviet Union fled upstage to be confronted by two rapidly converging walls; managing to squeeze through the narrowing gap just before one crossed in

81 The setting for *D.E.*, showing the moving walls and the suspended screen for projected titles

front of the other, he seemed to have disappeared when they separated and
moved on across the stage. In fact, he had simply concealed himself behind
one wall and exited with it.

Once again Meyerhold employed projected captions, this time on three
screens. As well as the title and the location of each episode, there were
comments on characters, information relevant to the action, and quotations

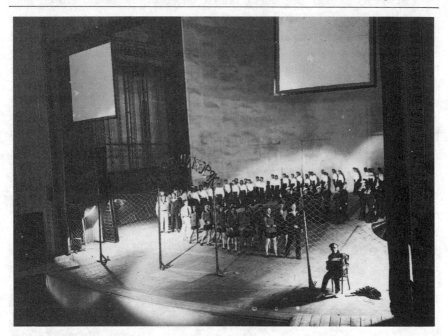

82 The Red Fleet in *D.E.*

from the written works and speeches of Lenin, Trotsky, and Zinoviev. The
aim was to point the political significance of the events onstage and to relate
them to as wide a context as possible.

The depravity of the Western world was portrayed in the now customary grotesque style, whilst the vigour of the young Soviet state was
expressed by marching and singing sailors borrowed from the Red Fleet
and real Komsomols performing biomechanics, acrobatic dances, and playing
football. Critics were quick to condemn this crude schematisation: not only
were the scenes in 'foxtrotting Europe' far more energetic and diverting,
helped greatly by the performance of the first jazz band to appear in Soviet
Russia,* but there was an obvious danger in representing a deadly political
enemy as a collection of emasculated cretins, cowards, and libertines. There

---

* The jazz band was assembled by the poet, Valentin Parnakh ('Parnok'), recently returned
from Paris where he had frquented Dadaist circles.

was plenty to ensure the success of *D.E.* with the public, not least the erotic dance numbers expertly choreographed by Kasyan Goleizovsky and exploiting the contrasting charms of Raikh and Babanova, but by all but his most devoted critics Meyerhold was accused once again of 'urbanism' and of 'infantile leftism' – Lenin's term for a naïve conception of the social situation that was bound to foster complacency. At a public debate shortly after the production's opening, Mayakovsky was particularly scathing in his criticisms. Meyerhold retorted: 'I am glad that Mayakovsky has finally broken his silence. Once he had written *Mystery-Bouffe* he retreated under his bell-jar, and clearly he finds it very comfortable to sit there and watch me fighting alone on the left front.'[27]

Meyerhold was right: no Soviet dramatist had emerged who could begin

83 Poster for the première of *Bubus the Teacher*, 1925

to rival Mayakovsky in artistic skill and political acumen, and now the repertoire situation was causing acute embarrassment. The time had come for more sophisticated material than either Faiko or the collective authors of *D.E.* had offered.

After several months of preparatory work, rehearsals, and revisions, Meyerhold revealed his next production to the public on 29 January 1925: a further play by Faiko called *Bubus the Teacher*. It was hardly the response the critics were demanding: yet another flimsy political farce depicting the exhausted last fling of the rulers of an imaginary capitalist country on the verge of revolution, it invited the very schematisation of Western decadent types that Meyerhold had already exploited to its limits. The one exception was the character of Bubus himself, an intellectual idealist who vacillated ineffectually between two camps and found himself rejected by the revolution when it finally came. He was an individual embodying the conflict of class loyalties within himself, instead of displaying in two dimensions the attitudes of one particular side. In conception at least he represented a significant advance on the placard style of earlier Soviet theatre, a shift from crude agitation to more reasoned propaganda. Lunacharsky was prompted to coin a new definition for Meyerhold's style: '*sociomechanics*', meaning the study of character in its social context prior to creating stage portraits of hyperbolic dimensions that revealed socio-political causes and effects in all their complexity.[28] But Bubus apart, Faiko's play was so insubstantial that it presented no intellectual challenge whatsoever to Meyerhold. Once more brushing aside the protests of a mere author, he adapted the text to suit his own ends and developed a whole new range of production tricks to invest it with heavy significance, slowing the lively farce tempo to the turgid rhythm of melodrama.[29]

There was no production by Meyerhold that did not reaffirm his conception of rhythm as the basis of all dramatic expression, but in *Bubus* he restored it to the pre-eminence it had enjoyed in such pre-1917 works as *Tristan and Isolde*, *Dom Juan*, and *Orpheus*. With only the occasional break, every movement was synchronised with a musical accompaniment, the text being spoken as a kind of recitative against a melody in counterpoint. As in *D.E.*, lascivious foxtrots, shimmies and tangos were danced to jazz accompaniment of Valentin Parnakh's five-piece band located this time offstage; but most of the music was taken from Liszt and Chopin and performed by the pianist Lev Arnshtam at a concert Bechstein perched high above the stage in a gilded alcove ringed with coloured lights. Meyerhold intended the effect to be similar to the piano accompaniment in the silent cinema; by revealing the source of the music to the spectator, he hoped to counteract its stupefying effects and reinforce its ironical function.

In contrast to the uncompromising constructions of recent productions the setting was not so much a *machine* for acting with as a platform designed to enhance it, affording the maximum freedom for the actors'

84 *Bubus the Teacher*, Act Two

85 and
86 Shlepyanov's
costume design
for Kamperdaf
and Pastor
Süsserlich in
*Bubus the
Teacher*

expressive movements and gestures. Conceived by Meyerhold and executed
again by Ilya Shlepyanov, it consisted of a semicircle of suspended bamboo
rods completely enclosing a stage area covered with an oval green carpet
edged with cherry red. The back wall was adorned with flashing neon
signs and the whole picture was framed by an ornate false proscenium
arch. Properties were few, the most striking being a gilded fountain in the
first act. The mellifluous tinkling of the bamboo curtain at the entrance of
each character, the soft splashing of the fountain, the rhythmical flashing of
the neon all played their part in Meyerhold's complex orchestration.

The languid aristocrats moved in broad leisurely curves within the rounded
confines of their fragile stockade, their footfalls silent on the green carpet.
Faultlessly turned out, their fans, cloaks, top hats, walking-sticks, and white
gloves were the pretext for much elegant by-play. The style was authentic yet
satirically pointed in a manner that was openly indebted to the cartoons of
George Grosz. To define the style of acting that he required of his company
Meyerhold invented the term 'pre-acting', though, as he acknowledged, the
technique itself was by no means new and in his case owed much to his
study of the Japanese theatre some twenty years earlier.* Essentially, this
amounted to the actor employing mime before speaking his lines in order

87 *Bubus the Teacher*, Act One

* See pp. 39-40 above.

to convey his true state of mind. Justifying this technique in a booklet that was distributed to the audience, he wrote:

> Nowadays, when the theatre is once more being employed as a platform for agitation, an acting system in which special stress is laid on pre-acting is indispensable to the actor-tribune. The actor-tribune needs to convey to the spectator his attitude to the lines he is speaking and the situations he is enacting; he wants to force the spectator to respond in a particular way to the action that is unfolding before him . . . The actor-tribune acts not the situation itself, but what is concealed behind it and what it has to reveal for a specifically propagandist purpose. When the actor-tribune lifts the mask of the character to reveal his true nature to the spectator he does not merely speak the lines furnished by the dramatist, he uncovers the roots from which the lines have sprung.[30]

Unfortunately, this constant interpolation of mime emphasised rather than made good the vacuity of Faiko's text, and was seen by most critics as a regression to the self-indulgent aestheticism of Meyerhold's World of Art period. 'Sadko' of *Evening Moscow* remarked maliciously that 'at times it was like sitting in some provincial offshoot of the Kamerny Theatre'.[31] In 1962 Faiko himself recalled: '. . . it was as though the whole play was duplicated, performed twice, and so assumed a heavy, ponderous, totally decelerated tempo. I saw my light situation-comedy transformed into a slow-moving, pretentious, falsely significant production.'[32] Erast Garin writes: 'The public's reception of *Bubus the Teacher* was reserved; they quickly grew tired, just as one grows tired in an unfamiliar museum. It was a spectacle overloaded with skill, a production for the appreciation of actors and directors.'[33] The production was further undermined by a fundamental error in casting on Meyerhold's part. The leading role of Stefka had been conceived by Faiko with the grace and comic talent of Maria Babanova in mind, but to the actress's great chagrin Meyerhold insisted on casting Zinaida Raikh, who had made a triumphant debut the previous year as Aksyusha in *The Forest*. To make matters worse, Ilinsky, for whom Bubus had been created, took exception to the director's persistent attempts to place Raikh's indifferent performance at the centre of the production and walked out shortly before the opening night.[34] It was a loss that Meyerhold and his young company could ill afford, but three years were to elapse before Ilinsky was persuaded to return to play Famusov in *Woe to Wit*.

Even so, for all its shortcomings, *Bubus the Teacher* remained for Meyerhold and his company a valuable exercise in rhythmical discipline which told strongly in subsequent productions. Above all, it marked his 'rediscovery' of music, the vital component in his finest work yet to come.

IV

When Meyerhold staged Ostrovsky's *A Lucrative Post* at the Theatre of the Revolution in May 1923, marking the playwright's centennial, it was generally taken to be a routine production which as the company's Artistic Director he felt obliged to undertake. Why else should he, leader of the theatrical Left, choose to stage a social comedy written in the 1850s and part of the staple repertoire of the venerable Maly Theatre? In consequence, the production was almost totally ignored by the Moscow critics and Meyerhold's erstwhile supporter, Vladimir Blyum, attacked him in *Pravda* for 'this strange outburst of piety towards Ostrovsky, that apostle of the middle way and of philistinism in all its forms.'[35] But, as Maya Turovskaya has suggested, on this occasion Meyerhold was concerned less with programmatic statements than with behaving as a responsible artistic director by presenting a popular work that would be certain to appeal to a mass audience.[36] His judgement was vindicated: the production ran, and continued to run for the next thirteen years. In 1937 Boris Alpers went so

88 *A Lucrative Post*, Act Four, with Babanova as Polina

far as to describe it as 'one of the most profound and significant productions in the entire repertoire of the Soviet theatre'.[37]

Meyerhold's approach to the play was relatively straightforward; relying on the virtuosity of a number of his ex-students in the cast, notably Maria Babanova who concurrently was playing Stella in *The Magnanimous Cuckold*. He left Ostrovsky's text untouched and devised a scenario of restless movement in order to emphasise the uneasy relationships between the play's characters. In this he was assisted greatly by his designer Viktor Shestakov who created a clean, functional multi-level construction out of angular beams, plywood, metal, and linoleum. Against these surfaces the exact period costumes and authentic properties sprang into prominence, emphasising their anachronistic quaintness yet pointing the analogy with the nostalgia and materialism of the NEP period.[38] Whether this was the specific reason for the success of *A Lucrative Post* is doubtful, but to Meyerhold at least the production demonstrated the potential vitality of the nineteenth-century repertoire in the Soviet context. Nine months later he applied this lesson to the most spectacular effect.

On 19 January 1924, three weeks before his fiftieth birthday, Meyerhold confounded all expectations with his production of Ostrovsky's most popular comedy, *The Forest*. The previous year, in a centennial article in *Izvestia* Lunacharsky, still concerned at the paucity of new Soviet drama, had called on the theatre 'to go back to Ostrovsky' in order to learn from his achievements in the depiction of social reality.[39] Prompted partly by the Maly Theatre's recent traditionalist version of *The Forest*, Meyerhold's production was his own particular response to Lunacharsky's exhortation, a totally unexpected 'return to Ostrovsky'. Shortly before its opening, he told a meeting of Red Army drama organisers: 'We don't need to borrow anything from the theatre of the aristocracy and the bourgeoisie, but we must avail ourselves of the experience of the popular theatre of the past. . . What we need is a Red folk-theatre* (but not a Red cabaret), topical folk songs, and clowns of the kind found in Shakespeare or in travelling shows.'[40]

Soon after, in a debate on the production he said: 'A play is simply the excuse for the revelation of its theme on the level at which that revelation may appear vital today.'[41] In a collection of articles published in 1926 by the Meyerhold Theatre, Alexander Slonimsky wrote:

> *The Forest* reflects the revolutionary upsurge at the beginning of the 1870s, and it is for this reason that Meyerhold chose to stage this play in particular. In it the object of the satire is not the mercantile middle class as is usually the case with Ostrovsky, but the landowning gentry in decline after the abolition of serfdom. In Ostrovsky's 'mercantile' plays the status quo is depicted as awesome and triumphant, as firm as a rock. But in *The Forest* it is subjected to complete comic destruction. The forces of youth opposing the status quo act more boldly and decisively, and the finale yields them a relative victory.[42]

---

* As in the past, he used his favourite term 'balagan'.

In the light of this reading of the text Meyerhold saw an obvious parallel with the bourgeois habits and attitudes that had been granted temporary licence under the terms of NEP. Ostrovsky's genre portrayal of the bigoted country gentry was reinterpreted in terms of class conflict, with character development rejected in favour of the interplay of 'social masks'. The action was adapted to sharpen the conflict between Raisa Pavlovna Gurmyzhskaya, the autocratic mistress of the rich estate 'Tree Stumps', and Aksyusha, her young impoverished relative who serves as a maid of all work. According to Ostrovsky, Gurmyzhskaya, a widow in her early fifties, 'dresses modestly, almost in mourning'. Played by the twenty-year-old Yelena Tyapkina, her fat, ungainly figure was clothed either in a masculine riding habit or in dresses of hideous vulgarity; she brandished a whip, spoke in a gruff, drink-sodden voice, sang sentimental romances off-key, and pawed lasciviously at the foppish young wastrel Bulanov. On the other hand, Meyerhold rejected the conventional view of Aksyusha as 'tearful, sentimental, lyrical in mood'.[43] In her debut performance, Zinaida Raikh wore a bright red dress and white neckerchief, and played her with all the optimism and buoyant energy of

89 Poster for the première of *The Forest*, 1924

a modern 'komsomolka', 'conveying the sense of a strong, agile, properly functioning body.'[44]

Every principal character was costumed to reveal his or her essential nature: Bulanov adorned the estate in striped singlet and shorts; Milonov, an obsequious neighbour, was transformed into a parish priest complete with full regalia and attendant acolytes. Of less obvious significance were the wigs worn by a number of the characters: Gurmyzhskaya's was bright red, Bulanov's was green, whilst Milonov had both a wig and a beard made of the gold thread used to decorate Christmas trees. A number were discarded soon after the première. Ostrovsky's itinerant actors, Arkashka Schastlivtsev, the comedian, and Gennady Neschastlivtsev, the tragedian, were decked out in an odd assortment of garments from the theatrical rag-bag; Schastlivtsev was played as a down-and-out music-hall comic dressed in baggy check trousers, a short toreador's jacket, and jaunty, battered sombrero; his partner resembled a provincial ham in a voluminous

90 Igor Ilinsky
as Schastlivtsev

91 Ivan Koval-Samborsky as Petya and Zinaida Raikh as Aksyusha

dark cloak and broad-sleeved Russian shirt. By far the more successfully realised of the two was Ilinsky's Arkashka. As Meyerhold acknowledged in a lecture in 1936, his portrayal owed something to the example of Chaplin, whose films enjoyed great popularity in Russia in the twenties. Specifically, he referred to Chaplin's creation of his tramp character from the disparate elements of the little bowler hat, the cane, the gaping shoes, the flapping trousers, the toothbrush moustache, which in the aggregate 'are like nothing on earth'.[45] But, as Béatrice Picon-Vallin argues in her fine analysis of the production, Ilinsky's creation had a far greater complexity than Chaplin's, and was quite devoid of pathos: 'Unlike Chaplin, he is not a man-child but a grown-up child. He is interested in money, he gets drunk, expresses and gratifies sexual desires. . . A clown who is at times cruel (he burns Ulita's hand), inventive, insolent: he orchestrates the wave of destructive gaiety that invades *The Forest*. He combines naïveté and cunning.'[46]

In their relationship with each other, their remoteness from the petty everyday world, and their romantic championing of the true love of Aksyusha and her sweetheart Petya, the two actors were a conscious evocation of Don Quixote and Sancho Panza, or as Meyerhold later claimed, of the knight of Spanish 'cloak and sword' drama and the *gracioso* or buffoon of Spanish comedy.[47] It was these characters who above all attracted Meyerhold to *The Forest* in the first place, for as Rudnitsky says, they embodied one of Meyerhold's favourite themes: the triumph of the *comédien* over real life. This is already present in Ostrovsky, but in Meyerhold's interpretation they were elevated to the stature of Satan and the Fool, and they controlled not

92 *The Forest*, Episode Seven ('Arkashka and the Governor of Kursk')

only the fate of the inhabitants of 'Tree Stumps', but the whole mood and tempo of the production itself.

Since the point of the 'mask' is to identify the character immediately, its gradual revelation through behaviour could be discarded. Hence, Meyerhold was able largely to ignore the play's original time sequence and rearrange Ostrovsky's text according to the principles of cinematic montage. Altering little of the actual dialogue, he divided the original five acts into thirty-three episodes,* shuffling them into new order, and inserting pantomime interludes for the sake of effective contrasts of mood and tempo. As the film critic Lebedev wrote: 'Meyerhold's *Forest* isn't theatre at all but a film . . . Meyerhold cuts and edits his scenes like film; as in film he works through gesture; as in film he uses close-ups and long-shots; as in film he changes the location for each scene.'[48]

Each episode was preceded by a brief blackout, during which its title was projected onto a screen above the stage. After the prologue in which Milonov led the rest of the local inhabitants in hurried procession across the stage with ikons and religious banners (the traditional comic 'parade'), the play opened with the meeting of the two actors (the original Act Two, Scene Two). This long scene, in which they swap tales of their adventures on tour, was split into seven brief episodes and interspersed with the eight scenes at 'Tree Stumps' from Act One. From episode to episode Arkashka and Gennady gradually descended a curved catwalk suspended above stage

* Soon reduced to twenty-six, and eventually to sixteen.

93 Vasily Fyodorov's construction for *The Forest* (1924)

level, arriving finally at a turnstile (forestage left) representing the entrance
to 'Tree Stumps'.* The intervening episodes were played on the main stage,
area lighting being used (as in *Lake Lyul*) to pick out first one location then
the other. The leisurely tempo of the players' progress, further emphasised
by the miming of fishing, catching insects, and the like, contrasted abruptly
with the domestic bustle on the stage below in a manner that Meyerhold
himself later compared both to Eisenstein's use of 'collision montage' in the
cinema and to the episodic structure employed by Shakespeare and Pushkin.
In 1935 he commented: 'Each episode represents a complete dynamic whole
with its own plot, development and climax.'[49]

Once again, the proscenium arch was rendered redundant and the division
between stage and auditorium obliterated by the incursion of the catwalk and
the addition of acting areas adjacent to each stage box. The back-wall and
wings were left exposed, whilst the bare stage carried an assortment of real
objects (a pigeon-coop, a trellis, a see-saw, a washing-line, giant strides†
which served no decorative function but were there to be used simply as
the action dictated).

The neutral permanent setting with its dynamic function was a refinement of Meyerhold's earlier, more overtly constructivist manner. His use
of properties in *The Forest* was based on a similar principle. An assortment
of real objects with no obvious relationship was assembled onstage to be

* The settings and costumes were conceived by Meyerhold and executed by Vasily Fyodorov.
Beginning with *The Forest*, the designs for practically all Meyerhold's productions were executed
in accordance with his own precise instructions.

† Ropes and loops, suspended from a fixed pole.

utilised as required. Thus Aksyusha conveyed her disdain of Gurmyzhskaya by rhythmically beating laundry on the washing-line whilst retorting to her strictures; Bulanov betrayed his fatuity by discoursing with Gennady whilst balancing on two chairs. Most dynamic of all was the scene on the giant strides between the young lovers, Aksyusha and Petya:

> . . . they take off in pursuit of one another, leaving the ground and rising into the air to whirl out over the audience. The red blur of Aksyusha's dress stands out like a flame against the grey background of the stage. As they circle, the dynamism of this scenic invention infects their words, expresses their relationship, and in overcoming the law of gravity transforms it into an immense, powerful dream of liberty. First Petya, alone in the air, conjures up his dream of a boat journey from Kazan to Samara, from Samara to Saratov, and his word-movements become the equivalent of the journey itself. Then the two lovers 'circle like birds', a metaphor of love without an ounce of sentimentality.[50]

94 Ivan Pyriev as Bulanov with Mikhail Mukhin as Neschastlivtsev

Every device served both an ironic and a rhythmical function, sometimes helping to gloss over dialogue that was not consistent with Meyerhold's new interpretation of the play, and sometimes investing it with a significance that Ostrovsky had certainly never dreamed of.

In his desire to restore the full atmosphere of traditional comedy Meyerhold did not shrink from what Rudnitsky calls 'Aristophanic crudity'. Thus, in the episode 'Moonlight Sonata' Arkashka see-sawed with Gurmyzhskaya's

95 Episode Twenty-three, 'Moonlight Sonata', with Varvara Remizova as Ulita

pretentious housekeeper, Ulita, while she sang the romance 'Do not tempt me needlessly'; 'Every time Arkashka came down to the ground at his end of the see-saw and caused the housekeeper to fly up into the air, squealing and gasping, she was lifted off her end by the bump and her skirts rode right up, affording the audience a not altogether decent picture.' The scene ended even less ambiguously: Arkashka sat on his end of the see-saw and lit a cigarette, while Ulita was left stranded in mid-air gripping the thick beam tightly between her legs.[51]

The Forest provoked an unprecedented critical response and over fifty articles appeared in the months that followed the première, initiating a debate that continues to this day.[52] Apart from the 'Leningrad school', headed by Alexei Gvozdev, which invariably subjected Meyerhold's work to thoughtful analysis, the majority of the critics were either unequivocally antagonistic or confused by a production in which they could discern little resemblance to anything that Meyerhold had done before. Those on the 'left' could see little point in reviving *The Forest* in the Soviet context, regarding the production as a resurgence of Meyerhold's Petersburg aestheticism and accusing him of 'revisionism'; those on the 'right', predictably enough, were outraged at the barbarous liberties they felt he had taken with Ostrovsky's text. However, neither side succeeded in gauging the public's reaction or in influencing its

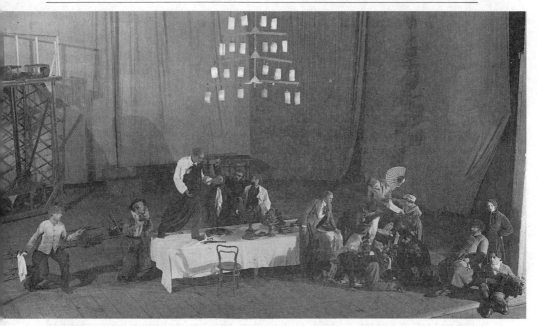

96 Finale: 'Don Quixote, or Tree-stumps again'

opinion: *The Forest* remained permanently in Meyerhold's repertoire for the next fourteen years, being performed over 1700 times.*

As Rudnitsky points out, the attitude towards Ostrovsky that Meyerhold had adopted was consistent with the changing mood of the left avant-garde: 'The days of wanton assaults on the classics were past, and the revolutionary poets were declaring their love for them . . . In their attitude one sensed a cheerful and rather vulgar familiarity.'[53] This is as good a description as any of Meyerhold's approach to the series of nineteenth-century masterpieces that he was to stage over the next eleven years. In his case, the familiarity was invariably the product of the closest scholarly acquaintance, which was more than could be said of the host of ill-conceived 'reinterpretations' of the classics now perpetrated by his imitators. The habit quickly assumed epidemic proportions and acquired the name of 'meyerholditis'. Ironically, in the course of time it was Meyerhold himself who was accused of propagating it.[54]

---

* A figure of 1700 plus is given by Rudnitsky and Garin. Presumably this includes the performances given on tour, since the number at the Meyerhold Theatre was 1328 (*Meyerhold II*, p. 528). In any case, it places *The Forest* far ahead of any other Soviet production of the period in popularity.

VI

Less than three months after the ill-received *Bubus* Meyerhold staged a production that won acclaim from all sides and marked a crucial advance in his production style. By 1925, despite growing misgivings within the Party, NEP was in full swing and over forty percent of retail trade was in private hands, much of it in the form of small businesses. It had spawned an alternative society, avid in its pursuit of Western fashions, nostalgic in its dreams of the old regime, and with a flourishing underworld of crooks, fixers and assorted parasites. For the zealous young satirists of the new Soviet theatre this presented an inviting target, though the risk remained of western-inspired decadence proving far more entertaining than Communist virtue, as Meyerhold's productions of *Lake Lyul* and *D.E.* in particular had already shown.

Presented at the Meyerhold Theatre on 20 April 1925, Nikolai Erdman's *The Warrant* was an altogether more complex and ambiguous work. Completed in 1924, *The Warrant* was the twenty-three-year-old Erdman's first full-length play, though he had already gained a considerable reputation as the author of numerous comic interludes, sketches and parodies performed in Moscow studio theatres and cabarets. One of these, *The Rhinocerotic Lover*, staged at Foregger's Mastfor studio in September 1922, was a parody of Meyerhold's production of *The Magnanimous Cuckold*.[55]

A satirical fantasy that immediately prompted comparisons with Gogol and Sukhovo-Kobylin, *The Warrant* depicts a typical group of 'internal émigrés' of the NEP period who still dream of the restoration of the monarchy, and preserve all the trappings and customs of the old order within the undignified confines of a communal flat in Moscow. In a series of hilariously involved peripeteia, Nadezhda Gulyachkina and her son Pavel seek to restore the family fortunes by arranging the marriage of Pavel's unprepossessing sister Varka to Valerian Smetanich, the son of prosperous bourgeois neighbours. As a dowry they offer Pavel's Party membership and the protection against the shocks of Communism that it will guarantee. Pavel's sole proof of his status is a warrant bearing his signature as chairman of the house committee, which, as it transpires, is forged by himself. The plan is foiled when Valerian chooses instead as his bride the Grand Duchess Anastasia, the miraculously surviving heir to the Romanov dynasty – only to discover that she is the Gulyachkins' cook, Nastya Pupkina from Tula. A lodger reveals all to the militia, but is sent packing: they have better things to do than to arrest these pathetic remnants of the past.*

The emblematic portrayal of character, the 'social masks' which Meyerhold

* For a translation of *The Warrant* see Nikolai Erdman, *The Mandate and The Suicide* (trans. Genereux, Volkov and Hoover, Ann Arbor, 1975).

97 *The Warrant.*
Varka (Zinaida
Raikh) and
Valerian (Sergei
Martinson)

had employed in all his productions of the Soviet period was entirely unsuited to *The Warrant*. Erdman's characters did not divide into the sharply contrasting social categories of *The Forest*, *D.E.*, or *Bubus*; instead they were all drawn from within the same narrow class, a series of subtly inflected variations on the one theme. The secret of Erdman's style lay in his ability to translate scrupulously noted details of petty bourgeois speech and behaviour into the most extravagant and arresting hyperbole without any sacrifice of authenticity. In effect, this was the style that Meyerhold had defined as 'the grotesque' fourteen years earlier in his essay *'Balagan'*, and which had so coloured his subsequent work. *The Warrant* gave him the opportunity to draw on all those years of accumulated experience and to apply it to a work of acute social observation.

Yet again, mime played a vital role in the production, in particular, sudden freezes that seemed to convey the characters' horrified subconscious awareness of their inescapable dilemma. Thus, says Rudnitsky:

> In Act One when Garin as Gulyachkin, in a kind of Khlestakovian ecstasy, surprised himself by blurting out the menacing and solemn words 'I am a Party man!', the fatal phrase made those around him and Gulyachkin

himself freeze in horror. Ivan Ivanovich, the lodger, at whom the threat was addressed, shrank back and cowered to the floor. Gulyachkin's mama and sister stood with their mouths gaping wide. Gulyachkin himself, unhinged by his own heroism, remained motionless in an unnatural pose that suggested both pride and terror. And then immediately this entire 'sculptural group', this monumental photograph of the explosion that had rocked the petit bourgeois world, glided slowly and smoothly into the depths of the stage on the revolve.[56]

The revolve was employed equally to hilarious comic effect. Immediately following his inadvertent proposal of marriage to Gulyachkin's sister, Varka, Sergei Martinson as Valerian Smetanich,

'. . . slowly reeling as though in a labyrinth of invisible blind alleys, exited slowly with downcast head. The action took place on the two contra-rotating revolves, with Valerian and Varvara finding themselves moving in opposite directions. Struggling to counteract the rapid motion of the revolve, the terrified philanderer, whose plans fell some way short of the hopes of his father, launched into frantic motion. Losing his balance, he swerved adroitly, first bending double and then seeming to sprawl headlong in mid-air.[57]

98 *The Warrant.* The wedding of Valerian Smetanich to 'the Grand Duchess Anastasia' (centre). Note Meyerhold seated at the bottom right-hand corner

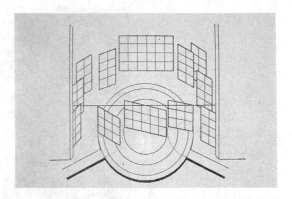

99 Plan of the setting for *The Warrant*

Meyerhold and his designer Shlepyanov devised a deep circular stage-area with two large concentric revolves and a series of tall varnished wooden screens that enclosed the action. Telling effects were achieved with these simple mechanical means: a petrified group would silently retreat, a gap would materialise in the seemingly impassable wall, and they would be 'hurled from the stream of life onto the rubbish dump of history'.[58] The revolves were also used to bear on the properties, employed sparingly but effectively 'both as instruments of acting and as a symbolic generalisation of a way of life'[59] A domestic altar complete with votive candles and horn-gramophone, a wrought-iron treadle sewing machine, a piano decorated with paper flowers, a banquet table with epergne and candelabra: these were the objects these doomed remnants relied on to preserve their delusion of permanency.

But unerringly satirical as Erdman's comedy was, it was far more than a merciless jest at the expense of a helpless foe. Pavel Markov, shortly to become literary manager of the Moscow Art Theatre, wrote shortly after the opening: 'The strength of *The Warrant* lies in the blending of satire with humour, of irony with lyricism. It is a lyrical satire. Essentially, this is dictated by Erdman's love of life and by his tenderness towards people, no matter how annihilatingly he may have depicted his heroes.'[60] In a public discussion of the production Meyerhold scorned the notion of 'tenderness', describing himself and Erdman as 'cynics and atheists'.[61] Nevertheless, there was no mistaking the powerful shift in mood that occurred as the production reached its denouement. Never was there a play at his theatre that so often reduced its audience to such helpless laughter,* but all the more disturbing were the emotions stirred by the final unmasking of Pavel and Nastya's pathetic delusions. There was little laughter at Pavel Gulyachkin's desolate closing line 'What's the point of living, mama, if they don't even bother

* The audience research group established at the Meyerhold Theatre recorded an average of 336 'laughs' during performances of *The Warrant*, or 92 an hour. This compared with 67 per hour for *The Forest*, 41 for *Bubus the Teacher*, and 30 for *D.E.*[62]

100 Madame
Gulyachkina at
prayer before
her horn-
gramophone

101 Erast Garin as
Pavel
Gulyachkin

to arrest us?' It was a sudden glimpse of the tragic aspect of the grotesque, which recalled Blok's bewildered Pierrot playing mournfully on his pipe at the end of *The Fairground Booth*. As Boris Alpers wrote: 'Meyerhold's satirical theatre, merry and irreverent in mood and capable of malicious ridicule at the expense of those individuals who were receding into the past, suddenly paused for reflection, broke off its laughter. Its performances began to move one. In its voice there began to predominate the note of tragedy.'[63]

A deep significance lay behind Erast Garin's interpretation of Pavel Gulyachkin, his first major role with the company. Following Igor Ilinsky's abrupt departure, his place in the company was filled by Garin. Rudnitsky writes:

> The buoyant, mischievous, charming Ilinsky, full of youthful energy, was replaced by the nervous, fragile, disturbingly grotesque Garin, with his sudden freezes into immobility. Energy was replaced by trance, the dynamic by the static, high-spirited playful humour by sombre and bitter satire. The highly talented Garin threw into sharp relief the growing divergence between Meyerhold's theatre and a changing reality.[64]

The Warrant marked Meyerhold's virtual rejection of placard drama and his return to a theatre of disturbing complexity; as Pavel Markov wrote, 'The production makes you think. It questions premises and proceeds by deduction.'[65] Significantly, Stanislavsky, who had not even taken the trouble to see *The Forest*, was deeply impressed and commented on the last act: 'In this act Meyerhold has accomplished what I myself am dreaming of.'[66*]

VII

The following season, for the first and only time Meyerhold entrusted a production to one of his pupils, Vasily Fyodorov. It was Sergei Tretyakov's 'drama of fact' *Roar, China!*, a play based on an actual incident on the Yangtse River in 1924 in which the captain of the British gunboat *Cockchafer* demanded the summary execution of two innocent Chinese coolies in reparation for the death in a brawl of an American business representative.

Shortly after the première on 23 January 1926, Fyodorov publicly disowned the production and resigned from the company. Subsequently, it transpired that large sections of the work were the result of Meyerhold's revision, notably the highly realistic portrayal of the Chinese coolies and the small part of the 'Boy', played memorably by Babanova.[68] By contrast, the scenes involving the Navy and the European business community were

---

* *The Warrant* remained in the repertoire for nine years, receiving its last performance in Moscow on 28 March 1934, by which time Erdman had been exiled to Siberia for writing 'anti-Soviet' fables.[67]

a throwback to the style of *Lake Lyul* and *D.E.*, emphasised the more by a setting divided across the middle by a strip of water with the looming gunboat upstage and the 'Chinese quarter' downstage.

Due largely to the interest provoked by the issues raised in the play at a time when the Chinese revolutionary movement was gaining momentum, *Roar, China!* was highly successful and formed part of the Meyerhold Theatre's repertoire when it went on its first foreign tour in 1930. Subsequently, the play was performed in numerous theatres throughout the Soviet Union and other countries.

Apart from *Roar, China!*, almost twenty months passed after *The Warrant* before Moscow saw another production by Meyerhold. His time was divided between work on Pushkin's *Boris Godunov* at the Moscow Art Theatre's Third Studio (Vakhtangov's theatre until his death in 1922) and on *The Government Inspector* at his own theatre. Sadly, *Boris Godunov* was never completed; Meyerhold returned to it with his own company in 1936, but again succeeded only in rehearsing certain scenes. The notes and eye-witness accounts of rehearsals that remain suggest that he might well have succeeded in achieving the long-overdue recognition of a dramatic masterpiece.[69]

102 *Roar, China!* The Navy and business community

The Government Inspector

In his review of *The Forest* Meyerhold's old Petersburg opponent Alexander Kugel wrote '. . . amongst us there are still many who were brought up on the exemplary works of Russian literature, and we regard such treatment of our great poets as unexampled barbarism'.[1] The charge was not new: many critics had protested in similar terms against the outrages perpetrated on *The Storm*, on *Masquerade*, and on *Tarelkin's Death*. But Meyerhold remained true to Mounet-Sully's dictum, 'Chaque texte n'est qu'un prétexte', claiming that '. . . the art of the director is the art not of an executant, but of an author – so long as one has earned the right'.[2] No production demonstrated this more resoundingly than *The Government Inspector*, which was presented on 9 December 1926 after over a year's rehearsal.

After the first performance of the play in April 1836, Gogol was so terrified by the outraged protests of conservative critics that he denied all satirical intent, saying 'Put two or three rogues on the stage and everyone flies into a rage and cries "we are not rogues!"'[3] Rejecting this excuse as disingenuous, Meyerhold attached far greater significance to what Gogol said eleven years later in his *Author's Confession*: 'In *The Government Inspector* I decided to gather into one heap everything rotten in Russia as I then saw it, all the injustices that are perpetrated in those places and in those circumstances where justice is most required of a man; I decided to hold up everything to ridicule at once.'[4]

As Meyerhold's co-adaptor, Mikhail Korenev said:

> The theatre was faced with the task of making *The Government Inspector* an accusatory production. Needless to say, our target was not merely peculation in some miserable little town in the middle of nowhere which has never got onto any map, but as far as possible the entire Nicholayan era, together with the way of life of its nobility and its officials.[5]

In fact, Meyerhold went so far as to project his whole production on the scale of the Russian capital, arguing that when Gogol was working on *The*

Government Inspector, 'he was burning with the desire to depict something from the life of St Petersburg'.[6]

In the original Petersburg production the cast paid little attention to Gogol's notes on character portrayal, reducing the play to a trivial farce involving stock characters, and with Khlestakov played, in Gogol's words, 'like some vaudeville rogue . . . the conventional swindler, that drab character who has appeared in exactly the same costume for the past two hundred years'.[7] It must have been harmless, because even stolid Tsar Nicholas was vastly amused and instructed the entire Royal Family and Privy Council to see it.

In Moscow a month later the play fared no better, even though the great Shchepkin played the Mayor. Gogol was deeply depressed and fled the country, to return only occasionally over the next twelve years. He continued to work on the text, seeking to eradicate the farcical elements that he considered had contributed to the burlesque of the first production. The final version published in 1842 contains numerous amendments, notably the insertion of the epigraph, 'Don't blame the mirror if your own mug is crooked', and the Mayor's aside to the audience in the final scene, 'What are you laughing at? You're laughing at yourselves!' Although this version is now accepted as canonical, it was not performed until 1870, by which time, says Korenev:

> Tradition unwittingly or perhaps, on the contrary, with most cunning malice
> aforethought, had set *The Government Inspector* on the rails of vaudeville and
> simple rib-tickling comedy and obscured its social significance; in their
> customary interpretation, the characters scarcely ever rose above the level
> of the conventional masks of light comedy.[8]

But new efforts were made to define Gogol's dramatic style, leading to the emergence of two further schools of opinion at the beginning of the twentieth century. First, there was the 'neo-naturalistic' interpretation which identified his theatre as the forerunner of the genre works of Ostrovsky, Tolstoy, Turgenev, and others, and was exemplified by the Moscow Art Theatre production of 1908. Second, there were the attempts of the symbolists (notably Rozanov's *Legend of the Great Inquisitor*, Bely's *Gogol*, and Merezhkovsky's *Gogol and the Devil*) to reinterpret *The Government Inspector* in the light of the writings of Gogol's late 'mystical' period, in particular the *Dénouement* to the play (1846), in which he represents it as an allegory of the Last Judgement with Khlestakov the personification of man's 'venal, treacherous conscience'.[9]

In 1908, Meyerhold expressed his admiration for Merezhkovsky's article, recommending it as a corrective to the entrenched views of the senior members of the Alexandrinsky company.[10] The manner of his work with Komissarzhevskaya suggests strongly that his planned production of *The Government Inspector* at her theatre in 1907 would almost certainly have followed the symbolist reading.

However, in 1926 Meyerhold rejected all such narrow interpretations, seeing the play as a unique synthesis of realism, hyperbole, and fantasy, and arguing that whereas Gogol's treatment was comic, the overall effect was disturbingly lachrymose. During a rehearsal he told his company:

When Gogol read Pushkin the opening chapters of *Dead Souls*, Pushkin (who, incidentally, loved a good laugh) grew steadily more and more gloomy until finally he was totally downcast. And when the reading was finished he said in a voice filled with melancholy: 'God, what a sad place our Russia is!' Gogol had achieved the desired effect: although the treatment was comic, Pushkin understood at once that the intention was something other than comic.[11]

These remarks set the tone for the whole production; early on, Meyerhold said 'We must avoid everything that is pure comedy or buffoonery. We must be careful not to borrow any commedia tricks, and try to express everything in terms of tragicomedy. We must steer a course for tragedy.'[12]

II

In his earlier interpretations of the classics Meyerhold, for all his startling innovations, had remained faithful to the printed text. Even in his 'montage' of *The Forest* he altered little of Ostrovsky's actual dialogue. But the breadth of his conception of *The Government Inspector* forced him to adopt an altogether freer approach. As the actor and director Mikhail Chekhov wrote:

He realised that to stage *The Government Inspector* and only *The Government Inspector* would be to torment himself with an unbearable vow of silence. *The Government Inspector* started to grow and swell until it split wide open; through the cracks there gushed a raging torrent: *Dead Souls*, *The Nevsky Prospect*, Podkolyosin, Poprishchev, the dreams of the Mayoress, horrors, guffaws, raptures, the screams of ladies, the fears of petty bureaucrats. . .[13]

Meyerhold's research for the production was characteristically scholarly and exhaustive, and would almost certainly have included Professor Ivan Yermakov's psychoanalytical study of Gogol's work and personality, published in 1924.[14] Working from a Freudian standpoint, Yermakov pays particular attention to Gogol's erotic fixations, but also lays stress on the thematic and lexical continuity of the writer's work as a whole. The work concentrates on *Dead Souls* and a number of the short stories, with only passing references to *The Government Inspector*, but it might well have encouraged Meyerhold to draw out the play's deeper meaning (not least its erotic aspects) by exploring the full range of Gogol's *oeuvre* and the circumstances of the writer's strange existence.* Pavel Markov, the literary director of the Moscow Art Theatre, wrote in 1927:

* Another production of *The Government Inspector* that was clearly indebted to Yermakov's work was Igor Terentiev's *Ubu*-like burlesque at the Leningrad Press Club in 1927, conceived as a slapstick challenge to Meyerhold's sombre vision of the play.[15]

103 *The Government Inspector*, Episode Five: 'Filled with Tend'rest Love'. With Raikh as Anna Andreevna (left)

> Meyerhold took Gogol himself as the theme for his production, switching the theme of the 'inspector' to that of Gogol destroyed by the age of Nicholas. Meyerhold's conception is one of love distorted, of spiritual emptiness, and of inner catastrophe. The 'eroticism' in the production, which caused such outrage at the early performances and subsequently has been considerably toned down, must be seen as essentially a protest against the perversion of love.[16]

In his now customary manner, Meyerhold divided the play into fifteen titled episodes, a sequence of fifteen separate vignettes that mainly followed the chronological sequence of Gogol's plot.[17] Whilst drawing on all six extant versions of the play, he took as the foundation for his grand design the first draft of the play which dates from 1835. He restored the scene in which Anna Andreevna boasts to her daughter of the cavalry captain driven to despair by her flashing eyes; the speech in which the Sergeant's wife offers to lift her skirts to show Khlestakov the bruises she has received from the Mayor's flogging; the comic dialogue where Khlestakov tries in vain to penetrate Doctor Hübner's German in order to extract a bribe from him. He introduced isolated lines from *The Gamblers*, *Marriage*, and *Vladimir of the Third Degree*, together with unmistakable touches from the *Petersburg Stories*. Moreover, on the departure of Khlestakov and Osip at the close of Act Four the theatre was made to echo with the ghostly jingling of harness bells, reminding the audience of the flight of Chichikov's celestial troika at the end of the first part of *Dead Souls*.

At first glance, the majority of these amendments seem to contradict Gogol's own revisions of the play, restoring the elements of physical comedy; but they were thoroughly consistent with the satirical style developed by Meyerhold in recent productions, in which pantomime and precise visual 'business', often with props, were employed to bring out the true significance of the action and the character's awareness of it. Thus, in Scene Five ('Filled with Tend'rest Love') the scale of Anna Andreevna's amorous fantasies about the Cavalry Captain was demonstrated by the sudden materialisation from behind furniture and out of cupboards of a band of adoring young officers serenading her to imaginary guitars, with the climax coming when the last of them, clutching a bouquet of flowers, emerged like a jack-in-the-box from the top of a cupboard and histrionically shot himself. When Khlestakov informed the Mayor that he lived 'to pluck flowers of pleasure', he immediately relieved himself of a gobbet of phlegm. Then during his drunken recital of his Petersburg exploits he idly drew Anna Andreevna's entranced little finger to his lips on a teaspoon.

The merest commonplace action was transformed into a studied pantomime: the ruminative, unison puffing of long pipes by the town dignitaries in the opening scene, the elaborate toilette of the Mayor before setting off for the inn, even the proffering of bribes to Khlestakov – all assumed the precision of a familiar ceremony, which exactly conveyed the ossified daily round of petty officialdom.

This emphasis on reiterated gestures formed the basis for the interpretation of character. In his notes to his actors Meyerhold supplied each character with a wealth of biographical detail that would have pleased Stanislavsky. The difference was that it was more idiosyncratic, more 'Gogolian' than Stanislavsky would have countenanced; he advised his actors 'to find a certain eccentricity within the limits of your own personalities – in your poses, in your gait, in the way you hold your pipe, in the way you gesture with your hands.'[18] The intention was not so much to furnish a broad base for the psychological interpretation of the role as to fix distinctive movements, poses, details of costume, and so on. Thus, Pavel Markov commented:

> Meyerhold looks at a person, an actor, with the eye of a painter, a draughtsman, or a cinema cameraman. He almost willingly sacrifices the effect of gradually uncovering the inner kernel of a personality. In a fleeting glance, a single movement, the drop of a hand, he reveals more than a normal observer would notice; he shows (or seeks to show) the fate of a man unfolding, and at the same time achieves a dazzling theatrical effect. . . The actor plays one and the same situation throughout an entire episode on the basis of the most precise rhythmical scheme which the director has presented to him.[19]

In working with his actors on this laconicism of style, Meyerhold urged them to study the films of Charlie Chaplin, Buster Keaton, and the director James Cruze, whose *Fighting Coward* was currently showing in Moscow.[20]

III

Proceeding from the assumption of a much grander location than Gogol's original small town, Meyerhold's portrayal of character was far removed from the traditional 'hemming and hawing idiots dressed up to look more idiotic still'.[21] For his visit to Khlestakov in his rat's nest under the stairs of the inn, the Mayor was arrayed in an ornate shako and voluminous cloak, looking like some august field-marshal from the glorious campaign against Napoleon.

104 Episode Four: 'After Penza'. With Nikolai Mologin as Dobchinsky (left), Pyotr Starkovsky as the Mayor (top left) and Erast Garin as Khlestakov (right)

The transformation of Anna Andreevna from the accepted stereotype was even more striking: Gogol's 'provincial coquette, not quite beyond middle age, educated half on novels and verses in visitors' books and half in fussing over the pantry and the maids' room. . .' became a 'Catherine the Great', a 'Provincial Cleopatra', a 'Russian Venus' with a lustrous black chignon, and shoulders of gleaming alabaster rising from the rich silks that swathed her voluptuous figure. It was a conception that certainly showed off Zinaida Raikh to the best advantage, but as Andrei Bely pointed out, she was in any case a creature straight from Gogol's own febrile imagination, one of the ladies from 'the town of N', who so excited Chichikov's erotic fancy at the Governor's ball in *Dead Souls*.[22]

The theme of sexuality was announced in Episode Five in Anna Adreevna's boudoir immediately preceding the materialisation of her band of admirers. Seizing on Gogol's note that 'She has four complete changes of costume during the play', Meyerhold made the Mayoress try on a whole series of dazzling silk gowns, stepping into the huge mahogany wardrobe to change them and rustling provocatively as she pivoted in front of the mirror in a 'firework display of dresses'. Her movements were eyed furtively by Dobchinsky, who was so bemused by the whole erotic sequence that he made a blind exit into the cupboard, from whence there emerged the first of the love-stricken officers. The allure of the scene was rendered even more disturbing by Babanova's portrayal of the Mayor's daughter, Maria Antonovna. On the one hand, she was made to act as a foil to her mother, setting off her voluptuous charms with her own innocence, her hair tightly plaited in absurd loops, and forced into ungainly girlish dresses with ankle-length frilly pantalettes underneath. On the other hand, she readily assumed the role of her mother's rival, wantonly flaunting her adolescent sexuality.

But true to the spirit of Gogol, this was hyperbole with a purpose. Whether all the finery represented a true picture of remote provincial life or Petersburg high society was beside the point; what it did represent was the bombastic Mayor and his feather-brained wife as they pictured themselves in their social-climbing dreams. When finally, the subterfuge was exploded, the Mayor lost his wits, to be removed raving in a strait-jacket by his own cloddish policemen, Anna Andreevna was borne away senseless on the shoulders of her faithful entourage of subalterns, like some fallen Racinian heroine, and the pure soprano voice of Maria Antonovna was heard singing a plaintive romance. To such heights had their deluded fantasies soared, that this grotesquely tragic end seemed fitting, even inevitable, and the audience had no need of the Mayor's chilling whisper 'What are you laughing at? You're laughing at yourselves!' to freeze the smiles on their faces.* Farce turned into nightmare as the church bells, ordered to celebrate Maria Antonovna's betrothal to Khlestakov, boomed louder and louder, police whistles shrilled, and a disembodied Jewish band

---

* In October 1846 Gogol wrote to Schchepkin: 'Pay particular attention to the closing scene; it is absolutely necessary for it to be vivid, even startling. The Mayor must be completely distraught and not at all funny.'

105 Garin as
Khlestakov

sent the guests on a frenzied *galop* through the auditorium. Simultaneously, a white screen rose in front of the stage, bearing the fatal announcement of the true inspector's arrival and then slowly disappeared aloft to disclose life-size terror-stricken effigies of the townspeople – condemned to eternal petrifaction.*

What of Khlestakov, the engineer of this whole nightmare? Meyerhold drew attention to his affinity with the card-sharper, Ikharyov, in *The Gamblers*,[23] but he gave him as many more aspects as he had once identified in Arlecchino and Dom Juan.† Leonid Grossman describes Erast Garin's first entrance: 'He appears onstage, a character from some tale by Hoffmann: slender, clad in black, with a stiff, mannered gait, strange spectacles, a sinister old-fashioned tall hat, a rug and a cane, apparently tormented by some private vision. He is a flâneur from the Nevsky Prospect, a native of Gogol's own Petersburg. . .'[24]‡

---

* In his *Dénouement* to the play Gogol describes the Dumb Scene as '. . . the petrification into which everybody is frozen by the announcement of the arrival of the true inspector who will exterminate all of them, wipe them from the face of the earth, destroy them utterly . . .'

† See pp. 108-109 above.

‡ From 1929 the role of Khlestakov was shared between Garin and Sergei Martinson. Contrasting the two, Alexander Matskin writes: 'Garin was more secretive; his Khlestakov was a gambler, a mystifier, a strange individual. Martinson was more open, more physiological; his Khlestakov was a figure from everyday life, enlivened by the actor's familiar comic absurdity.'[25]

And he had a double, an 'Officer in Transit' (sprung from Khlestakov's passing reference in the text to an infantry captain who had fleeced him at cards in Penza) with a pale lugubrious visage and a cynical daring reminiscent of Lermontov's Pechorin from *A Hero of our Time*. He was Khlestakov's taciturn accomplice in every enterprise. At the inn he set to work marking a park of cards; immediately Khlestakov's air of distraction vanished and he, too, became a sharp-witted swindler. On sensing the Mayor's servility towards him at their opening encounter, Khlestakov borrowed his companion's tunic, fur-collared cape, and tall shako, and 'Before our very eyes this timorous little fop, this most servile of civil servants was transformed into the phantasmagorical figure of the imposter.'[26] Later in Episode Eleven ('Embrace Me, Do') the pair of them danced a quadrille with Anna Andreevna and Maria Antonovna; whilst Khlestakov played the love-smitten gallant to mother and daughter in turn, his double looked on with a disdainful sneer, revealing the whole tawdriness of these amorous manoeuvres.

The 'Officer in Transit' was seen on the one hand as 'a mystical representation of everything that took place behind the scenes of Khlestakov's soul',[27] and on the other as 'an animated piece of furniture',[28] ready to provide the accessories for every transformation, an attentive ear for a soliloquy – even the occasional phrase in the rare event of words failing his garrulous companion.

Khlestakov had a different mask for every situation: Nevsky flâneur, ingenious card-sharper, timorous clerk, imperious general, adroit adventurer. He was all of these plus a Russian Munchhausen who elevated the lie to an art form. Yet on the words, 'Well how are things, Pushkin, old friend?' he lapsed into the melancholic reverie of a solitary poet and for a fleeting moment the audience was offered a glimpse of Gogol himself. Much was made of Meyerhold's 'mystical' interpretation of Khlestakov, but a thoroughly rational justification for it is supplied by Gogol:

> In a word he should be a type containing traits found scattered in a variety of Russian characters but which happen here to be combined in one, as is often the case in nature. There is nobody who for a minute, not to say several minutes, has not changed into, or gone on being a Khlestakov, although naturally he would be reluctant to admit it. We even make fun of this habit – but only, of course, when we see it in someone else. Even the smart guards officer, even the respected paterfamilias, even our friend, the humble man of letters, will sometimes turn into a Khlestakov. In short, there's hardly a single man who won't become him at least once in his lifetime – the only point is that he will change back again and carry on as though it had never happened.[29]

Erast Garin recalled in 1974: 'In the interpretation of the director there was hyperbole but no mysticism . . . the mystical interpretation of Meyerhold's Khlestakov by a section of the critics was a product of their own biographies; they were over-conscientious in the application of their literary education.'[30]

As a counterweight to the unrelieved corruption of the townspeople and the fiendish machinations of Khlestakov, Meyerhold interpreted his valet, Osip, as a vigorous positive character rather in the spirit of Aksyusha and Petya in *The Forest*. Rejecting the traditional picture of the scrofulous drunken rascal, he made him a red-cheeked country lad who sang traditional folk songs and emanated robust common sense. The text of his reminiscences of St Petersburg (at the opening of Act Two) was not changed, but he was furnished with the audience of a charwoman, borrowed by Meyerhold from *The Gamblers*, who pealed with laughter throughout.* Like the 'Officer in Transit' and Anna Andreevna's young officers – to say nothing of Doctor Hübner and his ministrations to the Mayor in Act One† – the charwoman both served a practical theatrical purpose (helping to avoid the soliloquy which Meyerhold considered outmoded) and accentuated the irony of the dialogue (Osip's contempt for Petersburg society). But further to that, her laughter served as a coloratura accompaniment to Osip's tenor recitative; one instance of the production's musical conception which is discussed below.

Meyerhold's most enigmatic addition was the figure of the 'Blue Hussar', a small captain in a light-blue uniform who appeared in three scenes and spoke no lines, representing perhaps yet another neglected suitor of the Mayoress and her daughter. 'What is this little officer, an empty space in the production?' – asked Mikhail Chekhov – 'Yes, of course, though not in the production but in the man himself. *The idea* of the emptiness and pointlessness of life, is conceived and manifested by Meyerhold to a degree of nightmarish reality.'[31]

IV

Meyerhold's version of *The Government Inspector* was considerably longer than the original, and his extensive use of pantomime and *tableaux vivants* made it longer still. In performance with two intervals it ran a fraction over four hours, ending after midnight.‡ Meyerhold wanted to use elaborate settings to evoke the atmosphere of the 1830s, but he needed to avoid lengthy scene changes which would have been inimical to the psychological effect of montage, and would have made the running time quite intolerable.

---

* 'We invented the Charwoman and then found a Charwoman in Gogol himself' (*Meyerhold II*, p. 132). In Scene Eight of *The Gamblers* Uteshitelny says: 'And on the stairs some charwoman, an absolute fright . . .'

† For a record of a rehearsal of this scene see *Braun*, pp. 221–30 (in this version the name 'Hübner' is rendered in the literal transliteration 'Giebner').

‡ Walter Benjamin, who was in Moscow in December 1926, recalls that when it opened the production actually ran for five hours, but was then cut by an hour.[32]

Accordingly, he devised a method of kinetic staging, similar in principle to the double revolve in *The Warrant*.*

The stage was enclosed by a semicircular, imitation polished mahogany screen containing a series of eleven double-doors (plus two more at either wing), surmounted by a dull green border and with three large suspended green lights. The centre section of the screen opened to admit a tiny truck-stage (4.25 by 3.5 metres with a one-in-eight rake) which rolled silently forward on runners to face the audience with actors and setting ready assembled. At the end of the scene the screen reopened and the truck retreated, to be replaced by another similarly prepared. All but four scenes were played on these trucks, with Episode Three in the inn ('After Penza') alone lowered from the flies. The remainder occupied the full stage area, with the final 'grand rond' overflowing into the auditorium. Bobchinsky's headlong tumble down the stairs of the inn continued right out of sight into the orchestra pit – a 'mise *hors* scène', as Eisenstein called it.

The full stage was used to striking effect in the episode entitled 'Procession' (the return from the hospital to the Mayor's house) when a tipsy Khlestakov in voluminous cloak steered an erratic course the length of a balustrade with a sycophantic *corps de ballet* of town dignitaries matching his every stagger. In 'Bribes' (Act Four, Scenes Three to Nine, staged simultaneously) the wooden screen was transformed into a cunning 'bribe machine': as Khlestakov lay stupefied on the empty stage in a flickering half light, eleven hands, seemingly conjured up by his drunken imagination, materialised simultaneously from eleven doors and apprehensively tendered eleven wads of banknotes which Khlestakov pocketed with the mechanical gestures of a clockwork doll.

Each scene on the truck-stage glided forward from the gloom like the reincarnation of a long-buried past, an exquisitely composed engraving projected out of its gleaming mahogany frame; a long pause was held for the image to register, then the tableau came to life. In a newspaper interview Meyerhold commented: 'Thanks to the method of staging that we have employed in the production, we have been able, in the language of the cinema, to shoot the principal scenes in close-up.'[33] This is well illustrated by Sergei Radlov's description of Episode Seven ('Over a Bottle of Fat-Belly') in which Khlestakov drunkenly expatiates on his Petersburg exploits:

> Crystal sparkles, blue and translucent; heavy silk, gleaming and flowing; the dazzling black hair and dazzling white bosom of a grand stately lady; a dandy,

* In the year leading up to the production Meyerhold parted company with a succession of designers. First to go was Ilya Shlepyanov, who had worked on *Bubus the Teacher* and *The Warrant*, next was Vladimir Dmitriev, who had designed *The Dawn* in 1920. A potential collaboration with Golovin and one of his assistants barely got beyond the discussion stage. Eventually, the designs were credited to Victor Kiselyov, though he did no more than faithfully execute Meyerhold's conception.

106 Episode Seven: 'Over a Bottle of Fat-Belly'. Khlestakov recounts his Petersburg
     exploits with the Blue Hussar (centre) seated next to Maria Antonovna and the Officer
     in Transit reclining extreme left

107 Episode Nine: 'Bribes'

romantically gaunt and drunk as only a Hoffmann could imagine, lifts a cigar to his languid lips with the gesture of a somnambulist. A silver bowl filled with pieces of fat, succulent watermelon. Enchanted objects, wobbling slightly, float from hand to hand, passed by servants in a trance. Huge splendid divans, like elephants carved from mahogany, stand poised in majestic slumber. What is this – *Caligari* run in slow motion by some lunatic projectionist?[34]

To some casual observers the profusion of lifelike detail seemed to suggest a rapprochement with Moscow Art Theatre naturalism, but in truth the picture was anything but naturalistic. The pot-belly of a wardrobe, the voluptuous curve of a Récamier couch, the deep rose-patterned back of a divan: they were all subtly exaggerated to enhance the poses of the characters and to imprint themselves more firmly on the retina of the spectator.

Above all, the truck-stage afforded no space for ill-considered, 'inspirational' movement. With thirty or more characters pressed together in a human pyramid, the merest deviation in timing or movement could destroy the whole ensemble. By this most practical device Meyerhold compelled his company to exercise physically the self-discipline that had always been the ultimate objective of biomechanics and all the experiments that preceded the formulation of that system. Freedom for self-expression in the creation of character and situation remained, but allied to extreme precision within the tightest spatial and rhythmical limits.

V

The powerful atmosphere and the sense of period of the production owed much to the complex musical score that accompanied it throughout.* It included arrangements of works by nineteenth-century Russian composers, in particular romances by Glinka and Dargomyzhsky sung by Babanova, and music specially composed by Mikhail Gnesin. Gnesin describes how the music heard during the celebration of Maria Antonovna's betrothal to Khlestakov was based on the little Jewish bands that Meyerhold recalled from the balls and weddings of his youth in Penza. It was similar to the music that Chekhov had specified as an accompaniment to Ranevskaya's agony in Act Three of *The Cherry Orchard*.[36]

Twenty years earlier, in his analysis of that same act Meyerhold had defined its musical structure, treating the actual music as one element in an overall rhythmical harmony designed to reveal the 'sub-text' of the drama.[37] Now he analysed and interpreted *The Government Inspector* in precisely the same manner, exploiting to perfection the principles that he had pursued originally

---

* In common with other major Soviet theatres, Meyerhold had at his disposal a small orchestra to provide a musical accompaniment for productions. For *The Government Inspector* it comprised 4 violins, 2 violas, 2 cellos, 1 double bass, 2 clarinets, 1 flute, 1 trumpet and cymbals.[35]

in 1905 with Ilya Sats at the Theatre-Studio and had refined further through his study of Wagner and Appia. Emmanuel Kaplan describes Meyerhold's 'orchestration' of Gogol's score in Episode One ('Chmykhov's Letter'):

Introduction. Dark. Somewhere, slow quiet music begins to play. In the centre of the stage massive doors swing silently open of their own accord and a platform moves slowly forward towards the spectator: out of the gloom, out of the distance, out of the past – one senses this immediately, because it is contained in the music. The music swells and comes nearer, then suddenly on an abrupt chord – *sforzando* – the platform is flooded with light in unison with the music.

On the platform stand a table and a few chairs; candles burn; officials sit. The audience seems to crane forward towards the dark and gloomy age of Nicholas in order to see better what is was like in those days.

Suddenly, the music grows quiet – *subito piano* – gloomy like the period, like the colours of the setting: red furniture, red doors and red walls, green uniforms and green hanging lampshades: the colour scheme of government offices. The music is abruptly retarded and drawn out expectantly; everybody waits – on

108 Episode Fourteen: 'A Fine Celebration!' The reading of Khlestakov's letter by the Postmaster, with the Mayor and Mayoress seated right and the Blue Hussar (Vladimir Maslatsov) extreme right

the stage and in the audience. Smoke rises from pipes and chibouks. The long stems 'cross out' the faces of the officials lit by the flickering candle flames; they are like fossilised monsters: crossed out and obliterated, once and for all. There they sit, wreathed in a haze with only the shadows of their pipes flickering on their faces; and the music plays on, slower and quieter as though flickering too, bearing them away from us, further and further into that irretrievable 'then'. A pause – *fermata* – and then a voice: 'Gentlemen, I have invited you here to give you some most unpleasant news. . .' – like Rossini in the Act One *stretta* with Doctor Bartholo and Don Basilio, only there the tempo is *presto*, whilst here it is very slow. Then suddenly, as though on a word of command, at a stroke of the conductor's baton, everyone stirs in agitation, pipes jump from the lips, fists clench, heads swivel. The last syllable of 'revizor' [inspector] seems to tweak everybody. Now the word is hissed in a whisper: the whole word by some, the consonants alone by others, and somewhere just a softly rolled 'r'. The word 'revizor' is divided musically into every conceivable intonation. The ensemble of suddenly startled officials blows up and dies away like a squall. Everyone freezes and falls silent; the guilty conscience rears up in alarm then hides its poisonous head again, like a serpent lying motionless, harbouring its deadly venom.

The dynamics of this perfectly fashioned musical introduction fluctuate constantly. The sudden *forte-fortissimo* of the Mayor's cry 'send for Lyapkin-Tyapkin!' The terrified officials spring up in all directions, hiding their guilty consciences as far away as possible – under the table, behind each other's backs, even behind the armchair where the Mayor was just sitting. It is like a dance-pantomime of fright. The District Physician begins to squeal on the letter 'i', first a long drawn-out whistle then jerkily on 'e' *staccato*, then the two 'notes' alternately rising and falling, whilst the next lines are 'embroidered' onto this background. In orchestral terms, it is like a piccolo with double bass *pizzicato*, just like the comic scenes in Rimsky-Korsakov's *May Night*. A sudden screech *glissando* from the Doctor and a new 'dance of terror' begins. The plastic pattern of the characters' movements corresponds to the rhythmical pattern of their voices. Their brief pauses seem to foretoken the dumb scene of the finale.[38]

Perhaps more than anything else it is this concept of 'musicality' that characterises Meyerhold's style – a style that has been described as 'musical realism' and which sets him apart from every other stage director of his time. Shortly after *The Government Inspector* had opened the composer and critic Boris Asafiev wrote:

To say or to express through music what cannot be conveyed through dialogue alone, to use music to attract and to beguile, to utilise it as a signal in order to alert the concentration – such is the range of music in drama. All this has featured in earlier productions by Meyerhold, the most symphonic of all being *The Forest*. But in *The Government Inspector* one is struck simultaneously by the scale, the mastery of form and the acuity with which the properties of music are utilised: to alert (by 'signalling'), to call, to lure and to hypnotise, to raise and lower the emotional current, to lend depth to the atmosphere and the action, to transform the comic into the horrifically bizarre, to lend the merest commonplace anecdote the tone of a psychologically significant event.[39]

When Meyerhold formed his association with the composer Vissarion Shebalin in 1929 they brought this style to a new level of refinement in a sequence of productions culminating in *The Lady of the Camellias* in 1934.

VI

There can be no doubt that Meyerhold's *Government Inspector* inspired a greater volume of critical literature than any other production in the history of the Russian theatre.[40] In the most unpredictable way, former allies and opponents of Meyerhold found themselves ranged up on the same side, both in support and in condemnation of his interpretation. Thus, the praise of Andrei Bely was predictable enough, but he could hardly have expected to be joined by Kugel, Lunacharsky and Mayakovsky. Meyerhold found the attacks of the 'left' especially hard to bear, particularly when they were directed at the performance of Zinaida Raikh. His retorts in open debate descended to a level of personal invective that drove the Association of Theatre and Cinema Critics to publish a protest against his 'unexampled anti-social attacks'.[41] The outcome of the affair was a lasting animosity that Meyerhold could well have done without in the years to come.

However, despite the violent criticism of its alleged 'mysticism', the attempts to discredit its author's political integrity, the hysterical protests at the liberties taken with Gogol's hallowed text, and the fears that it was too complex to be accessible to the average spectator, the work was performed regularly until the theatre's liquidation in 1938. Not only did it establish once and for all the creative autonomy of the stage director, it gave new impetus to the reappraisal of Gogol and other classics, although often in a superficial and opportunistic manner that by association was blamed on Meyerhold.[42]

One notable exception to this tendency was Shostakovich's first opera, *The Nose*, composed in 1928–1929 when he was working as a pianist at Meyerhold's theatre.* The libretto, based on Gogol's story of the same name plus fragments from *Diary of a Madman*, *Dead Souls*, *Nevsky Prospect* and *Old-world Landowners*, has a similar episodic structure to Meyerhold's *Government Inspector* and the musical affinity between the two works was confirmed at the time by Shostakovich himself: 'I treated Gogol's text symphonically, but not in the form of an "absolute" or "pure" symphony. Instead, my starting point was the *theatrical* symphony, as it is represented by the form of *The Government Inspector* in Meyerhold's production.'[44]

When the Moscow Art Theatre was preparing Bulgakov's version of *Dead Souls* in 1930, Stanislavsky took the production out of Vasily Sakhnovsky's

* Shostakovich recalls how he performed onstage in *The Government Inspector* as one of the Mayor's guests.[43]

hands because he objected to its Meyerholdian 'grotesquerie and fanciful-
ness'.[45] He also rejected the designs of Vladimir Dmitriev bcause they bore
the clear stamp of Meyerholdian eccentricity, and replaced him with the
tried and trusted Victor Simov.[46] Shortly before the much altered *Dead Souls*
finally opened in November 1932 Stanislavsky, who never saw Meyerhold's
production, said to the company:

> Gogol is first and foremost a Russian writer. . . Nowadays some people
> like to see Gogol as a Hoffmann. They try to turn him into a German
> Gogol. But in Gogol evil has a specifically Gogolian character. . . We are
> going to approach Gogol our way. Meyerhold's approach was through the
> stage props. We shall approach him through the actor.[47]

This troubled production, far removed from Bulgakov's original conception
and virtually a polemic against Meyerhold's *Government Inspector*, survived
all criticism to remain in the Art Theatre's repertoire up to the present day.

109 Part of the
concluding
Dumb Scene

The New Repertoire

When the Moscow Art Theatre opened its 1925–1926 season with Konstantin Trenyov's *The Pugachov Rising*, it confirmed the adoption of the new Soviet repertoire by every major Russian theatre except the Kamerny. This tendency was consolidated over the next two years by the widespread success of such plays as Trenyov's *Lyubov Yarovaya*, Gladkov's *Cement*, Bulgakov's *The Days of the Turbins*, and Vsevolod Ivanov's *Armoured Train 14–69*. Yet after *The Warrant* in April 1925 nearly four years passed before the production of another Soviet play by Meyerhold. Whilst Soviet society had outgrown the need for schematised propaganda pieces, few dramatists were writing with the social insight and poetic inspiration that Meyerhold demanded, and those who were either failed to deliver a completed script or fell foul of the increasingly repressive censor, the Glavrepertkom. A new play by Mayakovsky, to be called *A Comedy with Murder*, was promised first for 1926 then for 1928, but was never written;[1] insistent attempts to lure Bulgakov away from the Moscow Art Theatre were politely resisted by the dramatist;[2]* despite Meyerhold's urgent pleas, Erdman took three years to complete his next play after *The Warrant*, only for it to be banned in 1932 after lengthy rehearsals.

Possibly the greatest loss of all was Andrei Bely's dramatic adaptation of his novel *Moscow*. Mikhail Chekhov's 1924 production of Bely's *Petersburg* at the Moscow Art Theatre's Second Studio had been a depressing failure, but he was persuaded to return to the theatre by Meyerhold's treatment of *The Government Inspector*. Accepted for production in July 1927, *Moscow* was submitted to the Glavrepertkom but returned with the requirement that it must be presented 'in a completely realistic form with the elimination of all elements of mysticism and sadism'. It was further required that the play's

---

* This was hardly surprising; following the triumphant première of Bulgakov's *Days of the Turbins* at the Moscow Art Theatre in October 1926 Meyerhold had declared publicly that it should have been staged not by the Art Theatre but by himself, since 'he would have produced it in accordance with public opinion and not as the author wanted.'[3]

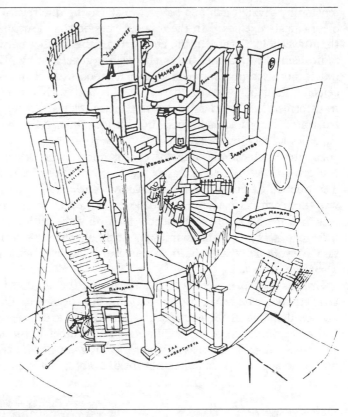

110 Meyerhold's
proposed
scheme for the
staging of
Andrei Bely's
Moscow

title be changed and that the 'external resemblance' between the character
Kierko and Lenin be eliminated, together with the description of him as
'a Bolshevik'.[4] Bely set about revising the text, greatly encouraged by
Meyerhold's vision of it as a montage of 'permanent action' set on a
vertical spiral of seventeen acting areas representing a labyrinth of rooms
that offered a composite picture of the contemporary Moscow intelligentsia.
It was, wrote Bely, 'a dynamic crescendo, presented in static form . . . if he
succeeds in staging it, this will represent a new achievement, not only for the
stage but also for dramatic art; dramatists will be able to write differently.'[5]
Meyerhold and Bely remained in close contact, and as late as 1930 a production of a revised version of *Moscow* was still being contemplated. However,
this exciting but highly problematic venture fell victim to an increasingly
hostile critical climate and rehearsals were never started.

A similar challenge to Meyerhold's inventive genius was posed by Sergei
Tretyakov's *I Want a Child*, which submits traditional attitudes towards love
and sexuality to rational scrutiny, and concludes by advocating selective
breeding, based on criteria of political (as opposed to racial) purity. The
communist heroine, Milda Griegnau is 'an agronomist who relieves her sexual

tension by giving birth to a baby, whilst paying due regard to the demands of practical eugenics.'[6] In the original version that Tretyakov submitted to the Meyerhold Theatre at the end of 1926 the conflict between the utopian radicalism of Milda and the squalid reality generated by NEP was depicted much more sharply, so much so that it stood little chance of satisfying the censor. Tretyakov agreed to rework the text with the result that it was transformed '. . . from an explosive political play about the conflict between frustrated utopianism and social destitution under NEP into a discussion of eugenics as such in socialist society.'[7] Even in this revised version the play encountered objections from the censor and it was December 1928 before Meyerhold was granted exclusive rights in the face of a rival bid from Igor Terentiev in Leningrad. With Tretyakov's enthusiastic support, his proposal was that each performance would be presented in the form of a discussion in which members of the audience (including the author) would be free to intervene, raising questions and suggesting alternative solutions. The actors, said Meyerhold, would need to recapture the improvisatory skills of the *commedia dell'arte*.

Crucial to the project was the setting – though 'setting' is a meagre term to describe what Meyerhold and his designer, El Lissitsky, now proposed. None of the constructivist architects and designers of the 1920s had a clearer vision of the organisation of volumetric space than Lissitsky, so he was a logical choice as designer for *I Want a Child*, even though he had no previous practical experience of theatre work. Between 1926 and 1928 he

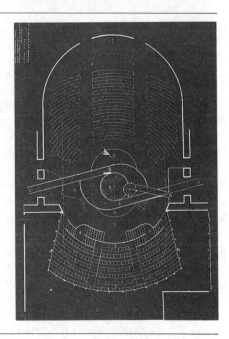

111 The ground
plan for *I Want
a Child*

produced five design variants for the production, but probably none of them bore much resemblance to what eventually emerged. As a logical response to Meyerhold's 'discussion' proposal, the final design amounted to no less than a total reorganisation of the theatre's interior. He described his concept in 1930:

> The stage is completely merged with the auditorium by the construction of an amphitheatre. A new acting area is created by building a 'ring' that rises from the orchestra pit. The actors enter from below out of the depths of the orchestra pit, from above out of the balcony, and from the sides across bridges: they no longer have anything to do with the stage itself. Props roll down ropes and disappear below after every scene. Light sources move with the actors, who perform on a transparent floor. The new arrangement of the acting area brings the actors closer to the audience on all levels, thus reducing the exclusivity of what used to be the front stalls.[8]

The plan envisaged the audience surrounding the performance on all sides, the vacated stage area being occupied by steeply raked bleachers, though it is not clear whether there was to be seating in the side balconies. The mobility of the lighting was to be achieved by a pulley system suspended over the audience.

By 1930 this visionary project was no closer to realisation and it was

112 Model reconstruction of El Lissitsky's construction for *I Want a Child*

decided to defer it until the rebuilding of Meyerhold's outmoded and inadequate theatre. This he never lived to see and a production was lost that, judging by the surviving plans, would have exemplified the spatial and functional concepts of constructivism to a degree that the theatrical work of Popova, Stepanova and Shestakov never did.[9]

From a purely architectonic point of view, *I Want a Child* represented the culmination of all Meyerhold's experiments with the performance space that extended as far back as *The Fairground Booth* in 1906 and the symbolists' utopian vision of a recovered 'sobornost', or shared, collective experience. However, in his recent book *Theatre as Action*, Lars Kleberg makes an important observation on the true nature of the performer-spectator relationship that was implicit in the *I Want a Child* project:

> The spectators would still gather together in order to be subjected – and perhaps again as representatives of the collective – to powerful effects from the stage. The point of departure, however, was no longer the postulated *unity* of the auditorium that was to be manifested and confirmed by the performance, but instead the socially based and by now undeniable *division* in the audience.[10]

This recognition, and indeed promotion, of inevitable audience division in an age, 'post-revolutionary and pre-Stalinist at the same time', is rightly ascribed by Kleberg both to the external causes of the rapidly growing social and cultural conflicts of NEP reality, and to the questioning by the theatre itself on a theoretical level of the very notion of the homogeneous audience.[11] Notwithstanding his early attempts to create a corporate experience with productions such as *Sister Beatrice* and after 1917 with celebratory works such as *Mystery-Bouffe*, *The Dawn* and *Earth Rampant*, the impulse to surprise, confront and disorientate was more native to Meyerhold's theatrical disposition, and it was this that characterised most of his work, not only before the October Revolution but again in the twenties from *The Warrant* onwards.

II

Such was the repertoire crisis at the Meyerhold Theatre in the late twenties that Meyerhold himself staged no new work to mark the tenth anniversary of the October Revolution in 1927. A plan to adapt John Reed's *Ten Days That Shook the World* did not materialise, and the best the theatre could offer was *A Window on the Country*, a 'political review' in the style of *D.E.* produced by twelve of Meyerhold's pupils. Aimed at propagandising the drive to modernise agriculture, it comprised a series of jejune sketches of peasants engaged in their traditional tasks and pastimes, interspersed with filmed inserts depicting the latest technological achievements.* Of all the productions at Meyerhold's theatre this was the only one that Stalin ever saw. He preferred the Bolshoi, the Maly, and especially the Moscow Art Theatre, where he is said to have seen *The Days of the Turbins* some thirteen times.† For Tatyana Bachelis this prompts the question:

> Supposing Stalin had seen not *A Window on the Country* in 1927 but one of Meyerhold's masterpieces of that period, say *The Warrant* or *The Forest* or, God forbid, *The Government Inspector*? I think it would have been even worse. The catastrophe in Meyerhold's life would have hit him even sooner – precisely because Stalin would then have seen works that were truly penetrating and dangerous. [13]

Meyerhold's problems had been exacerbated in 1927 by the departure from the company of Maria Babanova. As in the case of Ilinsky, the cause was Zinaida Raikh. Since playing Stella in *The Magnanimous Cuckold* and Polina in *A Profitable Job* Babanova had not received a single major role from Meyerhold, yet repeatedly she had outshone Raikh and won the devotion of the public and the critics alike. Paradoxically, whilst Meyerhold's admiration for Babanova's talent was unstinting and her loyalty to him constant, he developed the paranoid delusion that she was organising a campaign of disaffection against himself and Raikh. The situation came to a head when she became the object of regular demonstrative ovations at the final curtain of *The Government Inspector*, and Meyerhold accused her of sabotaging the production. Finally, when the company was on tour in Georgia he was driven to announce publicly that the company no longer needed Babanova, and in June 1927 she confirmed her resignation in a letter to the press. She moved to the Theatre of the Revolution and, unlike Ilinsky, never returned. 'And Meyerhold never regretted this – says Rudnitsky – seeming not to realise that with the departure of Babanova luck deserted his theatre.'[14]

In January 1928 Meyerhold revived *The Magnanimous Cuckold*, introducing amendments designed, as he said, to reduce the predominance of form over content. The part of Stella was now played by Raikh. Dimitri Talnikov, a penetrating critic but no great supporter of Meyerhold, wrote in *Contemporary Theatre*: 'Raikh moves ponderously over the construction and speaks her lines lifelessly; she lacks Stella's fire, her spiritual infectiousness, her youth. She is a woman of experience simulating naïveté and innocence, but no matter how much she rolls her eyes, nobody is likely to believe her.'[15]

The tone of Talnikov's review is a sample of what Meyerhold could now expect from many critics; yet the substance of his criticism holds good: despite Meyerhold's claims that Raikh had helped him to reveal the

---

* Filmed inserts were used by Meyerhold himself in *The Second Army Commander* and *The Final Conflict*, though they were never the major feature of the production that they were in Piscator's work in Germany.

† Rudnitsky also suggests that Stalin was deterred from visiting Meyerhold's theatre by the security risk posed by the absence of a state box with separate access. [12]

113 The 1928 revival of *The Magnanimous Cuckold*, with Raikh as Stella

tragic essence of Crommelynck's play,[16] the part of Stella was not within her range and the production itself now seemed little more than a quaint anachronism.

At length Meyerhold returned to the classics for his only new production of the 1927–1928 season. This time he chose *Woe from Wit*, Griboedov's satirical portrayal of Moscow society in the 1820s. It was a work that he had been contemplating since 1924, the centenary of the writer's death. He had first directed it in Kherson in 1903, when he had also played the part of Chatsky.

The production was a reinterpretation no less free than *The Government Inspector* had been and was inspired, said Meyerhold, by a letter from Pushkin to the Decembrist Alexander Bestuzhev, in which he wrote:

> Who is the intelligent character in *Woe from Wit?* Answer: Griboedov. And do you know what Chatsky is? A passionate, honourable, decent young fellow who has spent some time in the company of a very intelligent man (namely Griboedov) and has absorbed his thoughts, his witticisms and his satirical remarks. Everything he says is very intelligent, but to whom does he say it? Famusov? Skalozub? The old Moscow grannies at the ball? Molchalin? That is unpardonable. The first test of a man's intelligence is his ability to recognise whom he is dealing with, and to avoid casting pearls before swine like Repetilov.[17]

Proceeding from this, Meyerhold's aim was to set Chatsky apart from

114 *Woe to Wit*, 1928. Episode Six: 'The Lounge', with Ilinsky as Famusov (left)

the rest of society and relate him to the young radicals of the ill-fated Decembrist movement with whom Griboedov himself had been in sympathy, in order to convey the tragedy of a whole idealistic generation. Crucial to this interpretation was Scene Thirteen, interpolated between Act Three, scenes eight and nine of Griboedov's final version. While carefree couples danced to the strains of a Beethoven waltz in the ballroom of Famusov's mansion, Chatsky and the future Decembrists were seen declaiming radical verses by Ryleev and Pushkin in the adjoining library. The scene concluded with Chatsky quietly reading Lermontov's youthful lines, 'When I carry away to a foreign land . . . my restless woe, my delirious dreams . . .', poignantly prefiguring his own fate at the end of the play. As he finished, the music faded and the dancing couples froze in a reverence.[18] As they had done with *The Government Inspector*, Meyerhold and Mikhail Korenev took the three extant texts of Griboedov's play, and by cutting, rearranging, and adding other material they produced a new version in seventeen episodes. Meyerhold chose the more unequivocal title of the first draft *Woe to Wit*, implying 'woe to him who is incautious enough to exercise his intelligence'. All but the first of the episodes were given the title and setting of a part of Famusov's extensive mansion, thereby unfolding before the spectator a panoramic view of the manners and pursuits of Griboedov's society. However, in a number of episodes Meyerhold's interpolations had no organic relationship with the text, serving merely to heighten the local colour. They had neither the dynamic quality of the physical action in *The Forest* nor the complex metaphorical imagery of the tableaux in *The Government Inspector*.

This is all too clear from Meyerhold's description of Episode Seven: '*The Billiard Room and Library*', during which Famusov and Colonel Skalozub play billiards:

> This is a terribly boring scene. I can accentuate each couplet with a blow of the cue on a ball: 'He got a ribbon, I, a medal' . . . and rrraz . . . Then, 'An excellent fellow your cousin' . . . and again rrraz . . . Each such couplet has to be marked by billiard playing, then it will sound livelier. Otherwise, it is only philosophising. Here there can be an interchange of *raccourcis*,* when they put their hands in a particular way, at an angle . . . In general, playing billiards is very interesting, and I am astonished that it's not used in the theatre. I remember going specially to listen to that clicking of the balls.[20]

Diverting as such business was for the audience, it tended to retard the pace of the performance and did nothing to illuminate the play's meaning. The one notable exception was Episode Fourteen ('*The Dining Room*') where

115 Episode Fourteen: 'The Dining Room'

thirty-two dinner guests, seated bolt upright at a long table directly facing the audience, slowly relayed the false rumour of Chatsky's madness to the accompaniment of a tranquil nocturne by John Field; on the appearance of the solitary figure of Chatsky, they all raised their napkins as though in

* Meyerhold regularly employed the term '*raccourci*' in his work with actors. In French its literal meaning is 'foreshortening', but for him it had a particular significance, defined by Alma Law as: '. . . an "instantaneous, expressive moment of pose", related to the *mie* of the Japanese Kabuki theatre. It's what Alpers has in mind when he speaks in *The Theatre of the Social Mask* of the replacement of the acrobatic principle, "movement as an uninterrupted series of changes in the actor's position", in Meyerhold's productions in the twenties, by the principle of "distinct segments of movement always ending in a static position, a pose, a frozen moment of mime".'[19] Not only was this device influenced by the acting of the Japanese Kabuki, it also resembled the use of freezes by Keaton, Chaplin and others in silent cinema.

self-defence, hissing menacingly like snakes at bay. The critic Boris Alpers wrote:

> In the row of motionless, petrified figures behind the white table, in the measured lines punctuated with long pauses, relaying the rumour of Chatsky's madness, Meyerhold evokes the hallowed ritual of consuming not only food but a living man as well. Seated at the long white table, the guests of Famusov use their stone jaws to crunch both their food and Chatsky himself.[21]

In the interpretation of Chatsky by Garin, the utmost was done to emphasise his sense of isolation from Sophie, Molchalin, Famusov, and the rest. When he did speak to them, it was often whilst improvising at a grand piano. The music, selected and arranged by the composer Boris Asafiev, was designed to reflect the various aspects of Chatsky's character: Beethoven – his militant reforming zeal, Mozart – his Byronic *Weltschmerz*, Bach – his exalted humanity, John Field – his tender dreams of Sophie.[22] Effective though it was in reinforcing the production's strict chronometric scheme, this use of music found little sympathy amongst the critics, one of whom compared Garin to 'a piano-player at the pictures, illustrating his emotions'.[23] They were similarly perplexed by Meyerhold's depiction of Moscow society: on this occasion, he completely rejected the grotesque and presented Griboedov's gentry as robust, decisive and confident in their philistinism, leaving no hope that Chatsky's somewhat pallid idealism would prevail – which in the light of the 1825 débâcle of the Decembrist revolt was accurate enough.

The contrast between Chatsky and the world of Famusov was heightened by the costume designs of the artist Nikolai Ulyanov, who had first worked with Meyerhold at the Theatre-Studio in 1905. Rather than accept unquestioningly the convention of an authentic representation of Moscow society in the 1820s, he and Meyerhold chose to render its bold vulgarity in more expressive terms. In contrast to *The Government Inspector* the principle was not so much 'psychological' as 'cultural'. Whilst Chatsky wore a plain black velvet suit, the other guests of Famusov presented a riotous mix of styles and colours. To quote Ulyanov:

> Balzac, that authority on women and their fashions once wrote *Une Physiologie de la toilette*. The 'toilette' in *Woe to Wit* represents the physiology peculiar to a whole era or several eras. Did not Famusov's guests originate from three distinct turning-points in history: the Consulate, the First Empire and the restoration of the Bourbons? What a gaudy spectacle Moscow must have presented to the curious observer. To everything that Paris could offer, its fashions, the cut of its gowns, there was added something local, something 'home-made' – modifications and distortions that exaggerated an alien style taken on trust.[24]

The basic setting, a supposedly practicable construction by Victor Shestakov, was a typical example of the degeneration of constructivism to a design idiom devoid of all architectonic logic, since in performance the upper level and staircases were scarcely used. Its arbitrariness typified the production in general which, as Meyerhold himself admitted, was not an artistic success, suffering from 'false academicism' and a disproportionate emphasis on certain episodes. He later called it the 'Petersburg version' in order to emphasise its affinity with his pre-revolutionary work, and in September 1935 produced a second version, the 'Moscow version', which was dedicated both to the pianist, Lev Oborin (the original dedicatee), and to the Chinese actor, Mei Lan-fang, who had recently visited Russia and whose mimetic skill and rhythmical discipline Meyerhold held up as models to his actors.[25] The number of episodes was reduced from seventeen to thirteen, the construction assumed a more representational appearance, and Meyerhold claimed that he had strengthened the 'realistic aspects' of the production. However, with Garin, Raikh and Ilinsky replaced by inferior actors in the parts of Chatsky, Sophie and Famusov, it struck critics as no more than a routine revival and made little impact.

III

In July 1928, Meyerhold and Zinaida Raikh left the Soviet Union on holiday and spent the next five months in France. By that time, audiences at his theatre had dropped to less than three-quarters capacity, with box-office receipts falling at time to forty percent. This was due largely to the stale-ness of the repertoire which still contained such long-familiar works as *The Forest* and *The Magnanimous Cuckold*. With the failure of *A Window on the Country*, the theatre's financial position was all the more precarious. Scorning all available Soviet plays except the controversial *I Want a Child*, Meyerhold preferred to wait for the new works long promised by Erdman and Mayakovsky, and a Civil War tragedy commissioned from the poet Ilya Selvinsky. Meanwhile, he sought to bridge the gap by arranging a season for his theatre in Paris. But the 'Glaviskusstvo', the newly-formed state authority that controlled all the arts, twice ordered him to discontinue negotiations and even threatened to close his theatre if he failed to return and improve its position. After a violent controversy which rallied widespread support for Meyerhold and split even the ranks of the Glaviskusstvo, a special government commission was formed to investigate the Theatre's affairs. It condemned Meyerhold's negligence, but recommended a subsidy to cover outstanding debts and running costs for a further two months up to the end of November,* delaying its final decision on the theatre's future until his return.[26] The recommendations amounted to an ultimatum, which may have been motivated by the suspicion that Meyerhold was considering following the example of Mikhail Chekhov, the celebrated actor and artistic

---

* Since 1926 the theatre had borne the title 'State Meyerhold Theatre', and as such qualified for regular state subsidy.

director of the Second Moscow Art Theatre and a close friend of Meyerhold, who had decided to emigrate in August 1928.

Rather than risk losing his theatre, Meyerhold abandoned his plans for a Paris season and returned to Moscow on 2 December 1928, following convalescence in Vichy and Nice after a serious illness that had affected his heart and liver. Far from admitting his own financial negligence, Meyerhold straightaway complained of the state of the old Sohn Theatre (where only a hundred and fifty out of three hundred and ninety seats in the circle were usable) and demanded more storage and rehearsal space. On this, he said, depended the repertoire for the season, which he hoped would include *I Want a Child*, Erdman's *The Suicide*, and Selvinsky's *The Second Army Commander*.[27]

However, the first production proved to be the recently completed *Bed Bug*, which Mayakovsky read to the company for the first time on 28 December. Announcing his plan to stage it as quickly as possible, Meyerhold declared 'The repertoire crisis has been completely overcome (at least for the present). The theatre's confidence in the foremost experimental dramatist of the Revolution remains steadfast.'[28] After only six weeks' rehearsal, the play was presented on 13 February 1929.

In terms of theatrical innovation, *The Bed Bug* was one of Meyerhold's less significant productions, but of all the Soviet plays staged by him it was the one that has been most frequently revived. On the occasion of the director's sixtieth birthday Pavel Markov described Meyerhold as the 'director-poet' par excellence.[29] Not only was he alluding to his allusive, rhythmical style, but also to the remarkable proportion of poets amongst the dramatists staged by him. However, apart from Blok, Meyerhold held none of them in such high esteem as Mayakovsky. His immediate reaction to *The Bed Bug* was to hail it as 'a work as great and as significant as Griboedov's *Woe from Wit* was in its day',[30] and he immediately invited Mayakovsky to supervise the linguistic side of the production.

116 *The Bed Bug* (1929). Publicity leaflet by Mayakovsky

ЛЮДИ ХОХОЧУТ

И МОРЩАТ ЛОБ

В ТЕАТРЕ МЕЙЕРХОЛЬДА

НА КОМЕДИИ

КЛОП

117 *The Bed Bug*,
Scene One.
Left to right:
Bayan (Alexei
Temerin),
Madame
Renaissance
(Natalya
Serebryani-
kova),
Prisypkin (Igor
Ilinsky)

The first half of the play, which culminates in the riotous nuptials of lapsed party member Prisypkin and his manicurist bride Elzevira Renaissance, is a deadly accurate grotesque portrayal of the Soviet petit bourgeoisie. At Mayakovsky's suggestion, the young 'Kukryniksy' cartoon group was invited to design the settings, costumes and make-up. Nearly all the costumes and properties were bought over the counter in Moscow shops in order to demonstrate the pretentious ugliness of current fashions and the all too discomforting topicality of the satire – rammed home at the final curtain by the defrosted Prisypkin's joyful recognition of a whole audience of fellow bourgeois.

118 *The Bed Bug*.
Part Two. The
defrosting of
Prisypkin

Mayakovsky sets Part Two of the play fifty years in the future in a gleaming utopian paradise. Starting work on the play, Meyerhold said:

> The main purpose is to castigate the vices of the present day. In projecting us forward to 1979, Mayakovsky is forcing us to examine not a world transformed, but the very same sickness that is afflicting society today. . . Mayakovsky's aim is to show us that illnesses have deeply rooted causes, and take a great deal of time and a vast amount of energy to overcome.[31]

The costumes and settings for Part Two were the work of the Constructivist Alexander Rodchenko, making his debut as a theatre designer. They depicted an antiseptic, utilitarian vision of the future which seemed to contain a distinct hint of self-parody, entirely consistent with the ironic view of Meyerhold and Mayakovsky. But the critics were confused: some saw it as an inspired vision of advanced technology, some found it a lifeless abstraction, whilst some even reached the dangerous conclusion that it was a parody of the achievements of socialism.[32]

The music was composed by Shostakovich, still employed as a pianist at Meyerhold's theatre. As he recalls, the score was based on the marches of fire-brigade bands much admired by Mayakovsky.[33] Its strident cacophony was less to the taste of most critics. There was an ominous ring to the words of Robert Pelshe in *Contemporary Theatre*, the official organ of the Glaviskusstvo: '. . . we recommend Comrade Shostakovich to reflect more seriously on questions of musical culture in the light of the development of our socialist society according to the precepts of Marxism.'[34]

Despite widespread criticism, particularly of the contributions of Rodchenko and Shostakovich, *The Bed Bug* was a huge popular success, due largely to the inspired portrayal of Prisypkin by Igor Ilinsky. For another season at least, the Meyerhold Theatre was secure.

119 Shostakovich and Meyerhold, 1928

IV

Ever since the success of Bill-Belotserkovsky's heroic drama *The Storm* in 1925, the Civil War play had become a staple item of the Soviet repertoire: with its clear distinction between Reds and Whites, its epic heroism and suffering, and the personal memories that it evoked for many of its audience, it was a dramatic genre in its own right. Meyerhold had been the first to demonstrate its emotive power with his staging of Tretyakov's *Earth Rampant* in 1923, since when he had devoted his energies exclusively to comedy and satire. But in July 1929 he staged *The Second Army Commander*,* a Civil War tragedy in verse by the young poet Ilya Selvinsky. His aims were considerably more complex than those of most previous dramatists who had tapped the same source. Shortly after the première he wrote:

> In my play one can trace the problem of the leader and the masses, the problem of ideological imposture, the problem of technology opposed to poetic inspiration. There is the collision between the petit bourgeois revolutionary impulse and the proletarian, the contrast between misguided genius and competent ordinariness, the development of socialism into revolutionary praxis, and much more besides. . . But if you are looking for the general shape of the tragedy, its philosophical architecture, then I would say it is to be found in its dialectic.[35]

The play is set around the battle for the town of Beloyarsk in the early stages of the Civil War when the Red Army was still little more than a loose grouping of guerrilla units. The thesis and antithesis of Selvinsky's dialectic are represented by Chub, a partisan leader of peasant origins thrown up by the masses, and Okonny, an army clerk and one-time book-keeper who sees in the Revolution the means of self-realisation and glory. The one is laconic, straightforward, and limited in his horizons, the other is expansive, boldly imaginative, and highly versed in revolutionary rhetoric. Okonny usurps Chub's command by winning over the army with the appeal of his strategy, then causes the death of hundreds in gaining a victory of doubtful military value. He is arrested, and Chub, now more flexible and far-sighted, is restored to a new command, but only to be confronted by a 'new' Okonny, called Podokonny, the inference being that the dialectical process will continue. Selvinsky's portrayal of the two commanders is equally ironic, suggesting that the behaviour of both has its positive and its negative aspects. Taking the view that this simply obscured the intended 'dialectic', Meyerhold insisted on sharpening the antithesis by enhancing Chub's heroic

---

* In *Meyerhold on Theatre* and elsewhere the title is translated wrongly as 'Commander of the Second Army'. The point of the play is that one commander (Chub) is replaced by a second (Okonny).

120 *The Second Army Commander.* 'The Firing Squad'

stature and depicting Okonny as an egocentric adventurer riding to glory on the back of the Revolution. The character of Podokonny was eliminated and Okonny faced a firing squad at the end of the play. The changes were the outcome of long and bitter wrangles between the implacable director and the inexperienced dramatist. Selvinsky complained in the press that Meyerhold had reduced his text to 'agitational primitiveness', and broke off all relations with him. In 1967 Selvinsky recalled: 'He wasn't capable of arguing. He bombarded his opponent with paradoxes, disarmed him with humour, and always stuck rigidly to his principles.' Yet at the same time he confessed himself entranced by many of the effects that Meyerhold achieved, and conceded the considerable influence of the production on his later work.[36]

Meyerhold's production was a conscious revolt against the prevailing genre representations of the Civil War; it was an attempt to create, in Pavel Markov's words, 'a monumental musical tragedy'. The setting was of suitably heroic proportions and severity: with full use made of the forestage, the acting area was enclosed by a towering leaden-coloured screen which functioned as a sounding board for the frequent choral effects. Against it, a flight of steps descended from stage-left to right in a gradual spiral. Props were kept to a bare minimum, and the maximum emphasis was placed on

121 'The Sentries'

costumes and weapons. Devised by Meyerhold,* the setting was executed by Sergei Vakhtangov (the director's son) and the costume and lighting consultant was the prominent artist Petrov-Vodkin. In their furs and skins, criss-crossed with weighty ammunition belts, their assorted accoutrements and headgear sharing little in common save the Red Guard insignia, the partisans, ancestors of the modern Red Army, looked like the resurrected warriors of some ancient epic of the Steppe. Boris Alpers wrote:

> They are men who disappeared on the battlefields of 1918–19, the legendary heroes of a legendary time. If you removed their Caucasian hats and their sheepskin jerkins, you would find half-severed skulls, cloven heads, gaping breasts, torsos disfigured with a five-pointed star.
>   That is why they stand so still, holding their tall lances; that is why they move with such a slow and measured tread, the imprint of some strange reverie on every face.[37]

Inspired by the works of David, Velázquez (in particular, *The Surrender of Breda*), and Petrov-Vodkin, Meyerhold's scenic compositions achieved a stern hieratic grandeur. Aided by a powerful musical score by Vissarion

---

* In an interview Meyerhold described *The Second Army Commander* as 'my first independent work in the field of stage design', but, as we have seen, as early as *The Forest* in 1924 the concept of the setting was invariably his.

122 'The Meeting'

Shebalin, he kept a strict regard for the metre of Selvinsky's text and created what was virtually a dramatic oratorio. Much as critics objected to the play's historical inaccuracy, the schematised characterisation, the prolixity of Selvinsky's verse, and the feeble portrayal of Okonny, they were unanimous in their admiration for Meyerhold's staging of the ensemble scenes. In particular, they singled out the account of the Battle of Beloyarsk by a narrator with a refrain in mazurka time chanted by the entire company of fifty using megaphones, like the masks in Greek tragedy, to amplify their voices to awesome power.

The production was given its première on 24 July 1929 when the company was on tour in Kharkov. Contrary to Meyerhold's gloomy expectations, it proved successful and when it was staged in Moscow in the autumn it was recognised as the first serious attempt to create a Soviet tragedy.[38]

V

The huge popular success of *The Bed Bug* completely overcame all Maya-kovsky's reservations about playwriting; within seven months of its opening he had completed another play, *The Bath House*, described as 'a drama in six acts with circus and fireworks'. According to Mikhail Zoshchenko, Mayakovsky's first reading of the text to the company and Artistic Soviet★ of the Meyerhold Theatre on 23 September 1926 '. . . was a triumph. The actors and writers laughed uproariously and applauded the poet. They grasped the point of every single phrase. I have seldom seen such a positive reaction.'[38] But the Glavrepertkom failed to share their enthusiasm; it considered the satire far too provocative, and demanded numerous cuts before it passed the text for performance.[39] This reaction was a direct reflection of the opinion propagated by the Russian Association of Proletarian Writers (RAPP) that satire did nothing but harm the cause of socialism, and that art should depict only 'real life'. It is precisely this attitude that Mayakovsky is lampooning in Act Three of *The Bath House*, where the arch-bureaucrat, Pobedonosikov, and his retinue have just seen the play, and failed to recognise themselves in it. Pobedonosikov instructs the director on the theatre's proper function:

> In the name of every worker and peasant, I beg you not to disturb my peace of mind. What do you think you are, an alarm clock? Perish the thought! Your job is to beguile my eye and ear, not to assault them.

123 and 124 The Phosphorescent Woman (Zinaida Raikh) and Pobedonosikov (Maxim Shtraukh)

★ From 1928 onwards 'artistic soviets' were set up in all theatres. Their function was to supervise the selection and presentation of plays. In most cases, the chairman was nominated by the Party. The Soviet at the Meyerhold Theatre had more than sixty members.

. . . We need to rest after the discharge of our obligations to the state and society. Back to the classics! Study the great geniuses of the accursed past.

In the last act, when they are all ejected from the Phosphorescent Woman's time-machine which bears away the inventor and his proletarian friends to a Communist future in the year 2030, Pobedonosikov cries to the hack painter, Belvedonsky: 'Hey artist, seize the opportunity! Paint a real live man as he is mortally insulted!'[41]

By 1930, the influence of RAPP and its associated bodies in the other arts threatened to dominate Soviet criticism. As Rudnitsky writes, 'Using channels accessible only to themselves, they cleverly secured official support for nearly all their concrete recommendations, critical appraisals, and assessments of individuals.'[42] Their programme, essentially a rehash of Proletkult principles, advocated the true-to-life, positive portrayal of Soviet reality in a style easily accessible to the broad masses. Eventually, RAPP overreached itself in promoting its members' interests and in 1932 it was disbanded by

125 *The Bath House*, Act Three

the Central Committee of the Party. However, by that time its influence had been crucial in the evolution of the new, rigid code of Socialist Realism which was to stifle artistic expression throughout the Stalin period and continued to influence Soviet criticism long after that.

Meyerhold and Mayakovsky had already come under heavy fire from RAPP when they staged *The Bed Bug*. Now the bombardment was resumed even before *The Bath House* was seen by the Moscow public. Before Meyerhold's production, the play had its first performance on 30 January 1930 at the State People's House in Leningrad; it was greeted in the press with wholly negative criticism which made little effort to examine the problems posed by Mayakovsky's text. Then in the February number of *On Literary Guard* the RAPP critic Vladimir Yermilov published a preview totally condemning the play, even though he admitted to having read only a published fragment of the text.[43] For all its flagrant tendentiousness, Yermilov's article was republished in abridged form in *Pravda* on 9 March, thereby ensuring that the production opened a week later in an atmosphere of mistrust and hostility.

Almost without exception, the reviews were destructive; the play itself was seen as a malicious misrepresentation of Soviet officialdom, and its presentation a regression to the heavy-handed knockabout style of the early twenties. In so far as it is possible to tell from photographs and the objective accounts published, the production does seem in some respects to have resembled the 1921 version of *Mystery-Bouffe*, not to mention the agit-prop shows of the 'Blue Blouse' collectives which had come into being since then. Once again the 'Clean' were portrayed as a series of preposterous grotesques, whilst the 'Unclean' were an ill-differentiated series of komsomols in uniform blue overalls whose wholesome vigour recalled Meyerhold's students in *The Magnanimous Cuckold*. Zinaida Raikh, one of the production's few successes, appeared as the Phosphorescent Woman in a gleaming flying helmet and an alluring close-fitting space suit, the harbinger of a perfect socialist future.

Sergei Vakhtangov designed a setting that featured a towering scaffolding with a series of steps and platforms. In a number of scenes a huge screen in the form of a venetian blind with each slat bearing a political slogan was lowered from the flies. The walls of the auditorium too bore rhyming slogans by Mayakovsky, broadcasting the policies of the theatrical left and ridiculing the bureaucrats, the censor, RAPP, the critics, and the Moscow Art Theatre. Forced onto the defensive, Meyerhold and Mayakovsky had made the production as much a statement of their own principles as a denunciation of state bureaucracy.

Whilst conceding its imperfections, Meyerhold regarded *The Bath House* as the best of his four productions of Mayakovsky. Nevertheless, it was coolly received by the public, possibly because it seemed like a throwback to the agitatory clichés of the early twenties, possibly (as Rudnitsky and Fevralsky have both suggested) because its style was ahead of its time. In any case,

126 Act Six. The Departure of the Time Machine

poor attendances compelled the theatre to drop the production after only two seasons. It was a loss that hit Meyerhold hard, but incalculably greater was the loss of Mayakovsky himself, who on 14 April 1930 shot himself at the age of thirty-six. What drove Mayakovsky to this will always remain a matter for speculation, but some years later, recalling the campaign against *The Bath House*, Meyerhold said: 'It was nothing short of a stab in the back of Mayakovsky, the revolutionary – both by RAPP and by Yermilov, who clearly played the role of a modern d'Anthès* to Mayakovsky's Pushkin.'[44]

So close were Meyerhold and Mayakovsky – both as men and as artists – that to read Mayakovsky today is to sense the true atmosphere of Meyerhold's theatre. There were many reasons for Meyerhold's troubles in the thirties, but as significant as any was the loss at their very outset of his truest friend and ally, the only living dramatist he ever treated as his equal.

---

* Georges d'Anthès, the lover of Pushkin's wife, who killed him in a duel in 1837.

127 Meyerhold and Mayakovsky rehearsing *The Bath House*, 1930 (in conversation centre)

VI

Early in 1930, Meyerhold was finally granted permission to take his theatre abroad on tour. A section of the company left Moscow shortly after the première of *The Bath House* and spent six weeks in Germany, performing in nine cities including Berlin, Breslau, and Cologne. The repertoire consisted of *Roar, China!*, *The Government Inspector*, *The Forest*, and *The Magnanimous Cuckold*.[45] The public response was enormous, with a performance of *Roar, China!* at the Rheinlandhalle in Cologne attracting an audience of six thousand.[46] However, the critical reception was mostly negative and, in the case of the influential Alfred Kerr, downright patronising. There was a widespread feeling that Meyerhold's company had arrived too late and that those who had toured earlier, such as Tairov and Granovsky, had stolen his thunder. In the words of Norbert Falk, 'the original arrived in Berlin after the copies'.* One of the most intriguing assessments came from the early champion of Brecht, Herbert Ihering:

> Meyerhold has nothing in common with Piscator. On the contrary, through the style of acting he depoliticises even *The Government Inspector*, and he

* The one exception was Zinaida Raikh, who was highly praised for all her roles, notably Anna Andreevna in *The Government Inspector*.

reconstructs *The Forest* in accordance with formal principles. Meyerhold's theatre is a theatre of form. He bears the same relationship to Stanislavsky as Reinhardt does to Otto Brahm. Meyerhold was late in coming to Berlin, but his theatre is inseparable from the development of European theatre. This heroic creative achievement is, one might say, an aristocratic one. Essentially, it has no connection with the masses. Herein lies its tragedy, and particularly its tragedy within Russia.[47]

In May the company arrived in Paris, where it gave ten performances, starting with a public dress rehearsal on 16 June. *Roar, China!* and *The Second Army Commander* were banned due to their revolutionary content and *The Magnanimous Cuckold*, though announced, was not performed, leaving *The Government Inspector* and *The Forest*. The première of *The Government Inspector* was the occasion for a vociferous demonstration by a section of the Russian émigré community, which protested at Meyerhold's 'mutilation' of Gogol. Even so, the opening night at the modest little Théâtre de Montparnasse was a triumph. Ilya Ehrenburg recalls: 'There was Louis Jouvet, Picasso, Dullin, Cocteau, Derain, Baty . . . And when the performance ended, these people, gorged with art – one would have thought – and in the habit of carefully measuring out their approval, rose to their feet and joined in an ovation.'[48]

At the end of June the company returned to Moscow, while Meyerhold and Raikh remained in France on holiday until September. During the tour Meyerhold had been approached by an American impresario with a proposal for an American visit and had responded with a plan for a revival of *The Bed Bug* and a production of *Woe to Wit* with Mikhail Chekhov playing Chatsky in place of Garin who had now left the company. Perhaps still suspicious that, like Chekhov two years earlier, Meyerhold would remain abroad, the Glaviskusstvo denied him permission.* Whereupon he asked Bubnov, the Commissar for Enlightenment, to persuade the Politburo to allow him to spend a year in America studying its advanced technology in order that he might apply it to the reconstruction of the antiquated Soviet theatre. Not surprisingly, he was again denied.[50]

Certainly an American tour would have come as a welcome relief from the ever-pressing problem of finding suitable new plays. In November 1930, Meyerhold could offer nothing better to mark the thirteenth anniversary of the Revolution than a revised and updated version of the political review *D.E.* Shortly afterwards he turned to Vsevolod Vishnevsky, another of the new generation of Soviet writers, whose play *The First Cavalry Army* had been staged with great success at the Central Red Army Theatre the previous year. Vishnevsky's credentials could scarcely have been bettered: the son of

---

* Writing in 1954, Mikhail Chekhov claimed that when they met in Berlin in 1930 he warned Meyerhold of the danger he would face if he returned to the Soviet Union and urged him to emigrate. According to Chekhov, the suggestion was violently opposed by Zinaida Raikh, and Meyerhold resisted Chekhov's advice, saying that he had to go back 'as a matter of honour'.[49]

an engineer, he joined the army when still a schoolboy at the outbreak of war, and then in 1917 fought for the Bolsheviks; enlisting in the Red Navy, he was involved in some of the toughest campaigns of the Civil War as well as contributing dispatches to the Communist press. Subsequently, he recorded his experiences in a series of essays and short stories.

There is no doubt that when Meyerhold decided to stage Vishnevsky's *The Final Conflict*,★ it was in the hope that he had found a dramatist to replace Mayakovsky. What appealed to him was the extreme freedom of the play's form, which defied categorisation: it began with an elaborate

128 *The Final Conflict*, Last Episode

production number that parodied the Bolshoi Theatre's highly successful staging of Glier's ballet, *The Red Poppy*, a ludicrously idealised picture of life in the Red Navy. This was interrupted by sailors appearing from the audience and promising a real play about navy life. There followed a series of loosely connected episodes contrasting the adventures of debauched 'anarchist' sailors on the spree in Odessa with the cultured atmosphere of a seamen's club and the discipline and readiness of the Baltic Fleet.

The production as a whole was a dazzling display of theatrical tricks, but

★ Also translated as 'The Last Decisive'. The title is a quotation from the chorus of *The Internationale*.

in the final scene Meyerhold surpassed himself: a detachment of twenty-seven frontier guards and sailors held a beleaguered position on the first day of an imagined future war. Machine guns fired blanks directly at the spectators, artillery thundered from the back of the theatre, searchlight beams darted, and to the music of Scriabin's Sonata No.3 an actress planted in the audience was convulsed with sobbing on a prearranged cue. As the last survivor gasped away his life, a radio receiver blared out a trivial song by Maurice Chevalier. Summoning his remaining strength, the sailor painfully chalked on a screen:

$$162,000,000$$
$$-27$$

$$161,999,973$$

thereby demonstrating the value of the sacrifice and the will of the rest of the Soviet people to fight on. His task accomplished, the sailor died with a smile on his lips – then immediately stood up, advanced to the forestage and said 'Men and women – everyone who is ready to join in the defence of the USSR – stand up!' The audience stood without exception – but as one critic sourly observed, they would have stood at the end of Glinka's *A Life for the Tsar*.[51]

The impact of the final scene was conceded by most critics, but at the same time the play's ideological incoherence was heavily criticised. The most cogent opinion came from Pavel Markov:

> Just as in *The First Cavalry Army*, Vishnevsky employs the difficult and dangerous method of contrast, but contrast does not necessarily equal dialectical contradiction. On the contrary, it can easily turn into mechanical juxtaposition and the monotonous interplay of two or three colours. . . So far, Vishnevsky has composed only the sketches for a future symphony; put together to make a unified dramatic text, they jar on the ear because of their lack of inner harmony.[52]

But for all its incoherence and crude effects, *The Final Conflict*, with its combination of burlesque, low comedy, genre realism, melodrama, and tragedy, was a style of popular theatre close to Meyerhold's heart. The production opened on 7 February 1931. Ten days later Meyerhold wrote to Vishnevsky: '. . . Amongst Soviet dramatists you have every right to occupy the first place. Knowing your capacity for work, knowing your genuine ability to learn and improve yourself, I am convinced that your new play will be even more remarkable than the one we are performing with such pleasure at the present time.'[53]

Sadly, their friendship quickly turned sour when Vishnevsky's next work *Germany** failed to live up to Meyerhold's expectations and they disagreed

---

* Later retitled *Fighting in the West*.

violently over its revision.[54] Eventually, it was staged at the Theatre of the Revolution, and in 1933 Vishnevsky gave his most celebrated play *An Optimistic Tragedy* to Tairov of all people, who staged it with enormous success. In 1937 Meyerhold and Vishnevsky finally settled their differences and agreed to collaborate on a play about the Spanish Civil War.[55] But their rapprochement was too late, coming as it did barely three months before the closure of Meyerhold's theatre.

VII

Yury Olesha's *A List of Benefits*, first performed on 4 June 1931, was remarkable for being one of Meyerhold's very few 'chamber works', a production in which he made scarcely any attempt to stretch the resources of the traditional stage. The play tells the story of a fictitious Soviet tragedienne Yelena Goncharova who, feeling her creativity stifled by 'rectilinear, schematised works devoid of imagination', considers emigrating to Paris, the city of her dreams. But once there, she finds herself propositioned by a lecherous impresario, invited to perform a pornographic sketch in a music hall and enveigled into émigré society. Disenchanted and filled with remorse, Yelena finally joins a demonstration of unemployed workers, only to be accidentally killed protecting a French communist leader from an assassination attempt by a White émigré.[56]

129 Goncharova (Raikh) auditioning as Hamlet for Margaret, manager of the Globe Music Hall

130 Meyerhold and
Olesha.
Caricature by
Eric Mordmillovich,
1931

The central theme was only too familiar: Yelena Goncharova, who
appropriately played Hamlet, was an intellectual, an artist, whose sense
of individuality and capacity for reflection placed her at odds with society.
The genealogy was unmistakable: Konstantin Treplev, Pierrot, Ivar Kareno,
Arbenin, Chatsky, even Okonny. It was not surprising that Meyerhold was
drawn to the character of Goncharova (who was played with deep pathos by
Zinaida Raikh); her dilemma was familiar enough in Soviet society of the
late twenties and reflected the doubts of many artists close to Meyerhold. In
particular, there was Mikhail Chekhov, the greatest of Soviet Hamlets, whose
thoughts and experiences following his emigration in 1928 were relayed by
Meyerhold to Olesha, and were crucial to the play's composition.[57] Unlike
The Second Army Commander, Olesha's material was in no way amenable to
ideological polarisation, for its ambivalence lay within the very personality of
Goncharova, and Meyerhold's interpretation remained true to her dilemma.
At the close of the play the dying Yelena asks for her body to be covered
with the Red Flag, but all the banners are raised by the strikers to confront
the mounted police. Olesha's final stage direction reads: 'The unemployed
march. Yelena's body remains lying in the street uncovered. There are heard
the strains of a march.' It would have been simple enough for Meyerhold
to cover her and to play 'The Internationale', but on this occasion there
was to be no optimistic tragedy, no stirring call to arms, no affirmation

of solidarity. This time the audience were allowed to remain seated, alone with their contradictory thoughts.

In October 1931 the old Sohn Theatre was closed finally for renovation. It was destined never to reopen, so *A List of Benefits* became Meyerhold's last production in the ramshackle building that had witnessed his greatest triumphs.

'An Alien Theatre'

When the Sohn Theatre closed in 1931 Meyerhold and his company were left homeless until they moved into premises near the bottom of Gorky Street in what is now the Yermolova Theatre. Before they took up residence there in the summer of 1932 they spent their time on tour, first for three months in Leningrad and then for a further three months at a number of venues in Central Asia before returning to Moscow at the end of May. During this time no new productions were staged.

Originally, Meyerhold was allocated money only for essential repairs to the existing theatre; but he wanted nothing less than a completely new building, designed to his specification, with seating for three thousand spectators. This he announced only after demolishing the old building, calculating that the state would finance his new project rather than tolerate a ruined theatre in the very centre of Moscow.[1] His supposition proved correct; the Narkompros eventually endorsed the plan and financed it with a grant of one million roubles. However, endless delays ensued and the building was only just approaching completion when the Meyerhold Theatre was liquidated in January 1938. In consequence, Meyerhold was compelled to spend the final years of his life struggling to overcome the inadequacies of a theatre that was inferior even to the dilapidated Sohn. Though it had a capacity of over nine hundred and a correspondingly large proscenium opening, the new theatre was poorly equipped and had so little stage depth that the choice of plays was severely inhibited. So cramped were the premises that between twenty-five and thirty actresses were forced to share a single dressing-room and rehearsals had to be conducted away from the theatre in the premises of the Finance Ministry, two floors below street level.[2] These practical limitations ruled out all work of the scale that Meyerhold was contemplating for his new auditorium and were as much responsible for the gradual stagnation of the company's repertoire as the mediocrity of contemporary dramatic literature in the stifling climate of Socialist Realism.

The new theatre on Old Triumphal (later Mayakovsky) Square was

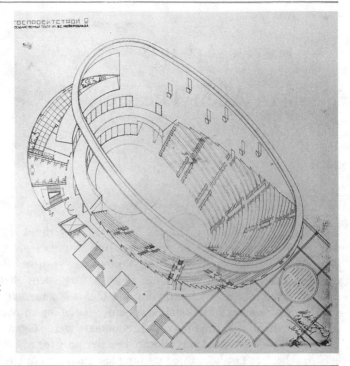

131 The new
Meyerhold
Theatre,
second variant
(1932).
Axonometric
drawing by
Barkhin and
Vakhtangov

designed by Sergei Vakhtangov and Mikhail Barkhin under the direct supervision of Meyerhold. In its third and final variant it took the form of a steeply raked, horseshoe-shaped amphitheatre seating one thousand six hundred spectators. The thrust stage was pear-shaped (24 metres deep and 7.5 metres at the widest point) with two revolves (the smaller downstage), both of variable level. There was no fly tower, scene changes being carried out on lifts beneath the stage. The entire auditorium was covered with a glass canopy with provision for stage-lighting from above. Immediately behind the stage was a wide arc of dressing-rooms affording direct access to the acting area. Directly above them was an orchestra gallery. To either side and to the rear of the main revolve there were gaps wide enough to allow the passage of motor vehicles. A configuration closer to a conventional proscenium stage could be obtained by installing portable seating downstage, up to the forward edge of the main revolve.[3] Viewed in the context of Meyerhold's earlier work ending with the unrealised production of *I Want a Child*, it is clear that the new theatre represented the culmination of all his experiments with scenic space and with the relationship between performer and audience. The project offers an intriguing comparison with the Total-Theater, designed by Walter Gropius for Piscator in 1927–1928. With seating for 2000 spectators, it incorporated variable performance areas and a series of seventeen slide or cine-projection points around the single-tier auditorium and in a suspended cabin.[4] We now know that Meyerhold met Gropius in Berlin in April 1930 and was shown a model of the Total-Theater, so it is possible that certain of its features became incorporated in the final design.[5] For financial reasons this project was never realised, so like Meyerhold, Piscator was denied the space in which to develop a new relationship with his audience.

132 The interior of the Tchaikovsky Concert Hall today

After Meyerhold's death the new theatre was extensively modified by another architect and opened in October 1940 as the Tchaikovsky Concert Hall. Since then, it has been used only occasionally for dramatic productions.

II

Ever since the triumphant première of *The Warrant* in 1925 Meyerhold had been trying to coax a further play from Nikolai Erdman, seeing in him and Mayakovsky his best hopes of creating a modern repertoire worthy to stand alongside his productions of Gogol, Griboedov and Ostrovsky. However, at the best of times Erdman was a painstaking stylist who completed work at the cost of considerable anguish and self-doubt, and now his problems were compounded by the tightening control exercised by the omnipotent Glaviskusstvo, an increasingly conformist press, and the artistic councils installed in all arts organisations and packed with time-serving nonentities. Beset by depression, it was not until the beginning of 1930 that he finally delivered to Meyerhold the completed text of *The Suicide*.

Set mainly in a communal flat, the action revolves around Semyon Podsekalnikov who out of a sense of discontent and self-loathing after a year's unemployment finds himself contemplating suicide, coerced by an

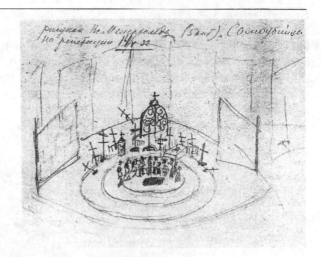

133 Sketch plan
for Act Five of
The Suicide,
1932

assortment of hangers-on, all of whom want him to commit this act in order to publicise their own personal grievances. Finally, Semyon baulks at their manipulation, whereupon it is reported that the idealistic Fedya Petunin, inspired by his example, has shot himself because 'life is not worth living'. With the exception of Semyon's hardworking and devoted wife Marya and the never-seen Petunin, Erdman presents an array of counterfeits: a living suicide, a phoney intellectual, a non-believing priest, a conformist protest-writer.[6] Yet his tragicomedy is aimed not so much at their ludicrous pretensions as at the everyday fear and misery that envelops them all and finally drives Semyon to ring the Kremlin, demanding that 'someone right at the top' be informed that he has 'read Marx and doesn't like Marx'. He is not even accorded the dignity of investigation: just as 'they' didn't even bother to arrest Pavel Gulyachkin in *The Warrant*, so 'the Kremlin' hangs up on Semyon in *The Suicide*.

Unsurprisingly, the play was banned by the Glavrepertkom when it was first submitted in September 1930. Reportedly, the committee's opinion was that 'It is necessary to experiment in the field of theatrical form, but to experiment in the field of politics is impermissible'.[7] However, a few days later Erdman read the text to a full meeting of the Meyerhold Theatre's Artistic Soviet which took the bold decision to defy the censor, approving it for production and 'for discussion in the working community of the major enterprises in the city of Moscow'.[8] Earlier in the year, however, influenced by the rumours that Meyerhold was contemplating an extended stay in the United States, Erdman had taken the precaution of offering *The Suicide* to both the Moscow Art Theatre and the Vakhtangov Theatre. The Vakhtangov abandoned it quickly enough, but Stanislavsky remained enthusiastic and, encouraged by the support of Gorky, appealed to Stalin to lift the ban. The General Secretary's reply, dated 9 November 1931, endorsed the Glavrepertkom's opinion but gave lukewarm permission for the theatre 'to make an experiment and demonstrate its skill', not excluding the possibility that it will succeed in its objective. At the same time, Stalin added, 'supervisors . . . versed in artistic matters' would be nominated, since '. . . I am no more than a dilettante'.[9]

Far from discouraged by this concession to Stanislavsky, Meyerhold decided to press ahead with his own production, issuing a public challenge on 21 January 1932 to the Art Theatre to engage with his company in 'socialist competition', and denying any 'counter-revolutionary' tendency in Erdman's play.[10] Rehearsals began in early May, continued for seven weeks and then resumed for a further ten days in August, concentrating on acts three to five. The surviving design sketches by Ivan Leistikov suggest a similar conception to *The Warrant*, with the use of concentric revolves and mobile screens. The part of Semyon was played by Igor Ilinsky.

Still denied formal approval for the production, Meyerhold took the unprecedented step of requesting a private run-through of the completed work without costumes or décor in the presence of members of the Party's Central Committee. Shrouded in secrecy, this took place in a workers' club at 11 p.m. on 15 August 1932.* Stalin was expected, but instead the Party group was headed by his close Politburo colleague, the ruthless Kaganovich. Apparently, the play was received well enough until the finale, but at that point Ilinsky as Semyon, following Meyerhold's direction, offered his revolver to Kaganovich and the others seated in the front row:

> They instinctively recoiled – Ilinsky recalls – 'Help yourselves, do help yourselves. . .' – I said, placing the revolver with great care on the floor. And I pushed it towards them with my toe to make it easier for them to 'help themselves'.
> Then I noticed the twisted expressions on the faces of the commission and how they began to exchange glances. And out of the corner of my eye I saw on Meyerhold's face a mixture of satisfaction and horror. He must have realised, couldn't help realising in that second, that this was the end for the production – and for the theatre as well. True, the theatre's end came rather later, but from that moment it was doomed.[12]

Kaganovich's rejection of *The Suicide* was immediate and unconditional. The production was halted, and the Moscow Art Theatre abandoned its rehearsals as well. For Erdman it was a catastrophe, but worse was to come. In October 1933 he and his co-writer Vladimir Mass were arrested, the immediate pretext being the actor Kachalov's recital at a Kremlin reception of a mildly satirical fable directed against Stalin, who was himself present.

---

* In John Freedman's biography of Erdman and in the recent Russian edition of his work the date of this event is given as October 1932. However, the fullest documentation of it is by Yury Zayats, who puts it at 15 August, following the final rehearsal earlier that day.[11]

However, as Freedman comments, by now *The Warrant* had attracted the censor's attention and there was the much more provocative text of *The Suicide* to take into account.[13] Within a week of their arrest Erdman and Mass were exiled to Siberia and it was not until 1942 that Erdman was assigned to the Song and Dance Ensemble of the NKVD and permitted to resume residence in Moscow. Whilst he continued to work in the theatre and cinema, he never completed another full-length play and died twelve years before the Soviet première of *The Suicide* in 1982 at the Theatre of Satire, staged in a heavily cut version by Meyerhold's pupil, Valentin Pluchek. Such was the fate of a work that Nadezhda Mandelshtam and others have described as the finest play of the entire Soviet period.

III

Deprived of Mayakovsky and Erdman, estranged from Selvinsky and Vishnevsky, rebuffed by Bulgakov, and despairing of finding any other Soviet dramatist worthy of production, Meyerhold commissioned the twenty-two-year-old Yury German to adapt his novel, *Prelude*, for the stage. The result was a dramatic text, much altered in rehearsal, that was set in Germany and amounted almost to a mirror image of *A List of Benefits*: a brilliant scientist Kelberg witnesses with growing horror the collapse of the German intelligentsia under the pressures of the capitalist system, and in the end feels compelled to emigrate to Soviet Russia. Presented on 28 January 1933, the production displayed in a number of its episodes all Meyerhold's impeccable style and sense of theatre, and again the critics remarked on the surprising degree of psychological penetration in the portrayal of the main characters. However, the work was modest in conception and could not overcome the inherent limitations of the textual material. It was of historical significance only for being the last play by a Soviet author to be performed publicly at the Meyerhold Theatre, fully five years before its closure.

Since *The Bed Bug* in 1929 every production by Meyerhold of a Soviet play had been met with severe criticism, whatever the public response had been. Of them all, only the two by Mayakovsky ever entered the repertoire of other Soviet theatres; the rest were staged by Meyerhold alone. At the Party purge of his theatre carried out later in 1933 he showed no signs of committing the anticipated act of contrition; on the contrary, he attributed his alleged shortcomings to external circumstances, excusing himself by saying: 'I cannot represent the great advances of socialist reconstruction with plywood scenery. I need new technical resources in a new building. The problems facing the theatre are problems of technology.'[14] In his concluding remarks the chairman said: 'As regards Comrade Meyerhold himself, without casting doubts on his past and without opening up his present for discussion, we are somewhat apprehensive about his future. We expect from Meyerhold determined application to the thematic material of socialist construction.'[15]

However, he once more sought refuge in the classics. In December 1932 he had revived his 1910 production of *Dom Juan* at the Alexandrinsky (now Pushkin) Theatre in Leningrad with Yury Yuriev at the age of sixty again playing the leading role. A year later, he produced a revised version of *Masquerade* (also with Yuriev) in the same theatre. Between the two, in April 1933, he had staged *Krechinsky's Wedding* by Sukhovo-Kobylin at his own theatre, and invited Yuriev to play Krechinsky.

By comparison with Meyerhold's earlier versions of the Russian classics, *Krechinsky's Wedding* was exceptionally restrained: the settings were simple with lighting the predominant means of expression, and pride of place was given to the minutely studied performances of Yuriev and Igor Ilinsky (who played Rasplyuev). Ilinsky writes:

> . . . with this production, Meyerhold undoubtedly advanced a further step towards profound psychologism and inner development of character. A new period seemed to have begun at the Meyerhold Theatre. This departure from the familiar Meyerhold of sensational bluff, the urge to shock and scandalise, might in the future have had a decisive influence on the development of his theatre.[16]

However, in 1937 when Meyerhold was showing visitors round the growing building of his new theatre, he enthusiastically described his plans for Pushkin's *Boris Godunov*, a new version of Mérimée's *Carmen* by Babel and Erdman, a revival of *Mystery-Bouffe*, *Othello*, and *Hamlet* – in Pasternak's translation and with settings by Picasso.* With that repertoire, one wonders just what course his work might have taken, once away from the confines of the Passage and out on the deep arena of the grand auditorium in Mayakovsky Square.

IV

Meyerhold worked for nearly a year on *The Lady of the Camellias*, the realistic comedy of manners that Alexandre Dumas fils had adapted from his novel for the stage in 1852. Presented on 19 March 1934, it seemed a curious, not to say dubious choice; Meyerhold justified it in an interview with Harold Clurman:

> I am interested in showing the bad attitude of the bourgeoisie to women. Marguerite is treated like a slave or a servant. Men bargain over her, throw money in her face, insult her – all because they say they love her. I was interested to show this because we, too, in the Soviet Union, have had a wrong conception of love and of women. Our attitude has been too biologic [sic]. . .[18]

* According to his assistant, Alexander Gladkov, Meyerhold discussed this project with Picasso in the summer of 1936. He also spoke of the possibility of Raikh playing Hamlet.[17]

He gave a similar explanation in an interview in *Izvestia*, citing the occasion in Geneva when Lenin was moved to tears by the play, and suggesting that he was responding to 'the artistic portrayal of the slavery of women under capitalism'.[19] But Joseph Yuzovsky was probably closer to the truth in his review of the production when he imagined Meyerhold saying 'I no longer desire ascetic self-denial of my heroes, my settings and my costumes. I wish my spectator joy; I want him to possess the world of beauty that was usurped by the ruling classes.'[20]

Rudnitsky does not disagree with this, but suggests that it was Meyerhold's considered response to the demands for harmony and balance, for optimism and a sense of *joie de vivre*, which the 'times' were now imposing on Soviet artists.[21] There may be some truth in this, but equally *The Lady of the Camellias* can be seen as an admission of weariness after years of struggling to extract something of worth from the contemporary Soviet repertoire. Perhaps above all, Meyerhold desired to see his beloved Zinaida in the classic bravura role of Marguerite Gautier. In his lengthy research for the production Meyerhold studied all the great interpretations of Marguerite, beginning with the creation of the role by Eugénie Doche at the Paris Vaudeville in 1852, but he readily acknowledged that his final conception was based on the performance of Eleonora Duse whom he had seen in St Petersburg in 1908. Even so, the production was by no means imitative or traditional; the prominent Russian director Leonid Varpakhovsky, who worked with Meyerhold on it, recalls:

> Instead of the feverish flush, the weak chest and the coughing, all suggesting sickness and a sense of doom, there was recklessness, gaiety, eagerness, energy, no hint of illness. Once more one found oneself recalling Meyerhold's words: 'In order to shoot the arrow, one must first draw the bowstring.' Marguerite's first entrance was preceded by a static scene showing her companion Nanine and the Baron de Varville in conversation. They spoke without exchanging glances from positions on opposite sides of the stage. Their conversation was desultory, with Nanine sewing and de Varville playing the piano. It was a *mise-en-scène* that gave this purely expository scene the necessary sense of alienation and coolness. Marguerite's unexpected appearance was in sharp contrast: dynamic in the extreme. She was returning home from the opera in the company of some young people whom she had invited to a fancy-dress evening. Marguerite, shouting words in Italian, rushed right across the stage from corner to corner, holding reins in which she had harnessed two of her youthful admirers. The two boys held top-hats high in their hands, whilst Marguerite brandished an imaginary whip.
>
> In making this entrance so stunningly unexpected, Meyerhold increased the distance that the actress had to travel in the course of the performance – from sickness to death. And in order to indicate the illness of the heroine from the very beginning, he made Kulyakbo-Koretskaya, who played Marguerite's companion, follow her closely, holding a warm shawl as though trying to prevent her catching cold.[22]

Many critics complained that Meyerhold, after all his 'reinterpretations' of the Russian classics, did not lay a finger on Dumas's questionable text. This was not true: his stage version included additional material from the original novel, as well as fragments from Flaubert and Zola, though this is not to say that the ideological balance of the play was significantly altered. However, the level of society was raised to the haute bourgeoisie, with Armand Duval's father becoming a 'powerful industrialist' instead of an assessor of taxes.[23]

The period was transposed from the 1840s to the late 1870s, the period of reaction and decadence that followed the defeat of the Paris Commune, which, according to Meyerhold, 'offers a more expressive phase of this particular period of society, . . . a period when the can-can was in full bloom'.[24] The 1870s also offered greater artistic possibilities, being the age of Manet, Degas, and Renoir: their works – particularly Renoir's – were carefully studied and copied in the scenery, properties, coiffures and costumes. Every possible source was consulted and all likely material photographed by Meyerhold's team of assistants: reproductions of paintings, cartoons, French fashion magazines of the period, even illustrations from *Punch* and *The Illustrated London News*.[25] Meyerhold insisted that his aim was not mere accuracy for accuracy's sake: 'The style of a period should come into being in space, not through the archaeological reconstruction of

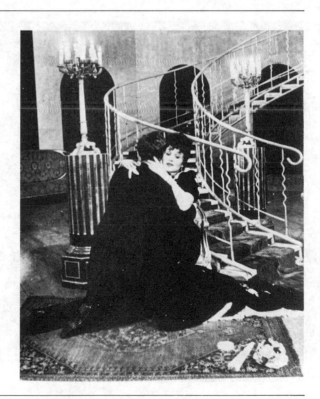

134 Zinaida Raikh
as Marguerite
with Mikhail
Tsaryov as
Armand (1934)

the period but through the creative work of the artist who has translated the language of a given culture into the language of his own perception.'[26] Thus, whilst certain of the actors' movements and poses were modelled on specific images, it was more important that they should convey an overall sense of the character in question. For example, Raikh's Marguerite was informed both by Meyerhold's personal recollection of Duse and by women in certain paintings by Renoir, notably *La Loge* (1874), *Le Moulin de la Galette* (1876) and the portrait of Jeanne Samary (1878). The principle was similar to that which had dictated the composition of his production of *Sister Beatrice* with Komissarzhevskaya in 1906 but its application was far more flexible and depended far more on the actor's own imagination, for whom the visual material was seen as simply the starting point for the creation of the character and the *mise-en-scène*.

The basic settings, executed by Ivan Leistikov, were simple and flexible, consisting largely of screens and drapes, but the properties were all exquisite period pieces, each serving a specific function and each emphasised through the use of spot-lighting. Dismissing the charges of some contemporary critics that all this finery was either a substitute for good acting or simply aesthetic self-indulgence, Rudnitsky suggests that Meyerhold's true aim was

135 *The Lady of the Camellias*, Act Four

to contrast the splendour of the clothing and furnishings with the meanness and cruelty of their owners.[27]

In Act Four, Meyerhold employed his favourite device of the staircase, this time a graceful spiral in wrought iron. Throughout, the limitations of the cramped box-stage were minimised by setting the scenes at a sharp angle to the proscenium line, thereby giving the spectator the impression of watching from the wings.* Most of the actors' movements, following the line of the setting, were diagonal, ensuring the spectator a three-quarters view which was more plastic and free from masking, even in extreme close-up. Thus, the production was conventionally representational yet conceived in the three-dimensional terms more commonly associated with the open stage.[28]

We have seen how the organising principle for virtually all Meyerhold's productions from 1905 onwards was music: music in both the literal sense and in the sense of 'musicality'. Remarkably as this style was demonstrated in *The Government Inspector*, for which the music was composed by Mikhail Gnesin, it reached even greater heights when Meyerhold joined forces in 1929 with Vissarion Shebalin, a composer whom, in theatrical terms, he ranked alongside Glazunov, Shostakovich and Prokofiev. Working together on *The Lady of the Camellias*, they achieved their most completely orchestrated composition.

From the early read-throughs of the play in Spring 1933 and throughout the company's summer tour Meyerhold required the involvement of two resident pianists whose task it was to help find appropriate music to accompany the reading of the text. Waltzes, polkas, romances and other pieces were culled from the works of Offenbach, Lecocq, Weber, Debussy, Ravel and even such minor composers of the period as Godard, Benjamin and Chaminade. Having assessed the effect of these temporary rehearsal pieces Meyerhold was able to transmit to Shebalin, who was engaged elsewhere, progressively more precise requirements for the final score. Here, for example, is an extract from a letter dated 16 July 1933:

> . . . 1 – Act Four begins with music. A can-can (or galop) begins before the lights come up. . . The character of this short introduction must be reminiscent of a traditional operetta finale in a scheme such as this: 8 beats: *forte*: major key; 16 beats: *piano*: major key; 8 beats: *forte*: minor key; 8 beats: *piano*: minor key; 8 beats: *forte*: major key; 16 beats: *piano*: major key; 8 beats: *fortissimo*: major key.
> You hear the music from behind the scenes, giving you the impression that several rooms separate us from the orchestra and that the intervening doors are being constantly opened and shut. Before the music has ended, it has served as a background for the first scene of this act. Length: 1 minute, 10 seconds.
> 2 – Between 'give me another ten louis d'or' (followed by a short pause) and before Gaston compliments Olympia on her 'charming party', a mazurka

---

* Meyerhold employed this device first in *A List of Benefits*.

(*brillante*), chic, danceable, with sharply accented impulses. Length: 1 minute, 30 seconds.

3 – Valse: dashing, nervous. Against this background, the scene between Armand and Prudence. Length 1 minute, 50 seconds.

4 - Second valse. This should be tender and lyrical. It begins at the end of Gustav's speech 'Injury to a woman . . .' Length: 2 minutes, 50 seconds.

5 - Supper-music: 'music for dessert'. Very graceful. Ice-cream cakes of different colours, garlanded with fruits, are served. You feel like saying: Shall they play a scherzo? No! Yes, a scherzo! No, not quite that. More expressive. Sober, with an undercurrent of a lyrical beat. Ah, how expressive music can be! This music should be divided into parts. It is a whole play in itself. Expressively tense (saturated with subtle eroticism). It should not soften the scene. On the contrary, it should be intensified, growing into a powerful finale, when Armand throws Marguerite to the floor, bringing everyone onto the stage as he throws the money in Marguerite's face. No longer is this a scherzo. Everything has gone wrong. Someone has put his foot in the ice-cream cake. Length: 3 minutes, 10 seconds.[29]

Altogether, Shebalin's final score for the production amounted to forty-seven pieces, only a few of which were repeats. Most were his original compositions, though some fragments from the original rehearsal music were incorporated. Thus, the whole tempo of the production was ruled by music, never used as mere background and frequently functioning in counterpoint to the actors' movements. With good reason, Varpakhovsky argues that in his collaboration with Shebalin Meyerhold inaugurated a whole new conception of music-theatre.

The production depended on Zinaida Raikh, who proved herself a born Marguerite, true to the spirit of Duse. So often, Meyerhold had been accused of distorting his productions for her benefit, but on this occasion her grace, beauty, and stage presence made *The Lady of the Camellias* the one unquestionable public triumph of the Meyerhold Theatre in the thirties – despite the predictably sour response from the majority of critics. The writer Alexander Afinogenov expostulated in his diary:

> *The Lady of the Camellias* . . . is the subtle poison of decay. This is how the old world lured people, with sparkle, velvet, silk, and shiny things . . . And the audience clap with delight and shout bravo . . . That's just the way that after the fall of the Paris Commune the bully-boys and their wives and prostitutes lived it up . . . And now this is being presented as a pearl of something. You are expected to take it as your standard and learn from it . . . Nonsense and tommy-rot! . . .[30]

Even so, when in the same year a dramatic adaptation of Balzac's novel *A Bachelor's Establishment* was presented by the Vakhtangov Theatre, the ironic advice given to visitors was: 'If you want Balzac go to Meyerhold, for Dumas fils go to the Vakhtangov.'[31]

V

With the site of his new theatre still little more than an empty space, and with no clear-cut plans for any new productions, Meyerhold accepted an invitation to direct Tchaikovsky's *The Queen of Spades* at the Leningrad Maly Opera, where it had its première on 25 January 1935. Under its Artistic Director, Samuel Samosud, the Maly Opera had established a reputation for innovation, being responsible for the first productions of Shostakovich's operas, *The Nose* (1930) and *Lady Macbeth of Mtsensk* (1934). Samosud agreed readily to Meyerhold's proposal for a complete revision of *The Queen of Spades*. Meyerhold reasoned that the libretto by Tchaikovsky's brother, Modest, was a crude distortion of Pushkin's original text, wholly motivated by his desire to gratify the prevailing taste for cheap romantic spectacle. Accordingly, he set out 'to saturate the atmosphere of Tchaikovsky's wonderful music . . . with the ozone of Pushkin's even more wonderful tale', enlisting the aid of a young poet, Valentin Stenich, to compose a new libretto.[32]

At the suggestion of Vsevolozhsky, the Director of Imperial Theatres, Modest Tchaikovsky had moved the period of the opera back from the 1830s to the last years of the reign of Catherine the Great, since it afforded greater opportunities for elaborate costume and spectacle. To avoid the social anomaly of Hermann, a poor officer of the Engineers, consorting with the nobility, he was transformed into an Hussar. But Meyerhold argued that this completely obscured a crucial point in Pushkin's story: the Countess exemplifies the hereditary society from which Hermann feels excluded; to penetrate it he needs the wealth that only luck at cards can bring him. He pursues Liza not because he loves her, but because through her he can discover the secret of the fatal three cards. Liza kills herself because she realises this, not because Hermann has killed the Countess.

Hence, Meyerhold restored the action to the 1830s and made Hermann once more Pushkin's poor Engineers officer, emphasising his isolation by depicting him as a brooding solitary of the kind who had dominated so many of his earlier productions. In his article on Meyerhold's revision of the opera Ivan Sollertinsky describes Hermann as 'a remarkable synthesis of the unbridled romantic hero: the "young man of the nineteenth century" consumed with Napoleonic ambition, demonic passions, the melancholy of Childe Harold and the introspection of Hamlet. . .'[33] Meyerhold himself compared him to Lermontov's 'Hero of Our Time', Pechorin, and to Pushkin's Yevgeny in *The Bronze Horseman*.[34] Stenich based his libretto on the poetry of Pushkin and his pleiad, in places incorporating fragments of their actual verses, though elsewhere retaining Modest's original text.

Inevitably, the result was uneven, and few critics conceded any stylistic improvement. But dramatically the new plot was far closer to Pushkin, with Liza assuming a role properly subordinate to the central Hermann–Countess conflict. Scenes devised by Modest Tchaikovsky simply for the adornment of the Imperial stage were removed entirely, 445 bars being excised from the score, and new words were set to the original music. Thus the opening scene in the Summer Garden, in which the exposition of the Hermann–Liza–Yeletsky triangle is interspersed with the coming and going of children and their wet-nurses, was replaced by Pushkin's original scene of the young officers gambling at Narumov's house with Hermann as an onlooker. The soldiers' song which is sung by the children in Modest's libretto was given to a girl wearing Hussar's uniform, entertaining Narumov's guests before they get down to the serious business of cards.

The ball was staged not with hosts of splendidly costumed extras, but as a series of intimate scenes with Hermann ever present, so that the audience could follow his conflicting emotions. The monarch who made a grand entry at the conclusion of the scene was not Catherine the Great but the uniformed figure of Nicholas II 'with the puffed-out chest of a sergeant major'.[35] In the final scene at the gaming house Hermann's fatal challenge was taken up neither by Yeletsky (as in Tchaikovsky) nor by Pushkin's famous Muscovite gambler Chekalinsky, but by a figure

136 *The Queen of Spades*. The Countess' Bedroom. Hermann and Liza after the death of the Countess

called 'The Stranger' invented by Meyerhold – a characteristic flourish which stirred memories of the infernal emissaries of his Petersburg days, yet was in no way inconsistent with the mood of Pushkin's tale which, said Meyerhold, is 'pure fantasy – there is nothing in it that resembles what really happens'.[36]

The settings were broadly representational, properties being employed with the same expediency as in *The Government Inspector* and *The Lady of the Camellias*. The designs by Chupyatov were not at all to Meyerhold's liking; they could not compare in elegance or architectural flair with what he was accustomed to in Moscow, though once again (in the Countess's bedroom scene) the curved staircase was in evidence. However, he compensated for the settings' limitations with his brilliant deployment of the huge chorus, rehearsing them with a care that they had never experienced, but to which they responded with enthusiasm.[37] Meyerhold describes his new approach to the problem of music and movement compared with his previous operatic work:

> In *Tristan* I insisted on the actor's movements and gestures synchronising with the tempo of the music and the tonic scheme with almost mathematical accuracy. But in *The Queen of Spades* I tried to allow the actor rhythmical freedom within the limits of the musical phrase (like Chaliapin), so that his interpretation, whilst remaining dependent on the music would have a contrapuntal rather than a metrically precise relationship to it, sometimes even acting as a contrast or variation, anticipating or lagging behind the score instead of simply keeping in unison with it.[38]

The one almost unanimous criticism of the production was that the new libretto deprived Tchaikovsky's score of much of its thematic logic, particularly in the exposition of the Hermann–Liza relationship. What is more, in his recent analysis of the Meyerhold–Stenich adaptation Isaac Glikman argues persuasively that Meyerhold's representation of the composer as a reluctant collaborator with his brother and Vsevolozhsky is at odds with the facts and was designed to validate his own approach. In fact, Tchaikovsky was co-author of the libretto and his own contributions endorsed Modest's approach to Pushkin's text. On the other hand, in common with other critics, Glikman sees considerable gains in restoring the action to the time of Pushkin, particularly as the social conflict embodied in the figure of Hermann gained greatly from the atmosphere of the repressive post-Decembrist period.[39]

Whatever their reservations concerning the liberties that Meyerhold took with the original libretto, few critics in 1935 disputed the dramatic gains or the production's overall fidelity to Pushkin. Here is Meyerhold's description of the closing scene:

> Hermann stakes such a huge sum of money that he cannot get the notes out of his pocket; he has to chalk the amount on the table. The others are afraid to play with him; many back away and he is left almost alone. He issues a general challenge.

137 The closing
scene in the
gaming house

A character steps forward who has not appeared before. I call him 'The
Stranger'. He steps forward and announces: 'I will play . . .' He comes up to
the table and starts to deal. But while the Stranger is approaching the table
and all attention is fixed on him and Hermann, the yellow-clad figure of the
Countess materialises unnoticed at the table; she sits with her back to the
audience, following the cards. Hermann cries: 'My ace!' . . . A long pause.
Then the silence is broken not by the Stranger but by the old woman saying
'Your Queen loses.'

Hermann shrieks: 'What Queen?' A further pause. Then again, the Old
Woman: 'The one in your hand, the Queen of Spades.' Pointing at the card, the
ghost of the Countess staggers back slightly, as though about to fall. Hermann
sees her in the same dress that she was wearing in the bedroom, and falling
just as she did when he pointed the pistol at her.

Blackout. Immediately a new setting: a ward in the Obukhov Hospital
with a bed jutting onto the forestage. Hermann is sitting on the bed. We
hear the same music as we heard in the barracks before the appearance of
the Countess's ghost. Hermann speaks the same words that she spoke then,
as though playing her role.

So ends Tchaikovsky's *Queen of Spades*. So ends Pushkin's *Queen of
Spades*.[40]

Of course, Glikman is right to point out that this is *not* how Tchaikovsky's
opera ends, but this does not detract from the bleak power of Meyerhold's
final image. What he achieved made a profound impact on the young
Shostakovich and encouraged the Maly Opera to invite him back to direct
Mussorgsky's *Boris Godunov* the following season. It also encouraged Stanislavsky to invite him to work at his Opera Theatre in 1938. Apparently,
the Meyerhold–Stenich version of *The Queen of Spades* is preserved in the
archives – awaiting an opera company with sufficient enterprise to revive
it.

VI

Two months after *The Queen of Spades*, on 25 March 1935, to mark the seventy-fifth anniversary of Chekhov's birth the Meyerhold theatre staged three of his one-act farces: *The Anniversary*, *The Bear*, and *The Proposal*, under the collective title *33 Swoons*. According to Meyerhold's calculations, there are no fewer than thirty-three occasions in the course of the three plays when a character swoons; hence his decision to make this the linking motif of the whole production. Each swoon was accompanied by special music – brass for the men and strings for the ladies – which subsided once the victim had recovered. Meyerhold was anxious to justify this as more than a mere theatrical device. The swoons, he claimed, were:

> . . . the manifestation of neurasthenia, which was most prevalent in Chekhov's day. Neurasthenia is a clear indication of the lethargy, the loss of will-power that is typical of Chekhov's characters. . . In the course of studying the age and society depicted by Chekhov, we assembled a wide variety of material that confirms the unusually high incidence of neurasthenia amongst the intelligentsia of the eighties and nineties (in the theatre there was even the special *emploi* of 'neurasthenic'). We know well enough what the social preconditions for such a phenomenon are.[41]

The explanation is laboured and unconvincing: it might perhaps be applied to Chekhov's full-length plays, in particular to a number of the roles that Meyerhold himself played, such as Treplev, Tusenbach, and Trofimov; indeed his portrayals were often described by the critics as 'neurasthenic'. But 'lethargy' and 'loss of will-power' are not the obvious terms that spring

138 Scene from *The Anniversary*

to mind when considering the violent eruptions that typify the characters' behaviour in Chekhov's farces. Convinced that the farces are more 'tragic grotesques' than 'jokes' (as Chekhov described them), Meyerhold equipped his actors with an abundance of hand-props, and invented endless business designed to help them betray the characters' inner emotions, whilst at the same time 'increasing the circulation of their vaudeville blood'. Thus, in *The Proposal*, Natasha and Lomov were made to fight over a napkin and tray while disputing the ownership of the meadows; in *The Anniversary*, the deputation of shareholders presented the Chairman Shipuchin not with an address and silver tankard but with a huge stuffed bear; at the close of *The Bear*, when the grief-stricken widow Popova finally ensnared the landowner Smirnov, she embraced him and with her free hand removed from the piano a bouquet of red roses which had lain there throughout, evidently left by another suitor.[42]

Meyerhold's tricks certainly yielded some hilarious moments, but the overall effect was to slow the pace with the sheer weight of ideas. He himself admitted to Alexander Gladkov:

> We tried to be too clever and consequently lost sight of the humour. We must look the truth in the face: the audience at any amateur production of *The Proposal* would laugh more than they did at ours, even though Ilinsky was acting and Meyerhold was the director. Chekhov's light, transparent humour was crushed beneath the weight of our theories and the result was a disaster.[43]

Sadly, this uncharacteristic production was to prove the last new work ever to be seen by the public at the Meyerhold Theatre and the role of Popova in *The Bear* the last that Zinaida Raikh would ever play. In 1935, the full implications of the First All-Union Congress of Soviet Writers held the previous year were becoming clear. Membership of the Union of Soviet Writers was to be mandatory for any writer who hoped to publish, and acceptance of the tenets of Socialist Realism a precondition of membership.[44] Thus, Party control was extended directly and formally to every area of literature, including of course the theatrical repertoire. In February 1934 Meyerhold's sixtieth birthday had been greeted with the routine panegyric in *Pravda*,[45] which was echoed fulsomely by other papers and journals. However, a year later when the inaugural list of People's Artists of the USSR was made public, the name of Meyerhold was an ominous absentee.*

At the beginning of 1936 the Party's campaign against 'formalism' in the arts took an ominous turn. Shortly after the creation of a new, considerably more powerful central controlling body, the All-Union Committee for Arts Affairs, there appeared in *Pravda* two editorial articles condemning productions of Shostakovich's opera, *Lady Macbeth of Mtsensk*, and his ballet, *The Clear Stream*.[46] Both were promptly removed from the repertoire. Then at the

---

* Prior to this the highest honour had been 'People's Artist of the RSFSR', which Meyerhold had been awarded in 1923.

139 Alexander
Tairov,
Edward
Gordon Craig
and Meyerhold
in Moscow,
1935

end of February, Mikhail Chekhov's former theatre, the Second Moscow Art Theatre Studio, and the Leningrad Young Workers' Theatre were both liquidated at the command of the Supreme Soviet and the Central Committee of the Communist Party.

With few exceptions, stage-directors took the first available opportunity to confess their past aberrations and affirm their faith in Socialist Realism. On 14 March 1936, Meyerhold spoke in Leningrad on the theme 'Meyerhold against Meyerholditis', but far from admitting his own mistakes, he accused his imitators of propagating 'Meyerholditis', the plagiarising and indiscriminate application of his formal devices with no comprehension of their logical motivation. Whilst acknowledging that some elements in his productions may have been unclear to the audience, he condemned unprincipled critics who made no serious attempt to interpret them. What is more, he boldly defended Shostakovich against the attacks in *Pravda*, and affirmed his right and the right of all artists to experiment.[47]

Simultaneously, a conference of 'workers in the arts' was convened in Moscow to discuss the implications of the attacks on Shostakovich and subsequent articles condemning formalism that had appeared in *Pravda*. Meyerhold was the target of many assaults, notably from the principal speaker, Johann Altman (the editor of *Teatr*), and from Radlov and Okhlopkov, two of the directors he had criticised in Leningrad. When he replied on 26 March 1936, he yielded little to his critics; indeed, what he said was tantamount to a total rejection of Socialist Realism and the official interpretation of the term 'formalism', his speech being marred only by an entirely gratuitous assault on Tairov. No one who heard it could have missed the withering sarcasm behind Meyerhold's remarks on simplicity in art, or have failed to be shaken by the fine, if ill-judged arrogance with which he asserted his creative independence. At a time of craven hypocrisy, self-humiliation, and universal suspicion, his open intransigence was without parallel amongst artists of his standing.[48] In the next number of *Soviet Theatre*, the organ of the All-Union Committee for Arts Affairs, the crudely-phrased, unsigned editorial stated that '. . . Beginning with his breakaway from the Art Theatre, Meyerhold in practice has always opposed his method not only to the naturalistic theatre but to the realistic theatre as well. To this day he has not rid himself of elements of the symbolist and aesthetic theatre, and most important of all, he continues to uphold them.'[49]

In response to charges that his was the only theatre in the entire Soviet Union without a Soviet play in its repertoire, Meyerhold announced plans for staging a modernised version of *The Bed Bug*, to be called *A Fantastic Comedy*, Mayakovsky's original sub-title. This was to be followed by a dramatic adaptation of Nikolai Ostrovsky's novel, *How the Steel was Tempered*. The Mayakovsky project was abandoned after preliminary rehearsals,[50] whilst *One Life* (as Ostrovsky's work was retitled) needed textual revision and was deferred to the following season. After a revival of *The Government Inspector* in April 1936, the second half of the year was devoted to rehearsals of Pushkin's *Boris Godunov*, for which Prokofiev composed the music. A number of scenes were rehearsed, but the production outgrew the theatre's cramped dimensions and finally was laid aside to await the opening of the new theatre. The accounts of the rehearsals reveal Meyerhold's profound insight into Pushkin's drama, conceived in 'the barbarous colours of freshly-painted sixteenth-century icons',[51] and suggest that the production could well have challenged *The Government Inspector* as his theatrical masterpiece.[52]

Before he resumed work on *One Life* Meyerhold made a further half-hearted attempt early in 1937 to stage a play that would meet with Party approval. Lydia Seifullina's *Natasha* is a chronicle play of a kind that was becoming all too familiar in the Soviet Union at that time. Natasha is the orphan of parents tortured and murdered by the Whites in the Civil War who shakes off the oppression of a kulak employer to become a labour hero on a collective farm. Meyerhold strove to reproduce the rural setting in all its lifelike detail, complete with apple trees and cabbage patches, but the result was an unworthy and embarrassing fiasco which was dropped immediately following the first dress-rehearsal. Unfortunately, Meyerhold's opponents could now claim justification for their assertion that he was incapable of staging a modern Soviet play.[53]

The need to make a success of *One Life* was now more acute than ever. Nikolai Ostrovsky, half-blind and crippled by wounds and illnesses incurred in the Civil War and the service of the Party, had inspired many millions of Soviet readers with his example, and on his death in December 1936 had become a national hero. The hero of *How the Steel was Tempered*, published in 1935, is Pavka Korchagin, a poor Ukrainian boy whose story follows closely that of Ostrovsky himself. No subject could have been more suitable for a play to mark the twentieth anniversary of the October Revolution. There can be little doubt that Meyerhold was profoundly moved by Ostrovsky's example in the course of their meetings in the final months of the writer's life, and unlike *Natasha*, the production of *One Life* was one that fired the imagination of the entire company. The author of the scenario, Yevgeny Gabrilovich, writes:

> It was truly the birth of a new revolutionary production, far removed
> from the earlier eccentricism, yet still with echoes of it in its depths. It
> was harsh, turbulent, romantic, violent – no other production of Nikolai
> Ostrovsky, either on the stage or on the screen, has approached it in my
> experience.*
> I vividly recall the episode when Pavka Korchagin was urging his comrades
> to resume work on the new railway line. They were all dog-tired, hungry,
> discouraged and bad tempered; nobody wanted to go out onto the site in the
> rain and cold. Then, after exhausting his vocabulary with descriptions of the
> international situation, jokes, and exhortations, Pavka slowly and tentatively
> began to dance. He danced all alone in the dim light of the damp barrack
> room, whilst his comrades on their bunks looked first with amusement then
> with growing amazement. He danced on and on, faster and faster, livelier and
> livelier, spinning and knee-bending, with no music, not even his own voice to
> accompany him. And then someone began to beat time with his hand on his
> bunk; then another, and then a third joined in the accompaniment. Another
> jumped down onto the floor and began to dance alongside Pavka. Others
> joined them, and the noise of the accompaniment grew louder and louder,
> with some of the lads now banging with their fists. And now it wasn't only
> Pavka dancing, but ten, fifteen, twenty others as well. Then slowly at first,
> but gradually more quickly and more violently, the beams of the spotlights
> began to move about the stage, as though they too were dancing. And now
> everything seemed to join in – the men, the lights, the drums, even the walls
> of the barrack room. Still there was no music – just the rhythmical sound of
> hands, fists, and drums. Then suddenly amidst this whirlwind and thunder,
> you heard from somewhere, very softly, as though in the very depths, in the
> heart of the hut, an old revolutionary song. It swelled and strengthened, and
> now the dancing and the banging fell silent. The men, hot and sweating from
> dancing, in their torn clothes and their remnants of boots, joined in this
> marvellous song, made up by their brothers and fathers in prison and exile.
> Then still singing, in the now motionless beams of the spotlights, they went
> out into the rain and the cold to work.[54]

Shortly before the anniversary celebrations in November the production was viewed by representatives from the Glavrepertkom; no serious criticisms were made and general approval was expressed by those present. However, it was suggested that the work needed further polishing, and in any case there

---

* There was a second version staged at The Moscow Young Workers' Theatre in 1937, followed since by numerous productions (including a ballet version). The novel has since been filmed twice: by Donskoy in 1942, and by Alov and Naumov in 1947 as *Pavka Korchagin*.

was no need to rush it on in time for the actual anniversary. So two weeks later, the production was shown again – this time to be severely criticised, not only by the President of the Committee for Artistic Affairs, Platon Kerzhentsev, but also by those who previously had voiced enthusiasm.[55] It was clear that a decision had already been taken about the Meyerhold Theatre's future which the likely success of an indisputably revolutionary, not to say Socialist Realist, production must not be allowed to prejudice. Evidently, it was deemed necessary to conceal *One Life* from public view and public opinion.

On 17 December 1937 *Pravda* published an article signed by Kerzhentsev, entitled 'An Alien Theatre'. The style was familiar enough:

> On the occasion of the twentieth anniversary of the Great Socialist Revolution only one out of the seven-hundred Soviet professional theatres was without a special production to commemorate the October Revolution and without a Soviet repertoire. That theatre was Meyerhold's theatre. . .
>
> Almost his entire theatrical career before the October Revolution amounted to a struggle against the realistic theatre on behalf of the stylised, mystical, formalist theatre of the aesthetes, that is, the theatre that shunned real life. . . [In its production of Verhaeren's *The Dawn*] his theatre made a hero out of a Menshevik traitor to the working class. . . *The Government Inspector* was treated not in the style of the realistic theatre, but in the spirit of the White émigré Merezhkovsky's book, *Gogol and the Devil*.
>
> It has become absolutely clear that Meyerhold cannot and, apparently, will not comprehend Soviet reality or depict the problems that concern every Soviet citizen. . .
>
> For several years [he] stubbornly tried to stage the play, *I Want a Child*, by the enemy of the people, Tretyakov, which was a hostile slur on the Soviet family. . .
>
> Systematic deviation from Soviet reality, political distortion of that reality, and hostile slanders against our way of life have brought the theatre to total ideological and artistic ruin, to shameful bankruptcy.
>
> . . . Do Soviet art and the Soviet public really need such a theatre?[56]

Clearly, the answer to this question was now considered beyond debate, but even so Meyerhold and his company were required to engage in the ritual process of self-examination and recrimination. In a three-day debate on 22, 23 and 25 December Meyerhold was given the opportunity first to respond to the charges in the *Pravda* article and then finally to answer the further criticisms that were aimed at him by members of the company in the course of the discussion.[57]

In his opening speech Meyerhold acknowledged his personal responsibility for the company's mistakes: in particular, their failure to work with such dramatists as Vishnevsky; their failure to seek the advice of Civil War veterans when working on *One Life*; their failure to establish contact with the young working-class audience; and their over-reliance on old successes in the repertoire. However, this fell far short of what was expected of him,

140 Meyerhold on the site of the new theatre, 1937

and in the ensuing debate speaker after speaker, a number of them his own actors, condemned his neglect of the repertoire, his egocentrism, his preferment of Raikh, his lack of forward planning, his hasty work on *One Life*. Alone amongst his accusers, the stage carpenter Kanyshkin pleaded that he be given the chance to prove himself anew in his new theatre.

Meyerhold's reply took up the entire final session, and the transcript of it runs to over thirty printed pages. At times bitingly sarcastic, at times robust in self-defence, he failed yet again to commit the act of total contrition that was customary in those frightening times. He conceded that the company's work had begun to weaken from 1933 onwards and that they ought not to have neglected 'average' Soviet writers; he conceded that the preparation of *One Life* had been over-hurried; he made the standard denunciation of the 'Judas Trotsky'. However, with the exception of *33 Swoons* he contested the charge of formalism, arguing that even in such productions as *The Magnanimous Cuckold* and *Tarelkin's Death* the approach to character had been profoundly realistic. He defended his right to experiment, though conceding that such work might be better conducted in laboratory conditions before audiences of specialists. He was, he said, experimental by nature: 'This is not so much my fault as my misfortune'. He argued that his love for Raikh as an artist was uninfluenced by his love for her as a person. He declared himself ready to engage in a searching examination of his entire working method and of 'everything concerning my world view', in the hope that he would 'still prove useful in the country of the Soviets in two or three years time'. Following the debate a resolution was drawn up endorsing every point in the *Pravda* denunciation. Whether the company ever voted on it is unclear, but in any case the outcome was a foregone conclusion: few would have risked siding with the valiant Kanyshkin.

On Saturday, 7 January 1938 the company gave its 725th and final performance of *The Lady of the Camellias*, with Zinaida Raikh still in the title role. The following day, after a morning performance of *The Government Inspector*, the State Meyerhold Theatre was liquidated and a ballet company took over its premises. The final week's repertoire tells its own story: *The Government Inspector, The Lady of the Camellias, Woe to Wit, Krechinsky's Wedding, The Forest*.

The Final Act

In the weeks following the liquidation of Meyerhold's theatre, few of his friends and associates visited him and Zinaida Raikh in their flat off Gorky Street:* some felt it tactful to stay away, others were anxious to avoid the risk of guilt through association.[1] Amongst those who spurned the danger were three in particular. Pasternak, by no means a close friend of the Meyerholds, was one of the first to call. Eisenstein, although himself extremely vulnerable since the banning of his film *Bezhin Meadow* the previous year, was soon to secrete the vast Meyerhold archive in the walls of his dacha, thereby ensuring its survival to this day.[2] Finally Stanislavsky, long regarded as Meyerhold's antipode, astonished all Moscow when in March 1938 he invited him to work as his assistant at his Opera Theatre. Thus Stanislavsky succeeded in confounding Kerzhentsev, who apparently was planning to assign both Meyerhold and Raikh to work in the run-down Lensovet Theatre in the outskirts of Leningrad.[3]

This apparent reconciliation of opposites was much less surprising than it seemed from the outside. For a start, though the two men rarely met for thirty or more years after the failure of the Theatre-Studio, and though Stanislavsky was scarcely ever seen at the Meyerhold Theatre, they shared a strong mutual respect, and Meyerhold never lost an opportunity to express his love and gratitude towards his first and only teacher. By contrast, the breach with Nemirovich-Danchenko was never mended, and Nemirovich made no secret of his dislike for Meyerhold's productions. From the mid-thirties Meyerhold and Stanislavsky had begun to see more of each other and share their thoughts on the future development of the Soviet theatre; there was even a plan to take *33 Swoons* for performance in Stanislavsky's flat when he was confined to bed through illness.

However, there is little evidence of any significant artistic rapprochement

* In Bryusov Lane, now 12 Nezhdanova Street. The building bears a memorial plaque and the flat is being converted into a Meyerhold museum.

between the two. Following his rehabilitation some Soviet critics sought to demonstrate Meyerhold's increasing preoccupation with 'psychological realism' in his late productions, but as Rudnitsky rightly observes, the fiasco of *Natasha* suggests that Meyerhold felt little commitment in that direction.[4] It is significant that even when describing Meyerhold's 'chamber' works staged within the confines of the theatre in Gorky Street, critics invariably recalled the sudden arresting image or theatrical stroke, seldom the complete psychological creation. On the other hand, although Stanislavsky may latterly have shown a serious concern with the physical aspects of acting, it was aimed primarily towards the greater stimulation of the actor's creative imagination, and in practice led to no radical change in production style. The ultimate objective remained the creation of an illusion of life; the relationship between performer and spectator was always rooted in empathy. As for Meyerhold, whilst it is true that, like the later Brecht, he was by no means averse to the emotional identification of the spectator with the character, he employed it consciously as a means of deepening the understanding of the production's overall significance, as one element amongst many. With Meyerhold, the character, even one as central as Khlestakov or Marguerite Gautier, was always viewed as a component part of the play's total meaning; with Stanislavsky, the merest servant or foot-soldier carried his autobiography complete with him on stage.

Similarly, with Meyerhold the basic dramatic unit was the episode, whereas with Stanislavsky it remained the act; the one dismantles reality, the other reproduces its flow. Then again, nowhere in Stanislavsky's writings does one find any analysis of audience psychology, the assumption being that if the actor's performance is 'truthful', then the spectator will recognise the truth and identify with it.* With Meyerhold, from as early as *The Fairground Booth* in 1906, the entire production was structured to stimulate and exploit audience reaction, confounding its expectations as often as it confirmed them. There is no reason to suppose that Meyerhold's theatrical philosophy would have changed had his dream come true and he had gained the freedom of the 'empty space' on Mayakovsky Square.

On 7 August 1938, Stanislavsky died. Yury Bakhrushin, his deputy at the Opera Theatre, recalls him saying shortly before his death: 'Take care of Meyerhold; he is my sole heir in the theatre – both here and elsewhere.'[5] Two months later, Meyerhold succeeded Stanislavsky as the theatre's artistic director. The appointment was confirmed by Nazarov, Kerzhentsev's successor on the Committee for Arts Affairs, Kerzhentsev himself having been dismissed for 'tolerating the pernicious Meyerhold Theatre for so long under his very nose.'[6]

Prevented by failing health from leaving his home and concerned at

---

* In *An Actor Prepares* Stanislavsky writes: 'the spectator . . . is like a witness to a conversation. He has a silent part in [the actor's] exchange of feelings, and is excited by their experiences' (trans. E. Hapgood, London, 1959, p. 197).

the inability of his assistants to execute his instructions, Stanislavsky had entrusted Meyerhold with the rehearsals of what was to be his last production, *Rigoletto*. It was presented under Meyerhold's supervision on 10 March 1939. The projected repertoire for the following season included productions by Meyerhold of Mozart's *Don Giovanni* and Prokofiev's new opera *Semyon Kotko*.[7] He also planned a revival of Stanislavsky's production of *Eugene Onegin* and a revision of his own earlier version of *The Queen of Spades*.

II

Three months before *Rigoletto* Meyerhold had presented a highly praised revision of his 1917 masterpiece, Lermontov's *Masquerade* in Leningrad, with the sixty-six-year-old Yuriev in his original role of Arbenin.[8] Soon there was confident talk of Meyerhold rejoining the company on a permanent basis; productions under consideration included *Hamlet*, Pushkin's *Boris Godunov*, Ostrovsky's *The Storm*, and several new works by Soviet writers. His proposed move to Leningrad had the enthusiastic support of Leonid Vivien, artistic director of the Pushkin Theatre, and was endorsed by the theatre's artistic council. Again it seemed that the Committee for Arts Affairs under Nazarov was favourably disposed towards his gradual rehabilitation and would uphold his appointment.[9]

Such hopes were encouraged by what appeared at the time to be a major shift in Party policy. In December 1938 Yezhov had been replaced as People's Commissar for Internal Affairs by Beria (and was to perish probably in January 1940 in the same way as his countless victims before him). At the XVIIIth Party Congress in March 1939 Stalin and others denounced the errors and excesses perpetrated by the NKVD during the period known as the 'Yezhovshchina'. Seemingly, the Great Purge was at an end, although we now know that the execution of Party members continued well after the conclusion of the Congress.[10] Concurrently, a new attitude seemed to have been adopted towards the arts and the intelligentsia. During the Congress Stalin had said:

> As regards the old pre-revolutionary intelligentsia who had served the capitalist and landowning classes, the old theory of mistrust and hostility was entirely appropriate. . . For the new intelligentsia we need a new theory, emphasising the need for a friendly attitude towards them, concern for them, respect for them and co-operation with them.[11]

The following month, the implications of this new line were developed in a series of public pronouncements by Alexander Fadeev, Secretary of the Soviet Writers' Union and a reliable voice of Stalinist opinion. In an article in *Pravda* on 16 April 1939 Fadeev called for greater trust to be placed in the arts: what is more, he sharply criticised the Committee for Artistic Affairs for seeking to remodel all theatre companies in the image of the Moscow Art Theatre, and advocated the renewed proliferation of theatrical forms. To many at the time this sounded like the official abandonment of the campaign against formalism which had culminated in the closure of Meyerhold's theatre.

At the end of April, during a week-long meeting of the Presidium of the Writers' Union chaired by Fadeev, Meyerhold's position was discussed at length and a more balanced view of his work was demanded. In his concluding speech Fadeev said:

> Meyerhold is an outstanding artist who continues to work in the Soviet theatre. His work must not be covered up. We need to have a clear attitude towards what he is doing and what he has done in the past, openly criticising what is incorrect and false but acknowledging what is forward-looking and capable of enriching the Soviet theatre.[12]

Around the same time Meyerhold himself was once again prominent in public debates. When he addressed the Writers' Union on 19 May 1939 he had regained sufficient confidence to criticise sharply the stifling effect of the Glavrepertkom on new writing. Citing the inspiring example of Dovzhenko's latest film *Shchors*, he called for a new popular heroic theatre that would burst the bounds of the 'box-stage' and free actors from the drudgery of 'rummaging around in narrow, everyday subject-matter'.[13] These were hardly the words of a supplicant for re-employment, so clearly Meyerhold had high hopes that he would soon be in a position to choose between the Stanislavsky Opera in Moscow and the Pushkin Theatre in Leningrad. But as we shall see, Fadeev, who had convened the discussion on 19 May, may already have known otherwise.

III

Despite the baleful presence of Andrei Vyshinsky, Prosecutor-General and Vice-Chairman of the Council of People's Commissars, it was in a mood of optimism that the first All-Union Conference of Theatre Directors opened in Moscow on 13 June 1939. Doubtless encouraged by the Party's apparent change of attitude towards the arts, a number of directors were surprisingly outspoken in their criticism of recent clumsy bureaucratic attempts to impose a crude version of Stanislavskian psychological realism as the norm for theatre production. Others were equally frank in their condemnation of the effects of the campaign against so-called formalism, launched in 1936, which had stifled true theatricality and experimentation, and had produced a style that, in the words of the critic Pavel Novitsky, could best be described as 'panic-stricken realism'.[14]

Inevitably, in this atmosphere Meyerhold was the focus of eager attention and high expectations. At the opening of the conference he was elected to the platform by acclamation from the floor, and on taking his place immediately after Vyshinsky, he was greeted with an ovation that the inexperienced chairman, Khrapchenko, was powerless to quell. Meyerhold himself tried in vain to direct the applause towards Vyshinsky, but the assembly would not be denied. During subsequent speeches on the opening day the mention of his name in speeches from Solomon Mikhoels and Alexei Popov was enough to prompt further vociferous demonstrations of support. By the third day of the conference Khrapchenko was so alarmed by this turn of events that he attempted to prohibit 'all applause, laughter and comments during speeches'. This ludicrous proposal was greeted with derision and the proceedings continued as before.

Originally, Meyerhold himself was not listed amongst the main speakers, and when at the start of the conference it was proposed from the floor that he contribute on the theme of 'performance style' he responded with uncharacteristic diffidence and surprise. However, he did undertake to participate in the debate after the main speeches. In the event, he spoke on 15 June for close on forty-five minutes.

141 Meyerhold
addressing the
Directors'
Conference,
15 June 1939

Until recently the contents of his speech have remained in dispute, and it was not until 1991 that the verbatim text was publis¹led together with Meyerhold's own notes and extracts from the contributions of other speakers.[15] This full version tallies with the extracts that had appeared in *Teatr* in 1974 and, interestingly, confirms the substance of the brief summary included by Alexander Kaun four years after the event in his *Soviet Poets and Poetry*.[16] Once and for all, it exposes as a complete fabrication the frequently cited version that Yury Yelagin claimed to have reconstructed from notes that he took at the conference and which he included in his generally unsound biography of Meyerhold.[17]

Sadly, the speech that Meyerhold actually delivered to his expectant audience at the Actor's House bears no resemblance to the defiant words that Yelagin sought to inscribe in legend. Over the years Meyerhold had proved himself as a formidable orator – erudite, acerbic and recklessly combative. But on this occasion all those qualities were missing, and his speech was sadly deferential, rambling and inconclusive. On such a clearly momentous occasion under the unsettling patronage of Vyshinsky it is understandable that Meyerhold should begin with the familiar sycophantic platitudes in praise of Stalin 'our leader, our teacher, the friend of toilers throughout the world', and then proceed to express his gratitude for the freedom (granted him in common with Shostakovich and Eisenstein) to work and correct past errors. Tactically at least, it made sense for him to apologise for exposing 'laboratory experiments' like *The Forest* and *The Government Inspector* to a wide audience. Such comments could well have served as the effective preamble to a bold exposition of what Meyerhold now envisaged as the programme for himself and his fellow directors in a new, more tolerant climate of opinion.

Undoubtedly, many regarded any creative freedom granted to Meyerhold as a clear indication of what they themselves might now hazard.[18] But those in the audience who had hoped for such a lead were gravely disappointed. Time and again, he approached such burning issues as the reinterpretation of the classics, the commanding role of the artistic director, the need to resist hack work, and the demand for a new heroic drama – only to lose himself in insignificant detail and inconclusive argument. His sorry performance ended lamely with a repeated citation of Dovzhenko's film *Shchors* as a model for the new heroic drama and a patriotic inspiration for all true citizens of 'the great Country of the Soviets'.[19] The speech was greeted with warm applause, but Meyerhold knew only too well that it had been a fiasco, and there was no disguising the dismay that many of his audience felt. The following day, in the course of a brave intervention from the floor, Isaac Kroll, a director at the Moscow Jewish theatre, said:

> It was the speech of a great man. Yet is seems to me that much of what we
> should have heard was not referred to by Vsevolod Emilievich. He made no
> mention of it. Like a mortally wounded lion, Vsevolod Emilievich was forced

to hide in the long grass. But if he has recovered and come out of the long grass, it should be not as a bedraggled cat, but as a mighty lion. Because it is as a lion that he is vital to Soviet art.[20]

The critic, Moissei Yankovsky, voiced similar sentiments.

> Yesterday from this platform, with the stroke of a pen Meyerhold destroyed everything that he has stood for throughout his life. Comrades, can we honestly agree that on the strength of what Meyerhold the man said yesterday Meyerhold the artist never existed? For that is what officially he announced to us. It would be wrong for us simply to try and ignore the vast riches that Meyerhold has bestowed on the history of our theatre. On the contrary, we must help Meyerhold now to understand what was and still is true in his work, and what can be discarded as dross. If Meyerhold – who to me seems to be in a state of confusion – cannot understand what has happened to him, then it is our task as critics and theatre specialists to help him. I call on you all to remember everything that he has given us and to help him find those positive things that should be preserved.[21]

In the days of the conference that followed by no means every speaker was as supportive of Meyerhold, and when Khrapchenko came to sum up the debate on the role of the director in Soviet theatre, his comments were blunt, sanctimonious, and sickeningly familiar in tone:

> Comrade Meyerhold . . . referred to his mistakes, but his admission of them was to an extent formal. The Party teaches us that it is not enough merely to admit our mistakes; we need to demonstrate their nature and their essence so that others may learn from them, above all our young people. We need to show them what such mistakes lead to, how they arise and where their true nature lies, why such mistakes are harmful and how they can be overcome. He said nothing about the nature of his mistakes, whereas he should have revealed those mistakes that led to his theatre becoming a theatre that was hostile towards the Soviet people, a theatre that was closed on the command of the Party.[22]

By this time Meyerhold was back in Leningrad, where he was directing a display of physical culture by students of the Lesgaft Institute. Khrapchenko's condemnation would have come as no surprise to him, but in any case how significant was it? How far did Meyerhold's fate depend on his making a satisfactory 'confession'? Angered as Vyshinsky was by the vociferous demonstrations of support for Meyerhold, were they in any way decisive? Recent evidence suggests that whilst the events at the conference may have hastened his actual arrest, in fact the die was already cast, and cast by Stalin himself.

IV

Following his speech at the Writers' Union in April, Fadeev had again advocated support for Meyerhold during a debate in Kiev. On returning to Moscow in the middle of May, he was summoned by Stalin and shown confessions recently extracted by the NKVD from the leading Soviet foreign correspondent, Mikhail Koltsov, and Belov, former Commander of the Moscow Military District, both of whom had denounced Meyerhold as a foreign agent and as a member of their own subversive organisation. 'Now I hope you can see who you were supporting in your speech' said Stalin. 'So, with your permission, we intend to arrest Meyerhold.'[23]

It was more than Fadeev's own life was worth to warn Meyerhold, and there is no evidence to suggest that he himself had discovered what lay in wait for him. But how else does one explain his demoralised performance at the Directors' Conference, which was quite at odds with the renewed confidence of his recent public utterances? Possibly he sensed that, regardless of the apparent easing of artistic policy, Stalin would never tolerate the return of such an undisputed leader as himself to the theatrical sphere. Certainly, this would make sense of the apprehension with which he begged the assembly to redirect its ovations towards 'our government, our Party, and towards him who inspires us artists to achieve great deeds in building a new communist society; towards him who created the constitution that in turn creates the conditions for we who have erred to correct our mistakes through our labour.'[24]

Meyerhold spent the night of 19 June 1939 in the Leningrad flat of Erast Garin and his wife, the film director Khesya Lokshina. Also present were Meyerhold's former students and actors, Yelena Tyapkina and Zosima Zlobin, together with the Director of the Lesgaft Institute. The evening started late and was convivial, with Meyerhold in good spirits despite reflecting ruefully on the Moscow conference. It was seven in the morning before he left to return to his flat on the Kharpovka Embankment in order to change before going on to rehearsal.[25]

At 9 a.m., Meyerhold was at home with his wife's sister and her husband when two NKVD officers arrived with a warrant for his arrest. The original order had been signed the previous day in Moscow by Beria. The signature was in blue pencil, indicating that the suspect was destined for execution. After a two-hour search of the flat, Meyerhold was conveyed to the Leningrad NKVD headquarters. Meanwhile, in the face of violent resistance from Zinaida Raikh, four officers carried out a search of their Moscow flat. Amongst the papers removed was the eleven-page draft of a letter of complaint about Meyerhold's treatment from Raikh to Stalin. Much as she reproached herself for this afterwards, its discovery by the NKVD

142 Meyerhold as
photographed
for the NKVD
dossier on Case
537, June 1939

obviously came too late to influence the decision to arrest Meyerhold, and
no reference is made to it in the record of his case. Whether it influenced
the treatment of Raikh is another matter. In the course of further searches of
their family dacha and Meyerhold's office at the Stanislavsky Opera Theatre
more letters to Stalin, Yezhov and Vyshinsky were discovered, but again
none was cited subsequently and their contents remain unknown.[26]

At 2 a.m. on 22 June Meyerhold left Leningrad under escort by train for
Moscow. On arrival there he was placed in solitary confinement in the 'inner
prison' of the Lubyanka. The preliminary case against Meyerhold, compiled
by NKVD Captain Golovanov and endorsed by Beria, was based on evidence
extracted from a number of other prisoners.[27] Principal amongst these were
the prominent journalist Koltsov and a young Japanese Communist Party
member, Yoshido Yoshimasu. Yoshido, who had served two terms of
imprisonment in Japan for his political activities, was arrested with an
actress, Okada Yosiko, in January 1938 whilst attempting to cross the Soviet
border on Sakhalin Island. Under interrogation in Moscow he was forced to
incriminate Meyerhold as an agent of Japanese intelligence who, amongst
other terrorist activities, was involved in plotting an assassination attempt
against Stalin when he visited the Meyerhold Theatre. At his subsequent
trial Yoshido retracted his confession, but was shot on 27 September
1939. Koltsov's confession cited Meyerhold's links with French intelligence
through the writer (and later Minister of Culture) André Malraux and Vogel,
director of the Paris review *Vu*. Koltsov also confirmed that Meyerhold had
helped an English journalist Fred Grey of *The Daily Mail* to make contact
with Rykov, the ex-Soviet Premier who with Bukharin and others had been
executed for treason following the final mass 'show trial' in March 1938. Grey
himself, whom Meyerhold and Zinaida Raikh had known as a friend since

1913, was expelled from the Soviet Union for alleged espionage in 1935.

In addition to Meyerhold's supposed links with foreign intelligence, the NKVD had forced others to testify to his involvement with the so-called Trotskyist right-wing counter-revolutionary organisation headed by Bukharin and Rykov. Specifically, it was stated that together with Trotsky, Meyerhold had defended the poet Yesenin; that he had attempted to stage Tretyakov's 'harmful' play *I Want a Child* and Erdman's *The Suicide*, 'which constitutes a counter-revolutionary slander against the Soviet power.'[28]

V

On 23 June Meyerhold was confronted by his first interrogator, Head of the NKVD Special Investigative Section, Kobulov. The greater part of the dossier on 'Case No. 537' consists of a factual record of dates, individuals, questions, answers and written statements. Normally, one would be left to infer the actual form of the interrogation to which the victim was subjected. In Meyerhold's case, however, we have the explicit account given by him in a two-part letter of appeal that he wrote to Molotov as Soviet Premier on 2 and 13 January 1940.[29] First, Meyerhold describes the effects of the 'psychological attack' that he underwent in the initial stage of his interrogation by Kobulov:

> Immediately after my arrest . . . I was plunged into the deepest depression, obsessed by the thought 'It serves me right'. I began to convince myself that the government felt that the sins I had committed had received insufficient punishment (the closure of my theatre, the dissolution of my company, the sequestration of the new theatre planned by me and under construction on Mayakovsky Square), and that I should undergo further punishment, which was now being administered through the agency of the NKVD. 'It serves me right', I convinced myself, and that 'I' split into two. The one began to search for the 'crimes' of the other, and when it failed to find them it began to make them up. In this process my interrogator proved to be a well-experienced assistant, so we set about inventing things together in close collaboration.

Meyerhold's first interrogation by Kobulov yielded a statement in which he confessed to being recruited for 'anti-Soviet' work in 1922–1923 by Mikhail Rafail, a Party worker who had met him through his involvement with the Theatre of the Revolution and later the Meyerhold Theatre.[30] As a direct consequence, all the leading Trotskyists had frequented his productions, and in 1934 Trotsky himself had facilitated the supply of military equipment for Tretyakov's *Earth Rampant*. 'In this way' – Meyerhold confessed – 'I found myself in the criminal orbit of these embittered and villainous enemies of the people.' Referring to further social contacts with other prominent political opponents of Stalin, together with Koltsov and the poet Demyan Bedny, Meyerhold stated that 'these gatherings over dinner had the undoubted aim of bringing together people of anti-Soviet inclination for the purpose of undermining the Soviet system.'

Under further interrogation on 27 June Meyerhold elaborated on his earlier confession, naming further Trotskyist contacts within the period 1923–1925 which led to his pursuing 'subversive work' in the theatre, one example being *Earth Rampant*, dedicated to 'Trotsky, first soldier of the Red Army'. He was, he said, encouraged to continue work of this kind in the years 1932–1935 by his further involvement with the 'right-wing Trotskyist organisation' which included Bukharin, Rykov, Radek, Milyutin and others. As regards his acquaintance with Fred Grey, Meyerhold admitted to re-establishing a 'criminal link' with him in 1928, though this amounted to no more than introductions to Soviet ministers (including Rykov and his wife) and a letter of reference supporting the extension of Grey's visa.

Following the second interrogation Meyerhold was returned to his cell and given a week in which to write out a full confession, naming all his confederates, known Trotskyists and other anti-Soviet individuals. In this statement Meyerhold included the prominent Party figures who had visited his theatre. Amongst them were such incriminating names as Trotsky, Bukharin, Kamenev, Smilga, Radek, Bubnov and Gamarnik – all opponents of Stalin. Perhaps ill-advisedly, he chose to include in this company the names of Molotov and Stalin himself.

Clearly this latest confession fell far short of Kobulov's requirements, so Meyerhold's interrogation was handed over to his subordinate Voronin. Working with one of two assistants (Rodos and Shvartsman) Voronin augmented the tactics of 'psychological attack' with 'physical methods' until a deposition was secured that met NKVD requirements. The first of the interrogations took place on 8 July and continued for eighteen hours, using a combination of the non-stop 'conveyer' method and actual physical torture. Meyerhold described this in his letter to Molotov:

> They beat me, a sick sixty-six-year-old man. They laid me face-down on the floor and beat the soles of my feet and my back with a rubber truncheon. When I was seated on a chair they used the same truncheon to beat my legs from above with great force, from my knees to the upper parts of my legs. And in the days that followed, when my legs were bleeding from internal haemorrhaging, they used the rubber truncheon to beat me on the red, blue and yellow bruises. The pain was so great that it was like boiling water being poured on the tenderest parts of my legs (I screamed and wept with the pain). They beat me on the back with the truncheon; they beat me about the face with blows from above – [they beat from me] all the strength of the last years of my life, . . .
> Lying face-down on the floor, I discovered the capacity to cringe, writhe and howl like a dog being whipped by its master.

Meyerhold was summoned again by his torturers on 14 July, this time for a session that lasted fourteen hours. Gradually, the whole improbable fabric of his confession and denunciation was put together: 'Whenever my imagination became exhausted my interrogators would work in pairs (Voronin and Rodos, Voronin and Shvartsman)* and draft the statements, sometimes rewriting them three or four times.'

At some point in August Meyerhold's physical state necessitated urgent treatment in the Lubyanka prison hospital. In the letter to Molotov, he wrote:

> When through lack of food (I was incapable of eating), lack of sleep (for three months),† from heart attacks at night and bouts of hysteria (floods of tears, trembling as though from fever) I became bowed and sunken, and my face was lined and aged by ten years, my interrogators became apprehensive. I was given intensive medical treatment (I was in the 'inner prison' which has good medical facilities) and put on a special diet. But that only helped to restore my appearance, my physical state; my nerves remained the same; my consciousness was still dull and confused – because the sword of Damocles was hanging over me; my interrogator threatened me constantly: 'If you refuse to write (meaning "compose"?!), we shall beat you again, leaving your head and right hand untouched but turning the rest of you into a shapeless, bloody mass of mangled flesh.'

VI

By 20 August the inquisitors had completed their work and the task of preparing the indictment was given to a new investigator, Shibkov. This process occupied the period from 22 September to 4 November, and at some point Meyerhold was moved from the Lubyanka to the nearby Butyrka Prison.‡

Following Meyerhold's arrest his family were denied any form of communication with him and were not even certain where he was imprisoned. On delivering winter clothes for him to the Butyrka in November, they were told that he had been transferred to the Lefortovo. There they were informed verbally that he had already been sentenced to 'ten years without the right of correspondence', which commonly meant execution (as it did in the case of Koltsov).

Meyerhold himself probably heard nothing from his family and was never told of Zinaida Raikh's fate. On the night of 14 July 1939 she was at home in their first-floor flat in Bryusov Lane. At about one o'clock in the morning two men entered by climbing up to the rear balcony and in a violent struggle stabbed her repeatedly with a knife. The Meyerholds' elderly housemaid was awakened by her screams but was beaten unconscious without catching sight of the intruders, one of whom escaped via the balcony whilst the other ran down the stairs, leaving traces of Zinaida's blood on the wall.

---

* Elsewhere, Meyerhold refers to a fourth interrogator Serikov.

† 'Three months' in the text. In fact, Meyerhold had been in prison for two months by this time.

‡ It is not clear whether he remained in solitary confinement.

The caretaker emerged just in time to catch sight of the two figures jumping into a large black car waiting at the corner on Gorky Street. On discovering Zinaida, he called an ambulance, but she died before reaching hospital.

Celebrated as she was, there was no announcement in the press and her burial on 18 July at the Vagankovo Cemetery was attended by only a scattering of mourners beyond her family. The word had come down 'from above' to stay clear; the actor Moskvin, a Deputy of the Supreme Soviet, told Zinaida's father 'The public refuses to bury your daughter'.[31] She went to her grave in the black velvet gown decorated with camellias that she had worn onstage as Marguerite Gautier.

Immediately following the funeral, Zinaida's son and daughter, aged twenty-one and nineteen, were given forty-eight hours to vacate the flat, despite the fact that legally it remained in Meyerhold's ownership. 'Your eviction is quite proper' was Moskvin's comment. Before they could remove the furniture, books and Meyerhold's extensive archive, they were being harried by a young woman, newly appointed to Beria's staff, who had been allocated half the accommodation, the other half going to Beria's chauffeur.

Before Zinaida's housemaid had fully recovered from the shock of the attack, she was arrested by the NKVD and questioned. She could remember nothing, but even so she found herself charged with some fictitious crime and sent off to a prison camp. Rumours circulated that the culprits were 'foreign agents', but eventually in the 1940s it was rumoured that a singer from the Bolshoi Opera and his son had been arrested and charged with the crime. Recently it has been revealed that they were in fact imprisoned in 1943, but for 'anti-Soviet propaganda and hostile activities against the Soviet state'.[32] To this day, no archive has revealed the identity of Zinaida Raikh's assailants, or for that matter the precise motive for her murder.

VII

In drawing up the indictment against Meyerhold, Shibkov did not resort to the methods of his fellow investigators, though the threat of renewed torture remained. At this stage Meyerhold attempted to modify some of his earlier incriminating statements and complained about lack of time to read through the draft in its entirety.

The principal points of his confession remained unaltered, but with one important addition. The final indictment dated 27 October stated that 'In 1930 Meyerhold was the head of the anti-Soviet Trotskyist group "Left Front", which coordinated all anti-Soviet elements in the field of the arts'. In July Meyerhold had denounced, amongst others, Ilya Ehrenburg, Boris Pasternak and Yury Olesha, and said that he had instructed Pasternak to recruit further writers with anti-Soviet views. A few days earlier, Isaac

Babel* had confessed under torture that he was the leader of the writers' section of this alleged anti-Soviet organisation within the arts, with Eisenstein responsible for the cinema and Mikhoels for the theatre, 'supported by Meyerhold'.[34] However, clearly it suited the NKVD to identify Meyerhold as the principal figure in this 'Left Front' conspiracy. Possibly, the original intention was to mount a further show trial, this time of artists, that would remove the entire Soviet avant-garde at a single stroke. However, this seems unlikely for, as Robert Conquest points out in *The Great Terror*, Stalin probably abandoned plans for further public trials soon after Beria replaced Yezhov as Head of the NKVD in December 1938, and decided that the time had come to curb the monstrous scale of the Great Purge.[35] Whatever the true explanation, none of the leading figures named by Meyerhold and Babel were ever arrested, though many other writers and artists were still to die or serve long years in the prison-camps.[36] Solomon Mikhoels, artistic director of the State Jewish Theatre, was murdered in a faked road accident in January 1948.

Whilst the show trials may have served Stalin's political purpose, they more than once caused considerable public embarrassment, most notably in March 1938 when Bukharin completely outfaced State Prosecutor Vyshinsky. Given the same opportunity, Meyerhold might well have equalled his performance, even though the final outcome would have been similarly unaffected.

On 9 November he was brought before Military Procurator Belkin, Deputy Commander of the Investigative Section Pinzura and Investigator Shibkov, for the purpose of confirming or denying what was contained in his earlier depositions. At the conclusion of a 'harsh interrogation' (apparently without further physical torture) he confirmed the essential facts admitted during the period 27 June–20 August, but asked leave to reread his statement in order to make certain additions and corrections. In a letter of appeal to the State Procurator dated 20 January 1940, he stated: 'At the interrogation on 9 November 1939 I again lost control of myself, my consciousness became blurred, I began to tremble hysterically and I was in floods of tears. . . In this state I should not have been asked to sign the statement drawn up on 9 November.'

The Military Procurator allowed Meyerhold's request, and a week later he was summoned by Shibkov to reread the statement. However, he was given no time to make any alterations and was deemed to have signed without reservation.

As far as the NKVD was concerned the case was complete, but on the same day Meyerhold was allowed to make a further statement. Written in his own hand, it is preserved in his dossier, countersigned by Junior Lieutenant Shibkov and dated 16–17 November 1939. In this courageous document Meyerhold makes no attempt to retract the confession of his own links with foreign intelligence and Trotskyist political circles. However, he

* Babel was shot on 27 January 1940.[33]

143 Meyerhold's repudiation of his confession, 16-17 November 1939

repudiates entirely all statements that might endanger the lives of others (Malraux, Ehrenburg, Pasternak, Eisenstein, Shostakovich, Olesha, Fedin, Vsevolod Ivanov and others), and rejects the idea of an anti-Soviet organisation within the arts.

Twice more Meyerhold wrote letters of appeal, first to the Military Procurator and then to the State Procurator, seeking to retract *in toto* all the confessions that he had made under torture, including those relating to his alleged links with Trotskyist elements and foreign intelligence. On 2 and 13 January he wrote the two-part letter to Molotov quoted above, describing the methods of his torturers and concluding: 'I repudiate the confessions that were beaten out of me in this way, and I beg you as Head of Government to save me and return me my freedom. I love my motherland and I will serve it with all my strength in the remaining years of my life.'

There followed one further appeal to the State Procurator on 24 January, but on the same day the indictment drawn up on 27 October was given final approval by the Military Procuracy and the date for Meyerhold's trial was set.

VIII

At its preliminary meeting on 31 January the Military Collegium of the Supreme Court of the USSR was presided over by the notorious judge Ulrikh, who had sent tens of thousands of innocent people to their death throughout the thirties. The court resolved to hear Meyerhold's case *in camera*, with no counsel for the prosecution or defence, and no witnesses. On the same day Meyerhold was formally served with the indictment and brought from the Butyrka to the cellars of the Military Collegium close to Red Square.

His trial took place the following day before Ulrikh, two military jurists, and a recording secretary. The typed summary covers five A4 pages, and the details suggest that the proceedings may have lasted rather longer than the customary ten to fifteen minutes. Meyerhold pleaded not guilty, and repeated his total denial of his earlier testimony, ascribing it to the methods used by his interrogators. His final address to the court was recorded verbatim:

> It is strange that a man of sixty-six should testify not to the truth but to what the investigation required. He lied about himself just because he was beaten with a rubber truncheon. It was then that he decided to lie and go to the stake. He is guilty of nothing, he was never a traitor to his country. He has a daughter who is a communist, whom he has brought up himself. He believes that the court will understand him and decide that he is not guilty. He has made mistakes in the field of art, and for that he was deprived of his collective. He asks the court to consider that although he is sixty-six, he still has sufficient energy and is capable of eradicating the faults that he has admitted. Recently, he has written letters to Lavrentii Pavlovich [Beria], Vyacheslav Mikhailovich [Molotov] and the State Procurator. He believes in the truth and not in God, because he believes that the truth will prevail.[37]

The court is not likely to have deliberated long over its verdict, which is recorded in hasty and crudely-formed handwriting. It concludes with the sentence: 'Meyerhold-Raikh, Vsevolod Emilievich, is to suffer the extreme form of criminal punishment by shooting, with confiscation of property. The sentence is final and not subject to appeal.'[38]

Meyerhold was shot the following day, 2 February 1940, in the cellars of the Military Collegium.

144 Confirmation of Meyerhold's execution, 2 February 1940

IX

For the next fifteen years all mention of Meyerhold's name was suppressed in the Soviet Union, and it was two years after Stalin's death in 1953, when Khrushchev became First Secretary of the Soviet Communist Party, before the first steps were taken to secure his rehabilitation. Even then, that process needed the courage of many people, principal amongst whom was Maria Valentei, Meyerhold's granddaughter. Thanks to her and others, the sentence pronounced by Ulrikh was finally quashed on 26 November 1955, and the lengthy and hazardous process of artistic rehabilitation could begin. Only now is that process nearing its completion with the full documentation of Meyerhold's work in the hands of Russian scholars, the founding of the International Meyerhold Arts Centre in Moscow,[39] and the recent retrieval of Meyerhold and Raikh's flat from the person who had occupied it continuously since its allocation to her by Beria in 1939.

Various versions of the circumstances of Meyerhold's death were given out, supported by falsified copies of his death certificate even after his legal rehabilitation. It was the summer of 1955 before the true date was named by a member of the Military Procuracy, though it was as late as November 1987 before Maria Valentei was given an actual certificate bearing both the true date and the tell-tale dash against the cause of death.[40]

The discovery of Meyerhold's grave was even more recent. On 14 June 1991 the paper *Vechernyaya Moskva* announced that a search of

KGB archives by the journalist A. Milchakov had revealed that following his execution Meyerhold's body had been cremated.[41] The ashes were deposited in 'Common Grave No. 1' in the cemetery of the Don Monastery, together with those of countless other victims from the period 1930–1942, of whom 493 have so far been identified. On a recently erected monument the inscription reads:

HERE LIE THE REMAINS OF
INNOCENT VICTIMS OF POLITICAL REPRESSION
WHO WERE TORTURED AND SHOT
IN THE YEARS 1930–1942
TO THEIR ETERNAL MEMORY

145 Common grave No. 1 in the cemetery of the Don Monastery

Conclusion

When Peter Brook staged *A Midsummer Night's Dream* in 1970 as a dazzling celebration of theatricality some critics were quick to identify the influence of Meyerhold, and the Stratford programme itself quoted his words on the spectator as the theatre's 'fourth *creator* in addition to the author, the director and the actor'. The attribution was entirely justifiable for, as Charles Marowitz wrote, Brook's radical reinterpretation of Shakespeare's over-familiar text used '. . . every scenic opportunity as a pretext for a theatrical riff'[1] – much as Meyerhold's irreverent version of *The Forest* had done forty-six years earlier, to provoke similar charges of 'aesthetic one-upmanship'.[2]

Understandably, the question of Meyerhold's influence on his contemporaries and his successors in the Soviet Union and abroad is one that has engaged a number of scholars in recent years.[3] What is more, directors as various as Joan Littlewood, Eugenio Barba, Ariane Mnouchkine, Anatoly Efros and Yury Lyubimov have all acknowledged his inspiration. And if plagiarism is a tacit form of homage, one need only cite the rash of 'Meyerholditis' that infected the Master's epigones in the 1930s, or more recent random borrowings such as the incorporation without apology of the episode of the Mayoress and her fantasy admirers in a Prospect Theatre production of *The Government Inspector* in the 1970s. Occasionally, the influence has been all too apparent, notably in the Realistic Theatre's 'in the round' configuration, 'appropriated without ceremony by Meyerhold's student Nikolai Okhlopkov' in 1932 from the unrealised project for *I Want a Child*.[4] Generally, however, such attributions are inconclusive and are prompted, as Lars Kleberg has remarked, by 'a certain comparativist mania for constructing causal connections and correspondences from insufficiently interpreted facts.'[5] In the case of Brook, Mnouchkine, Barba and others it is wiser to speak of an affinity, or kinship with Meyerhold, which expresses itself in shared objectives and, occasionally, in similar solutions.

In what does this kinship manifest itself? Is there one particular quality that serves to define Meyerhold's theatre and the theatre of those who have responded most creatively to his legacy? In an article celebrating the director's sixtieth birthday in 1934 Pavel Markov wrote:

> One might describe him as a director-poet. If there are in the theatre director-storytellers or director-rationalists, then one is entirely justified in regarding Meyerhold first and foremost as a director-poet. This is not to suggest that his poetic view is either sentimental or ineffectual. Meyerhold is a poet-satirist, a poet-pamphleteer, a poet of deep thoughts and passionate emotions. It was these qualities that impelled him to seize so avidly on the poetry of Blok.[6]

In referring to Blok, Markov is of course identifying the crucial turning-point in Meyerhold's career marked by his 1906 production of *The Fairground Booth*, a work that signalled his rejection of the sterile dogma of the symbolists, burst the confines of the proscenium arch and led him into the vertiginous domain of Harlequin. Paraphrasing the Polish philosopher Leszek Kolakowski, Jan Kott has written 'Tragedy is the theatre of priests, grotesque is the theatre of clowns.'[7] It was in the grotesque, the theatre of clowns, that Meyerhold found his true milieu and the natural expression of his world-view. To quote Harold Clurman, who observed his work at close quarters in the 1930s: 'He stamped the grotesque, the dislocated, the saturnine, the satirical grimace on his productions as hallmarks of contemporary civilization.'[8] As Jarry had done fleetingly in 1896 with *Ubu Roi*, Meyerhold rejected the theatre that counterfeited reality in favour of the theatre as an event, a here-and-now happening aimed at shattering the audience's composure. It remains a major contradiction in his career that in the decade leading up to the October Revolution he pursued this principle mostly within the sheltered confines of his studio whilst making his living by presenting ornately dressed spectacles on the Imperial stages before a public anaesthetised against shock by the pervasive lassitude of the closing years of Tsarist rule.

In invoking Blok as Meyerhold's exemplar, Markov is alluding to an even wider affinity than that suggested by their collaboration on *The Fairground Booth*. For as a poet of the theatre Meyerhold embodied a combination of qualities that was particular to Blok's verse: the sardonic, the lyrical, the poignant, the allusive, the vivid, the brutal, the disjunctive, the strident – all held in control by the rhythmical, the musical. In Béatrice Picon-Vallin's words, for Meyerhold music became 'the syntax of a language that is made ever more complex . . . The musical composition . . . serves to establish the relationship between gesture, space, colour, sound, dialogue, light, making a unity of them while still allowing each to maintain its own means of artistic expression . . .'[9]

It is easy enough to imagine how this integration of all the expressive means at the director's disposal was achieved within the strict discipline of such early productions as *Hedda Gabler* or *Sister Beatrice* – easy, too, to understand the reluctance of a company of actors to submit for long to such discipline at the cost of their creative independence. But there persists a view of Meyerhold as a dictatorial director, guilty of the 'reduction of actors to dehumanised puppets',[10] that is loosely employed to characterise his whole career. If this were the case, how does one explain his devotion from the early Petersburg years to the *commedia*, to the art of the *cabotin*, the strolling player, the juggler, the circus clown? How does one explain the central position of improvisation in his training programme? It is true that both before the Revolution at the Borodin Street Studio and from 1921 at his Moscow Theatre Workshops he schooled his students in strict spatial and rhythmical discipline, latterly through the seemingly mechanistic system of Biomechanics. Yet this was merely the means to an end, and the end was an ever greater precision of self-expression, all too necessary on the perilous construction of *The Magnanimous Cuckold*, the narrow spiral ramp of *The Forest*, the whirling revolve of *The Warrant* or the tiny truck-stage of *The Government Inspector*. Critic after critic bears witness to the gestural dexterity, the vocal invention, the comic virtuosity of Ilinsky, Babanova, Garin, Zharov, Martinson, Zaichikov, Tyapkina and others. Equally, those who witnessed Meyerhold's own 'demonstrations' to his actors describe a versatility amounting to genius that was inspiring to the gifted but enough to reduce the ordinary performer to paralysis. It was the lesser members of his company (in the latter years, sadly the majority) that he tended to shape in his own image.

Nor was his treatment of his actors consistent. As the unhappy fate of Maria Babanova shows, Meyerhold's artistic judgement was all too often distorted by his wilful promotion of Zinaida Raikh, an actress of distinctive talents but of limited range, who needed all the preferential attention that he gave to her.[11] Devoted as he was to the young and inexperienced, Meyerhold was frequently irrational and intemperate in his handling of established stars, and his theatre became the poorer for it.

Similarly, at a time when dramatists were struggling to find their voices within the new Soviet reality, Mayakovsky and Erdman were the only two to be accorded full respect by Meyerhold, whilst Bulgakov, the greatest exponent of the grotesque, kept a haughty distance from him. Apart from *The Magnanimous Cuckold* and *The Warrant*, Meyerhold's finest achievements in his mature years were his reinterpretations of the classics: *Masquerade*, *The Forest* and, outstandingly, *The Government Inspector*. More than any other works, it was these that called on the full range of his remarkable erudition and scenic invention, and presented the greatest challenge to his audience's preconceptions.

These productions exemplified Meyerhold's use of cinematic techniques: montage, fast cutting, slow motion, close-ups, freezes, and flashbacks.[12] As early as 1907 in his treatment of the episodic text of *Spring Awakening* Meyerhold had revealed an intuitive control of the staccato rhythm that in accelerated form was to energise the cinema of Eisenstein and other early Soviet film directors. When Sergei Radlov saw *The Government Inspector* and exclaimed in astonishment 'What is this – *Caligari* run in slow motion by some lunatic projectionist?', he was recognising the theatre's affinity with its sister art. Yet the debt was mutual: with Eisenstein, Yutkevich, Room, Ekk, Trauberg himself and others in mind, Grigory Kozintsev claimed in 1936 '. . . the real pupils of Meyerhold are working not in the theatre but in the cinema . . . Soviet cinematography has learnt far more than the Soviet theatre from the inspired work of Meyerhold.'[13] In an intriguing essay published in 1970 Leonid Kozlov speculates that Meyerhold was in fact the model for Eisenstein's portrayal of Ivan the Terrible and then concludes:

> Was not Eisenstein's film, *Ivan the Terrible*, – with its unbelievable richness in visual culture, with its special plasticity of the actor's art, with the enormous amount of, as it seems, inconceivable innovations and solutions for the art of film – was not his film a resurrection of the Meyerholdian heritage, of Meyerhold's experiences anew and on a new level? And is not the so-called, and as yet unexplained, 'theatricality' of this work further explained by the fact that Eisenstein's film art here absorbed Meyerhold's theatre, by making it harmonize with the laws of cinema?[14]

Again, it was Kozintsev who said: 'It is not only the footlights that he shattered nor only the curtain that he tore down; Meyerhold strove to obliterate the boundary that separates the theatre from life.'[15] In this he was successful both in the literal, architectonic sense and in the more elusive sense of infiltrating the audience's hidden emotions: its guilt, its fears, its appetites, its desires. The more bare the stage, the more ambiguous the characterisation, the more pervasive the music – the more the spectator's imagination was allowed free rein and the more the text eluded the grasp of the censor. In vain did the critics struggle to pin down the 'meaning' that Meyerhold discerned in Erdman or Gogol or Olesha: the meaning lurked somewhere in the mind of that 'fourth creator', evading the categories in which orthodoxy sought to confine it. This, finally, is the sense in which Meyerhold was the supreme director-poet – and as much as anything it may explain the fate that finally engulfed him.

Notes

The following abbreviations are used for works cited frequently in the footnotes:

V. E. Meierkhold – Statyi, pisma, rechi, besedy (Moscow, 1969, vols I and II)
  – *Meyerhold I and II*.
V. E. Meierkhold – Perepiska 1869-1939 (Moscow, 1976) – *Perepiska*.
Braun, E. (trans. and ed.), *Meyerhold on Theatre* (London–New York, 1969) – *Braun*.
Valentei, M. and others (ed.), *Vstrechi s Meierkholdom* (Moscow, 1967) – *Vstrechi*.
Rudnitsky, K., *Rezhisser Meierkhold* (Moscow, 1969) – *Rudnitsky*.
Volkov, N., *Meierkhold* (Moscow–Leningrad, 1929, vols. I and II) – *Volkov I and II*.

Chapter One Apprentice Years

1. The details of Meyerhold's early years are taken from Nikolai Volkov's biography, and from A. Gladkov, *Gody uchenia Vsevoloda Meierkholda* (Saratov, 1979).
2. *Volkov I*, p. 54.
3. Ibid., p. 57.
4. *Vstrechi*, p. 26.
5. See C. Schuler, 'Anna Brenko and the Pushkin Theatre: Moscow's first Art Theatre?' in *Theatre Survey*, vol. 33, no.1, pp. 85–105.
6. Ibid., p. 70.
7. See T. Makagonova, 'Arkhiv V. E. Meierkholda' in *Zapiski otdela rukopisey*, vypusk 42 (Moscow, 1981), pp. 128–9.
8. Ibid., pp. 88–9.
9. K. S. Stanislavsky, *Sobranie sochinenii* (Moscow, 1954–1961), vol. V, pp. 174–5.
10. *Perepiska*, p. 21.
11. *Meyerhold I*, p. 119 (*Braun*, p. 29).
12. Ibid., p. 120 (Ibid., p. 30).
13. N. Efros, *Moskovskiy khudozhestvenny teatr. 1898–1923*. (Moscow–Petrograd, 1924), p. 224.
14. *The Seagull*, Act One.
15. *Meyerhold I*, p. 75.
16. Rudnitsky, p. 17.
17. A. Gladkov, op. cit., p. 165.
18. Ibid., p. 164.

19. *Perepiska*, p. 29.
20. K. S. Stanislavsky, *Moya zhizn v iskusstve*, (Moscow, 1962), pp. 306–7 (this passage does not appear in the English edition).
21. *Meyerhold I*, p. 73.
22. See the exchange of letters between Meyerhold and Stanislavsky in January 1902 (*Perepiska*, pp. 35–7).
23. V. I. Nemirovich-Danchenko, *Teatralnoe nasledie*, vol. II (Moscow, 1954), p. 225.
24. See J. Benedetti, *Stanislavski* (London, 1990), pp. 118–19.
25. See letter to Chekhov, after 20 February 1902 in V. I. Nemirovich-Danchenko, *Izbrannye pisma*, vol. 1 (Moscow, 1979), p. 245.
26. *Volkov I*, pp. 138–9.
27. A. Gladkov, op. cit. pp. 184–5.
28. Quoted in *Teatralnaya zhizn*, 1990, no. 2, p. 22.
29. Quoted in *Rudnitsky*, p. 15.
30. A. Kugel, *Profili teatra* (Moscow, 1929), p. 66.
31. K. Rudnitsky, *Meierkhold* (Moscow, 1981), pp. 55–6.
32. *Perepiska*, p. 45.
33. For a complete list of all Meyerhold's productions see *Meyerhold II*, pp. 598–610 (a translation of this list from 1905 onwards is contained in M. Hoover, *Meyerhold – The Art of Conscious Theater* (University of Massachusetts Press, 1974).
34. See I. Pevtsov, 'Beseda ob aktere' in S. Tsimbal, *Tvorcheskaya sudba Pevtsova* (Leningrad–Moscow, 1957), pp. 213–14.
35. *Perepiska A. P. Chekhova i O. L. Knipper*, vol. II (Moscow, 1936), p. 371.
36. *Perepiska*, p. 39.
37. For an account of Meyerhold's first season in Kherson see N. Zvenigorodskaya, 'V nachale bylo . . .' in *Teatr*, 1990, no. 1, pp. 53–8.
38. Quoted by Alexander Gladkov, 'Meierkhold govorit' in *Tarusskie stranitsy* (Kaluga, 1961), p. 302.
39. See K. Rudnitsky, *Russkoe rezhisserskoe iskusstvo 1898–1907* (Moscow, 1989), pp. 300 ff.
40. Quoted, K. Rudnitsky, *Meierkhold*, cit., p. 60.
41. Ibid., p. 63.
42. Ibid., p. 62.
43. Cf. *Rudnitsky*, pp. 33–4; E. Welsford, *The Fool – His Social and Literary History* (London, 1935), pp. 305 ff.
44. 'Tovarishchestvo novoy dramy' in *Vesy*, 1904, no. 4, p. 37.
45. See J. West, *Russian Symbolism* (London, 1970), pp. 137–46.
46. Remizov, op. cit., pp. 38–9.
47. N. Zvenigorodskaya, 'Igra kolokolov' in *Mir iskusstv: almanakh* (Moscow, 1991), p. 484.
48. *Perepiska*, p. 45. For an expanded version of this analysis see *Braun*, pp. 28–9.
49. 'Vishnevy sad' in *Vesy*, 1904, no. 2, pp. 47–8.
50. See E. Polotskaya, 'Chekhov i Meierkhold' in *Literaturnoe nasledstvo (vol. LXVIII) – Chekhov* (Moscow, 1960), pp. 432–3.
51. Y. Bolotin, 'Provintsialnaya letopis' in *Teatr i iskusstvo*, 1904, no. 8, p. 178.
52. *Perepiska*, p. 43.
53. Ibid., p. 45.
54. Ibid., p. 48.
55. Unsigned review in *Tiflissky listok*, 28 September 1904, p. 2.

56. *Teatr i iskusstvo*, 1904, no. 42, pp. 749–50.
57. Quoted in *Mir iskusstv*, cit., p. 485.
58. Ibid., p. 490.

Chapter Two The Theatre-Studio

1. See K. Rudnitsky, *Russkoe rezhisserskoe iskusstvo 1898–1907*, cit., p. 311.
2. V. Nemirovich-Danchenko, *Teatralnoe nasledie*, cit., p. 283.
3. K. Stanislavsky, op. cit., pp. 337–41.
4. Quoted in M. Stroeva, *Rezhisserskie iskania Stanislavskogo 1898–1917* (Moscow, 1973), p. 148.
5. Quoted in K. Rudnitsky, *Russkoe rezhisserskoe iskusstvo 1898–1907*, cit., p. 315. For Maeterlinck's view see E. Braun, *The Director and the Stage* (London, 1982), p. 40.
6. K. Rudnitsky, *Russkoe rezhisserskoe iskusstvo 1898–1907*, cit., p. 314.
7. K. Stanislavsky, op. cit., p. 341. (In *My Life in Art*, London, 1962, pp. 429–30).
8. See letter to Stanislavsky, 8–10 June 1905 in V. I. Nemirovich-Danchenko, *Izbrannye pisma*, vol. 1, cit., pp. 391–412.
9. See *Rudnitsky*, pp. 48–9.
10. See *Meyerhold II*, pp. 30–4 (*Braun*, pp. 175–80); L. Freidkina, *Dni i gody V. I. Nemirovicha-Danchenko* (Moscow, 1962), pp. 207–10, 352 ff., 462.
11. Quoted in *Rudnitsky*, p. 49.
12. 'Nenuzhnaya pravda', *Mir iskusstva*, 1902 (vol. VII), no. 4, pp. 67–74.
13. See *Meyerhold I*, pp. 123–8 (*Braun*, pp. 34–9).
14. Ibid., p. 107 (Ibid., p. 41).
15. Ibid., p. 110 (Ibid., p. 45).
16. See C. Gray, *The Great Experiment – Russian Art 1863–1922* (London, 1962), Chapters 1–2.
17. *Meyerhold I*, pp. 108–9 (*Braun*, p. 43).
18. Ibid., p. 109, (footnote, loc. cit.).
19. Ibid., pp. 109–10 (Ibid., p. 44).
20. M. Pozharskaya, *Russkoe teatralno-dekoratsionnoe iskusstvo* (Moscow, 1970), p. 159.
21. Meyerhold spoke little or no French before he visited Paris in 1913 (see *Perepiska*, p. 153). However, Maeterlinck's 'Le Tragique quotidien' was published in Russian translation in *Mir iskusstva*, 1899, no. 2. *Le Trésor des humbles* appeared in its entirety in 1901 (translated by L. Vilkina as *Blazhenstvo dushi*), and was followed in 1903 by the first of six volumes of his complete writings, (Moscow, 1903–1909). Amongst the early critical writings devoted to him were: Hannibale Pastore, 'Maurice Maeterlinck', *Vestnik inostrannoy literatury*, 1904, September; Adolphe van Bever, *Maurice Maeterlinck – Kritiko-biografichesky ocherk* (St Petersburg, 1904).
22. See E. Braun, *The Director and the Stage*, cit., Chapter 3.
23. The passages are quoted from *Le Trésor des humbles* (Paris, 1896, 4th edition), pp. 181 ff.
24. *Meyerhold I*, p. 133 (*Braun*, p. 54).
25. Loc. cit.
26. Ibid., pp. 135–6 (*Braun*, p.56).
27. 'Po dorogam iskanii' in *Vstrechi*, p. 33.
28. Quoted in Yoko Chiba, 'Sada Yacco and Kawakami: Performers of *Japonisme*' in *Modern Drama*, vol. XXXV, no. 1 (March 1992), pp. 35–53. For a further

account of Sada Yacco and Kawakami's tour see L. C. Pronko, *Theater East and West* (University of California, 1967), pp. 120–3

29. Quoted in *Volkov II*, p. 51.
30. See *Tvorcheskoe nasledie Vs. E. Meierkholda* (Moscow, 1978), p. 121. Meyerhold's first direct experience of Kabuki theatre was in 1930 when he saw Tokujiro Tsutsui's troupe in Paris (see G. Banu, 'Meyerhold et le modèle du théâtre asiatique' in *Revue d'Histoire du Théâtre*, 1981, no. 2, pp. 121 ff).
31. *Meyerhold II*, p. 84.
32. *Meyerhold I*, p. 244.
33. Ibid., p. 245.
34. K. Stanislavsky, *Sobranie sochinenii*, cit., vol. VII, p. 325.
35. *Rudnitsky*, p. 49.
36. The dating of these dress rehearsals at the beginning of October in *The Theatre of Meyerhold* was incorrect. No first-hand account gives a precise date, but it seems likely that they took place shortly before 24 October.
37. Quoted in *Rudnitsky*, p. 62.
38. K. S. Stanislavsky, *Moya zhizn v iskusstve*, cit., p. 346.
39. See I. Pevtsov, op. cit., p. 227.
40. Quoted in M. Stroeva, op. cit., pp. 178–9.
41. Under the pen-name 'Avrelii' in *Vesy*, 1906, no. 1, p. 74.
42. Dated 31 January 1906 in *Perepiska*, pp. 60–1.

Chapter Three From Symbolism to the Grotesque

1. A. Gladkov, 'Meierkhold govorit', *Novy mir*, 1961, no. 8, p. 226.
2. Quoted by Meyerhold in letter dated 6 January 1906 (*Perepiska*, p. 59).
3. *Volkov I*, pp. 217–20.
4. *Perepiska*, p. 63.
5. See *Meyerhold I*, pp. 95–6.
6. *Perepiska*, p. 63.
7. G. Fuchs, *Die Schaubühne der Zukunft* (Berlin, undated but published 1904–1905).
8. See *Volkov I*, pp. 240–41.
9. Fuchs, op. cit., pp. 38–9.
10. Ibid., pp. 15–16.
11. Ibid., pp. 46–56.
12. Ibid., p. 66.
13. Ibid., pp. 72–3.
14. Ibid., pp. 77–9.
15. Ibid., p. 105.
16. For accounts of the Munich Künstlertheater see G. Fuchs, *Die Revolution des Theatres* (Munich–Leipzig, 1909, pp. 236–91; W. Fuerst and S. Hume, *Twentieth-Century Stage Decoration* (New York, 1929 and 1967), vol. I, pp. 45–8.
17. See *Tvorcheskoe nasledie . . .*, cit., pp. 125–6.
18. *Meyerhold I*, p. 104.
19. Ibid., p. 244.
20. Loc. cit.
21. Yu. Krasovsky, *Nekotorye problemy teatralnoy pedagogiki V. E. Meierkholda 1905–07* (Leningrad, 1981), p. 35.
22. Quoted in L. Freidkina, 'U istokov formalizma v russkom teatre', *Teatr*, 1937, no. 6, p. 72.

23. Letter (undated) quoted in D. Talnikov, *Komissarzhevskaya* (Moscow–Leningrad, 1939), p. 268.
24. Ye. Znosko-Borovsky, *Russky teatr nachala XX veka* (Prague, 1925), p. 271.
25. See *Perepiska*, pp. 73 ff.
26. Ibid., p. 367.
27. Yartsev's description, published in 1907, was quoted in full by Meyerhold in his *O Teatre*, Petersburg, 1913 (see *Meyerhold I*, pp. 239–42, *Braun*, pp. 65–8).
28. A. Kugel, 'Teatralnye zametki', *Teatr i iskusstvo*, Petersburg, 1906, no. 48, pp. 748-50.
29. G. Fuchs, *Die Schaubühne der Zukunft*, cit., p. 76.
30. See A. Kugel, op. cit., pp. 731-2; A. Rostislavov, 'Prizraki na stsene', *Teatr i iskusstvo*, 1906, no. 49, p. 768.
31. A. Matskin, *Portrety i nablyudenia* (Moscow, 1973), p. 201.
32. N. Berdyayev, *Sub specie aeternitatis (1900–1906)* St Petersburg, 1907, pp. 31, 32 (quoted in *Rudnitsky*, p. 78).
33. For accounts of these productions see E. Braun, *The Director and the Stage*, cit., pp. 87–8, 101–2.
34. Ibid., p. 247.
35. A. Tairov, *Zapiski rezhissera* (Moscow, 1921), p. 27.
36. See *Braun*, pp. 68–9; V. Verigina, *Vospominania* (Leningrad, 1974), p. 92.
37. *Braun*, p. 69.
38. *Meyerhold I*, p. 248.
39. Ibid., p. 55.
40. Ye. Znosko-Borovsky, op. cit., pp. 281–2.
41. K. Rudnitsky, *Meierkhold*, cit., p. 110.
42. 'Khudozhniki v Teatre V. F. Komissarzhevskoy', *Alkonost*, Book I (St Petersburg, 1911), p. 129.
43. See *Meyerhold I*, p. 248.
44. 'Moskovskie teatry – spektakli Peterburgskogo Dramaticheskogo teatra', *Zolotoe runo*, 1907, no. 7–9, p. 150.
45. T. Makagonova, op. cit., p. 145.
46. The following contain English translations of *Balaganchik*: C. Kisch, *Alexander Blok: Prophet of Revolution* (London, 1960); F. Reeve, *An Anthology of Russian Plays*, vol. II (New York, 1963).
47. See A. Blok, *Sobranie sochinenii v 8 tomakh* (Moscow–Leningrad, 1960–1963), vol. I, pp. 210, 227, 277, 287, 322.
48. *Meyerhold I*, pp. 228, 250 (*Braun*, pp. 70–1, 141).
49. Quoted in *Volkov I*, p. 280.
50. A. Deich, *Golos pamyati* (Moscow, 1966), p. 62.
51. *Vstrechi*, p. 40.
52. M. Fokin, *Protiv techenia* (Leningrad–Moscow, 1962), pp. 219–20.
53. *Vstrechi*, p.41.
54. *Rudnitsky*, pp. 92–3.
55. 'Moi portrety. Meierkhold', *Teatr i muzyka*, 1923, no. 1–2, pp. 427–8.
56. Letter to Alexander Gippius (20 January 1907) in Blok, op. cit., vol. VIII, p. 176.
57. *Meyerhold I*, pp. 208–9.
58. *Obozrenie teatrov*, 1907, no. 39, p. 6.
59. Blok, op. cit., vol. IV, p. 425.
60. See A. Bely, *Arabeski* (Moscow, 1911), pp. 311–12.
61. Blok, op. cit., vol. VII, p. 13.

62. See M. Beketova, *Aleksandr Blok* (Petersburg, 1922), p. 105.
63. *Rudnitsky*, p. 91.
64. *The Banquet Years* (London, 1959), p. 30.
65. *Meyerhold I*, pp. 226–7 (*Braun*, pp. 137–9).
66. Loc. cit.
67. A. Matskin, op. cit., p. 209.
68. See especially *Meyerhold II*, pp. 321 ff.
69. *Meyerhold I*, p. 251 (*Braun*, pp. 71–2).
70. L. Simonson, *The Stage is Set* (Revised and amended edition, New York, 1963), pp. 358–9.
71. See W. Volbach, *Adolphe Appia. Prophet of the Modern Theatre* (Wesleyan University Press, 1968), pp. 82–93.
72. Quoted in *Volkov I*, p. 284.
73. Quoted in M. Stroeva, op. cit., pp. 219–20.
74. See *Perepiska*, pp. 82–4.
75. *Meyerhold I*, pp. 105–42 (*Braun*, pp. 23–64).
76. See K. Rudnitsky, in *Tvorcheskoe nasledie*, cit., pp. 187–8 and *Volkov I*, pp. 304 ff.
77. See *Volkov I*, pp. 305, 308, 311.
78. For Meyerhold's impressions of Reinhardt's work see *Meyerhold I*, pp. 162–6; *Perepiska*, pp. 85–6.
79. See K. Rudnitsky, *Meierkhold*, cit., p. 129, and M. Slonim, *From Chekhov to the Revolution* (New York, 1962), pp. 164–7.
80. N. Volkova (ed.), *Vstrechi s proshlym – sbornik TsGALI* (Moscow, 1972), pp. 321-2.
81. Blok, op. cit., vol. V, pp. 194–5.
82. Quoted in *Volkov I*, p. 332.
83. *Obozrenie teatrov*, St Petersburg, 1907, no. 200, p. 14.
84. *Tvorcheskoe nasledie . . .* , cit., p. 227.
85. Valentina Verigina in *Vstrechi*, p. 44.
86. In *O Teatre* (*Meyerhold I*, pp. 237–57).
87. J. Leyda, *Kino* (London, 1960), p. 82.
88. *Volkov I*, pp. 334–5.
89. Blok, op. cit., vol. V, p. 200.
90. Quoted in *Alkonost*, (St Petersburg, 1911), Kniga I, p. 70.
91. Quoted in *Volkov I*, p. 335.
92. Ibid., pp. 341–3.
93. Ibid., p. 344.
94. *Meyerhold I*, p. 252.
95. *Volkov I*, pp. 345–6.
96. *Moskovsky ezhenedelnik*, 1907, no. 48, pp. 33–4.
97. Quoted in *Volkov I*, p. 346.
98. *Rudnitsky*, p. 109.
99. *Perepiska*, p. 108.
100. V. Verigina, op. cit., pp. 125–6, 144–51.
101. See A. Deich, op. cit., p. 58; *Meyerhold I*, p. 97.
102. *Perepiska*, p. 111.

Chapter Four Dapertutto Reborn

1. *Teatr. Kniga o Novom teatre*, St Petersburg, 1908. (*Meyerhold I*, pp. 105–42; *Braun*, pp. 23–64).
2. *Meyerhold I*, p. 141 (*Braun*, p. 62).
3. Ibid., p. 142 (ibid., p. 63–4).
4. *Peterburgskaya gazeta*, 24 April 1908, p. 2.
5. See *Rudnitsky*, pp. 114–15; V. Telyakovsky, *Vospominania* (Leningrad–Moscow, 1965), p. 167.
6. For a vivid eye-witness evocation of the Alexandrinsky Theatre at this time see Nikolai Petrov, *50 i 500* (Moscow, 1960), pp. 74–93.
7. Included in *Meyerhold I*, pp. 170–4.
8. Loc. cit.
9. See *Meyerhold I*, p. 338.
10. See *Volkov II*, p. 26.
11. I. Osipov in *Obozrenie teatrov*, 1908, no. 535, pp. 5–6.
12. *Vstrechi*, p. 48.
13. See *Rudnitsky*, pp. 117–20.
14. See *Perepiska*, p. 21.
15. *Volkov II*, pp. 40–1.
16. Ibid., pp. 83–4.
17. Ibid., pp. 35–9.
18. Letter to Lyubov Gurevich, *Perepiska*, p. 122.
19. See *Volkov II*, pp. 43–50; *Perepiska*, p. 123.
20. *Meyerhold I*, pp. 167–9.
21. *The London Mercury*, October 1935, vol. 32, no. 192, p. 537.
22. See K. Rudnitsky, *Meierkhold*, cit., pp. 153–4, 160.
23. *Meyerhold I*, pp. 143–61 (*Braun*, pp. 80–98).
24. Quoted from the English translation – R. Corrigan and M. Dirks (trans.) *Music and the Art of the Theatre* (University of Miami, 1962), pp. 14 ff.
25. I. Glikman, *Meierkhold i muzykalny teatr* (Leningrad, 1989), chapter 1.
26. R. Corrigan and M. Dirks, op. cit., pp. 17-18.
27. L. Ivanova, *Vospominania: kniga ob ottse* (Moscow, 1992), pp. 39–40.
28. *Meyerhold I*, p. 160 (*Braun*, p. 97).
29. 'V. E. Meierkhold i russky operny impressionizm' in *Istoria sovetskogo teatra – tom pervy* (Leningrad, 1933), p. 310.
30. *Meyerhold I*, p. 199.
31. A. Gozenpud, *Russky operny teatr mezhdu dvukh revolyutsiy: 1905–1917* (Leningrad, 1975), p. 277.
32. *Braun*, pp. 95–6.
33. *Meyerhold I*, pp. 198–9.
34. A. Gozenpud, op. cit., p. 277.
35. *Vstrechi*, p. 73.
36. *Tarusskie stranitsy*, cit., p. 307.
37. *Rech*, 5 November 1909.
38. A. Gozenpud, op. cit., p. 282.
39. 'V.S.' in *Teatr i iskusstvo*, 1909, no. 45, pp. 793–4.
40. 'Elgur' in *Obozrenie teatrov*, 31 October 1909, p. 7.
41. *Vstrechi*, p. 74.
42. Ye. Znosko-Borovsky, op. cit., p. 337.

43. For accounts of the Ancient Theatre see E. Stark, *Starinny teatr* (St Petersburg, 1922); Ye. Znosko-Borovsky, op. cit., pp. 333–43.
44. *Meyerhold I*, pp. 189–91. For Yevreinov's response to Meyerhold's criticism and for an account of the relationship between the two men see T. Pearson, 'Meyerhold and Evreinov: "Originals" at Each Other's Expense' in *New Theatre Quarterly*, vol. VIII, no. 32, pp. 321–32.
45. For a further account of *The Adoration of the Cross* see V. Pyast, *Vstrechi* (Moscow, 1929), pp. 169–80.
46. V. Shcherbakov, 'Po obe storony maski' in *Teatr*, 1990, no. 1, p. 64.
47. Ye. Znosko-Borovsky, op. cit., pp. 311–12.
48. V. Shcherbakov, op. cit., p. 64.
49. *Volkov II*, pp. 237–8.
50. See especially A. Matskin, op. cit., pp. 284 ff.; M. Davydova, *Ocherki istorii russkogo teatralno-dekoratsionnogo iskusstva XVIII – nachala XX vekov* (Moscow, 1974), pp. 164–8.
51. 'Die Abenteuer der Sylvester Nacht', *Fantasiestücke in Callot's Manier (Sämtliche Werke*, Munich–Leipzig, 1908, vol. I, pp. 339–75).
52. V. Shcherbakov, op. cit., p. 64.
53. *Meyerhold I*, p. 228 (*Braun*, pp. 140–1).
54. Ye. Znosko-Borovsky, op. cit., p. 303.
55. Quoted in I. Shneiderman, 'V.E. Meierkhold v rabote nad poslednem vozobnovleniem *Maskarada*' in A. Yufit (ed.), *Nauka o teatre* (Leningrad, 1975), p. 196.
56. In 'K postanovke *Don Zhuana* Moliera' (1910) – *Meyerhold I*, pp. 192–7 (*Braun*, pp. 98–103).
57. Loc. cit.
58. See L. Simonson, op. cit., pp. 204–16; K. Mantzius, *A History of Theatrical Art*, trans. L. von Cossel (London, 1905), vol. IV, pp. 100–4.
59. *Vstrechi*, p. 79.
60. See A. Kugel, 'Teatralnie zametki', *Teatr i iskusstvo*, 1910, no. 47, pp. 901–3; A. Benois, 'Balet v Aleksandrinke', *Rech*, 19 November 1910, p. 3.
61. *Meyerhold I*, pp. 195–6 (*Braun*, pp. 102–3).
62. Loc. cit.
63. Ye. Znosko-Borovsky, op. cit., p. 308.
64. See Ya. Malyutin, *Aktery moego pokolenia* (Leningrad–Moscow, 1959), pp. 112–13; *Aleksandr Yakovlevich Golovin – Vstrechi i vpechatlenia* . . . (Leningrad–Moscow, 1960), pp. 328–9.
65. N. Khodotov, *Blizkoe – dalekoe* (Leningrad–Moscow, 1962), p. 251.
66. *Meyerhold I*, p. 221 (*Braun*, pp. 133–4).
67. Ibid., pp. 218–19 (Ibid., p. 131).
68. Ibid., p. 221 (Ibid., p. 133).
69. See A. Matskin, op. cit., pp. 244–5, *Rudnitsky*, p. 139.
70. Op. cit., p. 3.
71. S. Volkonsky, *Chelovek na stsene* (St Petersburg, 1912), p. 78.

Chapter Five A Double Life

1. *Birzhevye vedomosti*, 1911, no. 12107.
2. Loc. cit.
3. Quoted in *Volkov II*, p. 165.
4. *Novoe vremya*, 6 January 1911.

5. *Volkov II*, p. 163.
6. *Vstrechi*, p. 75.
7. *Braun*, p. 82.
8. A. Golovin, op. cit. p. 84.
9. *Braun*, p. 106.
10. See I. Glikman, op. cit., pp. 139–40.
11. A. Golovin, op. cit., p. 262.
12. *Braun*, p. 106.
13. See A. Golovin, op. cit., p. 163.
14. Quoted in A. Gozenpud, op. cit., p. 299.
15. Ibid., p. 305.
16. M. Fokin, op. cit., pp. 500–1.
17. *Birzhevye vedomosti*, 1912, no. 12721.
18. *Studia*, 1912, no. 14.
19. *Meierkhold*, cit., p. 179.
20. M. Fokin, op. cit., pp. 501–3.
21. See A. Gozenpud, op. cit., p. 307; I. Glikman, op cit., pp. 176–7.
22. See V. Verigina, op. cit., p. 145.
23. *Peterburgskiy listok*, 11 February 1913.
24. Quoted in I. Glikman, op. cit., p. 181.
25. A. Golovin, op. cit., p. 127.
26. Quoted in I. Glikman, op. cit., p. 180.
27. Quoted in *Rudnitsky*, p. 162.
28. A. Gladkov, 'Meierkhold govorit', *Neva*, 1966, no. 2, p. 204.
29. *Yezhegodnik Imperatorskikh teatrov*, St Petersburg, 1913, vypusk IV, p. 136.
30. I. Glikman, op. cit., chapter 4.
31. *Birzhevye vedomosti*, 1913, no. 13407.
32. Diary entry 20 April 1913 (Blok, op. cit., vol. VII, p. 239).
33. Quoted in *Volkov II*, p. 273.
34. *Novoe vremya*, 19 February 1913.
35. *Braun*, pp. 144–5.
36. V. Verigina, op. cit., pp. 171–90.
37. *Braun*, pp. 119 ff.
38. Ibid., p. 124.
39. *Volkov II*, p. 291.
40. *Perepiska*, pp. 154–6.
41. Reprinted in A. Lunacharsky, *O Teatre i dramaturgii*, vol. II (Moscow, 1958), p. 165.
42. For a detailed account of *La Pisanelle* and Meyerhold's visit to Paris see G. Abensour, 'Meyerhold à Paris', *Cahiers du Monde Russe et Soviétique*, 1964, vol. V, no. 1, pp. 5–31.
43. For first-hand accounts of Meyerhold's Studio see A. Smirnova, 'V studii na Borodinskoy'; A. Gripich, 'Uchitel stseny' in *Vstrechi*, pp. 84–145; V. Verigina, op. cit., pp. 196–202, 205–14.
44. *Lyubov k trem apelsinam, Zhurnal Doktora Dapertutto*, 1915, no. 1–3, p. 140.
45. *Vstrechi*, p. 128.
46. *Lyubov k trem apelsinam*, 1914, no. 1, pp. 61–2.
47. Ibid., 1914, no. 4–5, p. 90.
48. For a fuller account of this presentation and other documentation of the Studio's activities see *Braun*, pp. 146–56.

49. *Vstrechi*, p. 93.
50. *Perepiska*, pp. 154, 388. See also B. Picon-Vallin, 'Meyerhold, Prokofiev et *L'Amour des trois oranges*' in *L'Avant-scène Opéra*, July 1990, no. 133, pp. 20–9.
51. A. Blok, op. cit., vol. IV, p. 576.
52. *Sovremennik*, 1914, June, pp. 120–1.
53. See V. Verigina, 'Vospominania o Bloke', *Uchenie zapiski Tartuskogo gosudarstvennogo universiteta*, vypusk 104 (Tartu, 1961), pp. 361–3.
54. *Sovremennik*, loc. cit.
55. A. Gripich, 'Uchitel stseny' in *Vstrechi*, p. 137.
56. *Meyerhold II*, p. 18.
57. For Meyerhold's comments on this project see *Lyubov k trem apelsinam*, 1915, no. 4-7, pp. 208–11 (*Braun*, pp. 151–3).
58. *Teatralnaya zhizn*, 1990, no. 2, pp. 22–3.
59. *Braun*, pp. 134–5.
60. J. Leyda, op. cit., p. 58.
61. *Teatralnaya gazeta*, 31 May 1915, p. 7.
62. A. Levitsky, *Rasskazy o kinematografe* (Moscow, 1964), p. 85.
63. Ibid., pp. 78–106.
64. J. Leyda, op. cit., p. 59.
65. Ibid., p. 81.
66. S. Ginzburg, *Kinematografia dorevolyutsionnoy Rossii* (Moscow, 1963), p. 303.
67. S. Yutkevich, 'V. E. Meierkhold i teoria kinorezhissury', *Iskusstvo kino*, Moscow, 1975, no. 8, p. 75. For an account of *The Picture of Dorian Gray* by Meyerhold see *Iz istorii kino*, no. 6 (Moscow, 1965) – *Braun*, pp. 305–11.
68. Interview in *Teatralnaya gazeta*, 7 August 1916, p. 15.
69. See A. Fevralsky, *Puti k sintezu: Meierkhold i kino* (Moscow, 1978), pp. 62–4.
70. *Novy zritel*, 1925, no. 18, p. 15.
71. *Perepiska*, p. 421; S. Yutkevich, op. cit., p. 76.
72. See also A. Fevralsky, 'Meierkhold i kino', *Iskusstvo kino*, 1962, no. 6, pp. 105–13.
73. For accounts of these productions see K. Rudnitsky, *Meyerhold the Director* (Ann Arbor, 1981).
74. For accounts of *The Storm* see *Meyerhold I*, pp. 285–93; *Volkov II*, pp. 403–15; *Vstrechi*, pp. 106–8; D. Kogan, *Golovin* (Moscow, 1960), pp. 38–41; *Rudnitsky*, pp. 185–92.
75. Quoted in I. Glikman, op. cit., p. 235.
76. For further accounts of *The Stone Guest* see I. Glikman, op. cit., pp. 198–241; A. Gozenpud, op. cit., pp. 345–54.
77. See T. Makagonova, op. cit., p. 121.
78. *Meyerhold I*, p. 298.
79. Ibid., p. 299.
80. Yu. Yuriev, *Zapiski* (Leningrad–Moscow, 1963), vol. II, pp. 201–2.
81. Ya. Malyutin, op. cit., pp. 99–100.
82. See *Volkov II*, p. 183.
83. *Meyerhold I*, p. 300.
84. *Meyerhold II*, p. 440.
85. I. Shneiderman, 'V. E. Meierkhold v rabote nad poslednem vozobnovleniem *Maskarada*' in A. Yufit, cit., p. 205.

86. For colour reproductions of many of the settings, costumes and properties see E. Lansere (ed.), *Maskarad Lermontova v teatralnykh eskizakh A. Ya. Golovina* (Moscow–Leningrad, 1941–1946).
87. Under the pseudonym 'Homo novus', *Teatr i iskusstvo*, 1917, no. 10–11, p. 192.
88. *Rudnitsky*, p. 203.
89. See I. Shneiderman, op. cit., p. 162.
90. For further accounts of *Masquerade* in works other than those cited see A. Matskin, op. cit., pp. 273 ff.; N. V. Petrov, op. cit., pp. 128–39; *Vstrechi*, pp. 111–13, 149–53, 159–63.

Chapter Six Revolution and Civil War

1. A. Lunacharsky, 'Yeshche ob iskusstve i revolyutsii', *Obrazovanie*, 1906, no. 12, p. 82.
2. Interview with 'N. M.', *Teatr*, 24 October 1913, p. 5.
3. Report by 'VI. S.', *Apollon*, 1914, no. 6–7, p. 109.
4. *Meyerhold I*, p. 318.
5. See K. Rudnitsky, *Meierkhold*, cit., p. 231.
6. See *Ocherki istorii russkoy sovetskoy dramaturgii*, vol. I (Leningrad–Moscow, 1963), p. 8.
7. *Nashi vedomosti*, 12 January 1918 (Quoted in *Rudnitsky*, p. 223).
8. A. Matskin, op. cit., pp. 300, 320.
9. For a further account see K. Rudnitsky, *Meyerhold the Director*, cit.
10. For a detailed account see I. Glikman, op. cit., pp. 244–69.
11. See *Vstrechi*, pp. 137–45; *Vremennik Teatralnogo otdela NKP*, 1918, no. 1 (November), pp. 24–9; B. Picon-Vallin, *Meyerhold* (Paris, 1990), pp. 76-80.
12. See D. Zolotnitsky, 'V. E. Meierkhold' in *Problemy teorii i praktiki russkoy sovetskoy rezhissury 1917–1925* (Leningrad, 1978), pp. 73–4.
13. See I. Glikman, op. cit., pp. 270–4.
14. See A. Fevralsky, *Pervaya sovetskaya piesa* (Moscow, 1971), pp. 60–2.
15. *Petrogradskaya pravda*, 5 November 1918, p. 2.
16. D. Zolotnitsky, *Zori teatralnogo oktyabrya* (Leningrad, 1976), p. 76.
17. Eye-witness account quoted by A. Fevralsky, op. cit., p. 73.
18. See Yu. Smirnov-Nesvitsky, 'Teatralnoe novatorstvo Mayakovskogo i revolyutsionnoe vremya' in *Teatr i dramaturgia*, vypusk 4 (1974), pp. 187–97.
19. A. Fevralsky, 'Misteria-buff' in *Spektakli i gody* (ed. A. Anastasiev, E. Peregudova, Moscow, 1969), p. 13.
20. Loc. cit.
21. *Zhizn iskusstva*, 11 November 1918, p. 2.
22. Quoted by Zolotnitsky, op. cit., p. 75.
23. See A. Fevralsky, *Pervaya sovetskaya piesa*, cit., pp. 201 ff.
24. B. Picon-Vallin, op. cit., p. 84.
25. For accounts of this period in Meyerhold's life see *Vestnik teatra*, 1920, no. 68, pp. 4–5; *Teatralnaya zhizn*, 1964, no. 14, pp. 28–9.
26. I. Ilinsky, *Sam o sebe* (Moscow, 1962), p. 106.
27. See Zolotnitsky, op. cit., p. 82.
28. See Matskin, op. cit., p. 319.
29. At a public debate reported in *Vestnik teatra*, 1920, no. 78–9, p. 16.
30. See *Perepiska*, pp. 191–4.
31. On 31 October 1920, quoted in *Vestnik teatra*, 1920, no. 72–3, pp. 19–20 (*Braun*, pp. 169–70).

32. Zolotnitsky, op. cit., pp. 107–8. For other versions see *Rudnitsky*, p. 244; Kh. Khersonsky, 'Vzyatie Perekopa i Zori', *Teatr*, 1957, no. 5, pp. 90–1.
33. *Vestnik teatra*, 1920, no. 72–3, p. 10; no. 75, p. 14 (*Braun*, pp. 173–4).
34. Quoted by Zolotnitsky, op. cit., pp. 102–3.
35. *Pravda*, 10 November 1920, p. 2.
36. Reported in *Vestnik teatra*, 1920, no. 75, p. 12.
37. *Vestnik teatra*, 1920, no. 76–7, p. 4.
38. For discussions of the role of Narkompros and the Theatre Department see S. Fitzpatrick, *The Commissariat of Enlightenment* (Cambridge University Press, 1970).
39. *Meyerhold II*, p. 360.
40. For an English translation of *Mystery-Bouffe* see *The Complete Plays of Vladimir Mayakovsky* (trans. G. Daniels, New York, 1968 and 1971).
41. *Pervaya sovetskaya piesa*, cit., p. 158.
42. N. Tarabukin, 'Zritelnoe oformlenie v GosTIM-e' in *Teatr*, 1990, no. 1., p. 96.
43. A. Fevralsky, *Pervaya sovetskaya piesa*, cit, p. 170.
44. *Vestnik teatra*, 1921, no. 93–4, p. 23.
45. For a detailed account of the liquidation of the R.S.F.S.R. Theatre no. 1 see A. Fevralsky, 'Teatralny oktyabr i Zori', *Sovetsky teatr*, 1931, no. 1, pp. 4–9.

Chapter Seven Biomechanics and Constructivism

1. See K. Rudnitsky, 'Portret Zinaidy Raikh' in *Teatralnaya zhizn*, 1987, nos. 21 & 22.
2. N. Volkov, *Teatralnye vechera* (Moscow, 1966), p. 285.
3. *Vestnik teatra*, 1922, no. 80–1, p. 22; no. 83–4, p. 22.
4. For a summary of Taylorism and Reflexology and a detailed exposition of Meyerhold's biomechanical 'études' see M. Gordon, 'Meyerhold's Biomechanics', *The Drama Review*, vol. 18, no. 3 (T-63), pp. 73–88. Additional photographs of the études are contained in *The Drama Review*, vol. 17, no. 1 (T-57). For further detailed accounts of biomechanics see Picon-Vallin, op. cit., pp. 104–24; N. Pesochinsky, 'Biomekhanika i teorii Meierkholda' in *Teatr*, 1990, no. 1, pp. 103–12.
5. From V. Fedorov, 'Akter budushchego', *Ermitazh*, 1922, no. 6, pp. 10–11 (for a complete version see *Braun*, pp. 197–200).
6. *Vstrechi*, pp. 322–3.
7. V. Meierkhold and V. Bebutov, I. Aksyonov, *Amplua aktera* (Moscow, 1922), p. 4. For a complete translation of *Amplua aktera* see M. Hoover, op. cit., pp. 297–310. Hoover also includes full biomechanics programmes and the curricula of Meyerhold's Workshop for the years 1922–1923 and 1927–1928.
8. See A. Trabsky (ed.), *Russkiy sovetskiy teatr 1921–26: dokumenty i materialy* (Leningrad, 1975), p. 355.
9. *Teatr*, 1922, no. 5, pp. 149–51.
10. *Teatr i muzyka*, 1922, no. 7, pp. 23–4.
11. For the relevant passages from Coquelin see T. Cole and H. Chinoy (ed.), *Actors on Acting* (New York, 1949), pp. 195–206.
12. E. Garin, *S Meierkholdom* (Moscow, 1974), pp. 28 ff.
13. *Vstrechi*, p. 125.
14. Ibid., p. 76. For a description of 'The Leap onto the Chest' see M. Gordon, op. cit., p. 85.
15. *Theatre Arts Monthly*, 1935, November, p. 874.

16. Quoted in N. Pesochinsky, op. cit., p. 104.
17. Loc. cit.
18. G. Gauzner and Ye. Gabrilovich, 'Portrety akterov novogo teatra' in *Teatralny oktyabr*, sbornik I (Leningrad–Moscow, 1926), p. 50.
19. See A. Gvozdev, 'Istoricheskiy rol teatra Meierkholda', *Sovetskiy teatr*, 1931, no. 1, p. 2.
20. 'Molozhe molodykh' in *Vechernyaya Moskva*, 9 February 1934.
21. Interview in *Teatr*, 24 October 1913, p. 6.
22. Quoted by Sergei Yutkevich in *Vstrechi*, p. 212.
23. *Teatralnaya Moskva*, 1922, no. 37, p. 10.
24. *Meyerhold II*, p. 47 (*Braun*, p. 204).
25. See V. Stenberg, 'O moei rabote c A. Ya. Tairovym i V. E. Meierkholdom' in *Sovetskie khudozhniki teatra i kino* (Moscow, 1979), pp. 218–20; A. Law, '*Le Cocu magnifique – mise en scène de Meyerhold*' in D. Bablet (ed.), *Les Voies de la Création théâtrale*, no. 7 (Paris, 1980), pp. 16 ff.
26. *Rudnitsky*, p. 261.
27. 'Zritelnoe oformlenie v GOSTIMe' in *Teatr*, 1990, no. 1, p. 97.
28. A. Gvozdev, *Teatr imeni Vs. Meierkholda – 1920–26* (Leningrad, 1927), p. 28.
29. *Izvestia*, 9 May 1922 (quoted in C. Lodder, *Russian Constructivism*, Yale University Press, 1983), p. 172.
30. *Izvestia*, 14 May 1922, p. 4.
31. E. Garin, op. cit., p. 50.
32. Quoted in M. Turovskaya, *Babanova: legenda i biografia* (Moscow, 1981), p. 24.
33. Op. cit., p. 34.
34. A. Law, op. cit., p. 23.
35. Meyerhold Archive, quoted in *Rudnitsky*, p. 269.
36. B. Alpers, *Teatr sotsialnoy maski* (Moscow–Leningrad, 1931), p. 34.
37. I. Ilinsky, op. cit., p. 154.
38. *Ermitazh*, 1922, no. 8 (4–10 July), pp. 3–4, 11–12.
39. *Teatralnaya Moskva*, 1922, no. 46 (27 June–2 July), p. 8.
40. A. Sukhovo-Kobylin, *Trilogia* (Moscow, 1966), p. 348.
41. Previously unpublished article in A. Trabsky (ed.), op. cit., p. 202.
42. See E. Garin, op. cit., pp. 58–61.
43. See Kh. Khersonsky, *Stranitsy yunosti kino* (Moscow, 1965), pp. 110–24.
44. See M. Zharov, *Zhizn, teatr, kino* (Moscow, 1967), p. 154.
45. For accounts of Eisenstein's work in the theatre see S. Eisenstein, *Izbrannye proizvedenia v shesti tomakh*, vol. V (Moscow, 1968), pp. 68 ff; Y. Barna, *Eisenstein* (London, 1973), pp. 46–72; L. Kleberg, *Theatre as Action* (London, 1993), pp. 77–89.
46. *Braun*, p. 311. For a discussion of the relationship between Meyerhold and Eisenstein see L. Kozlov, 'A Hypothetical Dedication' in L. Kleberg and H. Lövgren (eds.), *Eisenstein Revisited* (Stockholm, 1987), pp. 65–92.

Chapter Eight People's Artist

1. See *Perepiska*, pp. 218–19.
2. Quoted in 'Documents from *Novy Lef*' in *Screen Reader 1* (London, 1977), p. 300.
3. S. Tretyakov, '*Zemlya dybom*. Tekst i rechemontazh' in *Zrelishcha*, 1923, no. 27, p.6.
4. H. Carter, *The New Theatre and Cinema of Soviet Russia* (London, 1924), p. 78.
5. See E. Braun, *The Director and the Stage*, cit., pp. 163–6.

6. *Perepiska*, pp. 225–6.
7. D. Zolotnitsky, *Budni i prazdniki Teatralnogo oktyabrya* (Leningrad, 1978), p. 69.
8. *Zrelishcha*, 1923, no. 21, p. 8.
9. See Yu. Annenkov, *Dnevnik moikh vstrech* (New York, 1966), vol. II, pp. 60–1.
10. A. Fevralsky, *Zapiski rovesnika veka*, cit., pp. 239, 246.
11. Ibid., p. 238–9.
12. Ibid., p. 236.
13. Ibid., pp. 268–71. For an analysis of the records of audience reaction see the articles by V. F. Fedorov and subsequent discussions in *Zhizn iskusstva*, 1925, nos. 18, 20, 22, 23, 26, 27. See also L. Kleberg, *Theatre as Action*, cit., pp. 93–102.
14. See *Vestnik teatra*, 4 January 1921, no. 78–9, p. 15.
15. See A. Fevralsky, op. cit., pp. 247–9.
16. *Zrelishcha*, 1923, no. 60, p. 1.
17. *Vstrechi*, p. 298.
18. Ibid., p. 306.
19. *Zrelishcha*, 1923, no. 21, p. 8.
20. 'Constructivist Theatre as a laboratory for an Architectural Aesthetic' in *Architectural Association Quarterly*, vol. 11, no. 2, 1979, p. 25.
21. I. Erenburg, *A vse-taki ona vertitsya* (Moscow–Berlin, 1922), p. 114.
22. Letter to Meyerhold dated 5 March 1924, published in *Novy zritel*, 1924, no. 18, p. 16.
23. Ibid., pp. 16–17.
24. *Sobranie sochinenii*, vol. 8, (Moscow, 1966), pp. 336–7.
25. *Vstrechi*, p. 311; M. Zharov, op. cit., pp. 174–8.
26. Previously unpublished article in A. Trabsky (ed.), op. cit., p. 218.
27. *Novy zritel*, 1924, no. 29, pp. 13–14.
28. See A. Lunacharsky, op. cit., vol. I, pp. 374–6.
29. See A. Faiko, 'Tri vstrechi', *Teatr*, 1962, no. 10, pp. 121–2.
30. *Meyerhold II*, pp. 93–4 (*Braun*, p. 206).
31. Quoted in *Rudnitsky*, p. 331.
32. A. Faiko, op. cit., pp. 121–2.
33. E. Garin, op. cit., p. 101.
34. See M. Turovskaya, op. cit., pp. 66–74.
35. *Pravda*, 23 May 1923, p. 7.
36. M. Turovskaya, op. cit., p. 40.
37. *Teatr*, 1937, no. 1, p. 44.
38. See *Rudnitsky*, pp. 287–301.
39. *Izvestia*, 11–12 April 1923.
40. *Pravda*, 19 January 1924, p. 9.
41. Reported in *Novy zritel*, 1924, no. 7, p. 6.
42. '*Les* (opyt analiza spektaklya)' in *Teatralny oktyabr*, cit., p. 62.
43. *Meyerhold II*, p. 57.
44. Ibid., p. 70.
45. *Braun*, p. 319.
46. B. Picon-Vallin, op. cit., p. 203.
47. *Meyerhold II*, pp. 56–7.
48. *Kino-gazeta*, 19 February 1924.
49. '*Les*: annotatsia 1935 goda' in *Teatr*, 1990, no. 1, p. 116.
50. B. Picon-Vallin, op. cit., p. 178.

51. *Rudnitsky*, p. 315.
52. See Pesochinsky, '*Les* i yego kritiki' in A. Sherel (ed.), *Meierkholdovskiy sbornik*, vypusk pervy (Moscow, 1992), vol. II, pp. 94–100.
53. *Rudnitsky*, p. 302. For an extended analysis by Rudnitsky of *The Forest* see *Teatr*, 1976, no. 11, pp. 97–110, no. 12, pp. 65–106.
54. See Meyerhold's speech 'Meierkhold protiv meyerholdovshchiny' (14 March 1936) in *Meyerhold II*, pp. 330–47.
55. See J. Freedman, *Silence's Roar: The Life and Drama of Nikolai Erdman* (Oakville, New York & London, 1992). This is the first full-length study of Erdman in any language.
56. *Rudnitsky*, p. 340.
57. G. Shakhov, *Sergei Martinson* (Moscow, 1966), p. 33.
58. M. Zharov, op. cit., p. 184.
59. P. Markov, *O Teatre*, vol. 3 (Moscow, 1976), p. 289.
60. 'Tretiy Front. Posle *Mandata*' in *Pechat i revolyutsia*, 1925, no. 5–6, p. 289.
61. See O. Feldman, 'Otrazhenie nashei sudby' in *Teatr*, 1990, no. 1, p. 120.
62. 'Opyt izuchenia zritelnogo zala' in *Zhizn iskusstva*, 1925, no. 18, pp. 14–15.
63. B. Alpers, op. cit., p. 48.
64. *Rudnitsky*, p. 342.
65. P. Markov, loc. cit.
66. Quoted in P. Markov, *Pravda teatra*, cit., p. 43.
67. See J. Freedman, op. cit., pp. 7, 18.
68. See M. Turovskaya, op. cit., pp. 75–81.
69. See especially *Vstrechi*, pp. 278–89; *Meyerhold II*, pp. 373–418; P. Schmidt (ed.), *Meyerhold at Work* (Manchester, 1981), pp. 81–140.

Chapter Nine The Government Inspector

1. *Rampa*, 5–10 February, 1924, p. 7.
2. 'Meierkhold govorit', *Tarusskie stranitsy*, cit., p. 306.
3. Letter to M. P. Pogodin dated 10 May 1836 in N. V. Gogol, *Polnoe sobranie sochinenii* (Leningrad, 1940–1952), vol. XI, p. 41.
4. *Avtorskaya ispoved*, Gogol, op. cit., vol. VIII, p. 440.
5. M. Korenev, 'K postanovke *Revizora*' in E. Nikitina (ed.), *Gogol i Meyerhold* (Moscow, 1927), p. 78.
6. See *Meyerhold II*, pp. 145–6.
7. 'Otryvok iz pisma k odnomu literatoru', Gogol, op. cit., vol. IV, p. 99.
8. M. Korenev, op. cit., p. 77.
9. 'Razvyazka *Revizora*', Gogol, op. cit., vol. IV, pp. 121–37.
10. See *Meyerhold I*, p. 173.
11. *Meyerhold II*, p. 132, (*Braun*, p. 220).
12. Quoted by *Rudnitsky*, p. 352.
13. *Gogol i Meyerhold*, cit., p. 85.
14. See I. Yermakov, *Ocherki po analizu tvorchestva N. V. Gogolya* (Moscow and Petrograd, 1924). For a discussion of Yermakov and Gogol see R. Maguire (ed.), *Gogol from the Twentieth Century* (Princeton, 1974).
15. See K. Rudnitsky, *Russian and Soviet Theatre: Tradition & the Avant-Garde* (London, 1988), pp. 201–2; N. Worrall, *Nikolai Gogol and Ivan Turgenev* (London, 1982), pp. 111–12.
16. P. Markov, op. cit., vol. 3, pp. 382–3.

17. For details of Meyerhold's division of Gogol's text see B. Picon-Vallin, op. cit., pp. 276–7.
18. Rehearsal record in A. Trabsky (ed.), *Russkiy sovetskiy teatr 1923–1932*, chast pervaya (Leningrad, 1982), p. 275.
19. P. Markov, op. cit., p. 382.
20. See *Meyerhold II*, pp. 110, 112; Garin, op. cit., p. 123.
21. Korenev, op. cit., p. 79.
22. A. Bely, 'Gogol i Meyerhold' in E. Nikitina (ed.), *Gogol i Meyerhold*, cit., pp. 27–9. (The ball takes place in Part One, Chapter 8 of *Dead Souls*).
23. See *Meyerhold II*, p. 132, (*Braun*, pp. 220–1).
24. L. Grossman, 'Tragedia–buff' in *Gogol i Meyerhold*, cit., p. 42.
25. A. Matskin, *Na temy Gogolya* (Moscow, 1984), p. 179.
26. A. Lunacharsky, op. cit., vol. I, p. 402.
27. D. Talnikov, *Novaya revizia Revizora* (Moscow–Leningrad, 1927), p. 52.
28. Lunacharsky, loc. cit.
29. 'Otryvok iz pisma k odnomu literatoru', cit., p. 101.
30. Garin, op. cit., p. 148.
31. Quoted in *Rudnitsky*, p. 357.
32. W. Benjamin, *Moscow Diary* (Harvard & London, 1986), p. 32.
33. *Rudnitsky*, p. 353.
34. S. Radlov, *Desyat let v teatre* (Leningrad, 1929), p. 148.
35. See B. Picon-Vallin, op. cit., p. 350.
36. M. Gnesin, *Statyi, vospominania, materialy* (Moscow, 1961), p. 198,
37. See *Braun*, p. 28.
38. *Vstrechi*, pp. 336–7.
39. 'Glebov Igor' (pseudonym), 'Muzyka v drame' in *Krasnaya gazeta*, 30 January 1927.
40. For a comprehensive bibliography see S. Danilov, *Revizor na stsene* (Leningrad, 1934). For a scene-by-scene reconstruction of the production by Nick Worrall see *Theatre Quarterly*, vol. II, no. 7, pp. 75–95. Béatrice Picon-Vallin provides an exhaustive analysis in her *Meyerhold*, cit., pp. 264–339.
41. See *Rudnitsky*, p. 379.
42. See, for example, *Meyerhold II*, pp. 296–7.
43. L. Rudneva, 'Shostakovich i Meierkhold' in *Aprel*, 1992, no. 5, p. 225.
44. Quoted in L. Danilevich, *Nash Sovremennik* (Moscow, 1965), p. 34.
45. See A. Smeliansky, *Is Comrade Bulgakov Dead?* (London, 1993), pp. 194 ff.
46. Ibid., p. 196.

Chapter Ten The New Repertoire

1. See *Perepiska*, pp. 249, 412.
2. Ibid., pp. 265, 267.
3. A. Smelyansky, *Mikhail Bulgakov v Khudozhestvennom teatre* (Moscow, 1989), p. 135.
4. O. Feldman, 'Eta yego mechta ne osushchestvilas' in *Teatr*, 1990, no. 1, pp. 160–1 (contains a complete text of *Moskva*).
5. K. Rudnitsky, *Russian and Soviet Theatre*, cit., pp. 200–1.
6. Tretyakov, quoted in *Slyshish, Moskva?!* . . . (Moscow, 1966), p. 198.
7. L. Kleberg, *Theatre as Action*, cit., p. 106.
8. *Das Neue Frankfurt*, 1930, no. 10 (I am indebted for information on this project to Christina Lodder).

9. For an account by Alexander Fevralsky of this project see *Slyshish Moskva?!* . . . , cit., pp. 197–204.
10. L. Kleberg, op. cit., p. 103.
11. See L. Kleberg, pp. 103 ff.
12. *Meierkholdovskiy sbornik*, cit., vol. II, p. 11.
13. 'Meierkhold i Stalin', ibid., vol. II, p. 43.
14. K. Rudnitsky, *Meierkhold*, cit., p. 354. For a detailed account of the Meyerhold–Babanova dispute see M. Turovskaya, op. cit., pp. 93–109.
15. *Sovremenny teatr*, 1928, no. 9, p. 184.
16. Ibid., 1928, no. 10, p. 203.
17. See *Meyerhold II*, pp. 165, 322–3. For Pushkin's letter see N. Bogoslovsky (ed.), *Pushkin-kritik* (Moscow–Leningrad, 1934), p. 63.
18. See A. Law, 'Meyerhold's *Woe to Wit* (1928)' in *The Drama Review*, vol. 18, no. 3 (T-63), p. 104. This article contains a detailed reconstruction of the play, based on Meyerhold's unpublished rehearsal notes.
19. Ibid., p. 93.
20. Ibid., p. 97.
21. B. Alpers, *Teatr sotsialnoy maski*, cit., p. 71.
22. See B. Asafiev, 'O muzyke v *Gore umu*', *Sovremenny teatr*, 1928, no. 11, p. 223.
23. V. Blyum, quoted in *Rudnitsky*, p. 385.
24. *Russkiy Sovetskiy Teatr 1926–1932, chast pervaya*, cit., p. 289.
25. See A. Gladkov, 'Meierkhold govorit', *Novy mir*, cit., p. 228; *Meyerhold II*, pp. 322–3; G. Banu, 'Meyerhold et le modèle du théâtre asiatique', *Revue d'Histoire du Théâtre*, 1981, no. 2, pp. 139–42.
26. Announced in *Novy zritel*, 1928, no. 47, p. 16. The controversy is covered in detail in *Komsomolskaya Pravda*, 31 August–4 December 1928.
27. See interview with Meyerhold in *Komsomolskaya Pravda*, 4 December 1928, p. 4.
28. Interview in *Komsomolskaya Pravda*, 28 December 1928, p. 4.
29. See P. Markov, op. cit., vol. 2, p. 65.
30. *Meyerhold II*, p. 177.
31. Loc. cit.
32. See *Rudnitsky*, pp. 398–409.
33. See V. Katanyan, *Mayakovsky – literaturnaya khronika* (Moscow, 1956), p. 369.
34. *Sovremenny teatr*, 1929, no. 15, p. 235.
35. Quoted in *Rudnitsky*, p. 424.
36. *Vstrechi*, pp. 387–96.
37. *Novy zritel*, 1929, no. 40, p. 5.
38. For a detailed analysis of the play and production see P. Markov, op. cit., vol 3, pp. 601–11.
39. M. Zoshchenko (ed.), *Almanakh estrady* (Leningrad, 1933), p. 6.
40. See Fevralsky's commentary in V. Mayakovsky, *Teatr i kino* (Moscow, 1954), vol. II, pp. 505–8.
41. For English translations of *The Bath House* see G. Daniels, op. cit.; A. McAndrew, *Twentieth Century Russian Drama* (New York, 1963).
42. *Rudnitsky*, p. 421.
43. See Mayakovsky, op. cit., p. 509; *Rudnitsky*, p. 416.
44. Quoted by *Rudnitsky*, p. 420.
45. For a personal account of the tour see I. Ilinsky, op. cit., pp. 231–7.
46. See *Sovetskiy teatr*, 1930, no. 5, pp. 34–5, no. 11–12, pp. 45–6.

47. Quoted in V. Kolyazin, 'Meierkhold i Gropius', *Teatr*, 1992, no. 8, pp. 121–9, which summarises the Berlin critics' responses to the Meyerhold Theatre.
48. I. Erenburg, *Sobranie sochinenii v 9 tomakh*, vol. 8 (Moscow, 1966), p. 340. For an account of the Paris season see B. Picon-Vallin, 'Meierkhold glazami Zhuve' in *Meierkholdovskiy sbornik*, cit., vol. II, pp. 127–34.
49. See Chekhov's introduction to Yu. Yelagin, *Temny genii* (New York, 1955), pp. 15–17.
50. See Ibid., p. 128; Yu. Annenkov, *Dnevnik moikh vstrech*, cit., vol. II, pp. 85–7; *Mikhail Chekhov: literaturnoe nasledie v 2 tomakh* (Moscow, 1986), vol. I, pp. 390–1.
51. V. Kirshon in *Sovetskiy teatr*, 1931, no. 4, p. 18.
52. Ibid., p. 12.
53. *Meyerhold II*, p. 248.
54. See the account by Vishnevsky's wife, Sofia Vishnevetskaya in *Vstrechi*, pp. 405–14.
55. Ibid., pp. 556–7.
56. For an English translation of *A List of Benefits* see A. McAndrew, op. cit.
57. See N. Chushkin, *Gamlet – Kachalov* (Moscow, 1966), pp. 257–9.

Chapter Eleven 'An Alien Theatre'

1. See I. Ilinsky, op. cit., pp. 251–3.
2. See D. Zolotnitsky, 'V.E. Meierkhold – posledniy srok' in *Iz opyta sovetskoy rezhissury 1930-kh godov* (Leningrad, 1989), pp. 10–11; *Teatr*, 1990, no. 1, pp. 137–40.
3. For an account of the project by the architects see *Theatre Quarterly*, vol. II, no. 7, pp. 69–73.
4. See J. Willett, *The Theatre of Erwin Piscator* (London, 1978), pp. 116–18.
5. See V. Kolyazin, 'Meierkhold i Gropius', cit., pp. 121–9.
6. See A. Svobodin, Introduction to Nikolai Erdman, *Piesy, Intermedii, Pisma, Dokumenty, Vospominania sovremennikov* (Moscow, 1990), pp. 16–17. For an extended analysis of *The Suicide* see J. Freedman, op. cit., chapter 4.
7. See Yu. Zayats, 'Ya prishel k tyagostnomu ubezhdeniyu, chto ne nuzhen . . .' in *Meierkholdovskiy sbornik*, cit., vol. II, p. 120.
8. Ibid., p. 113.
9. N. Erdman, op. cit., pp. 283–4.
10. Yu. Zayats, op. cit., p.121.
11. Ibid., p. 122.
12. Quoted in N. Erdman, op. cit., pp. 384–5.
13. J. Freedman, op. cit., pp. 156 ff.
14. Reported by M. Glyarov, in *Rabis*, 1933, no. 11, pp. 34–5.
15. Quoted in A. Matskin, 'Vremya ukhoda' in *Teatr*, 1990, no. 1, p. 35.
16. Ilinsky, op. cit., p. 244.
17. See A. Gladkov, *Meierkhold* (Moscow, 1990), vol. 2, pp. 161–2.
18. *Theatre Arts Monthly*, 1935, November, p. 874.
19. *Meyerhold II*, p. 285.
20. I. Yuzovsky, *Zatem lyudi khodyat v teatr* (Moscow, 1964).
21. *Rudnitsky*, pp. 457–8.
22. *Vstrechi*, p. 476.
23. *Vstrechi*, pp. 500–1; *Meyerhold II*, p. 286–7.
24. *Meyerhold II*, p. 288, (*Braun*, pp. 274–5).

25. For a detailed account of this process see Varpakhovsky, *Nablyudenia, analiz, opyt* (Moscow, 1978), pp. 44–70.
26. Ibid., p. 46.
27. *Rudnitsky*, pp. 464–5.
28. For an analysis of Meyerhold's diagonal-staging method and of the musical composition of the production see L. Varpakhovsky, op. cit., pp. 72–132.
29. *Meyerhold II*, p. 287–92 (for a complete text of this and the second letter to Shebalin see *Braun*, pp. 274–8).
30. Quoted in A. Smeliansky, *Is Comrade Bulgakov Dead?* (London, 1993), p. 230.
31. *Molodaya gvardia*, 1934, no. 8, p. 131.
32. For a translation of Meyerhold's account of his revision and of his production see *Braun*, pp. 278–89.
33. *Sovetskiy teatr*, 1935, no. 1, p. 12.
34. Quoted in G. Lapkina, *Na afishe – Pushkin* (Leningrad–Moscow, 1965), p. 55.
35. I. Sollertinsky, *Kriticheskiye statyi* (Leningrad, 1963), p. 38.
36. From a rehearsal transcript in *Teatralnaya zhizn*, 1990, no. 2, p. 21.
37. See V. Bogdanov-Berezovskiy, *Vstrechi* (Moscow, 1967), pp. 102–6.
38. 'Meierkhold govorit', *Tarusskie stranitsy*, cit., p. 307.
39. See I. Glikman, op. cit., pp. 275–308. For a scene-by-scene reconstruction of the adaptation see L. Potapova, 'O nekotorykh osobennostyakh spektaklya *Pikovaya Dama* . . .' in *Teatr i dramaturgia*, vypusk 6 (1976), pp. 142–62.
40. *Meyerhold II*, p. 309, (*Braun*, pp. 288–89).
41. *Rudnitsky*, p. 475, *Meyerhold II*, p. 310.
42. See I. Yuzovsky, *Razgovor zatyanulsya za polnoch* (Moscow, 1966), pp. 245–62.
43. 'Meierkhold govorit', *Novy mir*, cit., p.228.
44. See M. Hayward & L. Labedz (eds.), *Literature and Revolution in Soviet Russia 1917–62* (Oxford U.P., 1963), chapters 4 and 5.
45. Quoted in D. Zolotnitsky, op. cit., p. 4.
46. 'Sumbur vmesto muzyki' (28 January 1936); 'Baletnaya falsh', (6 February 1936).
47. See 'Meierkhold protiv meierkholdovshchiny', *Meyerhold II*, pp. 330–47.
48. For the text see *Meyerhold II*, pp. 348–58, (*Braun*, pp. 289–300).
49. *Sovetskiy teatr*, 1936, no. 4–5, p. 2.
50. For details and rehearsal notes see *Meyerhold II*, p. 362–69.
51. J. Leyda, 'In Leningrad' in *Theatre Arts Monthly*, March 1935, p. 214.
52. See P. Schmidt, op. cit., pp. 81–140; *Meyerhold II*, pp. 373–418; A. Gladkov, 'Iz vospominaniy o Meierkholde' in *Moskva teatralnaya* (Moscow, 1960), pp. 366–76; G. Lapkina, op. cit., pp. 108–12.
53. See *Rudnitsky*, p. 485.
54. *Iskusstvo kino*, 1964, no. 4, pp. 68–9.
55. See *Vstrechi*, pp. 562–4.
56. The text is republished in *Meierkholdovskiy sbornik*, cit., vol. I, pp. 322–6.
57. For an abridged transcript of the debate see ibid., pp. 327–85.

Chapter Twelve   The Final Act

1. See *Vstrechi*, p. 565; A. Gladkov, *Meierkhold*, cit., vol. II, pp. 347 ff.
2. K. Rudnitsky, 'Krusheniye teatra' in *Meierkholdovskiy sbornik*, cit., vol. II, pp. 23–9.

3. Ibid., p. 22.
4. *Rudnitsky*, p. 487.
5. Quoted in *Vstrechi*, p. 589.
6. Loc. cit.
7. See I. Glikman, op. cit., pp. 345–7.
8. For an account of Meyerhold's rehearsals of *Masquerade* in 1938 see
   I. Shneiderman, op. cit., pp. 162–208.
9. See D. Zolotnitsky, 'V. E. Meierkhold – posledniy srok', cit., pp. 45–7.
10. See R. Conquest, *The Great Terror: A Reassessment* (London, 1990), pp. 438–41.
11. Quoted in M. Kotovskaya and S. Isaev (eds.), *Mir iskusstv* (Moscow, 1991),
    p. 414.
12. Ibid., p. 421.
13. Ibid., pp. 421, 435; *Teatr*, 1974, no. 2, pp. 36–9.
14. *Mir iskusstv*, p. 416.
15. Ibid., pp. 437–75.
16. *Teatr*, 1974, no. 2, pp. 39–44; A. Kaun, *Soviet Poets and Poetry* (Los Angeles,
    1943), pp. 96–7.
17. Yu. Yelagin, *Temny geniy* (New York, 1955), pp. 406–10.
18. See Vadim Shcherbakov's discussion of the conference in *Meierkholdovskiy
    sbornik*, cit., vol. II, pp. 216–24.
19. *Mir iskusstv*, p. 453.
20. Ibid., p. 455.
21. Ibid., p. 459.
22. Ibid., p. 461.
23. 'Iz vospominanii K. L. Zelinskogo ob A. A. Fadeeve' in *Teatr*, 1990, no.
    1, p. 144.
24. *Mir iskusstv*, cit., p. 442.
25. See Ye. Tyapkina, 'Poslednyaya vstrecha' in *Teatralnaya zhizn*, 1989, no. 5,
    pp. 7–8.
26. A different view of the effect of Raikh's letter to Stalin is taken by the
    Military Procurator who reviewed the case for Meyerhold's rehabilitation in
    1955. According to him, it was the 'direct cause' of his arrest, but if so, it must
    have been an earlier letter. None of these letters has ever been discovered. (See
    Teatralnaya zhizn, cit., p. 9).
27. Unless stated otherwise, all details of Meyerhold's case referred to below are
    taken from the account in *Teatralnaya zhizn*, 1990, no. 2, pp. 1–13, 33–4.
28. Meyerhold abandoned plans to stage *I Want a Child* in 1930. Work on *The
    Suicide* was halted following a run-through in the presence of Kaganovich and
    other Party functionaries in October 1932 (see p. 271 above).
29. First published in *Sovetskaya Kultura*, 16 February 1989, p. 5, and again
    in *Teatralnaya zhizn*, 1989, no. 5, pp. 2–3 (cited below).
30. Alexander Matskin, an authority on the period, describes Rafail as 'a long-
    forgotten rank-and-file Trotskyist'. See 'Vremya ukhoda' in *Teatr*, 1990, no. 1,
    p. 43.
31. Valentin Ryabov, 'Case No. 537' in *Ogonyok*, 1989, no. 15, p. 12.
32. Ibid., p. 11.
33. Also referred to in *Teatralnaya zhizn*, 1990, no. 2.
34. For an account of Babel's interrogation see *Ogonek*, 1989, no. 39.
35. See R. Conquest, op. cit., pp. 422–3.
36. The most recent assessment by the Union of Soviet Writers is that some 2000

literary figures alone were repressed, of whom about 1500 met their deaths in prison or in camps. (R. Conquest, op. cit., p. 297, quoted from *Literaturnaya gazeta*, 28 December, 1988).

37. *Teatralnaya zhizn*, 1989, no. 5, p. 1.
38. The record of the court proceedings is published in facsimile in *Teatralnaya zhizn*, 1990, no. 2.
39. See E. Braun, 'A New Meyerhold Centre in Moscow' in *New Theatre Quarterly*, vol. IX, no. 33, pp. 95–6.
40. For a detailed account of Meyerhold's rehabilitation see *Meierkholdovskiy sbornik*, cit., vol. I, pp. 23–157.
41. *Vechernyaya Moskva*, 14 June 1991, p. 6.

Conclusion

1. Review in *New York Times*, 13 October 1970, quoted in D. Williams, *Peter Brook – A Theatrical Casebook* (London, 1992), pp. 160–2.
2. Loc. cit.
3. See esp. K. B. Eaton, *The Theatre of Meyerhold and Brecht* (Westport and London, 1985); M. Hoover, op. cit., chapter 5; R. Leach, op. cit., chapter 9.
4. K. Rudnitsky, *Russian and Soviet Theatre*, cit., p. 198; see also N. Worrall, op. cit., pp. 149 ff.
5. L. Kleberg, *Theatre as Action*, cit., p. 142.
6. P. Markov, op. cit., vol. 2, p. 65.
7. J. Kott, *Shakespeare Our Contemporary* (London, 1965), p. 112.
8. 'Stage Figures', *The New York Times Book Review*, 2 December 1979, p. 51.
9. B. Picon-Vallin, op. cit., p. 395.
10. M. Billington, 'The Pope of E15', *The Guardian*, 29 March 1994.
11. See pp. 203, 243 above.
12. For a discussion of the cinematic elements in Meyerhold's theatre work see B. Picon-Vallin, op. cit., pp. 298–302.
13. Quoted in T. Makagonova (ed.), op. cit., p. 159.
14. 'A Hypothetical Dedication' in L. Kleberg and H. Lövgren (eds.), p. 92.
15. 'V. Meierkhold' in G. Kozintsev, *Sobranie sochineniy v 5 tomakh*, vol. 2 (Leningrad, 1983), p. 442.

Bibliography

What follows is a bibliography of the principal works devoted wholly to Meyerhold or containing significant reference to him. Newspaper and periodical articles are not included; for these the reader is referred to the notes above. For a complete bibliography of all Meyerhold's writings and other utterances published up to March 1974 see *Bibliograficheskiy ukazatel knig, statei, perevodov, besed, dokladov, vyskazivaniy, pisem V.E. Meierkholda* (compiled by V.P.Korshunova and M.A.Sitkovetskaya, Moscow, 1974). This is supplemented by the bibliography covering books published in the period 1974-1990 in *Meierkholdovskiy sbornik*, volume II (ed. A.A.Sherel, Moscow, 1992). Otherwise, the fullest list of works, including the principal periodical articles and an extensive range of background material is included in Béatrice Picon-Vallin, *Meyerhold* (CNRS, Paris, 1990).

ALPATOV, M. and GUNST, E., *Nikolai Nikolaevich Sapunov*, Moscow, 1965.

ALPERS, B., *Teatralnye ocherki* (2 vols), Moscow, 1977.

ALPERS, B., *Teatr revolyutsii*, Moscow, 1928.

ANNENKOV, Yu., *Dnevnik moikh vstrech* (2 vols), New York, 1966.

ASLAN, O. and BABLET, D. (eds), *Le Masque. Du rite au théâtre*, Paris, 1985.

BABLET, D. (ed.), *Collage et montage au théâtre et dans les autres arts durant les années vingt*, Lausanne, 1978.

BABLET, D. (ed.), *Les Voies de la création théâtrale 7: Mises en scène années 20 et 30*, Paris, 1980.

BARNA, Y., *Eisenstein*, London, 1973.

BASSEKHES, A., *Teatr i zhivopis Golovina*, Moscow, 1970.

BEKETOVA, M., *Aleksandr Blok – biograficheskiy ocherk*, Petrograd, 1922.

BENEDETTI, J., *Stanislavski*, London, 1990.

BENJAMIN, W., *Moscow Diary*, Cambridge, Mass.–London, 1986.

BEREZKIN, V., *Sovetskaya stsenografia 1917–1941*, Moscow, 1990.

BEZPALOV, V., *Teatry v dni revolyutsii 1917*, Leningrad, 1927.

BLOK, A., *Sobranie sochineniy* (8 vols), Moscow–Leningrad, 1960–1963.

BOGDANOV-BEREZOVSKY, V., *Vstrechi*, Moscow, 1967.

BRAUN, E. (ed. and trans.), *Meyerhold on Theatre*, London, 1991.

BRUKSON, Ya., *Teatr Meierkholda*, Leningrad, 1925.

CARTER, H., *The New Spirit in the Russian Theatre 1917–1928*, London, 1929.
CHUSHKIN, N., *Gamlet – Kachalov*, Moscow, 1966.
Cinema in Revolution (trans. D. Robinson), London, 1973.

DANA, H., *Handbook on Soviet Drama*, New York, 1938.
DANILOV, S., *Revizor na stsene*, Leningrad, 1934.
DAVYDOVA, M., *Ocherki istorii russkogo teatralno-dekoratsionnogo iskusstva XVIII – nachala XX vekov*, Moscow, 1974.
DEICH, A., *Golos pamyati*, Moscow, 1966.

EATON, K.B., *The Theater of Meyerhold and Brecht*, Westport–London, 1985.
EIZENSHTEIN, S., *Izbrannye proizvedenia v shesti tomakh*, Moscow, 1964–1971.
ERDMAN, N., *Piesy, intermedii, pisma, dokumenty, vospominania sovremennikov*, Moscow, 1990.
ERENBURG, I., *Lyudi, gody, zhizni*, Moscow, 1961.

FEVRALSKY, A., *Desyat let teatra Meierkholda*, Moscow, 1931.
FEVRALSKY, A., 'Meierkhold i Shekspir' in *Vilyam Shekspir 1564–1964: issledovania i materialy*, Moscow, 1964.
FEVRALSKY, A., 'Misteria-Buff' in *Spektakli i gody* (eds A.Anastasiev and E.Peregudova), Moscow, 1969.
FEVRALSKY, A., *Pervaya sovetskaya piesa*, Moscow, 1971.
FEVRALSKY, A., 'Prokofiev i Meierkhold' in *Sergei Prokofiev: statyi i materialy*, Moscow, 1965.
FEVRALSKY, A., *Puti k sintezu: Meierkhold i kino*, Moscow, 1978.
FEVRALSKY, A., 'Stanislavsky i Meierkhold' in *Tarusskie stranitsy*, Kaluga, 1961.
FEVRALSKY, A., *Zapiski rovesniku veka*, Moscow, 1976.
FOKIN, M., *Protiv techenia*, Leningrad–Moscow, 1962.
FREEDMAN, J., *Silence's Roar: The Life and Drama of Nikolai Erdman*, Oakville–New York–London, 1992.
FREIDKINA, L., *Dni i gody Vl. I. Nemirovicha-Danchenko*, Moscow, 1962.
FÜLOP-MILLER, R. and GREGOR, J., *The Russian Theatre, its Character and History*, London, 1930.

GARIN, E., *S Meierkholdom*, Moscow, 1974.
GINZBURG, S., *Kinematografia dorevolyutsionnoi Rossii*, Moscow, 1963.
GLADKOV, A., *Gody uchenia Vsevoloda Meierkholda*, Saratov, 1979.
GLADKOV, A., 'Meyerhold Speaks' in *Novy Mir 1925–1967* (ed. M. Glenny), London, 1972.
GLADKOV, A., *Meierkhold* (2 vols), Moscow, 1990.
GLIKMAN, I., *Meierkhold i muzykalny teatr*, Leningrad, 1989.
GNESIN, M., *Statyi, vospominania, materialy*, Moscow, 1961.
Gogol i Meierkhold (ed. E. Nikitina), Moscow, 1927.
GOLOVIN, A., *Vstrechi i vpechatlenia. Pisma. Vospominania o Golovine*, Leningrad–Moscow, 1960.
GOZENPUD, A., *Russkiy operny teatr mezhdu dvukh revolyutsiy (1905–1917)*, Leningrad, 1975.
GROMOV, P., 'Rannyaya rezhissura Vs. Meierkholda' in *Ocherki po istorii russkoy rezhissury kontsa XIX–nachala XX veka*, Leningrad, 1976.
GVOZDEV, A., *Teatralnaya kritika*, Leningrad, 1987.
GVOZDEV, A., *Teatr im. Vsevoloda Meierkholda (1920–26)*, Leningrad, 1927.

HAMON-SIRÉJOLS, C., *Le Constructivisme au théâtre*, Paris, 1992.
HOOVER, M., *Meyerhold – The Art of Conscious Theater*, University of Massachussets, 1974.
HOOVER, M., *Meyerhold and His Set Designers*, American University Studies, 1988.
HOUGHTON, N., *Moscow Rehearsals*, New York, 1936.

ILINSKY, I., *Sam o sebe*, Moscow, 1962.
Istoria russkogo dramaticheskogo teatra, vol. 7, 1898–1917 (ed. Ye. Kholodov), Moscow, 1987.
Istoria sovetskogo dramaticheskogo teatra, vols 1–4 (ed. K. Rudnitsky), Moscow, 1966–1968.
Istoria sovetskogo teatra, vol. 1 (ed. V. Rafalovich), Leningrad, 1933.
Iz opyta russkoy sovetskoy rezhissury 1930-ykh godov (eds D. Zolotnitsky & V. Mironova), Leningrad, 1989.

KHERSONSKY, Kh., *Stranitsy yunosti kino*, Moscow, 1965.
KHODOTOV, N., *Blizkoe – dalekoe*, Leningrad–Moscow, 1962.
KLEBERG, L. and LÖVGREN, H. (eds), *Eisenstein Revisited*, Stockholm, 1987.
KLEBERG, L., *Theatre as Action*, London, 1993.
KOGAN, D., *Golovin*, Moscow, 1960.
KOBRIN, Yu., *Teatr im. Meierkholda i rabochiy zritel*, Moscow, 1926.
V.F.Komissarzhevskaya: pisma aktrisy, vospominania o ney, materialy, Moscow–Leningrad, 1964.
KOZINTSEV, G., *Sobranie sochineniy v 5 tomakh*, vol. 2, Leningrad, 1983.
KRASOVSKY, Yu., *Nekotorye problemy teatralnoy pedagogiki V.E. Meierkholda 1905–07*, Leningrad, 1981.
KUGEL, A., *Profili teatra*, Moscow, 1929.
KULESHOVA, V. (ed.), *Khudozhnik i zrelishche*, Moscow, 1990.

LAPKINA, G., *Na afishe – Pushkin*, Leningrad–Moscow, 1965.
LEACH, R., *Vsevolod Meyerhold*, Cambridge, 1989.
LEVITSKY, A., *Rasskazy o kinematografe*, Moscow, 1964.
LEYDA, J., *Kino: a History of the Russian and Soviet Film*, London, 1960.
LODDER, C., *Russian Constructivism*, New Haven & London, 1983.
LUNACHARSKY, A., *Neizdanniye materialy. Literaturnoe nasledstvo*, vol. 82, Moscow, 1970.
LUNACHARSKY, A., *O teatre i dramaturgii*, vol.1, Moscow, 1958.

MAILAND-HANSEN, C., *Mejerchol'ds Theaterästhetik in den 1920-er Jahren*, Copenhagen, 1980.
MAKAGONOVA, T., 'Arkhiv V.E.Meierkholda' in *Zapiski otdela rukopisi, vypusk 42*, Lenin Library, Moscow, 1981.
MALYUTIN, Ya., *Aktery moego pokolenia*, Moscow–Leningrad, 1959.
MARKOV, P. (ed.), *Mikhail Tsarev: zhizn i tvorchestvo*, Moscow, 1983.
MARKOV, P., *O teatre* (4 vols), Moscow, 1974–1976.
MARKOV, P., *Pravda teatra*, Moscow, 1965.
MARTINEK, K., *Mejerchold*, Prague, 1963.
Maskarad Lermontova v eskizakh Golovina, Moscow–Leningrad, 1941.
MATSKIN, A., *Na temy Gogolya*, Moscow, 1984.

MATSKIN, A., *Portrety i nablyudenia*, Moscow, 1973.

MEIERKHOLD, V., *Perepiska*, Moscow, 1976.

V.E.Meierkhold: sbornik k 20-letiyu rezhissyorskoi raboty i 25-letiyu aktyorskoi deyatelnosti, Tver, 1923.

MEIERKHOLD, V., *Statyi, pisma, rechi, besedy* (2 vols), Moscow, 1968.

Meierkholdovskiy sbornik: vypusk pervy (2 vols, ed. A.Sherel), Moscow, 1992.

Meierkhold repetiruyet (2 vols., ed. M. Sitkovetskaya), Moscow, 1993.

MEYERHOLD, V., *Écrits sur le théâtre* (4 vols, ed. & trans. B. Picon-Vallin), Lausanne, 1973–1992.

MEYERHOLD, V., *La rivoluzione teatrale* (trans. G. Crino), Rome, 1962.

MEYERHOLD, V., *Textos teórios* (2 vols, trans. J.A. Hormigón), Madrid, 1970–1972.

MEYERHOLD, V., *Theaterarbeit 1917–1930* (trans. R. Tietze), Munich, 1974.

MEYERHOLD, V., *Le Théâtre théâtral* (trans. N. Gourfinkel), Paris, 1963.

Mir isskustv: almanakh (eds M. Kotovskaya and S. Isaev), Moscow, 1991.

NEMIROVICH-DANCHENKO, V., *My Life in the Russian Theatre*, London, 1937.

Vl. I. Nemirovich-Danchenko – Teatralnoe nasledie, vol. 2, Moscow, 1954.

Ocherki istorii russkoy sovetskoy dramaturgii (2 vols), Leningrad–Moscow, 1963 and 1966.

PERTSOV, V., *Mayakovsky v poslednie gody*, Moscow, 1965.

PERTSOV, V., *Mayakovsky – zhizn i tvorchestvo* (2 vols), Moscow, 1957 and 1958.

PETROV, N., *50 i 500*, Moscow, 1960.

I. N. Pevtsov – sbornik (ed. K. Derzhavin), Leningrad, 1935.

PICON-VALLIN, B., *Meyerhold*, Paris, 1990.

Pikovaya dama – sbornik statei i materialov, Leningrad, 1935.

POLOTSKAYA, E., 'Chekhov i Meierkhold' in *Literaturnoe nasledstvo*, vol. 68, Moscow, 1960.

POZHARSKAYA, M., *Aleksandr Golovin: Put khudozhnika. Khudozhnik i vremya*, Moscow, 1990.

POZHARSKAYA, M., *Russkoe teatralno-dekoratsionnoe iskusstvo kontsa XIX, nachala XX vekov*, Moscow, 1970.

Problemy teorii i praktiki russkoy sovetskoy rezhissury 1917–1925, 1925–1932 (2 vols), Leningrad, 1978.

PYAST, V., *Vstrechi*, Moscow, 1929.

PYMAN, A., *The Life of Alexander Blok* (2 vols), Oxford, 1979 and 1980.

RAKITINA, Ye., 'Lyubov Popova. Iskusstvo i manifesty' in *Khudozhnik, stsena, ekran*, Moscow, 1975.

Revizor v teatre im. Meierkholda, Leningrad, 1927.

RIPELLINO, A., *Il trucco e l'anima*, Turin, 1965.

RIPELLINO, A., *Majakovskij e il teatro russo d'avanguardia*, Turin, 1959 (translated into French as *Maiakovski et le théâtre russe d'avant garde*, Paris, 1965).

RODINA, T., *Aleksandr Blok i russkiy teatr nachala XX veka*, Moscow, 1972.

RUBTSOV, A., *Dramaturgia Aleksandra Bloka*, Minsk, 1968.

RUDNITSKY, K., *Meierkhold*, Moscow, 1981.

RUDNITSKY, K., *Rezhisser Meierkhold*, Moscow, 1969 (translated into English as *Meyerhold the Director*, Ann Arbor, 1981).

RUDNITSKY, K., *Russian and Soviet Theatre*, London, 1989.

RUDNITSKY, K., *Russkoe rezhisserskoe iskusstvo 1898–1907*, Moscow, 1989.

SARABIANOV, D. and ADASKINA, N., *Popova*, New York, 1990.
SAYLER, O., *The Russian Theatre under the Revolution*, Boston, 1920.
SCHMIDT, P. (ed.), *Meyerhold at Work*, Manchester, 1981.
SHEREL, A., *Rampa u mikrofona*, Moscow, 1985.
SMIRNOVA-ISKANDER, A., *O tekh, kogo pomnyu*, Leningrad, 1989.
SNEZHNITSKY, L., *Na repetitsiakh u masterov rezhissury*, Moscow, 1972.
SOLLERTINSKY, I., *Kriticheskie statyi*, Leningrad, 1963.
*Sovetskiy teatr: dokumenty i materialy – Russkiy Sovetskiy teatr: 1917–1921, 1921–1926,
    1926–1932* (3 vols, eds A. Yufit, A. Trabsky, A. Trabsky), Leningrad, 1968,
    1975, 1982.
STANISLAVSKY, K., *My Life in Art*, London, 1980.
STANISLAVSKY, K., *Sobranie sochineniy v vosmi tomakh*, Moscow, 1954–1961.
STROEVA, M., *Rezhisserskie iskania Stanislavskogo 1898–1917*, Moscow, 1973.

TALNIKOV, D., *Komissarzhevskaya*, Moscow–Leningrad, 1939.
TALNIKOV, D., *Novaya revizia Revizora*, Moscow–Leningrad, 1927.
Teatralny oktyabr – sbornik I (eds A.Gvozdev and others), Leningrad–Moscow, 1926.
TELYAKOVSKY, V., *Vospominania*, Leningrad–Moscow, 1965.
TRETYAKOV, S., *Slyshish, Moskva?!*, Moscow, 1966.
TUROVSKAYA, M., *Babanova: legenda i biografia*, Moscow, 1981.
Tvorcheskoe nasledie Vs. E. Meierkholda (eds L. Vendrovskaya and A. Fevralsky),
    Moscow, 1978.

Uchitel Bubus: spektakl Teatra im. Meierkholda (ed. V. Fyodorov), Moscow, 1925.

VAN GYSEGHEM, A., *Theatre in Soviet Russia*, London, 1943.
VAN NORMAN BAER, N. (ed.), *Russian Avant-garde Stage Design 1913–35*, London,
    1991.
VARPAKHOVSKY, L., *Nablyudenia, analiz, opyt*, Moscow, 1978.
VERIGINA, V., *Vospominania*, Leningrad, 1974.
VOLKOV, N., *Meierkhold* (2 vols), Moscow–Leningrad, 1929.
VOLKOV, N., *Teatralnye vechera*, Moscow, 1966.
V poiskakh realisticheskoy obraznosti. Problemy sovetskoy rezhissury 20–30 godov (ed.
    K. Rudnitsky and others), Moscow, 1981.
Vstrechi s Meierkholdom (ed. M. Valentei and others), Moscow, 1967.

YELAGIN, Yu., *Temny geniy (Vsevolod Meierkhold)*, New York, 1955.
YUFIT, A. (ed.), *Nauka o teatre*, Leningrad, 1975.
YURIEV, Yu., *Zapiski* (2 vols), 1963.
YUTKEVICH, S., *Kontrapunkt rezhissera*, Moscow, 1960.
YUZOVSKY, Yu., *Razgovor zatyanulsya za polnoch*, Moscow, 1966.
YUZOVKSY, Yu., *Spektakli i piesy*, Moscow, 1935.
YUZOVSKY, Yu., *Zatem lyudi khodyat v teatr*, Moscow, 1964.

ZAKHAVA, B., *Sovremenniki*, Moscow, 1969.
ZHAROV, M., *Zhizn, teatr, kino*, Moscow, 1967.
ZNOSKO-BOROVSKY, E., *Russkiy teatr nachala XX veka*, Prague, 1925.
ZOLOTNITSKY, D., *Budni i prazdniki teatralnogo oktyabrya*, Leningrad, 1978.
ZOLOTNITSKY, D., *Zori teatralnogo oktyabrya*, Leningrad, 1976.

Index